Spring vol. 78

POLITICS & THE
AMERICAN SOUL

A JOURNAL OF
ARCHETYPE
AND
CULTURE

Fall 2007

SPRING JOURNAL
New Orleans, Louisiana

CONTENTS

ARCHETYPAL REALITY IN POLITICS

JEROME S. BERNSTEIN

Today we can see just how strongly the negative pole of the archetype of the patriarchy has been activated when we consider the Iraq "war," which looks more and more like a quagmire; the promise of a "war on terrorism" which has no end; a ruling administration which may be the most secretive in the history of this country—and for good reason, given its penchant for breaking the law; a President who arrogates power and seems to consider himself to be above the law and who threatens to take away the rights of individuals which are guaranteed to them under the U.S. Constitution. Qualities associated with the feminine, e.g., Eros, and with the positive pole of the patriarchy, e.g., Reason and Justice, often seem absent from the prevailing *Zeitgeist* and spirit of the times.

In my view, however, while it seems that the negative pole of the patriarchy currently prevails, overshadowing other archetypal dynamics, at the same time we still can see signs of its weakening. Often with archetypal energies, as with some stars, we see a thrashing about and a burst of energy before they enter a waning phase. I think that is where

Jerome S. Bernstein is a psychologist and Jungian analyst in private practice in Santa Fe, New Mexico, who has written on political and clinical topics for over thirty years. His two books are: *Living in the Borderland: The Evolution of Consciousness and the Challenge of Healing Trauma* (Routledge, 2005) and *Power and Politics: The Psychology of Soviet-American Partnership* (Shambhala,1989).

we are today. A new psychic paradigm is about to emerge, and with it manifestations of new forms of consciousness.[1] We don't yet know what they will look like, and as I see it, this transition will not be a smooth one, but paroxysmal, accompanied by sudden and dramatic changes.

We are struggling these days to find a framework, a way to think about our current political events. C. G. Jung said that

> Our personal psychology is just a thin skin, a ripple on the ocean of collective psychology. The powerful factor, the factor which changes our whole life, which changes the surface of our known world, which makes history, is collective psychology, and collective psychology moves according to laws entirely different from those of our consciousness. The archetypes are the great decisive forces, *they* bring about the real events, and not our personal reasoning and practical intellect. … The archetypal images decide the fate of man.[2]

That is an audacious statement. What does it mean?

One meaning is that there is more to the picture than meets the eye. What are these potentially transforming archetypal currents hidden in the background? How might they transform the collective psyche?

ARCHETYPAL DYNAMICS ARE AT WORK

The Soviet Union collapsed abruptly on December 26, 1991. Its collapse was soon followed by the ending of the Cold War. At the time, everyone—politicians, think tank scholars, historians, military people, economists, the media—was utterly astonished at what had occurred. And they said so for about a year and a half. Then, in this vacuum of ignorance, the United States government stepped in and declared itself to be the victor of the Cold War. Once that happened, the same people who earlier had declared their mystification and amazement at these events began projecting their own analyses, interpretations, fantasies, and constructions onto them to explain why they had occurred, none of which came close to pinpointing what really had happened and why.

In the wake of the collapse of the Soviet Union, John Lewis Gaddis, a Yale professor and one of the pre-eminent scholars of the Soviet Union, asserted that:

> The end of the Cold War … was of such importance that no approach to the study of international relations claiming both

foresight and competence should have failed to see it coming. *None actually did so ... and that fact ought to raise questions about the methods we have developed for trying to understand world politics ....*

What is immediately obvious ... [is] that very few of our theoretical approaches to the study of international relations came anywhere close to forecasting *any* of these developments. One might as well have relied upon stargazers, readers of entrails, and other "pre-scientific" methods for all the good our "scientific" methods did; clearly our theories were not up to the task of anticipating the most significant event in world politics since the end of World War II ....

Dr. Gaddis concluded his remarks with the following observation:

My point ... is not to suggest that we jettison the scientific approach to the study of international relations; only that we bring it up to date by recognizing that good scientists, like good novelists and good historians, make use of *all* the tools at their disposal in trying to anticipate the future. That includes not just theory, observation, and rigorous calculation, but also narrative, analogy, paradox, irony, intuition, [and] imagination ....[3]

I would add to Dr. Gaddis' list of missing tools those that come from the field of analytical psychology, particularly Jung's theories of the collective unconscious and archetypes. What Dr. Gaddis is describing is the interplay of archetypal dynamics in the international arena, although this is not understood by political scientists because the vast majority of them know nothing about archetypal dynamics. When none of the known theories or political solutions seem to work in a given situation, it is highly likely that unrecognized archetypal dynamics are determining factors in what is or isn't taking place.

In broad terms we might say that some of the determining *archetypal dynamics*—it is important here to be able to think outside of the political science box and to use other tools as Professor Gaddis suggested—which played a critical role in the demise of the Cold War were the following:

1. The dropping of two atomic bombs on Japan at the end of World War II. It was the specter of the *archetypal image* of the scientific holocaust imprinted on the post-World War II

psyche that enabled both sides in the Cold War to refrain from engaging in nuclear "warfare." Each side with its tens of thousands of nuclear warheads "knew" that nuclear "warfare" meant the destruction of life itself and therefore there could be no victors.[4]

2. Until then, each side had engaged in the language of and identification with the hero archetype. However, the policy of "Mutually Assured Destruction" (MAD) did away with the ability to identify with the hero archetype (e.g., Ares/Achilles) because there could be no winners. This forced both sides towards the Athena pole of the archetype of war-peace (see below).

3. Since the possibility of warfare as it had been known up to the Atomic Age became psychically impossible (once the Self overruled the ego, as will be explained below), the possibility of acting out shadow projection through warfare also became severely curtailed, and thus thrust each side back onto its own shadow.[5] When democratic forces began to erupt in Eastern Europe in 1989-90, the Soviet Union *chose* not to intervene militarily on behalf of its "satellite regimes," as it had historically done since its creation in every instance except in the case of Yugoslavia. The choice not to intervene, which culminated in the dismantling of the Berlin Wall, reflected General Secretary Gorbachev's policy of facing the Soviet shadow.[6]

There are a number of other archetypal dynamics involved in the ending of the Cold War which might be identifed. For our purposes here, however, those already described above will give the reader a sense of the archetypal process at issue. The fact that most of the decision makers may not have been aware of the archetypal dynamics that likely guided their deliberations and actions is secondary, and does not change the nature of the archetypal process itself or the role it played in the ending of the Cold War.

Negative Pole of the Patriarchy

Western civilization takes its roots in Mosaic law, that is, the Ten Commandments handed down to Moses by God as recorded in Exodus. The Ten Commandments form the basis of a moral code and of a set of laws that are foundational in the Western psyche as well as in our system of laws. One characteristic of a code, however, is that it tends to be very resistant to evolutionary change over time. Another characteristic is that because the principles contained in the code are fixed and rigid—intentionally so—they just say what they say and no more. Thus, the *interpretation* of how and when a code is to be applied is determined by the one who claims possession of the code. That person, in turn, functions as if he were the voice of God, since, after all, he interprets the law of God.

The negative pole of the patriarchy is activated when moral codes are co-opted to support and justify political or personal goals. We see an example of this in Exodus 33 of the Hebrew Bible (the Old Testament). Even though God has just presented Moses with the Ten Commandments, including the stricture "Thou Shalt Not Kill," He then turns around and orders the Israelites to slay the Perizzites, the Jebusites, the Canaanites, and other tribes so that they may claim the land promised to Abraham, Isaac, and Jacob. Since the Mosaic Code set out in the Ten Commandments was given by God, it would appear that He holds claim to primary interpretation of it, including the admonition "Thou Shalt Not Kill," and He can violate the Code as it suits His whims without accountability. But then, in this example, we are talking about God Himself.

A more contemporary example of the activation of the negative pole of the patriarchy can be found in the Bush administration's double standard and double-speak in regard to the Geneva Convention and its policies on the treatment of prisoners of war. Vice President Cheney, former Secretary of Defense Rumsfeld, and former Attorney General Gonzales dismissed the Geneva Convention—which in fact had represented a great historical advancement in human consciousness—with a wave of the hand as irrelevant and antiquated—indeed, "quaint," to quote the former Attorney General. Ignoring the provisions of the Geneva Convention regarding how prisoners of war should be treated, the administration then proceeded to engage in a thinly veiled official policy of torture. It also condoned actions that involved human rights violations by countries like Poland and Romania, even though the U.S. had criticized these same countries for engaging in these kinds of activities during the Cold War. At the same time, the U.S. administration was doing this, however, it was chastising and holding other governments accountable for human rights violations.

POSITIVE POLE OF THE PATRIARCHY

In Greek mythology[7] the archetype of war-peace is represented by Ares, the God of War, and his sister Athena, who was born with a full suit of armor out of the head of Zeus, their father. Ares, as portrayed in the *Iliad,* is impulsive, immature, and hot-headed. He is ready to go to war over the smallest slight. His sister Athena, on the other hand, is both a warrior goddess and a goddess of peace and the arts. She is the goddess of prudent intelligence—a goddess of wisdom. Most important, she uses her warrior power to settle disputes and to uphold the law by nonviolent means. She also has the power to defeat—not destroy—Ares on the battlefield. In one encounter in the Trojan War, she knocks Ares to the ground on the plains of Ilium, and rebukes him for being an impetuous war monger. Looking down on him with contempt, she says, "Vain fool! Hast thou not yet learned how superior my strength is to thine?" Greek mythology is telling us here that without the presence of the reason and wisdom of the Athena pole of the war-peace archetype, Ares, or war, will run amok. She confronts his hot-headed attitude and his readiness to fight (go to war) at the slightest impulse or provocation.

Two characteristics of the archetype of war-peace are apparent here. First, Athena and Ares are brother and sister. They are linked to each other by blood, psyche, and spirit, and often they don't like being linked. Second, Athena is born out of the head of Zeus. Just like the moral codes of the Grecian and Roman world, she, the daughter of the patriarchy, is born from the mind (head) of the patriarch. But she is a woman and brings with her other dimensions of the arts and wisdom. She represents the beginnings of a feminine dimension to *Logos.*[8]

So, sister and brother—war and peace—are archetypally linked and bonded. An identification with either pole of the archetype (war or peace) can lead to dissociation—to profound grief and destruction. It is important to note here that "peace" in the archetypal context, as symbolized in the Ares-Athena link, is not the simple absence of war, but rather the *ongoing struggle (on the part of Athena) to contain and manage the instinct to war.*

We tend to think in terms of war *or* peace; we tend to think of "peace" as the absence of war. It is axiomatic in analytical psychology that when one identifies with one pole of an archetype, the opposite pole will be projected onto something else. For example, clinically, when someone is identified with being a victim, the figure of the bully often can be found lurking in the client's unconscious shadow. When we see a masochist, that person's sadistic side is not far away—it may appear either unconsciously in them, or perhaps in the person to whom they choose to attach. This dynamic is no less true in collective psychology—namely, the psychology of cultures and nations—and is also manifest in the political process.

Psychologically, this seemingly simple concept of "war-peace" versus "war *or* peace" takes one down radically different roads diplomatically, militarily, economically, and even environmentally. One pole (Ares) leads to the threat of war and war itself; the other (Athena) leads to carefully containing and channeling the instinct to war.[9] Implicitly, then, war *may* be necessary *after* all other attempts to contain the instinct to war have failed. In this context, the goal is not to totally vanquish the opponent but to contain the aggression sufficiently so that other means, such as (archetypally-based) diplomacy, can be employed to restrain further aggression. The first Gulf War (August 1990-February 1992) may be viewed as a case in point.

When the focus is on just one pole of the archetype—say, the peace pole—that unconsciously calls forth the other pole, war. For example, World War I was referred to at the time as "the war to end all wars." Many people believed this would be the case. At the close of the War, President Woodrow Wilson presented his "Fourteen Points" (as they came to be known) for the establishment and perpetuation of peace in the world. They were highly idealistic and reflected an identification with the peace pole of the archetype of war-peace. Ultimately the U.S. Congress refused to ratify the Fourteen Points and U.S. participation in The League of Nations (the Thirteenth Point). This doomed the League. Congress' primary concern was that the Treaty would curtail

Congress' authority to declare war. Wilson would not compromise on this point. President Wilson's identification with the peace pole of the war-peace archetype was likely a major contributing factor to the dynamics that resulted in World War II, just 23 years later.

The question then arises as to what might mitigate an identification with either the peace pole or the war pole of the war-peace archetype?

Moral Consciousness

As has been pointed out, moral codes emanate from the minds of humans, and they are dependent on the minds of humans for enforcement. These codes are laws, ideas; they are mental constructs, interpreted and backed by the authority holding forth that code. A positive example is the Geneva Convention on the treatment of prisoners of war; a negative example is the Bush Administration's official policy on torture (euphemistically labeled "extraordinary rendition").

Moral consciousness,[10] on the other hand, is a *psychodynamic process* connected to transpersonal energies. We all know that part of ourselves that goes beyond our rational mind, that transcends even our imagination—those experiences that our egos cannot explain. Moral consciousness refers to the connection with that dimension of God, or of the Sacred, that touches us with awe and is committed to the preservation of life.[11] Jung was alluding to a similar idea when he said that *Logos* "includes the idea of a universal being, and thus covers the fact that man's clarity of consciousness and rationality are something universal rather than individually unique." Jung clearly implies throughout his work that the roots of all moral consciousness are found in this transpersonal dimension—that is, beyond the human ego and the limits of our mind. At the same time, the ego is crucial in the struggle to connect with and apprehend moral consciousness.

Moral consciousness has the quality of thrusting itself upon the ego from deep within the Self. As a transpersonal force, it has the power to trump the ego and its mental constructs. The primary means by which this takes place is through a sense of violation—not the violation of a code, not even a violation against the word of God, but a violation against the essence of the Self. It is experienced as a violation of the essence of that which gives life, of all that is holy—by whatever name or means that we know it.

I believe that moral consciousness inserted itself into the 20th-century political process with the feeling realization that man had the literal capacity to destroy life itself. This is what was brought home *archetypally* to the political psyche (as well as to the personal and collective psyche) with the dropping of the atomic bomb on Hiroshima and Nagasaki.

We must never forget that the political mind cannot be separated from the psychological mind. First and foremost, we are psychological beings and our psychic nature as humans permeates all aspects of human functioning. Thus, in the political arena, although the human mind has always wrestled with moral questions, we were not fully equipped to wrestle with the question of *moral consciousness*,[12] as opposed to moral *ideas,* until we had within our grasp the capacity to destroy life as we know it. After the dropping of the atomic bomb, it would appear that archetypal forces—the Self—intervened and became the primary protectors of the continuation of life.

This became dramatically evident in the 1962 Cuban Missile Crisis as the military strategies put forth by both sides moved them toward the edge of the abyss. For the first time, however, moral consciousness appeared in this political drama, forcing both sides to look beyond political/military expediencies and acknowledge that the preservation of life itself was now at stake.

It is generally known that at the height of the crisis the political and military advisers on both sides advocated the use of nuclear weapons. Fidel Castro himself argued for launching a nuclear strike against the southern United States, even though such an act would lead to the obliteration of Cuba. This is what the war pole looks like when there is no Athena energy present. It looks like madness.

On October 26, 1962, General Secretary Khrushchev sent a letter to President Kennedy that is summarized in Robert Kennedy's book about the Cuban missile crisis.[13] There is no question that Khrushchev himself wrote the long and emotional letter. The emotion in it was directed at the death, destruction, and anarchy that nuclear war would bring to his people and to all humankind. That, he said again and again, and in many different ways, must be avoided. Robert Kennedy then goes on to quote Khrushchev:

> ... [W]e are of sound mind and understand perfectly well that
> if we attack you, you will respond the same way. But you too
> will receive the same that you hurl against us. And I think that
> you also understand this. ... This indicates that we are normal
> people, that we correctly understand and correctly evaluate the
> situation. Consequently, how can we permit the incorrect actions
> which you ascribe to us? Only lunatics or suicides, who themselves
> want to perish and to destroy the whole world before they die,
> could do this.[14]

We might say that Athena had entered Khrushchev's office.

Robert Kennedy reveals that the political establishment in
Washington considered Khrushchev's letter "unstable," "emotional,"
and "incoherent." This reveals a bias on the part of the U.S. political
establishment against feeling and a favoring of so-called rationality over
considerations of moral consciousness. It implies a denigration of the
ethical values found in moral consciousness. As it turned out, of all of
his advisors, President Kennedy himself was virtually the only one who
was compelled to act from the perspective of moral consciousness rather
than to make a so-called "strategic" response.

Since then, one could say that moral consciousness increasingly
has become a competing force on the world political scene carrying
great potential for political transformation. When looked at
psychologically, the demise of the Soviet Union may have resulted more
from moral consciousness and other archetypal forces than from any
given political strategy. This offers a partial, but crucial, explanation
as to how the upheavals within the Soviet Union that resulted in the
end of the Cold War could have taken place to the total surprise of *all*
of the political strategists in the West, notwithstanding the fact that
they had labored for years to bring about those very outcomes.
Apparently, another kind of force was in play—archetypal dynamics—
which went unrecognized.

Jung says of the collective unconscious and archetypes:

> There is nothing for it but to recognize the irrational as a necessary
> ... psychological function, and to take its contents not as concrete
> realities ... but as psychic realities, real because they *work*. The
> collective unconscious, being the repository of man's experience
> *and at the same time the prior condition of this experience*, is an
> image of the world. ... In this image certain features, the

> archetypes ... have crystallized out in the course of time. They are
> the ruling power. .... In so far as these images are more or less faithful
> replicas of psychic events, their archetypes ... correspond to certain
> general characteristics of the physical world ....[15](Emphasis added.)

At the level of collective consciousness, the 20th century ended in
a very different place from where it began: with the awareness that
nations—particularly ones possessing weapons of mass destruction—
can no longer afford to engage in absolute warfare where the enemy is
totally vanquished. That is, archetypally, nations can no longer afford
to identify with the war pole of the war-peace archetype. That was the
archetypal lesson "learned" from the Cold War.

From an archetypal standpoint, it would appear that the Cold War
ended because the United States and the Soviet Union held the tension
of the opposites, held the tension of—the hyphen between—the
archetype of war-peace and did not split it by identifying with only
one pole of it or the other. This constellated what Jung calls "the
transcendent function," which resulted in an unanticipated and
unimagined third outcome, the collapse of the Soviet Union.

What Jung has to say about the transcendent function is quite
instructive here:

> Once the unconscious content has been given form and ...
> meaning is understood, the question arises as to how the ego will
> relate to this position and how the ego and the unconscious are
> to come to terms. This is the ... more important stage of the
> procedure, the bringing together of opposites for the production
> of a third: the transcendent function ....[16]

Jung makes clear that it is the ego that must take over conscious
responsibility for moral consciousness from the unconscious. And this
is precisely where politics and political science are found lacking in
the current context.

Although in the above passage Jung is referring to an intrapsychic
process within an individual, the same dynamics can be applied to the
psychology of nations and political systems. That is what I have done
in the preceding material. But, as Professor Gaddis points out, as I noted
at the beginning of this paper, the ego (i.e., of political scientists,
politicians, and psychologists as a whole) has not done the work of
bringing to consciousness what seems to have taken place on an

unconscious level. With respect to the Cold War, it appears that the collective unconscious—the fates, the gods, grace, whatever one may call it—gave our species a pass in terms of launching nuclear holocaust and invoked moral consciousness in spite of our political will(s). We haven't fully grasped the meaning of this event, and therefore the ego— i.e., the conscious attitude and the scientific method found in the political science disciplines—is not yet ready to take over from the unconscious. This is of concern, since we may not be so lucky in the future.

MORAL CONSCIOUSNESS IN THE CONTEMPORARY CONTEXT

Unfortunately, we entered the 21st century with our power shadow intact, and the drama moved from warfare between nations to what we have erroneously come to call "the war on terrorism." 9-11 brought with it an opportunity not only to respond and to protect our nation and our people from unconstrained terrorist attack, but also to engage Eros and the positive pole of the patriarchy—an opportunity to differentiate between justice, represented by Athena, and war only as retribution. The Bush administration chose the latter: war as retribution.

There are a number of possible reasons why moral consciousness is not readily observable in today's national and international political spheres. I will mention only one seemingly glaringly obvious reason: the country's leaders are pathologically devoid of the capacity to feel. Specifically, I am referring to the former Secretary of Defense, the Vice President, and the President, all of whom have exerted enormous effort to conceal all *images* of the dead, dying, and wounded in this war, and have often lied about the use of torture as an articulated governmental policy.

Images, particularly those that depict archetypal dynamics (i.e., the sadistic pole of Eros), are crucial in penetrating ego defenses and activating compensatory archetypal energies. A turning point was reached in this regard when pictures from the Abu Ghraib prison in Iraq were released in April of 2004. These images invoked moral revulsion on the part of many. Support for the Iraq "war" and for the Bush administration has been on a steady decline since these images (as well as others depicting the callous incompetence of the government in the wake of Hurricane Katrina) emerged. Although moral revulsion is not the same as moral consciousness as I have defined it in this paper, it still reflects a shifting of psychic energy in a direction that could lead to moral consciousness.

ARCHETYPAL THEORY AND POLITICAL SCIENCE

It is my contention that archetypal theory broadens the comprehensive analysis of the dynamics underlying conflict. It is indispensable to the analysis, understanding, and treatment of intransigent international conflicts where political solutions have failed to ameliorate the problem. Two such arenas that come to mind are the Israeli-Palestinian conflict and Islamic Terrorism.[17]

In 1985 I made the following observations:

> ... [O]nce again [I am] reminded ... of what Jung has so often pointed out—it is man's unconsciousness that poses the greatest threat to life, and more specifically, his ignorance of the powerful forces of the collective unconscious. ... [A]rchetypal dynamics can be a primary source of tension between the superpowers and ... it is essential to bring that psychic substratum to bear. ...
>
> I believe that Jung's theories not only have a great deal to offer us ... but also that the time may have arrived when there can be a greater receptivity to his ideas in the world community.[18]

As it turns out, that was an overly optimistic view of the state of affairs at the time. In fact, there was a great deal of resistance in the Jungian community to stepping out of the clinical consulting room and to applying Jungian theory to "collective" situations.

While there are some who still feel this way, in today's world there is now a wealth of insightful and penetrating books and articles that apply Jungian theory to the *analysis* of collective situations and world conflict, as well as an articulated discipline pointing toward the *application* of Jungian theory to political science. However, this body of literature rarely reaches the outside world, and, as I have been reminded by a friend, talking to politicians and political scientists about Jungian theory and archetypes is a sure way to put them to sleep! Jung's son, Franz Jung, told me that one of his father's greatest frustrations was how to bridge the gap between his theories and their application to international conflict. There was Jung sitting variously with Churchill, Eisenhower, Dulles, and the like (Churchill did fall asleep while Jung was talking). They didn't grasp his psychology, and Jung did not know how to translate his theories into a form that could be applied to actual and potential conflicts.

Conflict theory viewed through a Jungian lens most often results in analytic models that are significantly, even radically, different from those produced within the extant political science framework.[19] The tools offered by Jungian psychology are needed whether the field of political science realizes it or not. There are myriad think tanks, as well as academic departments in many universities, with budgets in the hundreds of millions of dollars that focus on the application of every discipline imaginable, including psychology, to political science— every discipline, that is, except analytical psychology. To my knowledge not a single one of these resources applies Jungian theory to political science, in general, or to more specific conundrums such as the Arab-Israeli conflict and Islamic terrorism.

Archetypal theory applied to the Arab-Israeli conflict, for example, would yield analytical models that would focus on archetypal dynamics like the archetype of religion, the archetype of the patriarchy, and the resulting cultural complexes. On the surface, one might say, "Of course this conflict involves the patriarchy. Everyone knows that Jews and Arabs are cousins—Isaac and Ishmael, Jacob and Esau, and all that." True enough and well enough, but not enough. From an archetypal standpoint, the "father problem" between these two groups permeates every aspect of the conflict, including the political. This father problem—in which the patriarchal god promised the same land to two half brothers, and then countenanced one of the brothers being expelled from his biological father's home—is a psychological and *archetypal imprint* on the psyches of these two groups that will not go away.[20] Yet, according to a 2006 article in *The New York Times,* a report drafted by twenty scholars and other leaders, including Archbishop Desmond Tutu, Mohammad Khatami, the former Iranian president, and others, and endorsed by Kofi Annan, the United Nations Secretary General, emphasized that "the causes of tensions are primarily political, not religious ...." Kofi Annan went on to say, "The problem is not the Koran or the Torah or the Bible. Indeed, I have often said that the problem is never the faith, it is the faithful and how they behave toward each other."[21] One can almost hear massive archetypal icebergs crashing and grinding in this seemingly immutable problem. No wonder!

Treating the Symptom Instead of the Problem

Attempting to resolve problems that are fundamentally psychological and religious through political processes alone is like splinting a broken leg without first setting the bones. The Arab-Israeli conflict remains the oldest implacable on-going conflict in world history. It has withstood exiles and diasporas, crusades, endless invasions, and colonial occupations by all kinds of national and international powers and institutions. It has outlasted the Cold War, which the latter managed to grasp in its tentacles.

The implacability of the present-day Arab-Israeli conflict takes its roots in a history that dates back over three thousand years, and these roots are more religious than political. When a conflict is as intractable as this one and it still eludes all attempts at political solution, perhaps it would be wise to look for deeper, more elusive dynamics that perpetuate conflict—political power and pressure notwithstanding.[22]

In archetypal terms, the present day conflict dates to the beginning of Scripture. In the Hebrew Bible, God—Yahweh, as He is called— intervenes at several crucial points to lay the groundwork for conflict between Arabs and Jews.

1. Yahweh makes a divine promise to Abraham, declaring that "For all the land that you see, to you will I give it, and to your descendants forever. (Genesis 13: 14-16) This promise is repeated three verses later, when Yahweh tells Abraham that "I will ratify My covenant between Me and you and between your offspring after you ... as an everlasting covenant ... and I will give to you and to your offspring after you the land of your sojourns—the whole of the land of Canaan—as an everlasting possession." (Genesis 17: 1-8) The land given to the Chosen People, however, was already occupied—a theme which still echoes today in the problems in the Middle East.

2. Yahweh instructs the Egyptian slave Hagar, who has lived with Sarah and Abraham and is pregnant with Abraham's son, to return to them and submit to Sarah's abuse. (Sarah had driven Hagar from her home upon finding out she was pregnant with Abraham's child.) At the same time, Hagar is told that her soon-to-be-born son (from whom all Arab peoples

will descend) shall be named Ishmael "and over all his brothers shall he dwell." (Genesis 16: 9-12)

3. In a further piece of mischief, Yahweh himself later instructs Abraham that the Promised Land will pass through one side of his family and not the other. As to Abraham and Sarah's son Isaac, Yahweh says that he will "fulfill My covenant with him as an everlasting covenant for his offspring after him." As to Abraham and Hagar's son Ishmael, He says that Ishmael will "beget twelve princes and I will make him into a great nation," but the covenant will not extend to him or his descendents. (Genesis 17:15-17)

4. The conflict between Isaac and Ishmael (and their descendents today) is mirrored in the relationship between their mothers. As the wife of Abraham, a jealous Sarah demands that Hagar be driven from her home, "for the son of that slave woman shall not inherit with my son, with Isaac!' Abraham takes the problem of his wife's jealousy to Yahweh, who tells Abraham not to be "distressed over the youth or your slave woman: Whatever Sarah tells you, heed her voice, since through Isaac will offspring be considered yours." As a result of Yahweh's advice, Abraham banishes Hagar and Ishmael to the desert of Beer-sheba, where they found a new nation. (Genesis 21: 9-21)

5. Finally, the conflict between Isaac and Ishmael is further mirrored in the next generation, specifically in the relationship between Esau and Jacob, the twin sons of Isaac and Rebecca. While Rebecca is pregnant, she is told by Yahweh that "Two nations are in your womb; ... the might shall pass from one regime to the other, and the elder shall serve the younger." (Genesis 25: 23) Indeed, after the elder son Esau is cheated out of his birthright by his younger twin brother, Jacob, he marries a daughter of Ishmael, thus forming the family line that will become the Arab people. Jacob, who is later renamed Israel, continues the line that is to become the Jewish people. (Genesis 25-28)

The quotes in the preceding section are all from the Hebrew Bible, from "The Tanach," Stone Edition. For the faithful, this is Scripture, sacred writing, the word of God in written form. All three monotheistic religions—Judaism, Islam, and Christianity—refer back to this text, and to Genesis in particular, as the basis for their later Scripture. And all three embrace the Hebrew patriarchs of Genesis as their own.

And herein lies the problem: here is the patriarchal God, Yahweh, conspiring with His own chosen human patriarch, Abraham, who fathers two sons, half brothers to each other, promising to each the same land and the same status. Each will be the father of nations and kings, and through each will pass God's covenant with Abraham. But then He tells Abraham that it is through the descendants of his son Isaac that He will maintain His covenant in perpetuity. And neither Yahweh nor Abraham bothers to tell Abraham's other son, Ishmael, that a deal has been cut to make him the lesser of two equals.[23]

If this story were told to any of us as a personal story of individuals that we knew, would we not advise both sons that they had been set up for conflict by their father, who left each the same legacy and lands in two different wills, and who excused his conflicting mandates by saying that one brother would be more equal than the other? Would we not say to them that they should not be fighting with each other, but that they should look at the harm done to them by their common father and the conspiracies of their mothers (Sarah and Rebecca)? Would we not point out to them that they are both victims of treachery—by their father, their mother(s), and even God, Himself— and that to continue fighting over the same land promised to each of them is to perpetuate the treachery and insult visited upon them both by their father? And, let us remind ourselves, that this story and its plot are contained in Holy Scripture and are the foundation of all three of the monotheistic religions. Therein it has a hold on us—on all of us—beyond any other story which guides and governs our lives, our culture(s), and religion. It is imprinted in our individual and collective psyches and represents the archetypal core of the cultural complexes at the heart of the conflict.

The problem is that in secular American culture we tend to relate to such "stories" concretely rather than symbolically. In losing our connection with the symbolic, we lose our connection to the sacred. Over time we have, more often than not, come to relate to our Scripture, which provides the very mythological foundation of Western religion and culture, as if it is just made up of "stories" about historical events which have taken place in secular (rather than sacred) time. Their archetypal power thus lies hidden in the unconscious and is made manifest in our shadow projections.

We Americans are good at ignoring those parts of Scripture that don't suit us at any given moment. Our capacity to do so is greatly enhanced by the separation of religion and government that we have practiced, more or less successfully, for over the last 200 years. Indeed, most Americans believe that it is this very separation of church and state that was a major part of the creative genius of our founding fathers. Consequently, we, in attempting to resolve international conflict, typically pursue political goals in doing so, paying little, if any, attention to Jewish or Christian Scripture, and certainly not to the Muslim Qu'ran. Indeed, these sacred texts are seen as largely irrelevant in the pursuit of our power-based and political objectives.

However, such a separation between church and state has not historically existed in the world of Islam. Secular government is a relatively new construct in the Middle East, and one that did not emerge out of its own culture but was an alien invention imposed upon it by Western powers at the end of World War I and the collapse of the Ottoman Empire.

What we assume as a given—that Scripture has little or nothing to do with political reality in the modern world—is at the core of what the Islamic people see as Western blasphemy. For a people who organically do not separate religion and politics, Scripture is a sacred and divine promise. Until the West understands this fundamental fact, we will never have an adequate grasp of the question that we have been asking ourselves since September 11, 2001: "Why do they hate us so much?"

RELIGIOUS ROOTS

Although Israel is a society whose government, economy, and politics are modeled after the Western democracies, at the same time it has never fully transcended its psychic and religious commitment to its own Biblical history and Scripture. For a state where the people are overwhelmingly secular in terms of religious (non)practice, the degree to which it remains captive to its own religious roots is fascinating to contemplate. No matter how secular it tries to be, Israel is caught in the quagmire of its biblical (and thus archetypal) roots. And this takes us directly to the question of land: more than anything else, it is the sacred promise of land that lies at the core of the present-day Palestinian-Israeli conflict.

A central stumbling block to the "peace agreements" attempted between Israel and the Palestinians since the founding of the State of Israel in 1948, up to and including the last-ditch effort on the part of the Clinton administration at Camp David in December of 2000, was Israel's unwillingness to compromise on the "Settlements Issue."[24] The settlements in question are Jewish settlements, established by the Israeli government in the West Bank and Gaza Strip of Palestine. Under the 1979 Camp David Peace Accords, Israel had agreed that these settlements could become self-governed by the Palestinians. But shortly after the signing of these Accords between Egypt's President Anwar el Sadat and Israel's Premier Menachem Begin in 1979, Premier Begin's government nonetheless continued its policy of establishing Jewish settlements on the West Bank, the Gaza Strip, and the Golan Heights in Arab Israel. President Carter, the U.S. broker and signatory to the Camp David Peace accords, considered these settlements an egregious violation of the agreements.[25]

Since 1983, nearly 200,000 Jewish settlers have been moved into these lands and an additional number into the Golan Heights, formerly Syrian land annexed by Israel after the Six-Day War in 1967. At the present rate of expansion, it is estimated that nearly 400,000 settlers will occupy these Palestinian territories by the year 2005.[26] From the Palestinian and Islamic point of view, this constitutes a *de facto* Israeli occupation of Palestinian territory—lands that were to be an integral part of a future Palestinian state. Again in the Oslo Agreements of 1993, these lands on which most settlements continue to be built were already designated as Palestinian. The Oslo Agreements designated three zones in the disputed territories: (1) Palestinian; (2) Israeli; and (3) Shared. The implementation of these agreements broke down in 1998.

The aggressive expansion of Jewish settlements in the disputed territories was part of a focused and deliberate policy on the part of the Begin Government between 1979 and 1983. This policy has been carried out more or less without interruption by all successive Israeli governments. It is particularly noteworthy that Premier Begin never referred to these territories by their modern geographical names, but only by their ancient biblical names: "Judea" and "Samaria." He stated publicly and repeatedly that these territories—Judea and Samaria—belonged to the Jewish people by Biblical right and history. From his point of view, these claims were supported by Scripture. He made amply clear that he would not preside over the handing over of traditional Jewish territories to Palestinians or any other group for purposes of political expedience.

For the most part, the resolution of the religious dynamics of the problem will have to precede political agreement. Another way of saying it is that healing the religious problem will make political resolution more possible. An interim political accommodation in some cases might reduce hostilities sufficiently to permit a more in-depth process of addressing the religiously based dynamics of the conflict. But in most cases, lasting political resolution likely will not occur without first endeavoring to heal the 3,000-year-old religious conflict. This conflict is based upon insult and emotional wounding more than it is based upon politics. The psychological and archetypal reality is that whether or not we subscribe to any form of Judeo-Christian religion, this archetypal backdrop is at the roots of our culture, our values, and our politics, and it influences us all, collectively, on an unconscious and conscious level.

WHAT CAN ARCHETYPAL PSYCHOLOGY OFFER?

Because archetypal psychology deals with the transpersonal dimension in the form of "archetypes," it is particularly suited to help us understand this type of religiously derived conflict. Since all archetypes are bi-polar, there is always a tension that arises between the two poles of an archetype. Typically, and particularly in a political context, there is a tendency to split the archetype, e.g., "peace versus war" instead of "peace-war."

In the case of the Arab-Israeli conflict, archetypal psychology introduces the possibility that a neutral transcendent "third" will appear. By taking seriously scriptural history common to both protagonists, not just as story but as scriptural fact and archetypal imprint, a common sympathy may arise between the two antagonists, offering them a different problem upon which to focus (i.e., the problems created by the father Abraham and the father-god Yahweh, for example) that is beyond the dispute between themselves. This "common sympathy," which we see in the scene of Ishmael and Isaac together burying their father, can become an avenue for re-introducing feeling and relatedness into a situation that has been dominated by the emotion of hate. "Hate" is an emotion, not a feeling—it is a primitive emotional state unmediated by rationality.

The present dispute over Israeli settlements in occupied Palestinian territory—and now the "security fence" ("the wall" to the Palestinians)—is dominated by the emotionally based conviction held by both parties that the disputed territories were given to them by divine providence. For each, the other is wrong. But according to Scripture, the argument can be made that both are correct. Theoretically, this could make way ultimately for a more balanced negotiation, particularly if each could be made to recognize and feel that their deep injury derives in part from sources outside of the other.

By isolating the archetypal underpinnings of the conflict over this land, it would be more readily possible to recognize and isolate from the core problem the political mischief Western governments created after World War I, however conscious and unconscious: carving up territories; breaking promises (e.g., the Balfour Declaration by Great Britain promising a Jewish homeland in Palestine); the imposition of secular government on a culture for whom the separation of religion and government makes little sense, etc. It also would require the West to own up to its strategy of using the "protectorate" of Palestine as a political scapegoat for the expiation of its own guilt over complicity in the politics that brought about Hitler and the Holocaust. This guilt stems from the West's refusal to take preventive action, including its desire to keep its own borders closed to pre-World War II refugees and post-World War II survivors. The recognition by the West of its shadow projection onto Palestine could provide a basis for taking more political and material responsibility for the Israeli-Arab conflict. The more the Western governments take responsibility for their own role in the Middle East quagmire, the more pressure will be taken off Israel and the Palestinians, permitting differentiation of religious from political dynamics and thus a more reasoned and balanced discourse between these two parties.[27]

Taken to the limits of its potential, archetypal psychology could help the West to establish a much deeper sympathetic understanding of Islamic culture, in general, and Arab-Islamic fundamentalism, in particular, and could provide a basis for appreciating the woundedness that both sides experience. And for the Israelis, it could provide an avenue of discourse that allows for contained passion and ideas as a legitimate basis for communication between both sides, however painful the honesty.

A more sympathetic understanding on the part of Islamic fundamentalists (as differentiated from Islamic terrorists) would be harder come by, since they give the narrowest interpretation to their Scripture, the Qu'ran. Transformation of Arab-Islamic fundamentalism will have to come from the efforts of the more moderate Islamic clerics and governments. Key to their ability to do so is the capacity of the U.S. to better adhere to its own Judeo-Christian ethics and face the dilemma of its own power shadow in the Middle East. The role of the American government in arming both sides in the ten-year Iran-Iraq War of 1979, for example, and the resulting million-plus casualties, remains one of its most cynical and immoral acts in the eyes of Muslims throughout the Middle East, let alone what they think of the current "war" with Iraq. Such acts not only tarnish the image of the United States, but they also pull the rug out from under moderate and more progressive Islamic clerics and governments.

Although this cursory overview provides a sketch of how archetypal psychology might be brought to bear in the current crisis, obviously it is a long way from an applied technology. I hope that the reader can glimpse new avenues of possibility in the brief outline I've presented here. I am aware that this approach may sound naive. With regard to naïveté, I would offer up the history of real attempts at political resolution in isolation from other approaches and the three-thousand-year intractability of the problem.

Certainly most professionals involved in mediating the Israeli-Palestinian conflict have read the history of each of the protagonists, and some have even read their Scripture. But—and this is crucial—the approach I am advocating must be undertaken independent of any political regime. Otherwise the entire approach becomes *de facto* subordinate to political interpretation and agendas. This is the dysfunctional disembarkation point for the current (and past) crisis.

Integrating with Political Science?

Such an approach would require first developing theoretical and analytical approaches into an applied and predictable science. Just as clinical analyses are translated into treatment approaches for patients, so techniques could be developed vis-à-vis international conflict situations. Archetypal "science" has already been developed to a fairly sophisticated level, in Donald Kalsched's work on trauma and in how other analytical psychologists have applied his theories to various collective conflict situations,[28] in Renos Papadopoulos's ongoing work in "Terror, Trauma & Adversity-Activated Development," in Andrew Samuels' *Politics on the Couch*, and in Sam Kimbles' and Thomas Singer's work on "the Cultural Complex," among a number of others. The focus, however, would be shifted to the treatment and prevention of dynamics that lead to conflict and war, not on the treatment of individuals caught up in and traumatized by such conflict.[29] Its goal would be not the "prevention" of war, *per se*, but rather the anticipation of the constellation of the instinct to war and the exploration of the parameters of what is possible by way of containing and channeling this instinct.[30]

Next Steps

I would propose the establishment of a foundation(s)-funded research institute for the exploration and development of techniques based on Jungian theory and their application to international conflict. First steps, upon establishing such an institute, would be to bring together a group of Jungian scholars to develop an applied technology. Initial stages would not involve interface with other political sciences or even other psychological disciplines. We first need our own technology.[31]

The second phase would involve bringing in (not "going there") selected individuals from other schools of psychology, and from other disciplines, including political science, sociology, and game theory, among others, to engage in a collective analysis of a given problem, such as aspects of the Palestinian-Israeli dispute and the archetypal roots of genocide, or a predictive analysis of where the shadow of the American empire might be projected.[32]

The third phase would entail "field testing" of theoretical applications in applied contexts, i.e., how articulations of the problem and subsequent dialogue might shift as a result of an archetypal reframing of the issue under focus.

A fourth phase, perhaps simultaneous with the third, would be joint publications and the presentation of theoretical papers and the results of field testing with other non-Jungian institutes. It would also include the development of conflict resolution models jointly with non-Jungian institutes, making them available to politicians and conflict resolution professionals in the field. Lastly, it would entail the generation of outcome measures that could in most cases test the efficacy of the model(s) generated.[33]

In 1982—two years before Premier Gorbachev assumed power in the former Soviet Union—I conducted a study of superpower conflict from the perspective of Jungian psychology. The model generated in this study predicted the collapse of Soviet hegemony in Eastern Europe and the potential breakup of the Soviet Union itself. It also correctly asserted that the use of field war games between the armed forces of the Soviet Union and the United States could serve as a form of "ritual warfare" that would have the effect of dissipating the archetypal energies which impelled the two sides towards armed conflict.[34] Notwithstanding an enthusiastic response to several public lectures I gave on these issues beginning in November 1982 (at the height of the Cold War) at Brown University, in various venues in Washington, D.C., and at the Newport Institute, I could not get the ensuing book published prior to 1989. That was because the notion that archetypal dynamics were leading to the collapse of the Soviet Union, and particularly that ritual war games between the two sides of the Cold War was both feasible and desired, seemed too radical.[35] Radical or not, this was the model that was generated from an archetypal analysis of the Cold War. One can only imagine the impact that such a view might have had were there a conscious understanding of the archetypal dynamics that were actually in play and were those dynamics worked with consciously. The implications are pertinent not only in terms of the demise of the Cold War itself, but critically, in charting a coherent policy to lead the world in the post-Cold War era. The models that emerge when Jung's theories are applied to international conflict are both valuable and likely to generate unanticipated results and unimagined approaches.

NOTES

1. See, Jerome S. Berstein, *Living in the Borderland: The Evolution of Consciousness and the Challenge of Healing Trauma* (Routledge, 2005), Part 1.

2. C. G. Jung, *Collected Works*, trans. R. F. C. Hull (Princeton: Princeton University Press, 1953), vol. 18, para. 371 (all future references to Jung's *Collected Works*, abbreviated to *CW*, will be by volume and paragraph number).

3. See *Journal of International Security*, 17, no. 3 (Winter 1992/93): 5-58. The italics in this passage are those of Dr. Gaddis.

4. Notwithstanding the immorality and the horror of dropping the atomic bomb on Japan, that same immoral act can be viewed as essential from an archetypal point of view in order to avoid an even greater immoral act—the destruction of life itself through atomic "warfare" during the Cold War. See *Death's Dream Kingdom: The American Psyche Since 9-11* by Walter A. Davis (Pluto Press, 2006), p. 5, regarding moral considerations in the decision to drop the atomic bomb on Japan.

5. In Jungian terms, we would say that holding the tension of the opposites by *not* acting out through atomic "warfare" invoked the "transcendent function," which Jung describes as "the bringing together of opposites for the production of an unanticipated third." (*CW* 8 § 181)

6. See Jerome S. Bernstein, *Power and Politics: The Psychology of Soviet-American Partnership* (Shambhala, 1989). Again, as a reminder, it is essential to think *archetypally* and outside of the political science box. Here we are talking more about underlying and often unconscious psychic *dynamics* than we are about the science of cause and effect.

7. I say here that it is "necessary" to go to Greek mythology because, notwithstanding the very rapid evolution of American society and culture as a result of the influx and integration of myriad ethnic groups and cultures, Greek philosophy and archetypal symbolism, as reflected through Greek mythology, still remain the primary symbolic fonts for Western civilization, most particularly for its legal and ethical values and codes as reflected in its political systems. Also see, "On the Politics of Individuation in the Americas," by Murray Stein, in *The Cultural Complex: Contemporary Jungian Perspectives on Psyche and Society*, edited

by Thomas Singer and Samuel L. Kimbles (Brunner-Routledge, 2004).

8. Jung says that *Logos* "is ... a philosophical idea, an abstraction of ... son of God on the one hand, and on the other the dynamic power of thoughts and words." (*CW* 9ii § 293) Logos "includes the idea of a universal being, and thus covers the fact that man's clarity of consciousness and rationality are something universal rather than individually unique ... in the deepest sense impersonal ...." (*CW* 13 § 59)

9. See Bernstein, *Power and Politics,* especially Chapter 6 on war.

10. What Erich Neumann calls the "New Ethic." (See *Depth Psychology and a New Ethic*)

11. I am also distinguishing here between moral consciousness in Jungian terms and Freud's concept of the collective moral consciousness, i.e., the superego, which does not encompass the transpersonal/spiritual dimension. In Freudian terms, one could allude to the life instinct over the death instinct. I prefer Jung's formulation which is at once less and more defined than Freud's because it directly refers to God and suggests that moral concerns take their root in God's struggle with His own nature as reflected through His creation—life. In this context, the human psyche serves as *the* instrument for reflecting moral struggle within the godhead and on behalf of life itself. These notions and concepts are reflected throughout Jung's work but perhaps most deeply and passionately explicated in his *Answer to Job.*

12. The distinction here is whether the human ego, primarily through moral *ideas,* determines human behavior, or whether it is influenced, even trumped, by moral consciousness through a *feeling* realization of transpersonal struggle and need mediated through the human ego.

13. Robert Kennedy, *Thirteen Days* (New York: W. W. Norton & Co., 1969).

14. *Ibid.,* pp. 86-87.

15. *CW* 7 § 151.

16. *CW* 8 § 181.

17. For a highly illuminating and profoundly penetrating Jungian treatise on Islamic Terrorism, see the article by that title by Wolfgang Giegerich in *Jungian Reflections on September 11: A Global Nightmare* (Einsedeln: Daimon Verlag, 2002).

18. *Quadrant* 18, no. 2 (Fall 1985): 6-7.

19. See, Jerome S. Bernstein, *Power and Politics*; Anthony Stevens, *The Roots of War*; Luigi Zoja and Donald Williams, eds., *Jungian Reflections on September 11*; Thomas Singer and Samuel L. Kimbles, eds., *The Cultural Complex: Contemporary Jungian Perspectives on Psyche and Society*; and the works of Wolfgang Giegerich (Spring Journal Books), among others.

20. Eli Weisstub and Esti Galili-Weisstub cite the work of Vlamik Volkan who points out that the recent chapter involving "ethnic cleansing" in Kosovo and elsewhere in the Balkans traces its roots back to an event in 1389. (Weisstub and Galili-Weisstub, "Collective Trauma and Cultural Complex," in *The Cultural Complex*, pp. 164-65).

21. *New York Times*, November 14, 2006, p. A-3.

22. See Jung, *CW* 10 § 57.

23. This insult is later compounded by the conspiracies of his own mother against Esau. Yahweh has told her that Esau will serve his younger twin brother. Neither Yahweh nor his mother Rebecca bothers to tell any of this to Esau. The innocence of the player/victims in this drama is reflected in Genesis 25: 9-10: "Abraham expired and died at a good old age, mature and content. … His sons Isaac and Ishmael buried him in the cave of Macphelah …." A touching scene between half-brothers burying their father—just as it should be. But then, Genesis says: "After Abraham's death God blessed his son Isaac, and Isaac lived near the well of Lahai Roi." (Genesis 25: 11) No blessing for Ishmael, not even in this moment. Only silence from God. That is the end of Ishmael except for the record of his death at age 137, a recording of his descendants, and the statement, "He set himself to defy his brothers." (Genesis 25: 18) But there it ends, and there in another way it begins— three thousand years of fratricidal conflict between the descendants of these half-brothers that carries on to the present time right up to and through September 11, 2001.

24. In fact, the Israeli government did move a considerable distance toward compromise on the settlements issue in the negotiations at Camp David in 2000. Most tend to see Yasser Arafat as the stumbling block in them. However, the point here is an *archetypal* one, not a political one. It was the religious and biblical conundrum I have described that commanded the process and that ultimately sabotaged it, not unlike the stand-off described in Genesis. Indeed, one could virtually see that script as the unconscious wind in the background

that compelled a creative, yet ultimately failed, process. When he was in office, Menachem Begin, the former Prime Minister of Israel, stated quite openly and emphatically his intention that this should be the case and that Israeli settlements (in occupied territory) would be its primary political instrument.

25. It should be noted that the Camp David accords of 1979 implied, but did not expressly forbid the building of additional settlements.

26. I have not researched estimates beyond 2005. It seems to me that with these numbers the point is made.

27. There is always the question of degree to which the United States, as a matter of political expediency, actually desires a resolution of the Arab-Israeli conflict. The current Bush administration appears to be invested in maintaining the conflict in its current form—a "realpolitik."

28. See *The Cultural Complex* and *Jungian Reflections on September 11* for some essays dealing with the topic.

29. In a paper I wrote in 1991, I outlined a rather crude approach as to how to make a bridge from Jungian theory and analysis to applied techniques which can be measured by statistical and non-statistical means. The article can be found in *Carl Gustav Jung: Critical Assessments*, ed. Renos Papadopoulos, 4 vols. (London: Routledge, 1993). Also see "Victory in Iraq?: A Question of Moral Consciousness," in *Psychological Perspectives: A Journal of Global Consciousness*, no. 24 (1991).

30. Again, since "war," is an archetypal energy, it is not possible to get rid of it. It is possible to contain, channel, and in some cases, to transform it. This latter process *is* the goal of a "peace" technology.

31. See my call for the establishment of an "Office of Peace Technology," in *Power and Politics*, p. 179 ff.

32. When I was interfacing with a number of professionals, including politicians, political scientists, academicians, diplomats, conflict resolution professionals, and military personnel in the 1980s when I was living in Washington, D.C., I was surprised at the degree of receptivity to Jungian theory I found when I was able to articulate it in a coherent way.

33. As I have pointed out elsewhere, prevention technology, if it works, in most cases will not yield outcome measures, since, if they are successful, "nothing" will have happened!

34. See Bernstein, *Power and Politics.*

35. Those war games did take place between the Soviet Union and the United States and have continued with the Russian state in the post-Soviet era. See the Foreword by Senator Claiborne Pell, (D-RI), Chairmain of the Senate Foreign Relations Committee, to my earlier book *Power and Politics: The Psychology of Soviet-American Partnership.*

AMERICA: REDEEMER OR DESTROYER OF THE HIGHER DREAM?

ANNE BARING

> Redeem the time
> Redeem the unread vision in the higher dream.
>
> —T. S. Eliot, Ash Wednesday IV

Appalled by the carnage and chaos in Iraq, disillusioned with her government, America yearns for change. Can she make a quantum evolutionary leap—a leap that can redeem the "unread vision in the higher dream?"

The soul of America is a rich and vibrant one, a soul characterized by immense energy, pride, and trust in itself. It also carries a strong heroic element reflected in the deep and genuine devotion that many citizens feel toward their country, including the young men and women willing to sacrifice their lives for her. In America, there is a kindness, a basic openness, and a warm and generous response to others. Also living in America are some of the most creative and innovative people in the world whose awareness of the urgent need for a spiritual and

Anne Baring is a Jungian analyst and a retired member of the Association of Jungian Analysts (AJA), living near Winchester, England. She is the author and co-author of five books including, with Jules Cashford, *The Myth of the Goddess: Evolution of an Image*; with Andrew Harvey, *The Mystic Vision and The Divine Feminine*; and a children's book, *The Birds Who Flew Beyond Time*. Her website www.annebaring.com explores the issues facing us at this crucial time of choice.

political metamorphosis offers a hopeful perspective on the crisis of our times.

So many streams from different and older cultures have created the range and complexity of the American soul. It has been formed by the original inhabitants of this vast land whose soul was empathically linked to the magnificent and sacred landscape: the forests, lakes, mountains, and limitless great plains. Then came the first settlers who, often ruthlessly, displaced and decimated these people, desecrating their sacred spaces: the English, French, Dutch, and later German and Scandinavian settlers. Later came the slaves of the southern states forcibly abducted from Africa; the Irish fleeing starvation; Jewish refugees from Russian pogroms and the Nazi regime in Central Europe; Spaniards, Italians, Puerto Ricans, Greeks, and Chinese. More recently, Mexicans, Asians, Poles, Russians, and refugees from the Middle East are flooding into the country—all seeking a better life and, for many, refuge from persecution. The American soul is therefore an extraordinary blend of elements drawn from every continent superimposed on a primordial native soul—altogether a microcosm of the world soul.

Perhaps this is why the world has looked to America in hope and in trust as well as in admiration for the achievement of melding so many disparate elements into the United States—a democratic union of states that could agree to recognize the authority of one government. And why it is that Americans, having thrown off their subservience to a despotic government in the eighteenth century and fled many persecuting regimes since then, should have a deep sense of loyalty to the Constitution that was drawn up to protect their rights.

America is the richest, most powerful nation on the planet. Therefore the ethos she lives by and the values that guide her are of great significance for other nations. It has come as a shock to many Americans to discover that their government, while claiming to be acting beneficently for America and the world is, in fact, acting as destroyer of the very ideals and values it professes to serve. To many people outside America, it appears as if the American soul has succumbed to the spell of certain beliefs that endanger both itself and the world. What are these beliefs?

- The belief in technological and industrial progress—regardless of the threat of global warming or harm to the planet.

- The belief that America has the right to control the world through the exertion of military and corporate power.
- The belief that what is good for America is good for the world.
- The belief that God is on America's side.
- The belief that America must be victorious in war.
- The belief that the "war on terror" gives America the right to initiate pre-emptive, preventive, or punitive wars and to use nuclear weapons if she so chooses.
- The belief that America is above international law and need not be bound by the United Nations, the Geneva Convention, or the International Criminal Court.

SOLAR MYTHOLOGY AND THE STRUGGLE BETWEEN LIGHT AND DARKNESS

These contemporary beliefs carry the imprint of an archaic solar mythology that first appears in Bronze Age Egypt and Mesopotamia around 2000 BC and speaks of a cosmic battle between the forces of good and evil, light and darkness, portrayed as a battle between a god or hero and a great dragon, serpent, or monster.[1] This battle becomes the major theme of the hero myths of the later Iron Age, whether reflected in the Old Testament, the Greek hero myths, or the Indian epic, the *Mahabharata.* So enduring is its influence that it appears in modern guise in the contemporary struggle against the "Axis of Evil." The American soul is deeply influenced and driven by this solar mythology.

The word "myth" is generally used to describe something false, unreal. But myth in the Jungian sense can reflect an archetype that structures a whole evolutionary epoch, remaining active for millennia. Viewed from a long perspective of some four thousand years, solar mythology has inspired humanity's Promethean quest for freedom, justice, and power; its passionate quest for knowledge; its longing to transcend all limitations and alleviate the blind suffering and ignorance of the human condition.

Tracing the long trajectory of solar mythology, we can read the story of the heroic human ego striving to differentiate itself from the matrix of nature, to develop a sense of self, and attempt to master and control that from which it had emerged. The drama of the solar quest for light and enlightenment is the drama of the ego's quest for consciousness and the fear of falling back into darkness, into unconsciousness. The darkness had to be conquered for the light to prevail.

The integration of polarities is not a theme intrinsic to solar myth. Its primary theme is empowerment, ascent, achievement, conquest. It has helped the outstandingly gifted or heroic individual to differentiate himself from the tribal group, bestowing many benefits on humanity. It has inspired the American dream of rising through one's own efforts to the heights of achievement in myriad fields of endeavor. But it has also encouraged the belief that humanity itself is the solar hero, standing above all other species and having the right to exploit the resources of the planet for its own exclusive benefit, leaving other species defenseless against the onslaught of its perceived rights and needs.

There is still another aspect to this mythology, focused on the goal of territorial conquest. It has implicitly sanctified an ethos that strives for victory at no matter what cost in human lives and even now glorifies war and admires the warrior leader—the power of one man or one nation to lead, dominate, and control others. This archaic model of tribal dominance and conquest has inflicted untold suffering on humanity and now threatens our very survival as a species.

Unaware that our whole way of thinking has been formed by this mythology, America and, indeed, the greater part of the modern world, have fallen into the state of psychic inflation that the Greek tragedians called *hubris*—a state that was already clearly apparent in their time since they repeatedly drew attention to it. Like the Greeks, we ignore at our peril the message of Sophocles in his great play *Oedipus Rex* where Tiresias says to Oedipus: "You have your sight, but do not see what evils are about you."

Nowhere is solar mythology more active and this *hubris* more apparent and more dangerous than in the sphere of politics and religion. And no one was more aware of the dangers of this state of inflation than Jung when he wrote: "We are threatened with universal genocide if we cannot work out the way of salvation by a symbolic death."[2] On the eve of the outbreak of the First World War, as he recounts in *Memories, Dreams, Reflections*, Jung had a vivid dream:

> I was with an unknown, brown-skinned man...in a lonely, rocky mountain landscape. It was before dawn; the eastern sky was already bright, and the stars fading. Then I heard Siegfried's

horn sounding over the mountains and I knew that we had to kill him…On a chariot made of the bones of the dead he drove at a furious speed down the precipitous slopes. When he turned a corner, we shot at him, and he plunged down, struck dead… Filled with disgust and remorse for having destroyed something so great and beautiful, I turned to flee, impelled by the fear that the murder might be discovered. But a tremendous downfall of rain began, and I knew that it would wipe out all traces of the dead.[3]

Reflecting on the dream, Jung understood that it pointed to a problem that was being played out in the world. He realized that he had to sacrifice his identification with the solar hero and the inflated attitude that seeks power over others. He understood that when an individual or a nation does not become conscious of both the light and the dark, conscious and unconscious aspects of his/its behavior, the unconscious power-drive of the shadow may be projected onto an opponent and a crusade embarked on to eliminate an enemy. Hence the world is torn into opposing ideologies; hence walls, psychic and material, are built to separate enemies.

The solar era reflects an immense evolutionary change in human consciousness, the formulation of an entirely new perception of life that contrasts with an older lunar phase where humanity instinctively participated in an ensouled nature and attuned itself to the great rhythms of Earth and Cosmos. In that era the moon rather than the sun was the focus of consciousness.[4] With the rise and diffusion of solar mythology, coinciding with the advent of literacy, this sense of mythic participation gradually fades. Nature becomes something to be controlled by human ingenuity, to human advantage.[5] Earth, once alive with spirit, is desouled. Body is disconnected from mind, and mind from soul. The Biblical myth of the Fall describes this process of estrangement, separation, and loss—a stark reversal of the participatory way of knowing that characterized older, pre-literate lunar cultures.

Solar mythology had a profound influence on Middle-Eastern as well as European culture, impregnating Persian, Greek, Judaic, Roman, Christian, and Islamic cultures. As the solar age developed, the cosmic battle between the forces of light and darkness was increasingly projected into the world. A fascination with conquest gripped the imagination, leading to the creation of vast empires conquered by warrior-hero leaders. It was as if the human ego, identified with the solar hero or god, had to embody the myth in a literal sense.

The polarizing emphasis of solar mythology gradually created a fissure between spirit and nature, mind and body, which defined religious beliefs, cultural attitudes, and social customs. During this solar phase, the male psyche aligned itself with the supremacy of spirit and mind over nature, woman, and body, identifying man with the image of light and order and woman with the image of darkness and chaos. Woman, closer to nature than man, was named an inferior creation: nature, woman, and the body had to be subject to the will of man.[6] The unconscious identification of woman with instinct and nature was the origin of the negative projections onto her that were incorporated into social attitudes and customs—fused with religious beliefs—that endure to this day.

With the psychological insight that has become available to us over the last hundred years, particularly through the insights of Jung, we can understand that during the solar phase of our evolution a radical dissociation developed *within* the human soul between the growing strength of the ego—the light-bearing hero—and the older and greatly feared power of the unconscious instinct—the dragon that was identified with darkness. Mythologies, as well as religious beliefs and cultural habits of behavior, were built on the foundation of this dissociation.

The supreme achievement of the solar era was the emergence of a strong autonomous sense of self (ego) from the matrix of instinct and the development of the conscious, reflective, rational mind. But this had a high price. Firstly, the inflation of the ego as it drew away from its instinctive ground and began to assimilate a god-like power to itself. Secondly, the subjugation and repression of the instinctual, the non-rational, and the feminine which, identified with each other, were perceived as threatening to the hegemony of the masculine ego.

The unconscious conflict generated by this inner situation has, for millennia, been projected into the world as the drive for power, dominance, and control—whether in the religious or political sphere. Simultaneously, the need for the re-union of the dissociated elements of the soul has been deflected into the drive to impose unity on the world by the force of conquering armies and ideologies, whether religious or secular.

The atavistic behavioral pattern of predator killing prey, already deeply embedded in tribal rivalries and magnified by the polarizing effect of solar mythology, was incorporated into religious beliefs. This encouraged the persecution of people of a different faith and the evangelizing, conquering tendencies of Christianity and Islam as well as the struggle for supremacy between them. The "enemy" was identified with darkness and evil. The murder of heretics and apostates was sanctioned as something approved of by God. The idea that a particular belief system offered a superior path to salvation which excluded and demonized those following a different path was taught as part of a religious tradition, indoctrinating generations of children with this pernicious idea.

In the political domain, solar mythology ratified persecutory behavior towards the "dark" and so-called "inferior" or "primitive" (more instinctual) races that fell victim to the race for empire of the European nations. It was the primary influence on the secular totalitarian ideologies that ravaged the world in the last century because these ideologies separated the heroic race or "chosen" social group from those designated as sub-human and expendable. Wherever the word "purification" or "perfection" is mentioned, we may be sure to hear the call to eliminate the "impure" or "imperfect." The same tendency to demonize is reflected in the attitude of the fundamentalist Islamists to the *kaffir (kufr)* or non-believer; an attitude also found in evangelical Christianity where the long anticipated "Rapture" will ensure the salvation of the "chosen" group of Christians while the rest perish.

The problem for America and for all humanity seems to be that the civilizing influence of religion that emphasizes relationship, service, and compassion yields to the polarizing effects of solar mythology whenever unconscious survival instincts are aroused by leaders who name an enemy as "evil." Then, God may be co-opted by either side to support those who identify themselves with "good."

Closely affiliated with solar mythology is the myth of the redeemer, the solar hero. George W. Bush has assumed for himself a messianic role in delivering America and the world from the "Axis of Evil." Whether consciously or unconsciously, he identified himself with Christ when he said, "Those who are not with us are against us," echoing the words, "He that is not with me is against me." (Matt. 12:30)

From one side of the solar divide, Osama bin Laden was named as evil; from the other, he was hailed by his Wahhabi followers as the Mahdi, the saviour of Islam.[7] The aim of both solar heroes is the establishment of a global empire and the redemption of the world from evil. They and the millions who follow them, believing they are doing God's will, have, from a Jungian perspective, succumbed to an archetypal inflation, identifying themselves, their nation, and their religion with the light aspect of the Self and projecting the dark aspect onto their enemy. These possessed leaders believe that God Himself supports them since they are fighting His cosmic battle of good against evil. An archaic mythology has conditioned us to think only in oppositional terms—victory or defeat. Hence George W. Bush's words: "I will settle for nothing less than complete victory." Each solar hero is unaware that he is trying to destroy in his opponent a pattern of behavior that he cannot recognize in himself.

THE GOD-IMAGE OF THE SOLAR ERA

One of the most problematic legacies of the solar era is the monotheistic God-image shared by the three patriarchal religions—a paternal image that portrays God as transcendent to and separate from creation, thereby splitting nature from spirit. This belief effectively desacralized the phenomenal world and opened the way to its exploitation. It led to the fear and repression of the Feminine and prevented the emergence of a balanced culture which gave equal value to each archetypal principle. The developing ego "grew up" in the shadow of an image of deity that was utterly different from that of the earlier lunar phase where the image of the Great Mother embraced cosmos and nature and all life on Earth. This ancient and inclusive concept of spirit survived in Celtic Christianity until the seventh century AD and is reflected in the words of an Irish philosopher called John Scotus Eriugena (810-77) who lived at the French court in the ninth century:

> We should not understand God and creation as two different
> things, but as one and the same. For creation subsists in God,
> and God is created in creation in a remarkable and ineffable way,
> manifesting Himself and, though invisible, making Himself
> visible, and though incomprehensible, making Himself

> comprehensible, and although hidden, revealing Himself, and,
> though unknown, making himself known; though lacking form
> and species, endowing Himself with form and species; though
> superessential, making Himself essential...though creating
> everything, making Himself created in everything.[8]

Jung put this crucially important understanding into different
words:

> It was only quite late that we realized (or rather, are beginning to
> realize), that God is Reality itself and therefore last but not least
> man. This realization is a millennial process.[9]

From the split between creator and creation in the image of deity
has come the current scientific attitude that regards matter as inanimate
object split off from observing subject. From the belief in a monotheistic
God comes the conviction that there can only be one supreme truth,
whether offered by a religion, a scientific theory, or a political ideology.
Until the schism between spirit and nature is healed, the world will
continue to be fractured into competing "truths" that deluded and
inflated individuals will attempt to impose on others.

The belief that this material dimension (including matter and the
body) is not co-inherent with spirit, participating in the dimension of
spirit, and therefore sacred, led to them being regarded as inferior to
and separate from spirit; something in the Christian tradition that is
flawed, sinful, fallen. How then could all human life, all human
experience, be valued as something precious and sacred, an expression
and vehicle of spirit? How could the life of the Earth and all its species
be respected? How could people realize that we and all creation may
exist *within* the cosmic being of God or, as Jung put it, within the great
unifying field of the *unus mundus*?

SOLAR MYTH AND THE AMERICAN SOUL:
MILITARISM AND THE NEED FOR AN ENEMY

Much of the world now looks askance at America: resentful of her
power, mistrustful of her aims. And many Americans, sensitive to this
climate, ask "Why do they hate us so?" This question could be the
catalyst that opens the door to a change of consciousness. When a nation,
intent on attaining global hegemony or "full-spectrum dominance,"

identifies with the archetype of the solar hero, it will need to find an enemy on which to fix darkness and evil. The existence of this enemy will justify its transformation into an imperial power and the accumulation of a huge arsenal of weapons to pre-empt any future attack. Yet, the more inflated and hubristic it becomes, the more likely is it that it will draw nemesis upon itself, whether by attack from without or collapse from within.

After 9/11 the world held its breath. Would America be able to resist the instinct to retaliate? Could she enter into dialogue with the Islamic world? Could light shine in such darkness? But the moment passed...

It may be that the invasion of Iraq has done the world a great service by awakening people everywhere to the peril of allowing two leaders— George W. Bush and Tony Blair—to embark on a war that, far from spreading democracy in Iraq and adjacent countries, has destabilized them and antagonized the whole Muslim world.

"Operation Shock and Awe" focused only on the success of the invasion. The reconstruction of Baghdad was planned and handled with crass ineptness.[10] Nor was any value assigned to the unquantifiable laceration of the human heart that the invasion would engender for the traumatized veterans of the war, the parents who have lost sons and daughters, and the terrified people of Iraq, four million of whom have fled their homes, many of them now stateless and destitute.

During a talk given by the Dalai Lama in London in 2004, a question was asked about the advisability of the invasion of Iraq. The Dalai Lama simply replied, "Very bad karma; very bad karma." In the bloodbath of sectarian violence that Baghdad has become, in the tens of thousands of civilian lives lost, in the legacy of hatred, terror, lawlessness, and misery the war has engendered, we can now see what he foresaw.

American imperialism had its roots in the late nineteenth century at the time of the Spanish-American war when the Treaty of Paris of 1898 transferred the Spanish territories of Guam and Puerto Rico to American sovereignty as well as the entire Philippine archipelago of islands. As part of the treaty, Cuba agreed to America maintaining a naval base at Guantánamo Bay. The idea that America had a God-given mission to bring democracy to the world was first promulgated by Woodrow Wilson who saw himself as chosen by God to initiate this mission. "More than any other figure, he provided the intellectual foundations for an interventionist foreign policy, expressed in humanitarian and democratic rhetoric."[11]

At the end of the Second World War, America was the solar hero, in an atavistic sense the "primal male" — the only nation that had the atom bomb. She felt secure in her ability to confront all enemies. But her sense of pre-eminence was soon challenged by the Soviet Empire which exploded its own atom bomb in 1949. Immediately, Truman made the decision to develop a more powerful bomb, yielding to Teller's insistence that only the hydrogen bomb—a thousand times more powerful than the atom bomb—could protect America from an attack by the Soviet Union. Opposing Teller, Oppenheimer argued that the bomb, far from protecting America, would escalate the race for power among nations and lead to a catastrophic denouement. Regretting what he had engendered as "father of the bomb," he saw it as a truly demonic weapon: "an evil thing; a weapon of terror and aggression; a weapon for aggressors." Like Sakharov, who was ordered to develop the hydrogen bomb by Stalin, he recoiled from the horror that scientists had unleashed on the world.

In 1952 Teller's hydrogen bomb was detonated in the Pacific, in a three-mile-wide fireball that vaporized the island beneath it. In 1953 the Soviets detonated their first hydrogen bomb and two years later, another. Thus, powered by an unconscious addiction to solar mythology, the race was on to see who could "win" the nuclear race by building the greatest armory of weapons. Soon Great Britain, China, and France had the bomb; then Israel secretly developed it. World peace was now thought to be secured by the policy of "Mutually Assured Destruction" ("MAD").

As tension escalated in the Middle East, and America established many new bases on land that Muslims held sacred, Islamic nations were outraged by the West's political interference in "their" territory. Inevitably they sought to acquire the bomb. They found their hero in the Pakistani nuclear scientist, Dr. Abdul Qadeer Khan, who sold the plans for a nuclear reactor to Libya and Iran (as well as North Korea). America was drawn into the struggle to control the demonic weapon she had launched on the world. Einstein's prescient comment was ignored: "The unleashing of the power of the atom bomb has changed everything except our mode of thinking, and thus we head toward unparalleled catastrophes."[12]

Few governments acknowledged the enormity of what they were willing to inflict on a helpless civilian population in order to secure the survival of their particular nation. Each nuclear state was prepared to annihilate millions of innocent people and to pollute the Earth for generations in an exchange of nuclear missiles. For the decades of the Cold War the tension between competing empires and ideologies powered the escalation of military technology and, as this developed on each side, it was extended, in the Star Wars programme, to the race for control in space as well as on earth.[13] Arguing that the bomb would act as a deterrent, those promoting the arms race did not acknowledge that in an exchange of nuclear missiles, there would, as Jonathan Schell comments in his book, *The Fate of the Earth*, be no victor and no vanquished: both would be extinguished along with hundreds of millions of helpless civilians.

> The question now before the human species is whether life or death will prevail on the earth…No generation before ours has held the life and death of its species in its hands…In our present-day world, in the councils where the decisions are made, there is no one to speak for man and for the Earth, although both are threatened with annihilation.[14]

America now claims the right to make a pre-emptive nuclear strike and is adding to her nuclear arsenal which already comprises over five thousand multiple-megaton warheads and ten thousand nuclear warheads.[15] All this is enough to destroy the planet several times over. The existence of such a huge arsenal of weapons invites their use and encourages other nations to "join the club" of the nuclear nations.

Only a species completely dissociated from nature could collude in such madness. America leads this madness because she seeks world supremacy in order to control the resources vital to her economy. It is as if the violent assault on the elements of matter—itself the end-result of four thousand years of solar mythology—has split the human soul even further. Another symptom of madness is the fact that Christian fundamentalists welcome the prospect of a nuclear Armageddon, believing that it will hasten the "Rapture" and the Second Coming of Christ.

Between 1950 and 2006, staggering sums were spent on armaments and defense.[16] The proposed budget for 2008 is six hundred and forty-five billion dollars—nearly a hundred billion more than in 2007 and equal to the total sum spent on defense by all other nations put together. An additional hundred billion is demanded from Congress this year to finance the "surge" in Iraq.

While the financial demands of the military-industrial complex were growing, the plight of the poorest section of the American people was ignored. In a nation that proclaims freedom and justice for all, millions suffer from poverty, crime, drug addiction, lack of education, affordable housing, and medical care. They cannot live the American Dream. A UNICEF report in February 2007 showed the United States and the United Kingdom at the bottom of the list of the developed nations in the care and well-being of their children. The American soul appears to be split between a fundamentalist evangelical Christianity unaware of its power-driven shadow, and an aggressive Darwinian ethos that is addicted to consumption, winning, and supremacy. Decadent movies and videos—classified as "entertainment" and exported abroad —glorify male violence and imprint children's developing consciousness with images of sadism and torture.

During these fifty years, foreign policy became increasingly secretive, and the need for security began to erode the constitutional rights of the American people. Illegal operations (including enforced regime change and extraordinary rendition) were carried out abroad and kept secret. The network of naval and military bases established before and during the Second World War was expanded to number between seven and eight hundred in every continent except Antarctica. After 9/11 the prisoners incarcerated at Guantánamo Bay were denied the rights of prisoners of war established by the Geneva Convention.

From this imperial perspective the Iraq War can be viewed as part of a long-term strategy of increasing American power in the Middle East. Why else would America be building the largest embassy in the world in a protected enclave of Baghdad, supplied with electricity and water when, four years after the invasion, its citizens are barely supplied with either? On the one hand, America proclaims noble aims; on the other, she subverts the possibility of achieving them.

If members of the administration of George W. Bush had known the dangers of triggering a mass psychosis in the Muslim world by the decision to invade Iraq, would they have been so certain that the overthrow of Saddam Hussein would bring them victory, control of the oil in the Middle East, and a new regime in Baghdad that was compliant to their political aims?

Had they known anything about the dangers of aligning themselves with "good" and projecting their militarist shadow onto Al Qaeda, would they have formulated that phrase, the "axis of evil?" They could have heeded Nietzsche's warning: "He who fights with monsters might take care lest he thereby become a monster."[17]

From these facts it appears that successive administrations have, for the past fifty years, been intent on establishing a world empire—ostensibly with the aim of defending American interests and maintaining security for the world. The rise of militarism has led to the loss of civil liberties and is leading the country to bankruptcy. It has contributed to a dangerous increase in the power of the executive branch of government and the further transfer of power from Congress to the Pentagon, which appears to have become the virtual formulator and controller of foreign policy and expenditure. In psychological terms, it is as if the administration, in collusion with the military, has been acting like an autonomous complex that most Americans have no awareness of and over which, as the ability of Congress to check the power of the executive has weakened, they have no means of control. Fortunately, there are signs that Congress is seeking to regain the powers that the President and the Pentagon have appropriated. But the accusation that anyone who opposes the demands of the administration is unpatriotic may be used as a tool to sabotage this initiative.

The splitting and polarizing effects of solar mythology can help us to understand the situation in which America now finds herself and, with America, the world. Terrorism is not the only enemy. The real enemy is unconsciousness of the fact that the world is held hostage to an archaic mythology that carries a very dark shadow. Ever more dangerous conflicts will come into being until we develop insight into how we are in thrall to its archetypal power.

Millions of Americans take pride in the fact that their nation is the most powerful one on earth; millions believe that God has entrusted them with a mission to spread the Christian faith. How many are aware that America has, over the course of the last century, built up a world empire with totalitarian characteristics and that this is the reason why she is both hated and feared? America is still a democracy. She supposedly has a free press. With access to the facts there is a chance that the American people may be able to dismantle the military Colossus that now casts its paranoid shadow over the world, inviting a paranoid response.

John Quincy Adams warned America in 1821 that if she sought to become the dictatress of the world, she would no longer be ruler of her own spirit. America cannot be both a democracy and an imperial power. If Americans could challenge their government's imperial aims and dissociate themselves from them, the impact on the world would be incalculable. It would involve acknowledging the evil America has engendered in the ruthless pursuit of extending her corporate and commercial interests, her belief in "progress," and the furtherance of her political aims and religious beliefs.

Yet, it is important to remember that beneath the events of our time is the four-millennia-old history of solar mythology and the wound caused by the dissociation of human consciousness from the deeper, instinctive matrix of the soul and the split in the God-image between creator and creation. This history reflects an unconscious process whereby we lost our connection to Earth and Cosmos and became estranged from our deepest instincts, with the result that we are now possessed and driven by them—possibly to our own extinction. The predatory industrial culture we have created, although beneficial to ourselves in some respects, stands like a tyrant over and against nature, over and against the Earth and whatever threatens our supremacy as a species. There is an abysmal ignorance that Earth is primary and our survival is dependent on the well-being of the Earth's related systems.

In the Epilogue of his book, *The Passion of the Western Mind*, Richard Tarnas points to a process of awakening that is helping us to recover the ancient participatory way of knowing that was lost during the solar era. This is calling, ever more urgently, for its restoration at a new level that the philosopher Owen Barfield called "Final Participation."[18]

> As Jung prophesied, an epochal shift is taking place in the contemporary psyche, a reconciliation between the two great polarities, a union of opposites: a sacred marriage between the long-dominant but now alienated masculine and the long-suppressed but now ascending feminine...We seem to be

witnessing, suffering, the birth labour of a new reality, a new
form of human existence, a "child" that would be the fruit of
this great archetypal marriage.[19]

This epochal shift invites the mammoth task of redeeming the
unconscious shadow of the solar era and reuniting the dissociated aspects
of our soul. Jung's insight into the nature of the shadow is one of his
supreme gifts to our culture. But, as he wryly commented, "One does
not become enlightened by imagining figures of light, but by making
the darkness conscious."[20] Making the darkness conscious involves the
sacrifice of the ego that would continue in the same tracks of belief
and behavior as before, ignorant of the deeper archetypal forces that
control it from the shadow. Again, he wrote:

> This is an exceedingly dangerous time and we are confronted
> with a problem which has never been known in the conscious
> history of man. You cannot compare it with the early times of
> Christianity, because that movement did not come from the
> blood, but came from above, a light that shone forth. This is not
> a light but a darkness, the powers of darkness are coming up.[21]

Leaders carry and unconsciously act out the collective shadow.
Millions collude with their projections because they look to a leader
for security when survival instincts are aroused. Government
propaganda compounds both the fear and the illusion of safety. To
withdraw these projections and see clearly what the shadow is doing
depotentiates it, freeing us from being possessed by it. We have enough
consciousness now to make this choice, to shed light on our own
darkness. This involves dissociating ourselves as individuals from
collective beliefs that, far from eliminating evil, cause it to proliferate.
In Jung's words:

> The immunity of the nation depends entirely upon the existence
> of a leading minority immune to the evil and capable of combating
> the powerful suggestive effect of seemingly possible wish-
> fulfilments. If the leader is not absolutely immune, he will
> inevitably fall a victim to his own will-to-power.[22]

ALCHEMY: THE YOUNG KING AND THE NEW CONSCIOUSNESS

During the last fifty years or so, it seems as if we have been placed
in an alchemical retort, forced to live through the fire of transformation,

for the most part, unconsciously. The deaths, suffering, and destitution of millions of people created by wars and savage oppression, by the sale of arms, by corporate greed and corruption, and the ruthless despoiling and exploitation of the Earth call for a new kind of spirituality grounded in service to the Earth and all its species.

The new myth coming into being through the triple influence of quantum physics, depth psychology, and the ecological movement suggests that we are participants in a great cosmic web of life, each one of us indissolubly connected with all others through that invisible field. It is the most insidious of illusions to think that we can achieve a position of dominance in relation to nature, life, or each other. The belief that nations can continue to act as autonomous units, developing the power to destroy life on a colossal scale without their demonic inventions returning to them in the form of an enemy armed with precisely the weapons they have developed for their own protection, is not only an illusion but a pathology—a madness.

Now we are threatened with annihilation by weapons that may fall into the hands of individuals who will spare no effort to encompass the destruction of a hated enemy. Yet these enemies whom we hope to eliminate in the "war on terror" may be a manifestation of the split-off elements of the totality that are asking for recognition and integration. Evil will continue to confront us until we become conscious of the evil we unwittingly bring into being through our rape of the elements of matter and our wanton abuse and desecration of the Earth. Evil in this sense serves wholeness because it is driving us to integrate our unconscious shadow or face extinction.

Alchemy speaks of the Great Work. What might this be? We are embedded in the world of spirit. Our physical bodies carry cosmic elements that come from the stars. We are the living vehicle of spirit, but we don't know this. Spirit depends on us in this dimension to rescue it from the imprisoned or buried state to which we have consigned it. This work may be compared to the excavation of a precious treasure, bringing to conscious awareness the realization that the rejected feminine elements of spirit—nature, matter, and the body— participate in the unity and sacredness of all cosmic life. Alchemy describes an arduous process of attunement to this realization—arduous because it is so difficult to dismantle millennia-old habits of belief and behavior.

Alchemy gives us the image of an old king who has to die in order that his son may rule in his stead. These words accompany one of the beautiful illustrations to the sixteenth-century alchemical manuscript, *Splendor Solis:*

> The King's son lies in the depths of the sea as though dead. But he lives and calls from the deep: "Whosoever will free me from the waters and lead me to dry land, him will I prosper with everlasting riches." (illustration seven)

Today, the fate of our species, perhaps even the fate of the Earth, hangs in the balance. Will the American people choose to free the young king and the values he personifies from the waters of the deep or will they continue to live in thrall to the values of the old king—the power-seeking values that engender so much evil and suffering? Could the soul of America that has given sanctuary to so many different people and races find the insight and courage to make an evolutionary quantum leap, uniting the world in a transformation of consciousness that could draw humanity away from the brink of catastrophe and perhaps even redeem the unread vision in the higher dream?

The last words may be left to America's greatest sage, Thomas Berry:

> The time for action is passing. The devastation increases. The time is limited. The Great Work remains to be done. This is not a situation that can be remedied by trivial or painless means. A largeness of vision and a supreme dedication are needed.[23]

NOTES

1. See the Sumerian *Epic of Gilgamesh* and the Babylonian creation myth, the *Enuma Elish.* In Egypt, the myth of the Night Journey of the Sun.

2. C. G. Jung, *Collected Works*, tr. R. F. C. Hull (Princeton: Princeton University Press, 1953), vol. 18, para. 1661 (all future references to Jung's *Collected Works*, abbreviated to *CW*, will be by volume and paragraph number).

3. *Memories, Dreams, Reflections* (London: Collins and Routledge & Kegan Paul, 1963), pp. 173-4.

4. Jules Cashford, *The Moon: Myth and Image* (London: Cassell, 2003).

5. David Abram, *The Spell of the Sensuous* (New York: Vintage Books, 1996).

6. Plato's *Timaeus* and Genesis 1.

7. Lawrence Wright, *The Looming Tower: Al Qaeda's Road to 9/11* (London and New York: Penguin Books Ltd., 2006).

8. *Periphyseon: de Divisione Naturae* (Montreal: 1987, translated by I.P. Sheldon-Williams, revised by John O'Meara), p. 167. The same concept is found in Kabbalah.

9. Jung, *CW* 11 § 631.

10. Rajiv Chandrasekaran, *Imperial Life in the Emerald City: Inside Baghdad's Green Zone* (New York: Knopf, 2006), *passim*.

11. Chalmers Johnson, *The Sorrows of Empire: Militarism, Secrecy and the End of the Republic* (New York: Henry Holt, 2004), p. 48.

12. Albert Einstein, *The Expanded Quotable Einstein,* collected and edited by Alice Calaprice (Princeton: The Hebrew University of Jerusalem and Princeton University Press, 2000), p. 184.

13. The U.S. Administration is currently in negotiation with European and other governments to set up anti-ballistic missile stations, much against the will of the people of these nations.

14. Jonathan Schell, *The Fate of the Earth* (London: Pan Books, 1982), pp. 113, 116 and 188.

15. Chalmers Johnson, p. 64.

16. *Ibid.*, p. 56.

17. Friedrich Nietzche, *Beyond Good and Evil,* aphorism 146.

18. Owen Barfield, *Saving the Appearances,* 2nd ed. (Middletown, Connecticut: Wesleyan University Press, 1988), pp. 133, 186.

19. Richard Tarnas, *The Passion of the Western Mind* (New York: Ballantine Books, 1991), pp. 443, 444. See also *Cosmos and Psyche* (New York: Viking, 2006).

20. Jung, *CW* 13 § 335.

21. Jung, Nietzsche's *Zarathustra*, Vol. 1, p. 500.

22. Jung, *CW* 18 § 1400.

23. Thomas Berry, *Evening Thoughts* (San Francisco: Sierra Club Books, 2006), p. 19.

VIOLENT HEARTS:
AMERICA'S DIVIDED SOUL

LUIGI ZOJA

(Translated by John Peck)

DIVISION

*W*hy in every age is Odysseus called unique, timeless, and modern? Odysseus is at home in every era because he is complex, because many personalities belong to him. He is not incapacitated because of internal division or splitting. Instead, he thrives on it.

Each character in Homer is allotted a fixed set of adjectives which elaborate a single quality, and which are meant to help the oral performer of the poem by supplying rhythmic promptings and supporting his imagination during oral performance. But Odysseus is an exception. No single focus exists for his characterization, such as

A native of Italy and a graduate of the C. G. Jung Institute in Zurich, Luigi Zoja lectures, teaches, and maintains an active clinical practice in Milan. A former President of the International Association for Analytical Psychology, he has written a number of books, including: *Violence in History, Culture, and Psyche,* forthcoming from Spring Journal Books, March, 2008*; Ethics and Analysis: Philosophical Perspectives and Their Application in Therapy,* Carolyn and Ernest Fay Lecture Series in Analytical Psychology, No. 13, Texas A & M University Press, 2007; *Cultivating the Soul,* Free Association Books, 2005; *Jungian Reflections on September 11: A Global Nightmare* (as co-editor with Donald Williams), Daimon, 2002; *Father: Historical, Psychological, and Cultural Perspectives*, Routledge, 2001; *Drugs, Addiction and Initiation: The Modern Search for Ritual,* Daimon, 2000; *Growth and Guilt: Psychology and the Limits of Development,* Routledge, 1995.

physical prowess. Instead, a whole array of qualities is present, each of which mingles with the others: *poly-tlas* (he can bear many things), *poly-tropos, poly-metis, poly-mechanos* (he can cleverly invent or create many things, he can think his way through anything, he can travel anywhere)—which is to say, he has many identities.

Odysseus is fierce and destructive like the ancient heroes: in fact, we know that his name means "that which hates."[1] In the end, however, once he has conquered, he shows a surprising respect for the dead[2] and for the survivors.[3] His sensitivity to external enemies is a mirror reflection of his respect for internal adversaries. Odysseus battles outer opponents but also fights with himself, in that way opening a door onto a psychic dimension. While the masterworks of many national literatures ignore the soul's complexity, and the Hebrew and Christian scriptures enlist the soul in the service of the divine, Homer, the first great Greek author, and a man of the 8th century B.C., did not yet even know about the written medium, but already he tried to describe what today we call a psychological process. Perhaps out of respect for his attempts the whole West describes the inner world through a Greek idea, calling it *psychē*.

Naturally, Homer did not carry out a psychological analysis as we understand it today. Most likely, if had he employed modern psychological terms, imaginatively impoverished as they are, his narrative poems would have been entirely forgotten. He makes direct use of symbols, which say far more than do the abstractions which explain them. In that sense, the novelty of Odysseus is situated in the very language of human contradictions—the "I" that would but cannot, the compromises among internal pressures. He is a complex psychological character portrayed by Homer 2600 years before psychoanalysis.

The author whom we call Homer must have been an extraordinary poet and psychologist himself. He devoted fully half of his work to describing a single character—Odysseus—most likely attributing to him qualities that must have been his own: introspection and the ability to identify himself with others. He made the first attempt to tell the story, not of a war, a myth, or a god, but—to use the first word of the *Odyssey*—a man: *ándra*. And the man he described was not a unified being.

Confronted with mortal danger, not every Homeric hero goes on the attack like the figures in modern action films. Some of them, given to reflection, hang back. Odysseus, however, is reflective not only in the face of death, but rather consistently. In contrast to the ancient heroes, who immediately look for some way to impose themselves on an opponent, Odysseus knows how to listen for the voice of the other—the other within you, the other you have before you—to make his acquaintance. And, based on that new knowledge, to gain new opportunity.

To accept the soul's inherent division, to elaborate on it and turn it into a rich resource, is the new super-weapon. Odysseus is one figure and many figures (*poly-*) in one.

The fact that Odysseus disguises himself and uses a number of different names that are not his own is therefore not simply a narrative expediency. Odysseus epitomizes the "capacity to put on another man's clothes," sometimes to elicit his sympathy, at other times to psych him out and beat him at the first opportunity. This capability is the necessary presupposition either for the organization of a non-tyrannical society—like that of the Greeks—or for winning calculated victories over an enemy: a characteristic that has awarded the advantage to the West over millennia.

If a shadow happens to fall across the street, the dog either barks or does not bark. If something scares a man, he either cries "Help!" or he does not. But the man who has cried for help will go on asking himself, with one part of his mind, if that was the right thing to do. Only the stupid or the fanatical fail to realize that the inner voices that contradict each other are a great gift from the psyche.

Our major works of art tell us in various ways about our absurd ordinariness: only the gods are absolutely beautiful or entirely good. The superiority of human beings to the ingenious gods of antiquity rests, in a certain indefinable way, with a single attribute, that of being torn between opposite modes of being. Something of the same kind of superiority is true of artistic representation—its indefiniteness—next to the common kind, which is definite. Leonardo's "Mona Lisa" is a masterpiece partly because it expresses happiness and sadness at one and the same time, indistinguishably. As is Euripides' Medea for being simultaneously heroic and perverse, and Goethe's Faust for describing an ambivalent soul, a force that wills evil but works goodness. Truly great creations are embodiments of the intricate profundity of the human being.

Homer's figures are among the best known of all, even if no religion or powerful nation has adopted them. They are known because they are human, and in their mental processes we can still recognize ourselves. We take part in their dramas not only because of their staying power but also, as Bruno Snell has said, because of *recognition*. In line with Snell's idea, Jacqueline de Romilly has observed that Odysseus' admonition "Be patient, my heart!" initiated what today we call psychology.

Odysseus has returned to Ithaca, among the parasitical suitors who deplete its wealth and lie in wait for his wife. Furious to the core, he would like to grab the sword, revenge himself immediately: he is a *violent heart*. But he knows that would be suicidal. His heart cries out like a mother hound defending her young. Like the dog's master, Odysseus forces it to be quiet. He does not stop at simply chiding it. He knows that it is right, but that its rightness is only one among many good reasons for acting. Motive determines the objective, prudence decides on the timing. He orders his heart to sustain him.[4] Odysseus differs from conventional heroes because he listens, and also waits. Homer describes his thinking as being like a ball that volleys back and forth continually "between head and heart" (*kata phrena kai kata thymon*).

In Western tradition, division within the soul has been literally demonized; European languages define evil with terms like "de-vil," from the Greek *dia-ballo*, that which divides things. However, a conscious psychic division, accepted by the ego, is also our richness and humanity. It is the fertile field in which our ambivalence grows, our complexity, and, finally, our creativity. "Di-vision"—separation into two parts—is the necessary ground for "dis-course"—the word that runs or flows between two parties. The prefix here, *dis-*, is Latin for separation. Only that earth which has been divided by the plowshare can receive a seed.

Vertical division, those passages from one level of the soul to others more profound, may also correspond to *horizontal* divisions, in time. In this respect, too, Odysseus is the forerunner of Western vitality. His life is made up of radical shifts in activity and changes of place. He grew up on Ithaca. Then came ten years of war at Troy. Ten years of return voyaging came after that. Finally, his reign on Ithaca was to be followed, according to prophecy,[5] by another long voyage and another return. He lived with Penelope, then was a bachelor, one year with Circe and seven with Kalypso, before returning to Penelope. He went from being a king to being a wanderer and a beggar, then became king once more, and then a wanderer again, at long last making a definitive homecoming.

A pre-figuration of Western man? Better yet, a pre-figuration of the West's own West, the United States of America, where the courage and insatiable curiosity of Odysseus became the national soul. A way of being with no geographical or historical precedents.

Inheriting the command to "Go West!," the new man has stayed on the move. Arriving at the Pacific Ocean, the "West" was finished, but the "Go!" went on living. It wasn't just a practical command, it was a commandment, a mission. Not a journey, but America's stable essence—so much so that a foreign visitor on American highways is most likely to hear the police say, "Keep moving!"

The typical American citizen changes his place of residence as well as his marital status, sexual orientation, religion, and profession more often than citizens of any other country in any era. Changes them because of a belief in improvement or betterment, in a future greater than the past: a faith inconceivable to a Greek or an Italian, but obligatory to the Pilgrim Fathers and their descendants.

To accomplish this mission, however, one must divide up time: one must close the door onto the past, and leap the fence of the future. The search for purification from evil has driven the American legacy to attempt the elimination of the internal "other." But in this way, American identity thereby also denies one of its archetypal models: Odysseus. This liquidated factor returns as the "other" in time. The American search-mission abandons England as impure in order to build a pure society, but it also leaves a filthy past for a desired clean future, the spotless future that it wants. Time divides itself into separate times. In the United States, life can be diced up into very different periods, such that one cannot come to grips with them. The extraordinary legibility of spaces and times into which the American soul adventures at the behest of its original commandment is a possibility without equal, but also—something less talked about—an anxiety without definition. To pull up stakes, leave it all behind for the new thing, and with it, every time, a rebirth. But it is also a violence, a death of the preceding life. It is an endless revolution. And revolutions—as Solzhenitsyn has reminded us—are always violent: the old king, the outworn condition, must die. The anxiety of separation or division is therefore the absolute American anguish: an inner panic about losing identity, about taking on too much change, of falling into the void from having lived in too many spaces. Of discovering that a country that has stayed on the move everywhere no longer occupies any place. Mark Twain has Huck Finn end his story by saying that he intends "to light out for the territory"— that is, to vanish from the scene.

At the origins of Western history, the Greeks were divided into independent city-states. They frequently made war on each other. But these were wars in which little happened. The conquering city did not incorporate the defeated one. The dimensions of cities did not grow very much. Having invented democracy, the Greeks passed the better part of their time in the civic square discussing the nature of life in society. Each citizen had his own opinion: division was not functional, but it was vital. They very well knew that society, if it grew too large, risked becoming ungovernable and giving over power to a tyrant.

Every four years, the Greeks gathered together at Olympia: like champion duelists from armies, they gave themselves over to literary and athletic contest. Unity and division were two faces of their identity.

Once society had grown in scale, democracy was abandoned for monarchy. Much the same thing happened to the Roman republic. Western history must wait till the American and French experiments to see real pluralism again. History, however, has brought the two continents to deal with the problem of division in different ways. Europe was always divided into nations who were strong rivals. The infant French democracy immediately resisted internal squabbles. It suppressed them with terrorism, it projected them outside, contributing to a paranoid nationalism. Wars among the nation-states continued through the first half of the twentieth century. At that point Europe plunged itself without any illusions into a massacre bloodier than all the rest of human history: the two chapters of the European Civil War. Then it began to construct a federation that was post-national, post-ideological, post-religious, and post-heroic.

The United States, by contrast, did not meet up with genuine external threats: the first phase of its history did not lend itself to aggressive nationalism. The single mortal risk was internal division. The psychological denial of inner division ended up being projected onto society in the form of deadly confrontation between North and South.

The demonization of division was reinforced, the struggle against it became an absolute priority, and it has continued uninterrupted until today.

Such a fundamental American word as "divisive" is not translatable into the European languages. It simply is not to be found in dictionaries. This has its logic. The idea of "di-visive" does not belong to linguistics, but to liturgy. It represents the secular "de-vil" of the civil religion which every morning requires a prayer for an "in-divisible" America. Another European difficulty with the American language is the discovery that the substantive plural "United States" is followed by verbs in the singular number: "is," and not "are." History possesses the logic that grammar lacks; it was after the Civil War that the singular became the correct form.

The USA and Europe have therefore marched off in opposite directions. While from the beginning the United States was (were?) less aggressive and more tolerant, in a certain sense their positions today have changed places. The turning points are the Civil War in the United States and the two World Wars in Europe.

Today, concepts like "federal" and "federation" (from Latin *foedus*, oath) arouse different emotions in the European and American unconscious. For Europe these terms connote a secular concept, contractual in the way of civil marriage. It is a freely chosen union, which in the same free manner can be dissolved again. (Article 60, I, in the European Union Constitution [EU] very simply explains how to apply to exit the EU.) The American concept of federation instead remains quasi-religious, absolute, like Catholic marriage. The preamble to the Articles of Confederation of 15 November 1777 speaks of "perpetual union." The preamble to the Constitution of 17 September 1787 speaks of "a more perfect union." For the post-religious European, qualities like "perpetual" and "perfect" are not human but divine. From that viewpoint, therefore, the American Constitution contains no provisions allowing for exits from the Union because it is a religious document.

Psychodynamics, let us remember, function by reproducing oppositions. If consciousness accepts only one aspect of a polarity, the other aspect sets up a clamor in the unconscious, until repression no longer works and there will be some kind of explosion.

Issuing from the death of Greek democracy, the equilibrium between unity and division has suffered throughout the West, first in Europe and now even more so in America. America was born out of two originating traumas—religious separation, first from Rome and then from London, and separation of the thirteen colonies, first from the English monarchy—and then from two historical fractures—the Civil War, and an ethnic mix composed out of three hostile races. Because of these facts, America in its own collective unconscious has chiseled into stone the motto, *Never again division!*

Over time, this culture of unity at all costs has transformed itself into a one-sided negation of shadow, that is to say, denial of divisiveness or divisions, which are an ordinary human reality. And not only that. Being further along into a future that no one can escape, America is also experimenting for the first time with new kinds of division. It has met up with the war between the sexes, which had not existed before, new rivalries among ethnic groups, differentials between social classes which are growing with explosive speed, and a divide between free persons and persons in prison which has no historical precedent— indeed, proportionally eight times the number jailed in Europe. Analytical psychology has this to say about the situation: that whoever refuses to accept the presence of opposites is destined to meet up with them in pathological forms.

Perhaps it is no accident that the most typical new syndrome to come along in America has been that of Multiple Personality Disorder.[6] It prohibits the psyche from dividing within itself. Since many people are not going to be following orders, at some point they will definitely be calling in sick.

Even in war, the real winner is probably the unconscious, which manifests a crude, sarcastic irony. The major preoccupation of the politicians is that war, which bit by bit kills people, is going to be *divisive*. Yet as time goes on, war not only brings about death and division, it piles up literally divided corpses, blown to bits.

In modern wars, fewer and fewer victims are killed by conventional weapons, and always more by bombs. It is said that human tools are extensions of the human body. So too are weapons: if the sword is an extension of the arm, the rifle is an extension of the sword. But a bomb strikes at random because it has lost even this shred of meaning: it is simply the extension of hatred.

To the dead blown into a hundred pieces it is simply impossible to offer even the proper rites of burial. The dignity of such ritual, even in Homer's day, was still more sacred and inviolable than the respect for life itself. Having made it a priority to multiply our terrifying violence by technological means, we are at the same time stripping ourselves of those burial customs which not even the Neanderthals did without.

Ex Uno Plurimi: From One, Many

Spanish colonization attempted to transfer over the Ocean its original unity: one nation, one church, one king. It even ignored sexual division. Its ships carried only men to America's shores. These men killed off the native males and forced the women to become servants and concubines, as well as mothers of their bastard sons, only sometimes making them their legitimate wives.

It thus gave birth to a legitimate society into which children were born illegitimate as a rule. This foundational contradiction has subjected Latin America to an original inferiority when challenged by the Northern hemisphere, more than has either military or economic confrontation. This stain has made the presence of sin and darkness—of the *shadow*, already accepted with resignation out of Catholic tradition—as customary and inevitable as the change of the seasons.

How different were the Anglo-Saxon immigrants to the New World! They were fleeing the corruption of the Roman Church and the British monarchy. They were dedicated to re-establishing both society and religion. They arrived as families, and they chose to keep sexuality in the channels laid down by God. (This program carries out a project I cannot give time to here—namely, the influence on American psychology not of Homer's *Odyssey* but rather of Virgil's *Aeneid*, that success story of national foundation and Westward conquest, its subjection of native peoples on new territory for a divinely ordained mission. The Trojan exile mission was in fact inscribed in Latin on the Great Seal of the United States and on the dollar bill.)

The colonists inaugurated a grandiose political experiment: a system of government made up of free and equal individuals, who did not accept the dictates of external tyrants. But they were also trying out a grandiose *psychological experiment*, a system of government for the soul which eliminated the corresponding internal tyrant, evil itself, which they had left behind them with the rulers of Europe.

The foundational project of the United States was not only a political one, as it was for most other countries, but a missionary and puritanical one. It was the project which today is called *civil religion* and its continuation. From the viewpoint of analytical psychology, the project of a radical elimination of evil—that is, the definitive separation and negation of the so-called *Shadow*—is unavoidably dangerous. Rather than erased, the shadow is displaced, collectively projected onto societies which are different. The extremist psychological project complicates the political one. The omnipotence of the goal sooner or later meets up with impotence. It feels constrained to take measures that become ever more radical, and more violent, and in the end to introduce, under the forms of violence, precisely that evil which it wanted to do away with.

In a simple society, one is better able to cultivate the need for purity. This the colonists understood very well, and so, in contrast to the Spaniards, they sought to keep themselves distinct from the natives, based upon motives that were moral rather than political. The original geographic and demographic circumstances of the USA differed from those of all other conquering peoples known to history. Over time, Americans were able to incorporate new territories into the Union without any apparent compromises, placing the native peoples on reservations. The political enterprise and the psychological project seemed to proceed hand in hand, confirming each other in perfect alternation. It was possible to push the collective shadow ever farther off in the process of exclusion, just as it happened with the Indians.

This process gave birth to more than just a new society. It also brought into being the first collective soul that would not compromise with the shadow. However much the American founders did not run away from the fact that the Union could victoriously compete with the European powers, they preferred to avoid them. Contact with the games of power could soil their hands. No other people that came before them had thrust the contaminating shadow so far away from themselves. Evil was projected first on England and its monarchy. Then— continuing the English tradition of the "Black Legend" by constructing a negative myth shored up by gossip as much as by history—a black shadow was cast onto Spain, gradually spreading itself over the Spanish-speaking Catholic countries at large.

America's political officialdom sought to construct a geography that suited this projection. The Monroe Doctrine (the 2 December 1823 Annual Message to Congress) has been analyzed numberless times as a political manifesto. What ought to interest us as well is that it is also a psychological manifesto. The tendency toward purity becomes global: the Americas will remain democratic, while the rest of the world will fall under the shadow of geography and history. Without an Iron Curtain (the ocean supplied a wall), this doctrine anticipated the psychology of the Cold War.

But the Americas embraced many peoples, whom it was not possible to "purify" by moving them around like the tribes of Native Americans. The relationships with these peoples could not be avoided. The Big Stick of Teddy Roosevelt had not yet been named, but it was leaning against the frame of the door which stood open. The success of foreign policy in an expansive political program came along with a failure in political psychology: that failure followed from the psychic tendency toward "purity" which had given shelter to splitting and division.

In a certain sense, American armed forces—in accord with America's absolute historical exceptionalism—have always carried out "police actions." An army can either be victorious or suffer defeat. A police battalion, on the other hand, has no plans for anything except victory. Its only contingencies concern the different possibilities for timing and the measures to be taken. This view of the American military has de-legitimized its enemies and transformed military campaigns into attempts at destroying the shadow: the dark wilderness of the Native American tribes, the darkness that has corrupted many Latin-American regimes, the imperial blackness of international Communism. Ultimately the two World Wars were wars for the Europeans, but were perceived as a round-up of outlaws by the American Armed Forces.

Only the Civil War was a military undertaking in the full sense of that term: it was witnessed and endured directly by the civilian population, and it called the country's boundaries into question and placed the country in mortal danger. While the outcome was not the defeat of a national enemy, but rather the preservation of the country's original unity, memory of the war has not nourished the myth of the good nation that defeats evil ones, but instead a myth of the unity that vanquishes division.

The psychological history of the tendency to purify oneself of shadow accounts for several current events better than political history does. In contrast to all other countries, the United States has carried out the greater part of its territorial expansion by monetary purchase, even when this apparently was not necessary because it had already (as with Mexico) taken the lands by conquest. There is no need to explain this as a calculated move. Naturally the payment corresponds to a contractual acceptance of new frontiers, and makes it more difficult to put them back into question. But from a psychological point of view, the donation of payment enhances the tendency to purify the soul; even if the conquest was accomplished through violence, that act gets projected into the distance, into a past that is already over with, which is replaced by a present based on economic relationships. If a particular affair has been tidied up and finished off, it is better for both parties. At the price of dividing time into distinct epochs, division is foisted off: even the enemy apparently agrees.

In Europe, and particularly in the Catholic countries, it is difficult to understand how America's practice of capital punishment could have enjoyed such widespread support in a democratic country. We are prone to think that state-sponsored violence will habituate people to view violence as a normal, daily fact. But the historical experiences of the two continents are quite different. In America, capital punishment has been the expression of the local seats of power, the individual state governments or even the sheriff. In taking that route, the collective unconscious plays out, albeit in a juridical fashion, the ancient ritual of the scapegoat and its corresponding expulsion of the shadow. In Europe, however, capital punishment has represented the maximum form of deterrence and arbitrary jurisdiction by non-democratic power. One of the typical formative texts read by my generation was called, *Letters from the Resistance by Those Condemned to Death*. For years, the European continent was sealed off by the forces of Nazi-fascism, and those condemned to death were condemned politically. In the collective unconscious of Europe, the abolition of capital punishment and the abolition of tyrannies are one and the same thing. At the dawn of the modern West, these positions were reversed. In representing the American Revolution, Thomas Paine gave two speeches (on the 15th and 19th of January 1793) at the French National Assembly, futilely pleading that the former king Louis XVI not be put to death.

This rapid survey of the relationship between violence and the Puritan splitting-off of the shadow would not be complete without a brief nod toward the power given by the United States to the idea of Social Darwinism and the concept of Manifest Destiny. Social Darwinism was one of the most dangerous of all ideologies (its final fruit in Europe was Nazism), but it attained great popularity in being presented as a *science* that anticipated sociology, anthropology, and genetics.

These two ideological gods were able to sink roots into the American collective unconscious because they were, in several respects, a secular and extremist transformation of Puritanism. Those who are destined to be God's Elect become the darlings of both nature and history. In this fashion, the idea of superiority was no longer placed in check by Judeo-Christian compassion. The problem of the shadow became more intricate through social complexities: immigration brought into the USA ever fewer Anglo-Saxons and ever more people from Eastern and Central Europe, and over time has brought even more non-Europeans. The Puritan distortion did not really disappear, but slid into the unconscious, while the new "science" inherited the responsibility for housecleaning and decontamination. Evolutionary science seemed to guarantee that the "inferior" races would be wiped out. Assisting in this transformation had nothing to do with moral choice, because the sheer weight of already given conditions was to blame. No individual was violent—no, it was "natural evolution," with which one could collaborate.

It led people to believe that things were arriving at a stage very near the summit of progress, so that social progressives were often pushing in this direction more than were the conservatives, paradoxically. One example would be those who, following the Civil War and wishing to provide a solution to the problem of the Afro-American population, promoted the return of the blacks to Africa. On the one hand, they were trying to find some kind of generous action to take, one that would alleviate their guilt for the participating in the institution of slavery. On the other hand, the unconscious fantasy probably was that of freeing themselves from the African shadow (therefore the unconscious double meaning in the name "Liberia").

* * * * *

Erich Neumann, Jung's disciple, observing that the victors over Nazism were mounting the threat of nuclear weapons, wrote a short book in 1948 that proposed a *new ethic*.

The Judeo-Christian tradition appeared to be increasingly less adapted to a technological mass society. The distinction between good and evil had passed directly from religion over into politics. The refusal to recognize that evil was a part of one's own psychology, and the projection of this rejected evil onto the opposing group, transformed the moral distinction into one more instrument of intolerant and implacable struggle. Technical progress—and ideology, which as Solzhenitsyn has said, becomes, in its turn, a multiplier—changed conflict into extermination.

The only real alternative to catastrophe was through the way of psychology. This means two things. First of all, it was necessary to confront the problem of good and evil on individual terms: condemnation of the group is not a distinction between good and evil but an evil in itself. Second, if a good intention produces violence, conscious understanding of one's intentions is not enough. The responsibility for violence cannot be suppressed. If the responsible party among two adversaries is always "the other," that other is not to be found in the enemy but in the unconscious. The new ways of proceeding along this path—into the individual person and into what is unconscious—render evaluation and judgment much more difficult. But there is no other alternative. Collective justice has executed far too many injustices.

* * * * *

We have returned to what was said in the first part of this paper. The opponent, the adversary, the enemy is within us. The recognition of that truth makes one sad. Walter Benjamin has described melancholy as a necessary suffering of the historian. History is a carpet woven out of devastations and assassinations, over which rides the chariot of the conqueror in triumph. Whoever wishes to understand Carthage must enter into bereavement. The Romans, in an act of prudential wisdom, stood another man next to the triumphant conqueror in his chariot, a double, or "other," whose task it was to whisper into his ear that he was mortal, and that successes come and go like the wind.

In the history of my own country, the Roman Empire declared a *Pax Romana*, paid for with slavery and massacres. What followed was a drunken binge from which we have had to purify ourselves. The voice of the shadow in the chariot was right. During the fourteen centuries that followed the empire, we were divided and subject to foreign domination. That is enough time to get used to feeling the weight of history and its responsibility, time to grow sad and a bit reasonable.

Could it be that one of America's problems is that the carpet of victims beneath its wheels is still too fresh, that its triumph is still rolling along, and that the excitement arising from all this has not had a chance to subside into melancholy? The heart of America is submerged in the center of history. And so we come to the impossible question: is it possible to be powerful and just at the same time?

* * * * *

Just as with the assignment of capital punishment to a single person, so too with war (which condemns a collective to death): in Europe war could be decided by rulers, while in the United States it has had to gain public approval. A book like the recent *Just and Unjust Wars: A Moral Argument with Historical Illustrations* by Michael Walzer, is therefore profoundly American and civic in its aim of discussing when a war is moral. But can war, today, be moral?

The ethic that sets out to talk about a just war—and not *inevitable* war, or war *justified by the absence of alternatives*—is, unfortunately, still the old collective ethic, seeking some kind of collective punishment. Technical progress has multiplied atrocity almost beyond limit. At the end of the 19th century, war unavoidably killed civilians, but at least 90% of the dead were soldiers. Things rapidly reversed themselves between the First and the Second World Wars: in the First War, 8.6 million soldiers compared to 6 or 7 million civilian victims, and in the Second War, 17.1 million soldiers compared with 20 to 27 million civilian dead. Today the majority number reverses the earlier ratio exactly: 90% of the dead in our wars are civilians. Acceptance of violence, atrocity, and procedures of mass destruction is the hidden shadow of the argument of *Just Wars*.

The American military today has the ability to avoid, and indeed a preoccupation with avoiding, civilian casualties, more than any military organization in human history. If, notwithstanding this, we are mindful of the massacres in Iraq, we must conclude that in modern warfare the slaughter of innocents is no longer a chance or collateral occurrence, but the unavoidable essence of conflict.

A central criterion for evaluating war is the proportionality between war aims and human costs. If the human costs of war today cannot be controlled by the authorities who decide to wage war, then we must reconsider the very idea of the just war, because whoever makes the decision can no longer know what he is doing, or evaluate it properly, and therefore cannot actually authorize it.

What Erich Neumann has called a New Ethic demands of anyone a personal assessment, and Odysseus already knew that this calls for *time.* The psychic processes of the unconscious cannot be accelerated.

The memoirs of Traudl Junge—who was Hitler's personal secretary from 1942 until his suicide in 1945—are instructive and excruciating. What she learned little by little during the years following the war, and narrates, is frightening. But the most tremendous thing has required her to wait another half century of living, in order to fully portray the evil that she had encountered and with which, even if in a minimal way, she had collaborated. Her adversary, the person she most despised, was not some crude Nazi, but the girl whom she herself had been. Slowly, Traudl Junge had accomplished the ethical *personalization* that Neumann describes.

She was trying to forgive herself for saying to herself that she was too young at the time and that she did not know what was going on. One day, on the street, she saw a monument to Sophie Scholl, one of the young people martyred in the White Rose resistance to Hitler. Reading Sophie's dates of birth and death, she noticed that they were the same age, and that on the very day when she began working for Hitler, Sophie had been sentenced. She realized that the fact of having not chosen to do evil does not take away responsibility. She discovered another person within herself, an accomplice to assassination by omission. She also discovered that we are morally divided within ourselves over the course of time. Perhaps this fact already invalidates capital punishment: even the worst criminal, given time, is able to become a just man. By taking such a man's life, we also kill that just man who probably is growing in him but who is still an infant.

Hitler, Junge tells us, was directly moved when he sensed that certain of those who carried out his orders felt compassion for the victims. "You understand," he told them, "that it is necessary to sacrifice one's feelings for the common good. When everyone comes to see the results, they will understand that it was worth the suffering. In the meantime, you must not feel guilty, I assume the responsibility."

These are the collective norms of the old ethic. Someone takes on the charge of evaluating things for us. Of deciding if war is just. Or if eugenics—of which genocide is the extreme manifestation—is a good thing. Naturally, war and eugenics are collective operations and demand collective judgments; but the assessment is collective because it is functional, not because it is moral.

I go in fear of that adjective "just." It is something far too lofty to be pressed into service by something as base as war. It becomes dangerous, like an explosive device. It transforms a murderous impulse into something acceptable. What a strong temptation that is, just as strong as the one to obey those people who say that they know what the collective good is and take responsibility for it: they seem generous twice over, because they busy themselves with the good of the collective and even offer to carry the charge of our conscience. They offer us inner calm, untroubled by division.

It becomes easier to kill, when this kind of inner agreement prevails. And still easier, if one can say

> that even one's enemies
> Had rather have us win than him they follow.
> . . . If you fight against God's enemy,
> God will, in justice, ward you as his soldiers.
> If you do sweat to put a tyrant down,
> you sleep in peace, the tyrant being slain.
> —Shakespeare, *Richard III*, Act V

I do not know in any definitive manner whether any killings are ever justifiable. I do know, however, that no one ought to sleep in peace after having taken a life.

Editor's Note: "Violent Hearts" was originally delivered at the conference "Violent Hearts: The Divided Soul of America" at the University of Houston, December 30-October 1, 2005.

NOTES

1. Homer, *Odyssey,* Book XIX, ll. 406-409.

2. *Ibid.*, Book XXII, ll. 411 ff.

3. *Ibid.*, Book XXII, ll. 371 ff.

4. *Ibid.*, Book XX l. 18.

5. *Ibid.*, Book XXIII ll. 264-284.

6. *Diagnostic and Statistical Manual of Mental Disorders IV*, 300.14.

7. Michael Walzer, *Just and Unjust Wars: A Moral Argument with Historical Illustrations* (New York: Basic Books, 2006).

THE SOUL OF TERROR/THE TERROR OF SOUL

RONALD SCHENK

For Beauty's nothing
but beginning of Terror we're still just able to bear.
　　　—Rilke
The wise man laughs only with fear and trembling.
　　　— Baudelaire

TERROR AS POLITICAL

The word "political" comes from the Greek word for city, *polis*, which originally referred to a "ring-wall." The postmodern political theorist, Hannah Arendt, takes Aristotle's reference to man as *zoon politikon* or "political animal" to indicate that humans are fundamentally social beings. For the ancient Greeks and Romans, "to live" was "to be among men." "No human life, not even the life of the hermit in nature's wilderness, is possible without a world which directly or indirectly testifies to the presence of other human beings."[1]

Ronald Schenk, Ph.D., is a Jungian analyst practicing, teaching, and writing in Dallas and Houston. He has written three books: *The Soul of Beauty: A Psychological Investigation of Appearance,* regarding psychology as an aesthetic enterprise; *Dark Light: the Appearance of Death in Everyday Life*, a series of essays on culture and imagination; and, *The Sunken Quest, the Wasted Fisher, the Pregnant Fish: Essays in Postmodern Depth Psychology.*

Arendt uses the word "action" to indicate that specifically human activity which has to do solely with the need for social organization. The *polis*, as opposed to the private realm, provides the public space where such action can be undertaken. Political activity is beyond necessity, separated from the household of possible "futility" in the struggle for survival. The polis is where individual excellence (*arete*) can be shown, memory achieved, and immortality approached. The political realm is a place for the action of self disclosure within the encircling wall which opens up to a form of "organized remembrance." Politics is a kind of *thiasos*, a community based on a notion of theater— assuming a sense of "reality" by seeing and being seen.

For Plato, this action is a matter of creation, fabrication, or craftsmanship. (*Republic,* 420) The essence of political life becomes a show or display that is a "making," a making of appearance for an "other" in the service of remembrance. Here Arendt finds a place for violence in political life; "violence, without which no fabrication could ever come to pass, has always played an important role in political schemes...." This sense of political life provides a mold or form which fits the modern terrorist. The terrorist acts in a violently performative manner in the service of a higher cause, not for the sake of winning ground, but for the purpose of being seen by an other, the community of humans and gods that make up his/her world.

TERRORISM AS ARCHETYPAL

In 1926 Max Ernst painted a tableau of the Virgin Mary spanking her young son, Jesus, perhaps in punishment for his play habits. Legend has it that as a child, Jesus was instructed by his mother to include other children in his play. Subsequently, he asked three mates to play with him, and all refused because of his low birth. Jesus retaliated by creating a bridge of sunbeams crossing over a body of water and using it to get to the other side. The three declining children tried to follow, but the bridge disappeared and they drowned.

Beating as prelude to flagellation symbolizing sacrifice, betrayal from an intimate source, and the show of violence as a move toward political justice—all are themes of what we now call terrorism.

The story of Jesus can be seen to reveal more about terrorism. He was born amidst a setting of violence in which children were slaughtered, presenting a gruesome image of dismemberment and sacrifice. He gave up his trade as a carpenter at a young age to become a vagabond teacher of spiritual and political doctrine. Among his teachings were radical claims that he alone knew the kingdom of God and lived on earth in God's place. He urged his followers to give up their present and future security, to live every moment as if it were their last, and to give up their life for him.

As part of his message, Jesus used violent metaphors and acted violently. He claimed that his life itself was a weapon and that he was a "sword." He instructed his followers to sell their robes and buy a sword with the money. (Luke 22: 35-6, 38) He was quoted as saying

> Think not that I am come to send peace on earth: I came not to send peace, but a sword. For I am come to set a man at variance against his father, and the daughter against her mother, and the daughter in law against her mother in law. (Matthew 10:34)

In another version of this speech he asserts, "It is dissension which I have come to cast upon the earth: fire, sword, and war." (Gnostic Gospel of Thomas 16) He acted with righteous anger, creating havoc within the temple, literally turning the tables on the moneychangers, and he prophesied outright its destruction.

Jesus died as a suicidal martyr, a bloody sacrifice in the tradition of the scapegoat or *pharmakon,* the figure that is cast into the desert carrying all of the sins of the community. His burial was not successful, and subsequently he became an inspiration for bloodshed and torture that has lasted for centuries. His teachings, which went against common preconception and expectation turned rational modes upside down through paradox and parable. His life, as well as his imagistic death, was a symbolic message, meant as hyperbole, and enacted for a larger audience.

Jesus had a spiritualized agenda of overturning the power structure so that no other obligation was important except that owed to God. His teachings carried an ontological message of terror, "Wake up! Give up your life!" that burst through the prevailing symbolic order and the mundane experience of everyday life. He associated with those in the lower social classes, and it was toward them that he oriented his agenda as political. He was singular in his orientation, tolerating no deviance: "I am the way, the truth, the life: no man cometh unto the

Father, but by me." (John 14: 6) In Revelations, the climactic chapter of Jesus' story, the world is cast in image after image of violence and destruction brought about by the King of Kings with a sword emerging from his mouth, dressed in garments dipped in blood.

To begin our exploration of terror by seeing Jesus, held by many as the arch representative of peace, as a terrorist in his own way, helps us to sense how, as a universal metaphor, terrorism works in a paradoxical and deceptive manner. It operates from a firm base of comfort and security to reveal an underlying pool of fear and trembling. It is action meant as message for an audience, and it combines the political with the spiritual.

Coming closer to home, the notion of terrorism can be further expanded by looking into the background of three contemporary English words: "thug," "zealot," and "assassin." "Thug" was the name given to members of a terrorist group in India that existed from as early as the 13th century until the 19th century. The word originally meant "deceiver." In everyday life, thugs were models of propriety, known for such virtues as industry, temperance, generosity, kindliness, and trustworthiness. In their shadow life, they were followers of the earth goddess, Kali, the great divinity of life and death, sustenance and destruction. As members of a secret sect, they believed that Kali demanded blood in order to keep the world in balance. Thugs would choose their victims from among fellow Hindu travelers on the road, gain an intimate connection with them as they travelled together, and then strangle their victims with a handkerchief. The corpse was gashed and gutted, and the blood and guts let into the earth as a sacrifice to Kali.[2]

"Zealot" was the name given to a group of Jewish terrorists operating in the Holy Land in the centuries of Roman occupation.[3] The Zealots and another terrorist group, the Sicarii, targeted Roman or Jewish individuals whose high station of government official, priest, or landowner served to maintain the status quo. The tactics of the zealots were to carry out murder by dagger in broad daylight often on holy days when Jerusalem was crowded with pilgrims. The murderers would then make their escape in the midst of the panic they had created.[4]

Flavius Josephus, an ancient Hebrew historian, describes the scene,

> The Sicarii committed murders in broad daylight in the heart of
> Jerusalem. The holy days were their special seasons when they
> would mingle with the crowd carrying short daggers concealed
> under their clothing with which they stabbed their enemies.
> Thus, when they fell, the murderers joined in cries of indignation,
> and through this plausible behavior, were never discovered. The
> first assassinated was Jonathan, the high-priest. After his death
> there were numerous daily murders. The panic created was more
> alarming than the calamity itself; everyone, as on the battlefield,
> hourly expected death. Men kept watch at a distance on their
> enemies and would not trust even their friends when they
> approached.[5]

The word "assassin" comes from the name of a group of Muslim
terrorists operating during the 12th century. This was a Shiite sect,
rebelling against rival Sunni rulers who wanted to purify Islam and
return it to a single fundamentalist community in the form of a state.
The assassins placed young men in the service of religious or political
leaders in power, and over the years the young men would acquire the
trust of their masters. At an appropriate occasion, usually on Muslim
holy days and in a highly public place, the royal court or a venerated
site, the man in service would stab his master with a dagger in full
view with the expectation of being killed himself. In this way he became
a martyr demonstrating symbolically his spiritual truth and attaining
a paradisiacal afterlife.

A pattern emerges from these three originating terrorist groups in
which violence takes place in an intimate setting and is performed in
a ritualistic manner meant as a symbolic gesture to create an effect serving
a larger spiritual/political truth.[6] Out of the origins of terror in these
three religious traditions we see the inevitable connection between
violence and the sacred.

TERROR AND THE DIVINE

In the Hindu text, *Bagata Gita*, the hero, Arjuna, surveys the field
of impending battle which he is about to enter and loses heart. He
can't tolerate the loss of innocent life and the splitting of family and
friends that war involves. The god, Krishna, tells him he is confused.

(Y)our sorrow is for nothing. The truly wise mourn neither for the living nor for the dead.

There was never a time when I did not exist, nor you nor any of these kings. Nor is there any future in which we shall cease to be.

Just as the dweller in this body passes through childhood, youth, and old age, so at death he merely passes into another kind of body....

Bodies are said to die, but that which possesses the body is eternal. It cannot be limited, or destroyed. Therefore you must fight.

Even if you consider this from the standpoint of your own caste-duty, you ought not to hesitate, for, to a warrior, there is nothing nobler than a righteous war. Happy are the warriors to whom a battle such as this comes: it opens a door to heaven.

But if you refuse to fight this righteous war, you will be turning aside from your duty. You will be a sinner, and disgraced. People will speak ill of you throughout the ages. To a man who values his honour, that is surely worse than death. The warrior-chiefs will believe it was fear that drove you from the battle, you will be despised by those who have admired you so long. Your enemies, also, will slander your courage. They will use the words which should never be spoken. What could be harder to bear than that?
Die, and you win heaven.[7]

This passage sets out the paradigm for righteous warfare and holy terror practiced by Hindu, Jewish, Christian, and Islamic warriors and terrorists alike. Fight for the higher cause, and you will be victorious.[8] He who slays, slays not; he who is slain, is not slain. James Hillman has said that through religion a warrior class serves the human condition, and through the virtues of the warrior—courage, persistence, nobility, honor, loyalty—war finds its place in the human psyche.[9] The terrorist considers him or herself a holy warrior.

The Old Testament is filled with accounts of the military struggles of the Children of God. Abraham (Genesis 14) struck an enemy encampment at night with a small group of men in a guerilla attack. God made a deal with the Children of Israel in exile, be mine and I will be yours and provide you with the Promised Land as you conduct "Holy War" in my name. "I will send forth my *terror* before you, and I will cast into panic all the peoples among whom you pass, and I will cause all thy enemies to flee before you." (Exodus 23: 27) Moses' resume includes the role of military leader when he was still an Egyptian. While leading the Children of Israel through the desert, his followers, the sons of Levi, slaughtered three thousand worshipers of the golden calf. Joshua sacked the cities of Jericho and Ai and established the precedent of carrying into battle the Ark of the Covenant, or *shekinah*, the place where God dwells. God lives right on the battleground. Whether through commando raids such as those perfected by Gideon, or individual acts of terrorism such as that of the heroines, Jael who drove a stake through the head of an enemy commander while he slept (Judges 4: 17-22; 5: 24-27), and Judith, who pretending to be an informer, seduced an enemy general and beheaded him in his sleep. Samson pulled down the "world trade tower" of the Philistines, David conducted insurrectionist hostility, and both David and Saul carried on conventional warfare.

War in the name of God was inherent to the life of the Israelites. "The Lord is a man of war" (Exodus 15: 3), and he commanded his children to engage in genocide. (Joshua 6: 21) The word "Israel" came to mean "God fights," and one of the Psalms in praise of God is a song of revenge against the Babylonians: "Happy shall be he who takes your little ones and dasheth them against the stones." (Psalms 137: 9)

In 610 A.D. Muhammad received the revelation of the Koran, left his home in Mecca and, as a military leader, developed a stronghold in the town of Medina. Through various military campaigns he had conquered Mecca and most of western Arabia before he died in 632. Muhammad established the tenet that government is inextricably associated with religion, and in the early stages of Islam the entire Muslim community was under one ruler, an ideal for which contemporary Muslim terrorists still strive. In the Muslim world, religion, government, and war have been intrinsically connected from the start.[10]

The word "Islam" is a cognate to the word for peace, *salam*, which is related to the Hebrew *shalom*, Allah is merciful and compassionate, and he forbids the slaying of a soul which he has made sacred. But then there is a catch, "except by right."[11] Violence is condoned in defending home and faith. *Jihad*, meaning "striving in the path of God," is sanctioned "to suppress tyranny, insure the right of the individual to home and freedom within his own nation, prevent persecution in religion, and guarantee freedom of belief to all people"[12] *Jihad* came to indicate a political as well as religious act, the armed struggle for the defense or advancement of Muslim power in government in the face of threat of government by infidels. The Koran states,

> God has bought from the believers their selves
> and their possessions against the gift of Paradise;
> they fight in the way of God; they kill, and are
> killed; that is a promise binding upon God
> in the Torah, and the Gospel, and the Koran;
> and who fulfills his covenant truer than God? (I, IX: 112)

> When you meet the unbelievers, smite their necks,
> ...And those who are slain in the way of God, He
> will not send their works astray.
> He will guide them, and dispose their minds aright,
> and He will admit them to Paradise (II, XLVII: 4)

The Koran contains detailed accounts of how, where, and when to fight, the battle always in the name of God, with an emphasis on discipline, persistence, patience, and self-sacrifice, all qualities of Islamic fundamentalist terrorists. The Koran reflects its Hindu predecessor, the *Bagata Gita*, in its admonition to the holy warrior to kill and be killed for the supreme life in Heaven. Central tenets are that God himself is to be feared, not the enemy infidels, that life on earth is a delusion, and that the true life awaits the Believer in the paradisiacal afterworld. Again, from the Koran,

> As for those who disbelieve in God's signs, for them awaits a
> terrible chastisement;
> God is All-mighty, Vengeful. (I, III: 3)

> God warns you that you beware of Him,
> And unto God is the homecoming. (I, III: 26).

> Those who fear their Lord—for them shall be gardens
> underneath which rivers flow, therein dwelling forever—a
> hospitality God Himself offers. (I, III: 196)

> So let them fight in the way of God who sells the present life for
> the world to come;
> And whosoever fights in the way of God and is slain, or conquers,
> We shall bring him a mighty wage. (I, IV: 76)

> The enjoyment of this world is little;
> the world to come is better for him
> who fears God...
> Wherever you may be, death will overtake you (I, IV: 79)

What we call suicide is martyrdom for the fundamentalist Islamic terrorist, pleasing to God in that if he is victorious over God's enemy, he is given license to leave an existence which is but a prelude to an eternal life.

Perplexing to Westerners, the Koran embodies a sense of time different from the linear notion of beginning, middle, end. In the Koran, only the present moment is real. To God, the matter of the hour is but a twinkling of the eye, for He is ever creating each point in time and space at every moment. The Koran, written in imagistic style rather than narrative, moves grammatically from talking about the Day of Judgement as future, "Upon that day...the Trumpet shall be blown...and upon that day We shall present (Hell) to the unbelievers" (I, XVIII: 99), to announcing it in the present tense, "The Hour has drawn nigh: the moon is split." (II, LIV: 2) For the terrorists following the Koran, the Day of Apocalypse is already at hand. We are always living as if it were our last day, and what the West calls terrorism is only one more act in a war that is *already* occurring in the perpetual struggle for the soul of Islam.

In summary, a review of three major religions tells us that the sacred is dangerous and that those who consider themselves on the side of God are licensed by their holy scripture to "smite the necks" of those they believe to be unbelievers.[13] What makes the terrorist different from the conventional warrior or the guerilla warrior is that the goal of the terrorist is not military, but propaganda victory. The terrorist acts for a larger audience, both earthly and divine. Terrorists think through representational images and stage events that make symbolic statements. The terrorist is a performance artist, creating a spectacle for an effect that will outlast immediate consequences and leave the audience shaken.

FEAR AND TREMBLING

For the Greeks, terror existed in a condition of *tromokratia* where there is no order, and control is beyond human means. The word "terror" is derived from the Latin *terrere* which means to cause to tremble. "Tremble" comes from *tremere*, referring to tremor, specifically the trembling of the earth. *Terrere* is derived from its root, *"terra"* or earth, which in turn comes from a Greek word, *tremos* which again means "quaking" or "quivering," like the earth disrupted. *Tremos* is the root of the English word "trauma." From the etymological origins there is the sense of the earth itself as source of terror.

When the earth quakes, we tremble and shake. The Greeks had a god for earthquakes, Poseidon, called "Old Earth Shaker," in his earth-father form. The word "shake" is related to the Hebrew *shekinah* meaning "where God dwells." "Yet once, it is a little while and I will shake the heavens... and the earth and the sea and the dryland; And I will shake all nations." (Haggai 2: 6-7) The bass singing this recitative, standing in for the voice of God in Handel's "Messiah," sings in 16th-note melismas upon the word "shake" telling us every Christmas and Easter that the Lord will act as a terrorist. God does so in many ways—famine, pestilence, flood, and fire, but most of all, He will shake up the world with the coming of his Son, the Messiah. The idea is echoed in the Gospels—the Coming of Christ is indicated by the shaking of both heaven and earth. Where the water is troubled, there is God. Where there is terror, there is God, or when we are terrorized, we all become shakers.

The root of the word religion, *religio*, means to "bend back," as to a more fundamental plane of existence, so that it is as if when we are terrorized, our foundations tremble and we are shaken back to our roots. Traumatized with a glimpse of infinity dismembering our identity, we become "fundamental," shaken to our foundational being. All shook up, we are engaged in a religious experience.

The theologian, Rudolph Otto, in exploring the irrational aspect of the divine, described the "holy" as a *mysterium tremendum*, a "tremendous mystery" which we might say acts like a terrorist.

> It may burst in sudden eruption up from the depths of the soul
> with spasms and convulsions, or lead to the strangest excitements,
> to intoxicated frenzy, to transport, and to ecstasy. It has its wild

and demonic forms and can sink to an almost grisly horror and shuddering. It has its crude, barbaric antecedents and early manifestations, and again it may be developed into something beautiful and pure and glorious. It may become the hushed, trembling, and speechless humility of the creature in the presence of—whom or what? In the presence of that which is a *mystery* inexpressible and above all creatures.[14]

Even the goddess of love and beauty, Aphrodite, carries an aspect of terror, as those involved where love goes wrong can attest. She was born from the severed genitals of Uranus and the chaos of primeval waters. In Hesiod's account, her children were Terror and Fear. She was called the "black one," also known as "Aphrodite of the Grave" and "Grave Robber," and wreaked terrible revenges on those who defied her. Claire Lejeune writes,

This Beauty is sovereign, because it is unforeseeable and inescapable. Against its possible victory, our defeat, we arm ourselves; we turn from terror to terrorism. The ultimate object of human fear is Beauty; nothing is more disarming, more ravishing, than its eruption in our lives.[15]

The sense of the irrational as connected with the divine carries over into the seeming irrationality of terrorists and our sense of them as "diabolical;" but the devil, as Fallen Angel, has a dual character. The Greek word *diabolein* means to "tear apart," but this is an action characteristic of the Judeo-Christian God. The psalm promising destruction of the heathen declares, "Thou shalt break them with a rod of iron: thou shalt dash them in pieces like a potter's vessel." (Psalms 2: 9)[16] Ferocity or fury is in the character of Lucifer, but "Lucifer" means the "light bringer." The word "satan" means "one who obstructs," or "accuser," but Satan was originally considered to have been sent to earth by the Lord to carry spirit energies that organize natural processes. In this sense, the possessed mentality of terrorists can be thought of as mediation by the divine, or in William Blake's words, "Terror, the human form divine."

TERROR AS OTHER: THE TERROR OF THE STATE

The literary critic, Terry Eagleton has written of Lacanian thought, "Like God, the Real for Lacanian thought is the unfathomable wedge of otherness at the heart of identity which makes us what we are, yet which—because it involves desire—also prevents us from being truly identical with ourselves.[17] One way the divine makes itself visible as terror in human form is through the chaos hidden in all human gestures toward order. Mythically, chaos marks Beginning, and order emerges only from its turbulent ground. All gods, as creatures of excess, surpass human understanding. Such human institutional structures as those of religion, economics, and justice, necessarily created through will, inevitably involve transgression and violation as earthly matters are pressed by the spirit of will to give shape to what is ultimately ineffable.

The concept used by philosophers of the Enlightenment to indicate the indescribable is that of the "sublime." Edmund Burke, the 18th Century English philosopher, wrote a treatise on aesthetics in which he associated the sublime with terror.[18] For Burke, the sublime was impressive, vast, ruggedly magnificent, infinitely fearsome, inducing feelings of wonder, astonishment, and awe. Eagleton describes it as

> any power which is perilous, shattering, ravishing, traumatic, excessive, exhilarating, dwarfing, astonishing, uncontainable, overwhelming, boundless, obscure, terrifying, enthralling, and uplifting….a glimpse of infinity which dissolves our identity and shakes us to our roots.[19]

From this perspective, terror, as intricately connected with the sublime, is the base of all power, and by extension, most significantly, religious, economic, and political power. This idea was soon to be echoed across the English Channel with the temporary founding of another Western democracy through what is paradoxically known as the "Reign of Terror." One of the architects of that bloodbath, Robespierre, thought of terror as a consequence of the general principle of democracy applied to the needs of the nation.

> The mainspring of popular government in time of war is both virtue and terror: virtue without which terror is fateful: terror without which virtue is helpless. Terror is nothing but prompt, severe and inflexible justice: It is thus emanation and emanation of virtue.[20]

Alexis de Tocqueville, whose grandfather was beheaded during the Reign of Terror and who observed American democracy in its early stages, envisioned the potential banality of mind he saw in the future of

American democracy as a "terror which depresses and enervates the heart," giving voice to the violence which underlay the nation and its political institution.[21] It is this invisible violence, the "other" of social order, that cultures throughout the ages have symbolized through blood as sacrifice.

BLOOD

Divinity demands something from humans, and the terrorist reminds us that the sacred is sealed in blood. The Hebrew god, Jahweh, honors the offerings of the hunter Abel and not the farmer Cain. God wants blood. Abel becomes Cain's sacrifice. God gets blood. God demands a blood sacrifice from Abraham and gets it. The Hebrew words for "to make a covenant," *karat berit*, mean to literally "cut" a deal. The cut of circumcision becomes a covenant. God cuts words into stone for Moses. Moses cuts an animal in two, passes fire between its parts, and casts the blood toward the people. Through the "blood of the covenant" (Exodus 24: 8), God's children live for him, and bloodletting in the name of God carries over to transgressors who would be given by Him "into the hand of them that seek their life; and their dead bodies shall be for meat unto the fowls of heaven, and to the beasts of the earth." (Jer. 34: 20)

Blood is symbolic of sacrifice which is associated with the word "sacred," representing the mode of giving back to the gods, reciprocating their favor. The root of the word "sacred," the Latin *sacer*, means "holy," but also "devoted to deity for destruction," "accursed," "detestable," and "criminal." The Greek root, *ieros* means "holy," but also relates to death and taboo animals. The root syllable *sac* also refers to the last spinal bone, the sacrum, called the "holy bone" which gives rise to our word, sacroiliac. The notion of sacred means to get to the "bottom" of things, the dirty side of life, which borders on death as well as on the divine. The sacred is the "sack" or pouch that carries the gore and guts of the animal as well as the head of the slain enemy offered in sacrifice. Blood represents life having passed through death to become sacred. The suicidal terrorist performs and provides a double sacrifice, himself and his victim.

The institutionalized Hindu worship of Kali featured a great temple festival in which hundreds of animals were slaughtered and the blood let into a deep pit filled with fresh sand that sucked up the blood and then was buried in the earth to create fertility.

> Today the temple of Kali at the Kalighat in Calcutta is famous for its daily blood sacrifices; it is no doubt the bloodiest temple on earth. At the time of the great autumn pilgrimages to the annual festival ... some eight hundred goats are slaughtered in three days. The temple serves simply as a slaughterhouse, for those performing the sacrifice retain their animals, leaving only the head in the temple as a symbolic gift, while the blood flows to the Goddess. For to the Goddess is due the life blood of all creatures —since it is she who has bestowed it.[22]

As we know from the universal ritual practice of pouring blood libations into the earth, earth wants blood, earth gets blood. Life and death come from the same source.

Divinity, both heavenly and earthly, evokes terror through a call for blood mirrored in the actions of the terrorist. The terrorist brings us to body and a violent propensity for body rending which lies in the domain known by some as "the feminine." Archetypally, the terrorist can be seen as a form of "son-lover" to the great earth goddess. In the myth of Adonis, the young man becomes the beloved of Aphrodite. Against her wishes he goes out on a hunt and is gored to death by a boar, and Aphrodite is thrown into grief. In ancient Egypt, Adonis was associated with the corn god, and at the harvest women of the community would shave their heads or prostitute themselves in lamentation for the dismembered god seen in the sickled, ground grain. In the ancient Mideastern cultures, the son-lover was Attis and the goddess Cybele. Attis was thought to have castrated himself, and, on the "Day of Blood," a high priest would cut his arms, while lower priests would dance in ecstasy, gashing their bodies and spattering blood on the alters. In Syria, laymen would be moved by the dances of eunuch priests to castrate themselves and spend their lives dressed in female attire. The Egyptian god, Osiris, consort to his sister, Isis, was dismembered by his brother Set in the form of a boar. Set scattered the pieces of Osiris' body, but Isis, in mourning, gathered them, reforming the god. In the annual festival, human sacrifice was performed in imitation of the violent death of Osiris, and pieces of the body scattered while farmers beat their breasts in lamentation. Seeing through the images of Jesus' crucifixion and the Pieta, as well as terrorist bombings with scenes of grief and mourning, we can detect the savage violence and lamentation in the ancient rites and rituals of the son-lover.

THE TERRIBLE GOD

Terror opens us to a larger image of the conjunction of life with death, fertility with dismemberment, intimacy with violence, and the sublime with the uncertain. Through the vivid spectacle of terror as a body-rending spectacle of red blood flow amidst bits of bone and flesh to appease the gods, the form of another divinity emerges. It is a youthful, effeminate face, now bearded, now beardless, framed by an entwined serpent, revealing the god who exposes the joy of terror and the terror of joy, Dionysus. He was the invigorating and ravishing god of wine, divinity of the drum beat and the dance, but also of human savagery and lust for blood from within intimate settings. The classicist W. F. Otto characterized him as "the god of the most blessed ecstasy and the most enraptured love. But he was also the persecuted god, the suffering and dying god, and all whom he loved, all who attended him had to share his tragic fate....."[23]

> And the inner force of this dual reality is so great that he appears among men like a storm, he staggers them, and he tames their opposition with the whip of madness. All tradition, all order must be shattered. Life becomes suddenly an ecstasy—an ecstasy of blessedness, but an ecstasy, no less, of terror.[24]

In the terrorist we see Dionysus, god of wine and blood, dance and dismemberment, and theater, especially tragedy. As "the Great Loosener," he liberates from cares but also dismembers. He dissolves form and notions of linear progression, transgressing over boundary, licensed and unruly, emancipated from the ground of reason to the passions of the animal and the guile of the serpent. Intimate and alien, suddenly appearing and disappearing, Dionysus presides over what Terry Eagleton refers to as

> that orgy of un-meaning, before the dawn of subjectivity itself, in which bloody stumps and mangled bits of bodies whirl in some frightful dance of death. It is a dark parody of carnival—a jubilant merging and exchange of bodies which like carnival itself is

never far from the graveyard. The orgy dissolves distinctions between
bodies, and thus prefigures the indifferent leveling of death.[25]

Of all the gods, the "most terrible, although most gentle, to
mankind," the dual aspect of Dionysus is evident in the stories of his
birth. In one version, Zeus, in the form of a snake, fathered Dionysus
with the goddess Persephone. In jealousy, Zeus' wife Hera had the
infant torn into pieces by the Titans. Zeus swallowed the baby's heart
and fathered him a second time with the human female Semele. Semele,
after being impregnated by Zeus, was tricked by the still-jealous Hera
into getting Zeus to grant any wish. In her naivete, Semele wished to
see Zeus in his true form. Being human, she could not survive the sight
of the god in his divinity and was turned into flame. Zeus again rescued
the infant, carried him to term in his thigh, and "born again," Dionysus
was given to foster parents to raise for a time as a girl.

The story of Dionysus as *ur*-terrorist is told by Euripides in his
play, *The Bacchae*. Dionysus, disguised as an effeminate foreigner from
the east, enters the city of Thebes, and finding himself not honored
there, casts a spell upon the women so that they leave their looms and
shuttles, go off into the hills, and become initiates in his mysteries.
Dionysus demands to be worshipped as a god, and the young king,
Pentheus, refuses. Pentheus is a violent, arrogant, stubborn man,
arbitrary, intolerant of tradition, impious, immoderate, and disdainful
of any power except that which he derives from his station as king. He
has nothing but contempt for tradition and a hidden fear of anything
pertaining to the "other." When he hears of the havoc being wrought
in his city, Pentheus can only think by way of rigid forms, and insists
on meeting the challenge of Dionysus with the conventional symbols
of man-made power—manacles, chains, traps, nets, hangings, and
prison. Pentheus is the embodiment of *amathia*, the condition of self
unknowing where action is taken from an ungovernable ignorance of
self and of necessity. Dionysus, disguised as a stranger, is taken prisoner,
but as prisoner turns terrorist, crying, "Let the earthquake come! Shatter
the floor of the world!"[26] He causes the palace to be razed to the ground,
and the chorus cries in dismay at its tottering and collapse as it goes
up in flame ignited by a thunderbolt.

The *maenads,* or female followers of Dionysus which include
Pentheus' mother Agave, with serpents for headbands dancing to drum
and flute, call upon the city to honor Dionysus.

> O city,
> With boughs of oak and fir,
> Come dance the dance of god!
> Fringe your skins of dappled fawn
> With tufts of twisted wool!
> Handle with holy care
> The violent wand of god!
> And let the dance begin!
> He is Bromius who runs
> To the mountain!
> Where the throng of women waits,
> Driven from shuttle and loom,
> Possessed by Dionysus! (108–119)

Dionysus is the god of madness, and with his appearance comes the question of madness and what it is. In the background of the question of madness, we can see the relativistic essence of terrorism. Pentheus sees the revels of Dionysus as a kind of mad possession, but from Dionysus' standpoint, it is daily, ordinary life, business as usual, the shuttle and the loom, which is mad. The elders of the city consider it mad of Pentheus not to pay attention to the traditional relationship between men and gods, while he takes them for lunatic old men in suggesting he give up his power.

Dionysus turns our perspectives upside down and gives us double vision. After he has arrived with the intent to possess Pentheus, Dionysus calls for Pentheus to come out so that Dionysus can see him. Pentheus, king of Thebes, then emerges wearing a dress and wig of long blonde curls, a cross-dresser. He stammers,

> I seem to see two suns blazing in the heavens,
> And now two Thebes, two cities, and each
> With seven gates. And you—you are a bull. (918-920)

Dionysus frames this vision as that of the god, unlike before when Pentheus was "blind." Dionysus teaches us to see with multiple eyes, the dual vision of the gaze of imagination—not literal, not abstract—but matter and spirit at once.

Dionysus lures Pentheus into following him into the hills to witness the revels of the women. He becomes the poet of revenge as the women that were hunted by Pentheus turn and become the hunters, their desire echoed by the Chorus.

When shall I dance once more
With bare feet the all-night dances,
Tossing my head for joy
In the damp air, in the dew,
As a running fawn might frisk
For the green joy of the wide fields,
Free from fear of the hunt,
Free from the circling beaters
And the nets of woven mesh
And the hunters hallooing on
Their yelping packs? And then, hard pressed,
she sprints with the quickness of wind,
bounding over the marsh, leaping
to frisk, leaping for joy,
gay with the green of the leaves,
to dance for joy in the forest,
to dance where the darkness is deepest,
  where no man is. (862 – 878)

Pentheus is finally treed like an animal and falls to his death by dismemberment at the hands of his crazed mother foaming at the mouth as she tears the limbs and head from her child's torso.

Euripides' play tells us that the "life force" *zoe* embodied in Dionysus carries its own violent surprise which comes bursting forth as if from out of the earth. Its chaos cuts through the rational barriers of personal ego and collective order based upon reason in the service of certainty. Dionysus asks us to abandon homeland security and demands his place among the psychological necessities we call gods. Openness to the terrible powers of this surreptitious *daimon* winding its way across the earth brings a form of compassion for life and also reflects a kind of "wisdom," or *sophia* or self knowing, based on an awareness of one's own nature and place in the scheme of things. The play ends on a ground of uncertainty.

The gods have many shapes.
The gods bring many things
To their accomplishment.
And what was most expected
Has not been accomplished.
But god has found his way
For what no man expected. (1387- 1393)

The ways of the gods are not the ways of humans. "What is most expected" is not accomplished, and instead what is "found" is "what no man expected." Terrifying, indeed.

A terrorist is terrifying because, like Dionysus, he or she works from a place intimate with the subject in order to achieve his or her ends violently. Wine dissolves our boundaries to create intimacy, but also drives us mad. In the myth of the Middle Eastern goddess Inanna, dirt from under the fingernails of the god Enki is used to form the *kurgarra* and the *galatur*, creatures who, "like flies ...slipped through the cracks of the gates," and terrorize another son/lover, Dumuzi.

For Jean Paul Sartre, identity cannot be separated from the surrounding world. We are who we are, always in relation to an "other." Dionysus, the effeminate male god, reveals Pentheus, the macho man, as "other," a man in women's clothes. Augustine confesses that God is, "one who fills me with terror and burning love: with terror in so much as I am utterly other than it, with love in that I am akin to it."[27]

If social structures hold their own terror concealed, and terror its own order, then Pentheus embodies the terror of the state, and Dionysus the order of the mysteries within chaos. Ultimately, what makes terrorism most terrifying is that the terrorist is at once something totally other than his subject, and at the same time akin to it, terrorist and victim always reflecting something of each other, each a "trace" of the other, each complicit in the act. Jacques Derrida characterizes terrorism as an autoimmune crisis, an aspect of a system turned against itself. Finally, terrorism serves to turn the tables on our values, pulling out our underlying secrets in a maneuver presented by John Milton in his character, Satan, the fallen, formerly foremost angel, who declares, "Evil, be thou my good."

NOTES

1. Hannah Arendt, *The Human Condition* (Chicago: Univesity of Chicago Press, 1958), p. 22.

2. The myth upon which this practice was based states that Kali at one time had killed a gigantic monster that devoured humans with her sword, but their drops of blood simply turned into more monsters.

Kali solved the problem of multiplying demons by licking up the blood of their wounds.

3. The criminal, Barrabas, who was released by Pilate according to the Roman custom of letting a prisoner go at the time of the Jewish holiday, a reverse form of scapegoating, is thought by some to have been a zealot. Ironically, Jesus, took his place on the cross.

4. The origin of the ideology and tactics of the Zealots and Sicarii extended back to the time of Moses, when the Children of Israel were still wandering in the desert. Phineas, a high priest, was incensed by the unfaithful and licentious acts of God's children. Taking the law into his own hands, he murdered a tribal chief and his concubine with the head of his spear which he used as a dagger (*sica*). This act prepared the way for God to command the Holy War (*herem*) against the Canaanites for possession of the Promised Land.

5. As quoted by David C. Rapoport in "Fear and trembling: Terrorism in Three Religious Traditions," *The American Political Science Review*, Volume 78, p. 670.

6. Thomas Singer and Samuel Kimbles, *The Cultural Complex: Contemporary Jungian Perspectives on Psyche and Society* (London and New York, Brunner-Routledge, 2004); Thomas Singer, "The Cultural Complex and Archetypal Defenses of the Collective Spirit," *The San Francisco Jung Institute Library Journal*, Vol. 20, No. 4, 2002, pp. 5-28; and Thomas Singer, "Unconscious Forces Shaping International Conflicts: Archetypal defenses of the Group Spirit From Revolutioary America to Confrontation in the Middle East," *The San Francisco Jung Institute Library Journal*, Vol. 25, No. 4, 2006, pp. 6-28, have framed terrorism through the psychoanalytic constructs of "complex" and "defense," placing the phenomenon within a conceptual structure of psychopathology. In this paper I am taking an archetypal approach which I believe to be more psychologically encompassing in that it is closer to the experience of terrror itself and sees through to a spiritual intention at its roots.

Archetypes are structures of action, consciousness, and image which have similarity across culture and time. They are universal metaphors out of which we live our daily lives. Every conscious moment, large and small, from giving birth to crossing the street or washing the dishes has an archetypal dominant which informs it, making it in a sense "larger than" we know. Images which indicate archetypal patterns are often in the form of gods and goddesses. Those religions with pantheons of multiple gods are more helpful in this way in that each god represents a distinct archetypal realm or world. The personified gods Kali, Dionysus, and Christ represent ways of being that we would think of as a separate "worlds" of being. We might think of them as distinct ways in which the world reveals itself to us. Although each world is separate and distinct, they do not exist in isolation but will of necessity interact with others through innate structures, hence the victim is always linked to the perpetrator.

7. *The Song of God: Bhagavad-Gita*, translated by Swami Prabhavananda and Christopher Isherwood, with an Introduction by Aldus Huxley (New York: New American Library, 1951), pp. 36-39.

8. The right of just war was advocated by Cicero, St. Ambrose, and St. Augustine as well as Mohammed and has been exercised throughout Judeo-Christian as well as Islamic history.

9. "Wars are not only man-made; they bear witness also to something essentially human that transcends the human, invoking powers more than the human can fully grasp. Not only do Gods battle among themselves and against other foreign gods, they sanctify human wars, and they participate in those wars by divine intervention." James Hillman, "Wars, Arms, Rams, Mars: On the Love of War," in *Facing Apocalypse*, Valerie Andrews, Robert Bosnak, and Karen Walter Goodwin (eds.) (Dallas: Spring Publications, 1987), p. 120.

10. The merging of government and religion is not altogether foreign to Americans as witnessed in the Puritans who founded their colony merging the notions of government, religion, and economics into one structure.

11. Koran VI: 152. All quotes of the Koran are taken from *The Koran Interpreted, A Translation by A. J. Arberry* (New York: Simon and Schuster, 1955).

12. Abd-al-Rahman Azzam, *The Eternal Message of Muhammad* (New York: New American Library, 1964), p. 129.

13. Regina Schwartz (1997) has made the point that when a religion is monotheistic, the people identifying on the one hand with God and with land on the other, violence is the inevitable result.

14. Rudolf Otto, *The Idea of the Holy*, trans. by John W. Harvey (New York: Oxford University Press, 1958), pp. 12-13.

15. As quoted by Ginette Paris in *Pagan Meditations* (Dallas: Spring, 1987), p. 157.

16. In Handel's *Messiah* the very next word after this declaration is "Hallelujah," again an indication of a celebration of God's violence.

17. Terry Eagleton, *Holy Terror* (Oxford: Oxford University Press, 2005), p. 43.

18. *Philosophical Enquiry into the Origin of our Ideas on the Sublime and the Beautiful* (1757).

19. Eagleton, p. 44.

20. Andrew Sinclair, *An Anatomy of Terror: A History of Terrorism* (New York: Macmillan, 2003), p. 76.

21. Alexis De Tocqueville, *Democracy in America, Vol. II* (New York: Vintage Books, 1990), p. 330.

22. As quoted by Erich Neumann in *The Great Mother* (Princeton, NJ: Princeton University Press, 1963), p. 152.

23. Walter Otto, *Dionysus: Myth and Cult*, trans. and with an Introduction by Robert B. Palmer (Bloomington: Indiana University Press, 1965), p. 49.

24. Otto, p. 78.

25. Eagleton, pp. 3-4.

26. Quotes from *The Bacchae* are taken from *Euripides V of the Complete Greek Tragedies*, edited by David Grene and Richmond Lattimore (New York: Washington Square Press, 1968), p. 585.

27. As quoted by Eagleton, p. 72.

Politics and Jungian Analysts:
An "Enterview" with Jan Bauer and Lyn Cowan

ROBERT S. HENDERSON

Editor's Note: These interviews with Jungian analysts Jan Bauer and Lyn Cowan were conducted by Robert Henderson over the course of several months in 2006-2007 for publication in this issue.

Jan Bauer, M.A., is a Jungian analyst working in both English and French in Montreal, Canada. Born and raised in the United States, she attended Sarah Lawrence College and obtained Master's degrees from the Sorbonne and Boston University before receiving her Diploma from the C. G. Jung Institute in Zurich. She has served as the Director of Admissions and the Training Director of the Inter-Regional Society of Jungian Analysts. She is the author of *Impossible Love: Or Why the Heart Must Go Wrong* (Spring Publications, 1993) and *Alcoholism and Women: The Background and the Psychology* (Inner City Books, 1985).

Lyn Cowan, Ph.D., is a Jungian analyst in Minneapolis, Minnesota. Born and raised in New York, she graduated from the University of Minnesota, obtained her Ph.D. from Union Institute, and received her Diploma from the Inter-Regional Society of Jungian Analysts. She has

Rev. Dr. Robert S. Henderson is a Pastoral Psychotherapist in Glastonbury, Connecticut. He and his wife, Janis, a psychotherapist, are co-authors of *Living with Jung: "Enterviews" with Jungian Analysts: Volume 1* (Spring Journal Books, 2006). Volumes 2 and 3 are forthcoming, in 2008 and 2009, respectively.

served as both the Training Director and President of the Inter-Regional Society. She is the author of *Portrait of the Blue Lady: The Character of Melancholy* (Spring Journal Books, 2004)*; Tracking the White Rabbit: Essays in Subversive Culture* (Routledge, 2002); and *Masochism: A Jungian View* (Spring Publications, 1982); she also served as the editor of *Barcelona 2004: Edges of Experience—Memory and Emergence* (Daimon, 2006).

Robert Henderson (Rob): Over the years, I have often heard that Jungians do not share their political views. Have you found that to be true in your experience, and, if so, why do you think that is the case?

Jan Bauer(Jan): First of all, the archetype of the analyst is not at all a political one but one connected to the Healer, whether shaman, priest, doctor, etc. Of these, the analyst is especially concerned with the inner life. Therefore, by definition, analysts do not speak with authority from a political point of view. They can only speak with authority about their own domain. I think the fact that Jung was so badly burned by his political experiences during WW2 has also left its mark on Jungian analysis and had repercussions in our world that until very recently tended to encourage avoidance of "collective" concerns.

It's only been since the Republican take-over of politics in the U.S. that I've encountered a lot of political discussion and concern among analysts. And then, it's mostly as citizens, not as analysts, though we all like to add our bit of psychological speculation into the discussions of the administration in Washington, etc. And it's true there are more and more analysts speaking up professionally about politics and the world situation, and I think this is good as long as it doesn't veer too much into personal opinion and away from psychological observation. I personally find it annoying when an analyst gives a lecture on a subject he/she knows well and then can't resist adding a lot of their own political views into it.

I'm not sure we Jungians had any political views as long as we, along with our collective peers, could still enjoy the image of ourselves as having participated in all the important battles of the 60's and 70's. Racism, feminism, etc. But, I think that's true of lots of us pre-baby boomers and baby boomers that make up the largest proportion of the Jungian analyst population.

I remember going to the C. G. Jung Institute in Zurich in 1974 at age 31—just arriving there, with no pre-contact or warning, and saying I wanted to become an analyst. I was quickly told I would need some analysis first, and so I got a job and got an analyst and then began training a year later. In those years, it was easy to work in Zurich, easy to gain admission to the Institute. So much, to return to the political-psychological, for my particular experience in getting to Zurich and living there. But, I do think lots of us, especially American ex-pats, were looking for some steady fathering that Zurich represented and that the Institute carried very well with its patriarchal organization and attitudes. There were few influential women apart from Jung's "daughters," Marie-Louise von Franz, Barbara Hannah, etc., and the "'fathers," i.e., our analysts of the time, all seemed absolutely imperturbable and serene and all knowing.

On the one hand, I'm very grateful for those years and those analysts. They truly believed in the psyche and were able to impart its importance in an environment that allowed full expansion of all psychic madness, weirdness, and beauty, without the interference of the world. Especially the American world, with its mobility, chaos, and uncertainty. I know I had fled my own dysfunctional family to be there, and I think I wasn't alone among the foreigners in that. Also, Swiss society is so closed and Swiss German such an obstacle that it was easy to remain outside of it all and just concentrate on analysis and the inner world. Many of us sorely needed a secure structure created by the Zurich "fathers" to grow and learn to be; we were not about to challenge their dominion or get into "politics" of any sort, even regarding the Institute.

It was just in later years, returning to North America, that I began to see the shadow of the isolation of Zurich and the very patriarchal attitudes that were inherent in Jungian ideas of the time. Still, I remain grateful for those years of "time out" of the world. They were precious, and I realize just how much when I see my own patients struggling to have an inner world in a society that keeps nipping at them to buy, work, and keep moving. But I think it is true that the idea of "time out" is deeply part of the Jungian ethos in a sense of countering the "madding crowd" extraversion of American culture, in particular, and Western culture in general. The good part of this is its emphasis on the inner world. The shadow part is that it creates a sense of belonging to a "special" world apart where outer things are sometimes seen with skepticism, even contempt.

On the other hand, since the mid-80's and my participation in the Inter-Regional Society of Jungian Analysts, both as a regular analyst and on the Executive Committe for many years, I have seen changes in this particular Jungian attitude. Candidates have become more demanding, more critical, and this is good. There is more "Eros" of a sibling kind and less dependence on parental supervision. This is true in Zurich, too, where it finally led to a revolution that started the new International School of Analytical Psychology (ISAP) where a sense of equality and openness is much more present than it ever was at the Institute when I was there. I think this movement speaks of a tendency towards more awareness of political realities and more willingness to get involved at a nitty gritty level in them.

Lyn Cowan (Lyn): Speaking from my own little corner of the world, I think it *used* to be true that Jungians did not share their political views, at least in public. But it seems that in the last 5 years or so—not coincidentally since Bush took over in 2001—politics in *any* venue has become discussable (and "cuss-able"). (Jungians don't talk about their religious beliefs, either—and this is still a much closed personal area, in my experience.) My mother taught me that there were three topics you should never discuss in public: religion, sex, and politics. (Which left, as I understood quickly, nothing of interest to talk about.)

Neither religion nor sex is off-limits anymore, but politics still has a subtle "no trespassing" sign for many people, even in casual conversations. Do we not want to offend? Do we not want to be offended? For me, I used to worry about what people would think of me if I expressed a political opinion that contradicted theirs, an unmistakable sign of a complex being activated. In my case, it had much to do with my personal father complex. As I've come to understand a bit more about my complex and its effect on me, I've become less anxious about expressing my political views. (The complex is depotentiated, but I still have trouble managing my basic homicidal urges!)

Perhaps in former times—before we entered the Dark Ages (i.e., before Bush the Son)—there wasn't so much obvious pathology pervading national politics and high-placed politicians. Nor did it seem very relevant to the work of analysis, since the material of the individual psyche, even though it had an archetypal ground, was assumed to be primarily formed, informed, or deformed by personal experiences in personal relationships (with parents, spouses, lovers, siblings). One could relate individual experience to the archetypal Great Mother and understand that individual's complexes about the personal mother, about the material world, about related mothering and nurturing/ withholding dynamics. But to my knowledge, not too many of us put together the Great Mother with the Democratic party, or the Authoritarian Father with the Republican Party, and tried to understand an individual's psychic structure through their political loyalties, ideas, and family political "case history."

I think it was Andrew Samuels who first began pushing hard to put "politics on the couch," in his phrase, and for us to incorporate the analysand's political experiences into analysis. James Hillman has been putting politics and depth psychology together for a long time. Ron Schenk has gone public with his views. Increasingly, others are doing the same. I think it is also the case that as the world has "shrunk," what happens politically in my country has serious implications for colleagues and friends in another. I remember being in Zurich during the Watergate hearings and Nixon's impeachment proceedings, and ordinary Swiss people expressed their admiration with the open way in which the American system corrected itself. But now people around the world just look on in horror as the American system seems to have shut down, or is apparently collectively unwilling to correct itself.

It may be that we as Jungians are talking more personally to each other now about politics because the stakes are higher and our patients are being impacted in a way they have not been before. Individual pathology in high political places is more widespread, more dangerous, and more reflective of our collective psychic life. The very practice of our profession has been profoundly and negatively impacted by political decisions, such as managed care, rules of confidentiality, therapist liabilities, etc.

I think the traumatizing effects of recent politics on the national psyche is only partly a result of the 9/11 attacks; the greater part is a result of the way the Bush administration has interpreted, exploited, and used the 9/11 catastrophe to justify whatever Bush wants to do, while keeping us in a catastrophic mentality that has practically destroyed the political imagination. No one (including Democrats) seems to have real political vision, an imaginative vision of what we as a country might be or become or what our constructive place in the world might be. The quality of unconsciousness is remarkable and frightening. There is also a pronounced psychopathic streak in Bush and his immediate circle, and this, I think, is reflective of a growing trend in psychopathic attitudes visible in large segments of the American population—religious fundamentalists, corporate criminals, and corrupt politicians in all parties. (Why, there are some people out there who still try to dope racehorses!)

As an analyst, as a citizen, as an individual, I can't help but be shaken and affected by what goes on around me, even if it is happening on the other side of the world in Iraq, or Lebanon, or Darfur, since Donne's line is still true: "no man is an island." So I am affected by everything my government does or does not do. This requires a constant ethical consideration of how I live my personal life in small ways as well as how I vote, and these personal decisions are complex and difficult. We need to talk to each other as Jungians because we can't afford to be unconscious of what is going on either in our leaders or in ourselves. (And as we know as analysts, wherever we are unconscious, our patients suffer.) For myself, I would go quite crazy in a matter of hours if I didn't have a close friend or two with psychological savvy to go on a rant periodically about the latest insanity coming out of Washington or Iran or my local City Council (which is also occasionally incapable of reasonableness). Unfortunately, I now go on a rant every 15 minutes, which has wrecked my schedule.

Jan: Lyn filled in a lot I didn't around the contributions of Jim Hillman and Andrew Samuels and also around the particular situation that Bush politics has created in the U.S., both in general, in spreading national paranoia and encouraging psychopathy, but also in directly influencing the practice of therapy with intrusive political moves.

In Canada and Europe, these intrusions are far less felt in analytical circles. So the necessity to get in there and be involved politically is less felt. On the other hand, I think that both Europeans, and Canadians to a slightly lesser extent, have been generally more aware of the rest of the world and more conversant with politics than Americans for a long time. I don't think, for example, that American abuse of power is new, it's just more blatant, and we can't ignore it any more because it actually affects middle-class Americans and professionals now, while before it just affected the poor, the wrongly colored, the wrongly religious, and people in other countries.

I was amazed and embarrassed by my own ignorance when I arrived in France in the early 60's and realized that everyone talked about politics all the time. This was quite a change from my college friends who at the same age were talking about beer and football games or getting "pinned." I'm not saying the French were always right. They weren't. They had all sorts of skewed prejudices about the U.S., and they did a lot more talking than acting, so it also made me appreciate the civil involvement of so many Americans who just get out there and do things instead of yakking about them and complaining.

Lyn: Jan, I loved your comments on Zurich, both from your baby-days and now as Grande Dame involved in the new life of the new Institute. I remember, too, there was a brief, rather abortive movement to create a "social life" among candidates when I was there, begun, naturally, by Americans, who were also the only ones interested, and then not too many. So while the initial Questionnaire of interests was a very clever hoot, I don't think anyone answered it, so nothing happened. (I was one of the authors of the Questionnaire, seduced into participating by some of the extraverts, mainly to escape the crushing isolation of an ex-pat's life in Zurich). I hated the isolation at the time, but have long since recognized its necessity and extraordinary productivity in terms of my own "settling into myself."

When I first started analysis in late 1965, I was already being impacted psychologically (unconsciously) by the then-nascent women's movement, so there was a political aspect to my analysis from the very beginning, although it was never articulated as such. And much of my own personal psychology became clarified through the political currents at work at the time. The theme of justice was always a huge one for me, and it was then being played out on a national scale in the civil rights movement, the women's movement, and the beginning of the Vietnam War protests. Since Jungian analysis has, as Jan pointed out, been focused almost exclusively on the "inner" world of the individual, there was nothing being written about the "outer" world to which one could look for some parallels, or amplification, or even a context for one's own neurosis. (Except the great, slightly weird stuff from Jung on UFOs, etc.)

Much of this has changed within Jungian circles, but there is still, I think, a large shadow consisting of unrecognized power drives in the Jungian community. This is true of any organization or institution, but because Jungians keep emphasizing Eros and relationship, the power drive stays in the shadow, and comes out in all sorts of political machinations in all Jungian institutes, and can be sometimes quite lethal. There are some, but I don't know too many analysts who can handle the political shadow, or even recognize it when it is at work amongst us. We imagine that if our motives are pure (or close to it), our actions will be helpful. But whose motives are so pure? I think it may have been von Franz who said (but maybe she wasn't the first) that it was better to do the wrong thing for the right reason than the right thing for the wrong reason. Motives, then, matter, and political motives matter, most of all, when it comes to affecting any kind of serious political change.

Jan: Lyn, great stuff here. Your comments about political awareness in your analysis and what the world changes would mean for you. You were much more aware of this than I and it's pertinent. And yes, to the power shadow of us all. The dangers of "innocence," etc.

Rob: One could assume that if our country were to have a woman as President, the force of the feminine would be impactful throughout the collective policies and decisions. What difference could you see it making if we had a woman President?

Jan: When I think of Ireland, Germany, Chile, Israel, Iceland, England, Canada, the Philippines, Pakistan, and others, I don't see a very big difference in the "womanness," only in the "person-who-is-also a woman." Sometimes better, sometimes worse than the men who went before. I think it would be the same if a woman were elected president of the U.S.

I have to say, Rob, the question I find more important here is why, exactly, has it been such a problem to elect a woman for the last 200 years in the U.S.? Or, being more realistic, since we got the vote in the 20's? When I was growing up, it never occurred to me that women could be president. Feminism changed that, or was supposed to. Yet, feminism has been much less present in many of the above-mentioned countries, and they don't have heart attacks at the idea of a woman in charge.

At the same time, more than those from any country I know, American women throughout our history have been incredibly active in changing our society through social groups and civic activities and volunteer work. All "unofficial," and yet central to our values and society today. Kind of like the nuns in Quebec who ran everything, education, health, and religion, while the men officiated at the top in pretty outfits or ran off into the woods to cut wood and bond.

Which leads me to think or surmise that there might be a North American connection here. And from there I would go on and talk about *puer* culture in which everyone is less secure in their sense of identity than people from older countries. De Tocqueville said it, others after him, our very democracy, a society of "winners," and our mobility creates anxiety all the time, and the only way to counter this is to invest in persona trappings that say exactly who you are and where you belong. Even though we are fast rolling into a permanent plutocracy, it's still a younger one than elsewhere, and the need to keep proving worth through material stuff remains paramount.

I am frequently impressed when in Europe or when talking in depth to women from other societies, whether European or Russian or Islam, how much more sure of themselves the women are there. Much less burdened with obsessions around looks, around guilt at not being a perfect mother, lover, etc. Less tortured by the fears of not being "right." Of course they have problems, both personal and political too, but not the same very personal, individual self blame at not being ideal that seems to be a genetic part of North American womanhood. Certainly that is also a heritage of the Puritan obsession with self improvement that expresses itself today in all the self-help books, Oprah, etc. And it's not all bad.

It's what makes American prosperity too. The need to go ever farther and better.

But, still I wonder if this obsession with perfection hasn't made politics much less appealing to American women than to women elsewhere. No where else is a woman in public service and in the public eye so dissected, criticized, and judged on her personal characteristics, looks, voice, hair, age, boyfriend, or family, etc. Forget her ideas, her visions, her convictions, she looks mousy, or frazzled, or has on the wrong color, and bam! for the votes.

Men get it too, I know, and more and more in the age of CNN and FOX NEWS. But less than women, and when they do, they nearly always have a woman next to them to assure them of their value, unlike many women who, because they are successful in power, are very often single!

So, I really think that our society punishes women in public power more than men and more than in many other countries.

And this, I think, comes from our basic insecurity. I think we want men as leaders because we are simply not secure enough as a society to get out from under the need for an old-fashioned male at the top leadership. Yes, there are more and more women in positions of power in private enterprise, but there are fewer in politics than there were 20 years ago. Somehow leading a cosmetic empire or even a brokerage house is ok but not the country. We may have gotten rid of the king, but we still want a daddy. Just a nice one this time, one "like us," a regular guy, and not a snobby, mean one like the old English king.

Pleasing men is, alas, still a primary concern for most of the young women I know or treat, as much as it was for my generation, and often even more so. If that is the case, then how can women elect a woman?

In a mobile, changing society where loneliness and anxiety are epidemic, something needs to stay stable and the same. I would propose that one of those things in the States is a need to have a dad (Reagan, Bush, Sr.) or big brother (Clinton, Bush, Jr.) at the top. It's where our "modern" society reveals itself to have a very regressive shadow.

Thinking more psychologically, the "feminine" was never valued in the U.S. to start with. The *anima* was in the wilderness, and it was not loved. It was exterminated. The masculine, the pioneer, the white ego was scared and reacted by stamping out the feminine, whether in himself, in the Amerindians, the animals, the trees, or the women and slaves. I think that the American ego is still scared of the feminine, still a male adolescent proving itself in the world and unable to cope with the subtleties and "irrational" aspects of the feminine. (Witness the reaction to Kerry's anima, Teresa!)

Older countries have usually made more peace with the anima; though it may be repressed and abused, it is still a given and not something to be a cause of shame and avoidance. I.e., they are more at ease with sexuality, with appetites, with sensuality, with the arts, with nuance, and human rights, while we're at it.

So the only woman who could be elected would have to be a woman without very much anima, therefore femininity. Condi Rice would do fine—all the right persona attributes of a woman with nary a stroke of real anima except, probably, in her music. And we come full circle. If a woman were elected, her femininity would make little difference because the only kind of femininity that would be valued would be as it was expressed through her looks or in her domestic skills.

I think the American anima is the "sister." Not lover, nor mother. In my experience, American women are the most apt to befriend other women, to make "sisters" of them, to organize with them, rather than see them as mainly rivals or mothers/daughters. Unlike French women (the first) and Quebecers (the second), for example. This has resulted in incredible social groupings from the League of Women Voters, to NOW, to PTAs and even to American Women's Associations all over the world. With men, however, I fear the "sister" has always been a younger one. A sidekick, helpmate, comrade in adventure and effort, but not taken seriously enough to be considered a leader in a man's world. A woman presidential candidate would have to have, therefore, qualities of a good sister, friendly, smart, open, feisty, not too sexy, and not too motherly.

Lyn: On the prospect of a woman becoming president: it is hard to stay psychological and not purely political on this one!

And this question is a hard one, as Jan said, and I think she's pretty well covered a lot of the ground in answering it. I, too, question whether "the feminine" (and I am not sure anymore what that is, exactly) has any real force or impact on the American (or North American) psyche. "She" has been banished for so long no one notices she's missing. Even getting the vote 86 years ago hasn't changed much, since women have only had men to vote for, with a few exceptions. Those exceptions have been noteworthy—in my time alone, Barbara Jordan, Patricia Schroeder, Nancy Pelosi, Hillary Clinton, Dianne Feinstein—but these women *are* exceptions, not the rule. But to think that Anima will return in the form of a "woman president" and so humanize us and restore a sense of stability, reliability, sanity, clear priorities, and relational management (all of which the Great Mother can do) is wishful thinking. As Jan pointed out, "anima" in this collective psyche is the lover/whore, not the sustaining mother. And lover/whores can never be trusted, which may be why there hasn't been a female president since Day One, and it is an uphill climb for Hillary.

As many parts of the world have discovered, having a woman as leader does not cause mass heart attacks. But neither does it solve much on the world stage, although individual countries may have benefited in certain ways. Our ideas of "leadership" in America are still formed by 19ᵗʰ-century cowboy images, gun-totin' tough guys who can hold their liquor and keep women "in their place." (Their place has never been executive board rooms, where they are still ridiculously small minorities, certainly not in positions of political leadership: even with a few female governors, there are only 16 senators right now, and certainly not in the armed forces—again, the one or two exceptions of high-ranking officers highlight the aberrations, and there is no joint chiefs possibility).

George the Small has done nothing to change this image and everything to reinforce it, with catastrophic consequences, deepening the insecurity (as Jan also rightly says) that has always characterized the American male with his dreaded "impotence" and the American female with her dreaded "masculinization." The religious right that supports Bush and his cowboy pals (who can't shoot well anyway, as we know from Dick Cheney's mistaking his friend for a duck) also has psychologically violent ideas about women and will not vote for one. And as Jan noted, I think correctly, American women in general, liberal or otherwise, have been pressed back into earlier roles and value systems which they mistake as "natural" to women (youthful appearance, the whole narcissistic schtik of presenting oneself as sexually desirable to a man, and the giving up of one's ability to think independently). Women, too, support a masculinized culture which provides a "place" for everyone according to gender.

Unambiguous gender is the mainstay of those in need of security (which is at least partly why the very idea of gay people is so threatening). And therein lies the impossible rub—we still make gender the most important thing, which is why we are stuck asking questions like this: what about a woman president, how can marriage be "protected," how to defeat "the gay agenda," etc. In short, as Jan already said, even if a woman were to become president, she would be presiding over a male-dominated culture of which she herself is a product and can be expected to have a vested interest in supporting, not changing, it.

Of course, we hope—hope, hope—that such a woman would at least introduce some "softening" effects: not as "feminine" weakness, but as a means of relating to people and ideas that can provide an alternative to the harsh militarism that always seems characteristic of Republican administrations, and could restore a sense of courage to the Democrats, many of whom seem unable or afraid to just come out and clearly say what they think (without having to draw their guns). (Only women Democrats, by the way, seem to really "get it" and are unafraid to speak their minds. And unlike a lot of their colleagues, they have minds to speak.) Most mothers (and all women are mothers whether they have literal children or not) are courageous when it comes to protecting their young, while men's courage seems to be activated in behalf of ideals and principles. Nothing wrong with that, but it's often the young who get sacrificed for these principles, when there might be another way to both protect the young and stand for the principle. (And wouldn't *that* be a revolutionary idea?)

In summary, I think Americans might like the novelty of a woman president because they like novelties of any sort. And since George the Small has so demeaned the office with his adolescent narcissism, it would be a treat to have a *psychologically adult woman* in the oval office. (There must be a forgotten reason why the office is oval, from "ova," egg-shaped, clearly designed as a woman's space.) But I would not want a woman who is a Dubya-clone or Republican lackey or anyone from Texas except Molly Ivins or Ann Richards, and they are both dead. God save us from creatures like Harriet Meiers, erstwhile nominee for the Supreme Court, who thought Bush was "the most intelligent man" she'd ever met. So being a woman isn't enough, just as being a man isn't enough—*individual psychology always trumps gender.* There is no guarantee anything will improve, get worse, change, or really affect anything in any way if a woman is president. But I think what *will* happen—and this is BIG—is that the collective imagination will be freed to move toward new possibilities, since we will have a whole new image of what a president can *look* like.

[Second political aside: Having expressed my dour outlook on the prospect of things not changing much with a woman president, I should note that right now there are more women candidates running for office here in Minnesota than just about ever before, and all but one has a good mind, good ideas, and has managed to combine thoughtful policy ideas with strong conviction in a non-belligerent tone. Interesting, also, is the fact that they are all running on the Democratic ticket (while we have a Republican governor and one Republican senator): for governor, attorney general, senator, and some important House seats. (The one exception is a Republican woman who is a mindless fanatic concerned with, as one person put it, "God, guns, and gays," and who needed Dubya himself to come visit for a fundraiser. All these candidates have a good chance to win since the majority seems to be disgusted with current leadership (or lack thereof). Psychologically, it does seem to point to a restoration of anima concerns and values (at least, here in the Northland). This is the state, after all, that gave us Eugene McCarthy, Hubert Humphrey, Walter Mondale, Paul Wellstone—each of whom was more led by anima than by fake cowboy, boot-stomping gun-slinging attitudes, and each lost in their bids for president, being perceived as "weak," "appeasing," or downright wimpy. (Wellstone never got to run, having been killed in a plane crash a week before the last senatorial election in which he was a candidate—and few supporters believe it was an accident.)

Update after the Minnesota election: Most of the women made it, including the brainless one who soon made national television news by endlessly pawing Bush at the State of the Union Speech, and thereby discredited herself in her home state. She has not been seen or heard from since. I have even forgotten her name.]

Gloria Steinem and Nancy Pelosi would make good presidents, and also Anna Quindlen, but she's probably not interested. I myself would be a good president—George the Small has set the bar soooooooo low —but I am not willing to give up Saturdays at the racetrack.

Second thought on a woman becoming president: a Jungian friend of mine once said that the Republican Party was a manifestation of the Dominating Father archetype, while the Democratic Party was a manifestation of the Great Mother archetype. I think this is one way, and probably an accurate one, of talking about the political situation in psychological terms. Of course, there is a complication here, which is that even a Democratic male president easily falls prey to the Dominating Father archetype (except for Bill Clinton, who seemed to be a strange cross between a helpful older brother and a Don Juanabee. John F. Kennedy was in fact a helpful older brother and a playboy— which takes more money than Clinton had). But in terms of party platforms and policies, it does look like a Republican "Father" and a Democratic "Mother." Since mothers have never been well regarded in this country—hence the guilty need for Mother's Day, which came long before Father's Day—there is compensation at work here.

Putting a woman in the White House could mean a huge shift in the collective psyche, an attempt to get some equilibrium back, since the psychic scale has been so heavily weighted with male power, desires, values, and methods. But again, it depends so much on the psyche of the individual woman, and whether she unconsciously works to preserve the status quo, or whether she is conscious and courageous enough to work towards a shift in the country's psychological perspective, i.e., to govern with a new style of leadership. This new style could also come from a male president, but since it hasn't happened since 1789, it's not likely to start now.

[Political aside again: George Washington would have much preferred to be an innkeeper for tourists in Saratoga Springs, NY, a possibility he worked hard for in 1783. He couldn't get anyone to sell him the land with the springs on it, so he went back to Mt. Vernon and reluctantly took the job when Congress asked him to be president in 1789. So we have to thank the tiny group of anonymous settlers and Native Americans of Saratoga for giving us our first president. But the REAL lapse, the failure to seize the moment, is Martha's, who could have said, "Look, George, you keep trying and follow your bliss up there in New York, and I'll be president. I need to get out of the house more."]

Jan: Very nice reflections, Lyn, all very right on and your off-the-tip-of-your-finger knowledge of particular names of women in U.S. politics is very impressive.

Just one correction: I didn't say the American anima was lover/whore.

Although that plays out in all male psyches probably everywhere, I do maintain that the more American version of the anima remains the sister, and preferably the little sister. Helpful, appealing, sometimes surprising sidekick but, as you say, "in her place."

Lyn: Correction noted. I must have projected my own idea into yours. And thanks for the compliment, but my knowledge of women in politics pales next to your psychological insight, which is really deeper than mine. I slip into being an historian too much and get polemical.

But I disagree that the American version of the anima is the sister, big or little, although it is true that "she" takes many forms and at times is more dominant in one aspect than another. But overall, from the beginning, the American male simply hasn't known what to do with "her" — the anima has always been split, I think, into the lover/whore, or more accurately perhaps, the wife/whore. Since Puritan days the woman has had to be "pure" — virginal, "clean," "wholesome," etc. Not like a sister but like a lover who remains virginal. The Artemis figure is the most hidden, most unconscious, and therefore most powerful of all feminine figures in the American male psyche, which is why we have so much trouble with issues that fall under her purview, such as abortion, birth control (especially for teenagers), lesbian sexuality, the environment of the natural world, etc. Artemis is the lover who slays. (The fascination continues with women who kill their husbands or lovers being labelled "evil," while those who kill their children are merely "insane.") Artemis is the virginal lover/wife who becomes the whore in order to be controllable. Rather than deal with the split anima, the figure of Hera emerges to fill the cavernous split and thus promotes things like the absurd Defense of Marriage act, since she is the ultimate monogamous wife who runs a tight ship known as marriage and knows her place and allows men to publicly exalt her, while they slip off in secret to visit the altar of the "loose" one who seduces and satisfies and makes no demands, but can never be acknowledged.

I'm oversimplifying all this, but hey, maybe we ought to get the jump on Rob and talk about where the political Animus is these days!

Jan: Mmm, you're right. About wife/whore, not lover. Right about Artemis in American psyche. Buttttttttt. I still say the "sister" is a strong one. And don't forget, after all, that Artemis *is* a sister goddess. Sister to Apollo and patron goddess to groups of young women, "sisterhoods!" In the States, you can't ignore the groupings of women who work together, volunteer together throughout our history in a way that no other culture has. And women appreciated as sexless companions of men, in work, in adventure, are legion.

Lyn: Well.....I guess I could concede a little to the sister figure — you make a good point. Still.....(I'm like a nasty pit bull when I get on to something)......I think the way women perceive themselves and the way men perceive them are two very different constellations in the psyche. Women may be more likely to be informed by the sister archetype, but I still think it is hard for men to see actual women as sexless even while they might be appreciated as companions. There is also the resistance aroused in men when women do come together in groups, especially for purposes of social change that also affect the collective psyche. Such groups have often formed in spite of male resistance. I'm thinking of women suffragettes who were arrested, beaten, and force-fed for silently picketing Wilson's white house. The "sister" looks different to women than she does to someone like, say, Elmer Gantry! (One of my all-time favorite movies, by the way: Burt Lancaster at his smarmy finest; Jeanne Craine, pure and innocent.)

Rob: I have a sense that when our country sees shadow in our President, like we did in recent history with Nixon and Clinton, we want them to go away; so they resign or we impeach. Or when people have pointed out Bush's shadow, we want them silenced. What do you think this reveals about the United States?

Jan: If, as some analysts have pointed out, maturity is not perfect balance but an ability to tolerate circulation between the shadow and light, then we are not very mature as a country. We seem to go to extremes in both cases. Exaggerating the sexual shadow of Clinton, exaggerating the leadership capacity of Bush.

But I think we did not exaggerate with Nixon. We had the Watergate hearings; we followed seriously as a country the unfolding of a complicated situation of abuse of power and came to a logical conclusion for impeachment. I don't think there's any comparison at all with the Clinton shadow where witch hunting trumped due process and sexual escapades and voyeurism obliterated any capacity of the public to react with common sense and reflection on the real gravity of the situation. I don't think there could be a Watergate today, or rather, there have been so many abuses already on the part of the administration as to the legal system and the Constitution, but the public seems totally unconcerned. At least the public not involved with either Move On or support Karl Rove.

But returning to your question regarding the denial of the shadow as an American way of life. Yes. The good side of this has given us American optimism and openness to the new, uncomplicated by unpleasant lessons of the past. I realized this when I was living in Europe and everyone, from cab drivers to university professors, had a more cynical view of things, seeing cabals everywhere, never believing that what you see is what you get. This was cynical, yes, but they also had a much better education about history, knew better the facts, both glorious and infamous of their own countries, and had little illusion about politicians' virtue. It was when I began to realize, in spite of my self, that my country had not behaved generously at all times and in all places. It was a loss of innocence. But why did I have to go to Europe or read Chomsky and company to realize this?

When I was growing up, the teaching of history was still very white-washed, perhaps it still is. Is it our American mobility and chronic insecurity about our roots and belonging that make it necessary to deny bad things and keep facing the future with a hopeful grin? A kind of Willy Loman syndrome? Or simply the meshing of Calvinism and capitalism where whether you belong is a question of money and mansions and things, and huckstering the agreed-upon way to succeed?

Psychologically, I think we are very much a sensate type country, giving us our amazing capacity to do, to act, to master material reality and live in the present. But this also leaves out both the judgment functions, thinking and feeling, which would bring some historical perspective as well as respect for social continuity and heritage and taking care of the vulnerable. We have become so much a Winner Society, more and more Darwinian where shadow is simply relative. I.e., if you win, it matters little what shadow you have and what it took to get there. Shadow is the poor, the weak, the wrong color, or the failure, and we distance ourselves as quickly as possible from such. Shadow is our sending the boys and girls to Iraq where it doesn't matter if they get killed or maimed because they won't cause anyone any trouble and they weren't expected to count in a winners' world anyway.

In this sense, I think Bush is the perfect American, and it's not for nothing people vote for him. He incarnates the loser who is a winner. The rather stupid, not very refined, ordinary guy who triumphs over the ones who speak well and make people feel inferior. And he triumphs by money and stubbornness, something all Americans can aspire to. In a perverse way, he is like little Hans in the fairy tales who triumphs over his more favored brothers by enlisting help from unexpected places (i.e., avoiding Congressional oversight, ignoring the Constitution, and other annoying mainstream barriers), and I think people admire this sort of Wild West behavior a lot more than punctilious respect for tradition and law.

In both Europe and Canada, I'm struck at how obedient people are. In one sense, this can be stifling, but, as a community, it makes for a feeling of security and safety. People don't just barge in, help themselves, and go where they feel like no matter what the signs. Americans do that, all over the world. We're used to just following our impulses, consider it conformist and silly to not walk on the grass if we feel like it. We're not particularly polite or respectful of other cultures' taboos and have little sense of shame about not respecting protocol. On the contrary, we revel in it; it's what makes for that puer charm.

Now, again, this makes for an interesting ability to think out of the box and not be stopped from invention and trying new things. And, it makes for corporations and leaders who don't give a second thought about getting what they want in any way they want.

I don't think that the shadow for Americans is greed, lawlessness, grandiosity, or lying. I think the real shadow is being a loser and a failure. That, I think, is what Americans would find truly intolerable, and Bush knows this very well and is determined to not be either, no matter what the evidence to the contrary.

Lyn: Jan's thoughts on the American shadow are so meaty I have no bone to pick. (I would just expand on one of her salient points: that the dominant sensate function by which the collective American psyche operates consciously leaves out the judgment functions of thinking and feeling. Americans love the feeling of loving, and very much like to see themselves as loving, but the real work of love conflicts with the sense of entitlement that most Americans have.)

You can't be sacrificially loving and have someone else in the center of your life if you are taking up all the space and feel you have a right to do so. The culture of narcissism, as someone called it years ago, has created a shadow of indifference and carelessness, as Jan noted. (And there is not just one American shadow, there are many—and that's why it's getting darker around here!) So there is a conflict between the American collective self-image as a loving, caring, generous people and an opposite reality that is driven by (again, as Jan said) the absolute need to win, to be successful, to win, win, win, and to build yourself up so no one can tear you down. No love comes out of this.

On the thinking side—well, there isn't any, or much, of real quality. In politics, as in mainstream psychology, we haven't had a really original idea in decades. America has always had a tradition of anti-intellectualism (Tom Jefferson and other smart guys notwithstanding). I remember in the 1952 presidential election, Adlai Stevenson was ridiculed for being an "egghead" — as if it would be much better to have a dummy for president.

Thinking is very much a shadow aspect for Americans, which is why most of the great presidents—all terrific thinkers—are considered great: they carry the *positive* shadow of creativity that comes from informed thinking (Washington, Lincoln, Jefferson, and FDR). Then there are those very smart presidents (Adams, Wilson, Kennedy, Carter, Clinton) who were not great and so embodied the conflict Americans have with thinking: yes, they are smart and we're proud of them, but they are too smart for their own good, so we find sins (usually sexual ones) to accuse them of.

One thing that is perpetuating American's shadow problem is its deepening ignorance of history and culture, which makes it more difficult to value thinking—because we have little to think about. With so little knowledge of the past, beginning with our own, and so little absorption of culture, particularly in the form of literature (real literature, not pulp fiction, with which I have no argument, but it doesn't necessarily teach about life the way Shakespeare or Toni Morrison or Tennessee Williams or Joyce Carol Oates does).

That American penchant for living in the future does give us a wonderful optimism and creative thrust, but it also leaves us little to fall back on when there is a need to reflect and remember. We have a remarkably poor national memory, largely because we have so little knowledge or understanding of what went before—again, nothing to think about.

Our history *is* much of our shadow. This is why, I think, it is so easy now for America to jog happily behind a two-bit dictator who calls himself "The Decider," who is the exact image (the perfect American, as Jan said) of the anti-intellectual, ignorant, narcissistically self-preoccupied, indifferent, careless American who loves to see himself as loving while other people's children die.

Speaking of dictators, the way in which Hitler came to power is instructive in that it remarkably—too remarkably—parallels the machinations that went into getting Bush into office the first time. And now, thanks to Dubya, we too have a "Homeland" *über alles*. Of course, being Jewish, I have a serious persecution complex, so I may be a little melodramatic. But I'll be on red alert watching where the next concentration camp (outside of Guantanamo) will be built for Americans who are caught thinking. (George Orwell has turned over hundreds of times in his grave already, poor soul.)

Jan: Reading Lyn's very juicy words (never mind the meat, they go down fast), and reflecting on my own, they both seem so harsh and leave me wondering about our eager criticism and how we got there. Then a very Jungian conclusion about the extremes occurs to me. I think Jung's basic tenet about neurosis being a question of blockage and unbalance and loss of circulation applies here. There is a Polynesian tale about a great goddess who came along and gave the people all they wanted: prosperity and comfort and wealth. Abundance.

Then after a certain time, the people rose up and killed her, and balance was restored as poverty and deprivation returned to create balance in the collective.

I think our collective abundance, especially 20th-century prosperity of a kind never before seen in history, has doomed us to our present blindness.

Very few individuals or families deal well with great wealth. We know that from observation and our analytical practices. Great wealth isolates, creates entitlement, lack of incentive, and lack of necessity. In fact, in studies at the Menninger Clinic, the statistically largest percentage of psychopaths was found among the very rich elements of the population. At Menninger, the staff speculated that this was mainly because for the very rich, there are rarely serious consequences to their behavior.

So, I think we can apply this to a certain extent to a country. The incredible wealth and prosperity that the U.S. created and lived in for the past 50 years has made us isolated from the necessity to empathize with other cultures, including our own poor, entitled and narrow-minded and careless. You have to visit middle class people in other "rich" countries, such as Canada, France, and Germany, to see the difference. American homes are simply incredibly full of things and gadgets and modern "conveniences" that most people outside of the States would consider exotic luxuries.

So I think the rule of the extremes prevails. Too much poverty and suffering or too much wealth and prosperity both create the conditions for anti-social, anti-community behavior.

Now, I know this is less true as we get into the 21ˢᵗ century and Americans fall behind in all standards of social and economic well being. But, there are still enough extremely well-off people to carry the ball into narcissistic anti-social behavior.

As with individuals, perhaps the only thing that would create a major shift in these selfish values would be a disaster. But what kind? Katrina certainly didn't make a dent in the *zeitgeist*. Maybe a huge economic depression in which even the richest were touched? And people started needing each other?

Lyn: Jan, excellent point about abundance leading to blindness (metaphorically, not medically). I was also struck by your realization about the harshness of our responses, and that makes me stop and ask myself where is it coming from in *me?* I don't know for sure—but I am thinking that this harshness, almost a condemnation of attitudes in which I sit in a "superior" viewpoint, is really a slice of that collective shadow: a condemnation of attitudes which I do not see myself harboring, and therefore I am right (righteous) to condemn them.

A lot of my own hard criticism of what goes on politically comes from my fear and insecurity, rising not only from a personal neurosis (early family dynamics, my own odd character traits, unfilled needs, etc.), but from my shaky demographic position: an older Jewish lesbian in a culture which disparages (at best) all three categories. (And there is still enough anti-Semitism to go around, even in 2007.) I want acceptance, so I condemn any attitude that is not accepting.

I was at a regular get-together with some long-time friends last week, when somehow we got into a discussion about the Middle East situation (after a rather hilarious Bush-bashing session). One of our number, a woman about 50-ish, whom I know as an acquaintance more than a friend, and who has done some pretty heroic things in her life (overcoming serious abuse, alcoholism, chronic illness, among them), said she thought the whole problem of the Middle East was that Israel was a state that had been imposed on the Palestinians and if there were no Israel, there would be no problem.

Well, she's mostly right—no Israel, no problem. That was the extent of her position on a Mideast political policy—and she is not a stupid person. But the scope of her ignorance was breathtaking, and her inability or unwillingness to deal with the reality of the last 60 years of American, European, Jewish, or Arab history was stunning.

She did not understand, for example, why the Jews didn't "just go home" after World War II — "home" to Germany, Poland, Hungary, etc. She knew nothing about American or Canadian immigration policies during WWII, nothing about the historical relationship between Jews and Muslims in the Mideast, nothing about the UN resolution which also created a Palestinian state along with Israel in 1948.

She didn't know every Arab country attacked Israel at its inception, or that those Arab countries supported the Nazi regime. But not knowing all that, she became quite entrenched in her position, got fairly worked up, irritable and defensive, trying to convince us as we tried to talk about the political and psychological flaws in her argument, which was, in a nutshell, that the Jews brought all their troubles on themselves. Now, this is the kind of naive, ignorant kind of non-thinking, know-nothing, "its-really-simple" kind of approach that drives me insane.

It also mirrors exactly the kind of simplistic, childish approach to complex human reality that marks the way Bush and his gang go about things. (Like Nancy Reagan's solution to the drug problem: "Just say no.") This woman, convinced of her loving acceptance of "everyone" without knowing who they are or what they need, reveals an undifferentiated attitude nearly identical to that which she rejects, and reveals the American shadow as rigid, petulant, and childish—quite different from the way Americans also are: easy-going, good-humored, capable, accepting of "diversity."

Since I, too, am often rigid, petulant, and childish, I'm allowed to criticize. And it is true that even though there are many faults that can be laid at America's "golden door," there is absolutely no other country on the planet that makes a better hamburger. Let's hope we never have to go to war to prove it.

Jan: I'm struck dumb (well, almost...) by your words. At how open and true they are, and how anguishing. For you, for us, for the U.S.

If I were to put in my own *mea culpa*, it would go like this: Being an expatriate makes me feel both smug and guilty. Smug at realizing at age 18 that I did not want to live in a place where preppy competition on all levels seemed to erase the possibility of asking important questions and really reflecting on them. And ever since, smug at not being one of those who voted for the present administration and who appreciates the virtues of other places that take up less room and make less noise on the international scene.

Guilty at leaving and not being there to help bring about change. At the same time, I'm often appalled at how many expatriates seem to make a virtue of constantly dumping on the States and apologizing for American conduct. For me, I can only think that this simultaneous criticism and showy "*mea culpa* as an American" traces its roots to some Puritan compulsion for self improvement that we project on our country since we haven't succeeded in making ourselves into especially perfect human beings and aren't there to do our part to make change.

And yet, when we put aside all the negatives, there is still something about American energy, openness, and hopefulness that is refreshing, appealing, and unique. I often miss it, up here in this well-behaved, safe, and yet not very friendly, country.

Rob: What archetypes are driving that part of the American electorate who support a President like George W. Bush?

Lyn: This is a deceptively difficult question—at least for me, since I tend to get tangled up in my own strong emotions about contemporary politics and easily lose sight of the larger picture and its deeper currents. (Jan is much better at this than I am; even though her emotions are just as strong, she's more level-headed and insightful about collective movements.)

But I do think that the archetype of the Spirit (*animus*) drives people who voted for Bush. The spirit archetype gives energy to all lofty ideals and "lifts up" into airy generalities, away from the earthy details (which is much more the realm of the soul). The spirit archetype—at least in its darker side—tends to view things in moral categories: right and wrong, good and evil, light and dark. So it is not surprising that Bush (and his party) are interested in spreading democracy, saving the world, labeling whole countries good or evil. The spirit archetype informs the missionary zeal behind these ideas, a zeal which, like the spirit itself, knows no limits—so any means of accomplishing the spiritual goal are justifiable, such as invading a country without provocation, alienating all those political entities (like Iran or even Democrats) who oppose these spiritual ideals.

It may be that the spirit archetype is so powerful for so many people because it tends to fill a void, and the void I see it filling is one of meaningfulness in our collective life. I don't think the Christian story is as powerful as the lack of any story at all, a lack which drives collective attempts to give some purpose and meaning to our collective life. This lack is the result, I believe, of not knowing history.

I remember Jung saying that we think we are born with no myth and that we live without history, and this is "a disease, absolutely abnormal." Without knowing one's history, as a country or as an individual, or without even a *sense* of history and its importance in shaping our present situations, a void opens, with its attendant anxiety, even panic. It becomes very difficult to know what the *real* threat is, where it comes from, what its historical roots are, and what that might suggest for a plan to address it.

Bush is, like so many who support him, an ahistorical person who does not act from a psychologically grounded, reflective depth of knowledge and thought, but from a spiritual perch so high above reality that he (they) sees nothing except the endless sky and limitless possibilities of what he (they) can do—without counting the cost or weighing the consequences.

Some of this has certainly infected the Democratic party, which has (to my mind) been driven more by the archetype of soul, or anima. Historically, the party has attracted the poorer classes, the less powerful, the socially questionable, and, interestingly enough, the independent thinkers. They have always been sort of scrappy, messy in their infighting, ears relatively close to the ground. Their emphasis has been on relationship (they tend to an Aphrodite approach), on social issues, and domestic well-being.

These are concerns governed by the archetype of soul. The energy of the anima tends to move horizontally, between persons and groups, at ground level, while the energy of the animus tends to move vertically, from earth to heaven. It would seem that the task of our collective life is to reach a point of intersection—what we call "moderation," although I can't think of how this has been, or can be, possible, for when we reach that point, everything stops moving.

Ironically, the Democrats have, in the last century, produced the most intellectually gifted and philosophical presidents—qualities of the spirit. Presidents with minds like Wilson, Roosevelt, Kennedy, and even the pragmatist Clinton are (pardon the pun) head and shoulders above their Republican counterparts (Harding, Coolidge, Hoover, Eisenhower, Reagan, Bush I, Bush II), but they were also presidents who held power during times that required more soul, less spirit—

Wilson during WWI, Roosevelt during the Depression and WWII, Kennedy articulating a vision in the Cold War that Eisenhower could not, and Clinton, in perhaps a lesser crisis, restoring the economy that tanked in the late 1980s under first Reagan and then Bush I.

I would add that in addition to the archetype of the spirit that drives the conservative attitude in its Republican expression, it is a distinctly *saturnine* spirit, the archetype of the paranoid old man, Saturn, the misogynist god who rules prisons and money. And this spirit, as I said before, is beginning to infect the Democratic Party— witness the many newly elected Democrats who are socially conservative, in contrast to their party's history. So while I am quite happy overall with the outcome of the election (midterm election— 2006), I am not particularly optimistic that things will change soon or for the better, although perhaps at least a little bit of soul will be enough to get us turned in a productive direction again, and that turn begins in Iraq.

Jan: Wow, I think Lyn really nailed it. Very insightful, brilliant analysis I had not thought of at all. All I would add is more reductive: i.e., Republicans representing more the Father, Democrats more the puer/sibling. Father in so much as "law and order," "family values," and other Establishment, status quo slogans appeal to people's need for security, or appearance of. And though Bush Jr. tried, as Lyn said so well, to rule overtly from the spirit archetype, his father was still, I think, in the minds of many voters present as the "guarantee." The whole idea of dynasty representing a return of the repressed in our New World psyche.

However, another archetype I would mention would be the Salesman. Hermes, perhaps, but I don't think the Greeks really had a god who incarnated the Salesman archetype. It belongs to the age of capitalism and certainly reigns prominently in the American psyche. As the first MBA president, I think Bush managed to captivate a lot of people who identify with business and believe both that a "sucker is born every minute," or whatever P. T. Barnum said, and that government should be run like a corporation. All the people I know who vote Republican and for Bush (while holding their noses because they don't really think he has much class...), do so with conviction that freedom for business is the basic American value and should be our most important export as well as domestic pillar.

Democrats, on the other hand, I think, represent more sibling values. Ones of cooperation, mutual help, horizontal not vertical attitudes. Clinton was always more a brother than a father, feeling for people, going on about his dysfunctional family. (Interesting that Bush Jr. has never talked of his dysfunctional family, and it never really gets out just how awful Barbara has been—*noblesse oblige*—or what a terrible father he's been).

Lyn might point out that Clinton's feeling-ness was a reflection of soul, above all. Maybe so. But I think he really was more a "democrat" in the sense of wanting participation and equality for the citizens, his peers, more than secrecy and power which the negative father archetype seeks in the persons of Bush Jr.'s cabinet and White House.

I think the Salesman archetype is driving the country. Hermes IS the ultimate con-man, after all, which is how so many Americans perceive politicians—always trying to "sell" them something. Hermes was the god of thieves, con-men, and hucksters of all sorts, the patron of P. T. Barnums everywhere. The ancient Greeks considered Hermes the god of commerce—because he provides a hermetic language (concealing defective goods, obscuring intentions, fudging prices, etc.) and is happily duplicitous in his dealings. He is an amoral god and so not bound by ethical concerns of any sort. Definitely add The Salesman to the archetypal repertoire that drives the American political scene. And while I think Republicans tend to be more in thrall to this archetype than Democrats, the attitude is so ingrained in the American political psyche that it is really all-inclusive, and we all buy "the party line" at one time or another—no matter which party or line it is.

Rob: How have you found Jungian psychology helpful in your engagement with the outer world?

Jan: First of all, just to pass the time, I sometimes try to remember and imagine my life and world perspective "pre-Jung." And find it's nearly impossible. Impossible to see the world without interpreting it through ideas of shadow, archetypes, typology, and more clinical notions of neurosis—mine and others. Movies, politics, the neighbors, and my dog all get frequently splashed with Jungian colors. Often this is enriching. It helps me put events and people into a larger context and increases both my appreciation and understanding of them. Sometimes, admittedly, it's defensive. It puts things into a sort of box I can control, but interferes with just engaging with them and letting them unfold. The more stressed or frustrated I feel, the more Jungian psychology can become for me a defensive, "gottcha" way of coping with the Other. I imagine, however, this is true for all us; our way of seeing the world can be a curtain to open up or close off from the things going on outside.

In general, though, there is no doubt that I feel incredibly lucky to have found this particular *weltanschauung*. It adds dimensions and complexity and fascination to everything it focuses on.

More personally again, I definitely find that when I am doing my own inner work, taking the time to read and reflect on psyche, my dreams, and feelings and images as a way to restore my own psychic balance, then Jungian psychology not only serves as a precious guide to the inner world but helps create more openness and creativity in seeing the outer world. When I neglect this personal aspect, I find it is easy to slip into intellectualizing the terms and notions, short-changing both myself and others.

Finally, there is no doubt that being steeped day and night in my practice and other Jungian activities makes it sometimes difficult to engage easily and deeply with people who haven't a clue about it. This is an inevitable consequence of any vocation, I think. And I suspect it has less to do with Jungian psychology itself than the fact that many of those of us who "chose" it—or perhaps were chosen by it—were already searchers or outsiders from mainstream society, and that being analysts simply gave us a meaningful container to live out this archetype.

Lyn: Wow, what a question! It would take a book to answer fully, so I'll try to keep it down to a paragraph in the prologue to the first chapter of the book of the multi-volume set.

Like Jan, I find it hard to remember life "pre-Jung," and now can't really imagine how I could have lived any other way. For me, it wasn't just the ideas that gave me a means of engaging with myself and the outer world—although those ideas have become not merely mental constructions but the stuff of living, breathing imagination—it was originally my personal experience in Jungian analysis, which came before I read or knew anything about psychology. I don't think it was a very good analysis in terms of helping me understand myself or my inner world or how I "worked" as a personality. But it did open to me the possibility of what I came to understand as "the psychological life," and it was this possibility that opened the world to me, inside and out.

The rich perspective of Jungian thought has animated the world for me, giving value to what is usually not valued (the eccentric, the pathologized, the hidden and weak, the subjective, the visceral), and providing an objective point of reference in which I can see both myself and the other(s) in a relationship that always has a larger, deeper context. I don't always *have* this objectivity—but I know it's there, so even when I lose my bearings in the heat of conflict or an upsurge in my own neurotic eclipses, I know there is an objective point from which the situation can be observed, understood, analyzed, and felt. Though I am more passionate about some things than others—horse racing, politics, friendships, good literature, dixieland music, and Shrek movies—I see the world through a Jungian lens, from an archetypal perspective, which deepens significance, heightens meaning, and increases the enjoyment and pleasure of the world immeasurably. It also increases the anguish that much too, watching killing and violence on a monstrous scale go on around the world, where my psychological understanding does not necessarily alter the reality of those who suffer it.

Like Jan, I too tend to fall into a defensive position and use Jungian psychology wrongly when I forget what the terms of engagement are. But there is a built-in self-correcting attitude that is at the core of Jungian psychology. For me, this is perhaps the most compelling idea I take from Jung: the notion that psyche is not in us, not fragmented into bits and pieces individually parceled out, but that we are in psyche—*esse in anima*—that we have our being in soul. We are contained in it, it is not confined to us. So my engagement with the outer world—persons, ideas, animals, geologic forms, whatever is there that makes the world—is a natural and inevitable given, waiting for me to step into relationship with it, so to speak. I just need to remember to let it come into me on its own terms, and then the poet promises that all's well that ends well.

Rob: Thanks, Jan and Lyn, this has been much fun and very interesting.

Jan: Many, many thanks to you for all your patience and persistence in "sorting the seeds" of Lyn's and my verbosity!

Lyn: This has really been great fun. A bit brain-stretching at times, but it's good to preserve elasticity of all cells after you pass a certain age. As we say in horse racing, Rob: it's been a ride. Thank you!

HEADLINE:
"POLITICS BANISHES PSYCHOLOGY!"

Today it is a major challenge for anyone to carry on a civil political discussion. I would go a step further and suggest that it may be even more difficult to conduct a civil *psychological* discussion about politics. When I was in law school, my professors often discussed issues on which "reasonable minds may differ." As I see it, reasonable-mindedness is as much an expression of psychological activity as it is a requisite for civil discourse, so, as psychologists, we may well ask: Are "reasonable minds" at the forefront of discussions today about controversial issues such as gay rights, reproductive rights, physician-assisted suicide, the decision to invade Iraq and how to end the war, the role of religion in public life?

The United States has always been a contentious nation. From the shooting of Alexander Hamilton by Vice-President Aaron Burr in a duel, to the bloody and protracted Civil War, to the assassination of four presidents, to the attempts made on the lives of several others, to the impeachment of three (of which two went to trial and the third

John A. Desteian, J.D., is a 1983 graduate of the C. G. Jung Institute in Zurich and a practicing Jungian analyst and licensed psychologist in St. Paul, Minnesota. He is also a member of the Minnesota Bar Association. He is the author of *Coming Together-Coming Apart: The Union of Opposites in Love Relationships* (Boston: Sigo Press, 1990) and a contributor to *The Soul of Popular Culture*, M.L. Kittelson, ed. (Chicago: Open Court Press, 1998).

resigned), America has raged, and raged again, against itself. Debate and discourse have always been strident in U.S. politics, but this does not belie the current perception, shared even by some scholars, that *our* times are different, that a substantive qualitative and quantitative change has come over the country.[1]

Of course our times are different! A categorical change has taken place in the United States, a change that is evident in the angry faces and voices of politicians, public figures, and ordinary citizens. But it is not anger *per se* that makes our times different—the anger of the 1850s and 1860s, for example, was explosive, rending the entire nation. Rather, it is the psychological condition that the anger expresses that makes our situation today unique.

One might argue that the United States has ceased to be a psychological nation altogether. By the term "psychological nation" I mean that as a nation America was born out of the psychological development of the human race as it evolved from our ancestors' earliest religious rituals and philosophical wonderings about themselves and their relation to the world and the cosmos down to the 18th century. The constitution and Constitution of the nation continued to evolve over the next two hundred years, becoming more egalitarian in appearance and theory, if not always in practice. However, in the past thirty years, that advancement has been threatened by a reactionary— even atavistic—backlash against the evolution of psychological understanding as manifested in the significant changes that occurred over the course of American history, in such advances as universal suffrage, the end of slavery, equal protection under the law, and the recognition of a woman's reproductive rights.

These advances are the result of changes in the constitution of human consciousness and reflect a fundamental restructuring of what Wolfgang Giegerich calls the "syntax" (or *logical form*) of psychological thinking, a change that Giegerich speaks of as a dramatic shift from *mythos* to *logos*. That we are, as a nation, unaware that this change has taken place in the syntax, or form, of our psychological thinking is central to the problem of our time. There is a tacit assumption that *mythos* and *logos* can co-exist and that they can interact with each other, that the psyche is capable of holding simultaneously two fundamentally different organizing forms of consciousness. We are, thus, unable to appreciate the psychological consequences of attempting to paper over the cracks in the American psyche. Ordinary usage suggests that only *individuals* can have a psychology. However, the American experiment, it can be argued, is itself a psychological project, a child of psychological reflection, of *logos* (or the thought of the psyche). The nation's debates, policies, and actions are what Giegerich might call the "semantics" (i.e., *lexis* or *content*) of that psychological project.

The nation's original psychological venture was, above all else, an outgrowth of the upheavals in philosophy, religion, and economics that took place in Europe and the colonies between approximately 1500 and 1800. Those disciplines were, in effect, the "psychology" of the time, before the "science" of psychology proper came into being. The changes that transformed the economic, political, and religious horizons of those years reflected the evolution of Western consciousness, and were themselves a consequence of psychological reflection.

The United States could not have emerged had no new economic consciousness crystallized out of feudalism. The feudal economic system, in turn, could not have collapsed without a prior psychological shift in the general attitude towards authority (namely, the view of the feudal lord as absolute master), and the consequent emphasis on the status of the human *qua* human. This same shift in attitude to authority manifested itself within religious consciousness, precipitating the Protestant Reformation. Martin Luther undermined the authority of the Catholic Church by claiming that the individual had direct access to God without the intercessory mediation of a priesthood or the institution of the Church. Had there been no Reformation, there would have been no call for the freedom to follow conscience in matters of religious belief and practice, no migration of Pilgrims to the New World, and no discussion of the issue of the separation between church and state. This entire chain of historical events turned on one pivotal factor: a change in the constitution of Western consciousness, a change by which it became possible for the notion of authority to evolve into something beyond itself and thus complete the transition from *mythos* to *logos*.

Psychologically, documents such as the Constitution and the Bill of Rights (and consequently the makeup and *modus operandi* of the U.S. government—and of government in general—and its relationship to its citizens and the world at large) have served two functions. For the framers of the Constitution, these documents embodied the semantic consequences of the psychological changes that had taken place at that time. For us, in this and every other time since their creation, they serve as *an historical record* of these consequences.

To reiterate, then, there are two distinct dimensions of psychological thought: (1) syntax, or form, which has to do with the status or mode of thinking (in our time, thinking informed by *logos* rather than *mythos*); (2) semantics, that is, the contents of thought (the ideas that make up the fabric of political discourse, for example). As we have just seen, syntax influences semantics; the form of thought affects its content. In other words, *how* we are thinking changes *what* we think. ✳

A CASE STUDY IN THE PSYCHOLOGICAL ANALYSIS OF POLITICAL DISCOURSE

If psychology has something to say about politics, is the reverse also true? Does politics have something to say about psychology? And, if so, what?

President G. W. Bush once commented that he understood that the Iraq War was taking its toll on the American psyche. It would appear that he was really just referring to the fact the polls indicated that Americans were responding to the war in large numbers with considerably negative emotions. While emotions are indeed associated with the psyche, Bush's remark cannot be taken as a political commentary on psychology. Aside from this, it is common knowledge that politicians use psychological theories of learning, attitude development, and opinion formation to shape public opinion through carefully crafted propaganda, though we seldom get a first-hand look at this process in action. However, this use of applied psychology to elicit preferred responses (something done routinely in advertising) does not qualify as politics having something to say about psychology either. We have to look elsewhere, reading between the often vague lines of political discourse. If we do this, we find a particularly compelling instance of political commentary on psychology in a speech delivered by then-presidential advisor Karl Rove to the New York Conservative Party on June 22, 2005. This is what he said:

> ... [P]erhaps the most important difference between conservatives and liberals can be found in the area of national security. Conservatives saw the savagery of 9/11 and the attacks

and prepared for war; liberals saw the savagery of the 9/11 attacks and wanted to prepare indictments and *offer therapy and understanding* for our attackers. ... Conservatives believed it was time to unleash the might and power of the United States military against the Taliban; ... liberals believed it was time to ... submit a petition.[2] (Italics added.)

For psychology, the question is: Did we, as the audience, and Rove, as the speaker, *realize* the *psychological* import of his remarks? The stark contrast Rove drew between "conservatives" and "liberals" had the effect (and we might infer also the intent) of provoking intense reactions on both sides. It evoked taunting and derisive laughter from conservative commentators and partisans on one side, along with a sense of superiority, and it induced embarrassment and outrage among the affronted, maligned, "whining" liberal commentators and partisans on the other.

Senator Charles Schumer of New York, a Democrat, said, with all disingenuous sincerity: "In New York, where everyone unified after 9/11, the last thing we need is somebody who seeks to divide us for political reasons."[3] In a story written by Raymond Hernandez, we are told that

> Democrats seized on Mr. Rove's comments, clearly hoping to put Republicans on the defensive by issuing harsh criticisms throughout the day in press releases, at a hastily arranged news conference in the Capitol and in remarks delivered on the Senate floor. The parade of Democrats attacking Mr. Rove included Senators Charles E. Schumer and Hillary Rodham Clinton of New York, Senators Jon Corzine and Frank R. Lautenberg of New Jersey; and Senators Christopher J. Dodd and Joseph I. Lieberman of Connecticut.[4]

What passed for political discourse in response to Rove's statement, would, from a psychological perspective, be more properly described as emotion-driven posturing or histrionic speechifying, a kind of auto-erotic political exhibitionism. Like all forms of quasi-masturbatory behavior, it brought about a momentary orgasm of pleasure or a temporary release of tension at the expense of real thinking and understanding.

No one in the public arena appeared to pay any attention to the psychological meaning implicit in Rove's comments (which were tantamount to a *banishment of psychological understanding from political discourse*) when he said: "Conservatives saw the savagery of the 9/11 attacks and prepared for war; liberals saw the savagery of the 9/11 attacks and wanted to prepare indictments and *offer therapy and understanding* for our attackers ..." (italics added). At the semantic level, we could debate whether or not the content of this statement is true—whether conservatives are different from liberals in the way Rove asserts—or why Rove made the statement—whether his motives were pure or driven by political calculation. However, here I would like us, rather, to enter into Rove's assertion at the syntactic level and analyze what it has to say about psychological *understanding*.

We do not know whether Rove himself was aware of the psychological meaning of his statement, or whether he had ingested his own soporific bromide to such an extent that he was asleep to the psychological implications of his caricature. What we do know is that the ensuing storm of derision and protestations certainly did not concern itself with the psychological substance of Rove's assertions. In fact, Rove's salvo and the response to it show that he, his allies, his opponents, and popular political discourse itself had already banished psychological understanding and meaning from the political scene.

INCISIVE THINKING AND PSYCHOLOGICAL UNDERSTANDING IN AMERICAN POLITICS

Not only has psychological understanding been banished, but thinking itself has been precluded. Here I am not referring to thinking as we use it in common parlance, that is, thinking as the thinking function, or thinking up something witty to say (a frequent pastime in the public and political arena), or plotting ways to make others feel small, or daydreaming about buying a better car. The kind of thinking I am referring to here, the thinking that has been banished from popular political discourse, is *incisive* thinking, thinking critically about what is, what has been, and what will be said, enacted, thought. This sort of thinking cannot be conciliatory. It must be civil, but, like the incisor teeth, it is at the same time cutting, tearing, shredding, violent, and destructive—not of personalities, but of ideas.

Truly psychological thinking is incisive thinking—without this "cutting into" things there can be no psychological understanding. It is not the "nuanced" thinking that John Kerry was erroneously but successfully accused of in the 2004 presidential campaign. While incisive thinking may go on in academia, such thinking may not necessarily be *psychological*. For that, the reflective interplay between thesis and contradiction is necessary, and the totality of psychological activity—instincts, memories, emotions, and images, as well as incisive thought—needs to be the focus of attention. To find examples of incisive thinking and psychological understanding in American politics, we have to go as far back as the Federalist and Anti-Federalist papers written by the participants in the Constitutional Convention of 1787. Those expositions often express a back-and-forth between the nation's founders as they engaged in considering the United States as both experiment and problem. Now that psychological understanding and incisive thinking have been banished from the political realm, it is left to those *outside* the center of political activity to find both a language and a stance to speak on behalf of the exiled (incisive thinking and psychological understanding) and to speak against what lies behind that exile.

Another way to understand what is going on in American politics is to think of incisive thinking and psychological understanding as being subjected to a process of de-meaning, in both senses of that word: demeaning as *debasement*, as seen in the debasement implicit in Rove's caricature of liberals and the derision it evoked, and de-meaning as "*drained of meaning*" (and psychological understanding), as the following analysis illustrates.

When Rove said that the liberals in America wanted to "offer therapy and understanding" in response to the 9/11 attacks, he was not seriously suggesting that the liberals were literally calling for therapy to be offered to members of al-Qaeda and the Taliban. The very notion of offering therapy to one's sworn enemies is ridiculous, yet in juxtaposing therapy with the idea of understanding, Rove made both *appear* absurd with a not-so-subtle appeal to guilt by association. This would seem to be both the intent and the effect of Rove's coupling of therapy with understanding. However, there is nothing absurd about understanding an event or person psychologically, even one's enemies.[5] To understand something is not necessarily to condone or excuse it. Rove's rhetorical sleight of hand was clearly calculated to insinuate that those who would seek to understand the attackers are as absurd as those who would offer them therapy. It paints understanding with the same brush as therapy, evoking images of support and empathy (and, by extension, coddling and making excuses), and it thereby pre-empts the possibility of apprehending the word "understanding" in its full range of meanings. By association with the word *therapy* and the images it evokes, the word *understanding* becomes drained of all its meaning: it becomes de-meaned.

To get an even better understanding of the way in which language is de-meaned, we need to translate Rove's statement from another psychological angle as well. "Conservatives believed it was time to unleash ... might and power," while "liberals" wanted "to offer therapy and understanding for our attackers." The two contrasting characterizations counterpose *action* ("unleash[ing] ... might and power") and *understanding*, as if the two were in opposition to each other, and as if they represented an intrinsic hierarchical antinomy, namely, that understanding is *not action* (hence, *inaction*) and, by extension, antithetical to action, and that action (in Rove's sense of unleashing might and power) is the necessary and sole means to salvation and safety. In Rove's call to "action" we hear an echo from the cowboy movies of a bygone era: "Shoot first and ask questions later."

The justification behind the privileging of *Rove's particular brand of action* over the *action* of understanding is obvious: if one stops to reflect in a crisis, one may well be dead before one can formulate a measured response. In psychological terms, when a threat is perceived an instinct is triggered, and Rove's sort of action (unleashing the power and might of the United States) is the immediate instinct-generated response to the threat. From this perspective, it would *appear* to make psychological sense that "action" should have been the policy of choice for the Bush Administration, but this would hold true only under two conditions (neither of which existed at the time): (1) if the time frame were such that delay would have been disastrous; or (2) if pursuing the path of understanding precluded the taking of decisive action, that is, if the U.S. could not take military action *if* it engaged in an attempt at understanding.

We know that some amount of planning (though precisely how much and how competently has been the subject of considerable debate) went into the war against the Taliban after the 9/11 attacks. Thus, the facts make it clear that the immediacy of an instinctual response was not at play in the decision to wage war in Afghanistan. There was indeed time to ask questions first and shoot later, and the Bush Administration took that time to plan a strategy of response. Since there was time for strategizing, there was certainly time for understanding, assuming that the administration could reflect and strategize at the same time. The first of the two conditions, then, did not obtain, either logically or empirically.

The second condition (that is, understanding precludes "action") seems not to have prevailed either. In considering the proposition that the U.S. could not take action if it succeeded in understanding in *this* situation (the 9/11 attacks), we must first turn our attention to what it is that is to be understood. What is the object of our search for understanding? What are we trying to understand? I would submit that our efforts to understand in the wake of 9/11 might profitably have been directed towards the history of Western colonial and neo-colonial attitudes towards the Middle East and Islam; the religious, social, political, and economic interactions between the West and East; the dangers of inciting a population of desperate true believers, both within Islam and among the neoconservative ranks in the United States. That the Bush Administration did not consider these factors in its response to the attacks is telling. As with any situation viewed psychologically, what is excluded from thought (or reflection) is as significant as what is included. Given these considerations, it is by no means a foregone conclusion that understanding the attackers after 9/11 would have prevented the United States from taking action, but it would certainly have influenced the kind of action taken.

The Death of Psychological Understanding

We are now ready to reflect on the meaning of Rove's statement and its psychological implications. If we take him at his word, we must banish understanding from policy making and hence from our actions. *Action must be inoculated against understanding. Understanding must not be allowed to infect (affect) action. Action must be immunized against understanding.* Is this what Rove meant? If it was, would he want us to know that? Unfortunately, we are left with these questions unanswered. But if this is an accurate assessment of the implications of Rove's assertion—namely, that understanding does not qualify as an action, and that action is not to be informed by understanding—it says something about us and our nation's commitment to thinking psychologically. That Rove could get away with making such a statement and was not questioned in the public arena about its implications is an indication that we as a people tacitly acknowledge that the statement is true. Our silence is an obituary, a notice declaring that psychological understanding is dead, and therefore not a part of our public political discourse. That we are left unable to answer the questions just posed about Rove is one consequence of that death. Rove does not have to answer these questions because even as we ask them now, they are not being asked with the full weight of public pressure behind them to compel a response. From the fact that these questions have not been raised until now we can conclude that, as a nation, we do not know what questions to ask because we do not think incisively about what we are hearing and being told, about what we are seeing and doing.

What would have been the proper focus of our understanding in response to the attacks of 9/11? This question needs to be considered incisively and psychologically. Rove asserted that the liberals sought understanding *of the attackers,* and by coupling "understanding" with "therapy," he implied that "understanding" the attackers meant either supporting or empathizing with them, or, much worse, coddling them and looking for ways to excuse their behavior. Let us consider what "understanding the attackers" might mean if it is taken out Rove's equation and disconnected from the de-meaning association with therapy. We might begin by analyzing the dictionary definitions of "understand," namely: (1) to grasp the meaning of something; (2) to interpret in one of a number of possible ways; (3) to achieve a grasp of the nature or explanation of something; (4) to show a sympathetic or tolerant attitude toward something (*Webster's New Collegiate Dictionary*). We can insert these four definitions in turn into Rove's statement: (1) the liberals sought to *grasp the meaning of* the attackers (the meaning of their actions? of the consequences of their actions?); (2) the liberals sought to *interpret* the attackers *in one of a number of possible ways* (interpret their motivations? their intentions?); (3) the liberals sought to *achieve a grasp of the nature or explanation of* the attackers (the nature of their power? their attraction? their source of financing?); (4) the liberals sought to *show a sympathetic or tolerant attitude toward* the attackers.

The first three of these four possibilities make no sense if the object of "understand" is the attackers themselves rather than some aspect of what they did—actions, consequences, motivations, intentions, scope, attraction, source of financing, etc. Only the last of the four sentences makes sense without the addition of this kind of information. It is only this fourth sense of the word "understand" that keeps the focus on the attackers themselves, rather than on something relating to them or their actions. This eliminates the first three senses of "understand" and limits us to only one interpretation, namely that to understand the attackers means to show a sympathetic or tolerant attitude towards them. We have already inferred that Rove's intention, whether he was aware of it or not, and the effect of his statement, was to focus attention on the idea that the liberals wanted to be, and therefore *were*, sympathetic to and tolerant of the attackers.

That he coupled the word "understanding" with the idea of "offering therapy" not only reinforced the implication that the liberals were "tolerant and sympathetic" to the attackers, but also made the point indirectly that the liberals stood in relation to the attackers as *one in a position of trust or confidence who can make such an offer of therapy*, that is, as a friend, family member, or advisor. By extension, then, liberals are traitors whose tolerance of and sympathy for the attackers make them complicit in the attack, co-conspirators, or fellow-travelers, to use the term applied to liberals during the Cold War red-scare era of Joe McCarthy, Richard Nixon, and Roy Cohn.

Those who would dismiss this interpretation as far-fetched would do well to consider *Treason: Liberal Treachery from the Cold War to the War on Terrorism*[6] by Ann Coulter. She begins her book with the following:

> Liberals have a preternatural gift for striking a position on the side of treason. You could be talking about Scrabble and they would instantly leap to an anti-American position. Everyone says liberals love America, too. No they don't. Whenever the nation is under attack, from within or without, liberals side with the enemy. This is their essence. The left's obsession with the crimes of the West and their Rousseauian respect for Third World savages[7] all flow from this subversive goal.

Like Coulter, but using a linguistically more subtle form of insinuation, Rove surreptitiously introduces the notion of "liberal treachery," and effectively equates understanding the enemy with treason. This particular interpretation may have been lost on the "liberals," who are, regrettably, just as prone to avoiding incisive thinking as the "conservatives." The effectiveness of Rove's strategy rested upon the fact that the sentiments he expressed would be *emotionally and ideationally* familiar to those who he knew already held the belief that liberals side with the enemy and commit treason and who would hear the reinforcement of this belief in their own vernacular.[8] By virtue of this emotional familiarity, we might even infer that his speech was offered for its histrionic effect: theatrical, exaggerated, insincere, and unrestrained. Whether there is any truth to this supposition as to his motivation or not, the logical inference to be drawn from his remarks is that those who would engage in the activity of understanding the actions, motivations, intentions, scope, attraction, sources of financing, etc. of the attackers would be engaging in treason. Clearly, if one were to put the question directly to Rove, it is doubtful that he would answer with as much overt honesty *as to his subjective belief* as Coulter displays in her book. It is even questionable whether he consciously harbors such attitudes or convictions. But, in answer to the question immediately before us: *What is the proper object of our understanding in response to the attacks of 9/11?* Rove's answer would be: "Nothing!"

With the death of psychological understanding, political discourse is reduced to empty rhetoric, and Rove's comments on the differences between conservatives and liberals represent, on the collective cultural level, merely the logical and psychological vacuity of the prevailing political culture in the United States today. It is not as if Rove were the only producer of this kind of discourse. Those who characterize G. W. Bush as "crazy," whether this is meant as a derogatory epithet or as a psychological diagnosis, engage in equally vacuous political discourse. Of course, politics does not have to be empty-headed. It is so only because *we* choose to make it that way. While Rove's speech may be a far cry from the lofty *ideals* of the nation's founders as embodied in the Declaration of Independence and the Constitution of the United States, or as debated in the Federalist and Anti-Federalist Papers, it is very much in keeping with the histrionic tone that has characterized mundane political discourse in the United States throughout its history. (A discussion of the psychological dimension of the desire for empty-headed discourse must be postponed until another time.)

We are left with the conclusion that in our time the psychological function of political speech as histrionic rhetoric is merely to reinforce already held opinions and beliefs and to inoculate them with emotionally poisonous antibodies that immunize them from infection by opposing viewpoints. How did this change in the function of political discourse come about, and when? And what are the consequences of the attempt to banish psychological understanding from politics?

PSYCHOLOGICAL TRUTH: SELF-REFLECTIVE TRUTH-SEEKING

The most fundamental consequence of the banishment of psychological understanding from the political sphere is that along with it, psychological truth is exiled as well. In a political system in which psychological understanding plays no active role, it is not only the semantics of thought but also its syntax that goes into permanent eclipse.

Any discussion of psychological truth has to begin with an analysis of the notion of truth in general. And we cannot talk about the truth of anything without first understanding, or at least exploring, the different kinds of truth. A good starting point is the difference between truth in the material and the immaterial (that is, non-material) realms. A visual image, such as a photograph, belongs in the material realm, and its truth can be determined quite easily if the notion of truth is limited to accuracy in the representation and perception of material reality. This kind of truth does not interest us, though it might interest philosophers and experimental psychologists. Factual assertions such as "Columbus sailed into the Western Hemisphere in 1492 as he was searching for a route to the East Indies" or "The trash can has been placed at the curb to be picked up tomorrow" are true statements, but they are primarily descriptions of events that have occurred—and this kind of "historical" truth does not concern us either.

Can scientific knowledge be considered material truth? It has been argued convincingly that scientific knowledge is nothing more than a set of statements about preponderant probability in the physical universe and is based on a generally accepted consensus of perception. In fact, science does not purport to be, and is not really concerned with, truth at all, but rather with the establishment of the probability of a causal relationship between various physical phenomena, with the positing of hypotheses and the making of observations and measurements, and with the predictability, validity, and reliability of the conclusions and implications that arise out of them. Scientific knowledge might also thus be termed scientific fact. In reflecting on what constitutes psychological truth, then, we can eliminate scientific knowledge or fact, since scientific facts exist in relation to the material world and are the product of empirical observation. Alan R. White wrote in his 1970 book *Truth*: "I would like to suggest that *fact* is a notion which applies neither to items in the world, such as features, events, situations, etc., nor what is said about the world, like true statements, but to *what* the world is like, to *how* things, necessarily or contingently are."[9] White's assertion does not necessarily carry any weight in our discussion, but it seems as good a definition as any to adopt in determining what constitutes a fact. Given its predication on probability (and given White's definition), scientific fact can be characterized, for our purposes, as a contingent understanding of what the world is like or how things are, an understanding that can be "disputed, challenged, assumed, or proved."[10] We can thus talk about a scientific fact as being "objective," but only if we limit the meaning of "objective" to saying something true in a contingent sense about a material object or the mechanisms by which that object exists or moves in the perceptible world.

Unfortunately, the exclusion of scientific knowledge does not bring us any closer to positing a rigorous notion of psychological truth. If psychological truth is not fact or event, what then is it? Rove's assertions about conservatives and liberals *seem* to fall into the category of fact—a statement of what the world is like or how things are, necessarily or contingently, and capable of being disputed, challenged, or proved. Of course, since they lack any of the validity or reliability of scientific knowledge, they decompose as fact and must therefore be relegated to the realm of opinion and belief—and even prejudice—about what the world is like and how it operates. But when we begin to consider the status of opinion and belief (not to mention prejudice), we enter the immaterial (that is, non-material) realm, the province of thought, and here we finally encounter the possibility of positing our notion of psychological truth.

All manner of thought appears to begin as an empirical observation, which is then subjected to a process of abstraction to produce meaning in the form of opinions, beliefs, prejudices, or concepts. We say "*appears to begin*" because we know, as pointed out earlier, that everything we perceive is constituted equally of what we *ex*clude as what we *in*clude. Rove's statement, as analyzed above, serves as an example of this inclusion and exclusion inherent in the formulation and propagation of opinion and belief, but also of the subjectivity involved in abstract conceptualization. In the realm of immateriality, then, to opinion, belief, and prejudice we must add the entire domain of abstraction. Consider, for example, words such as the United States, truth, honor, patriotism, justice, equality, fairness, terrorism, religion—none of these abstractions has any materiality whatsoever, but are nevertheless the "flesh and bones" of American political discourse.

We are reminded here of Hobbes's discussion of the scope of philosophy in his *Logic*, where he asserts that philosophy, by his definition, excludes the immaterial or insubstantial, and thus God, religion, revelation, and theology.[11] Hobbes claims for himself the privilege of defining philosophy (itself an abstraction) in any way he chooses, and anyone who wants to challenge his philosophy must do so on his terms. If we extend this same nominalist privilege to Rove, we must conclude that like Hobbes, Rove is free to define (by inclusion, exclusion, or confinement) the objects of his perception "psychologistically," that is, in any way he (egoistically) chooses and for whatever purpose, and to fantasize about liberals and conservatives in whatever manner strikes his wish-fulfilling fancy.[12] Yet, to cite the subjectivity of Hobbes and Rove gets us, as before, no closer to a notion of psychological truth, since subjectivity renders the notion of psychological truth vaporous at best, and vacuous at worst. It is clear from the discussion of Hobbes and Rove that subjective judgments lack universality, originating as they do in the (ego.) But what would be the point of positing a notion of psychological truth if this truth were not intrinsically universal or universally applicable? It would appear, then, that we may have to abandon the notion of psychological truth altogether if we maintain that it consists in a set of contingent universal statements. Perhaps we need to take a different approach to truth, and for this we may borrow from Foucault, *mutatis mutandis*:

> The point of departure. My intention was not to deal with the problem of truth, but with the problem of [the] truth-teller or [of] truth-telling as an activity. By this I mean that, for me, it was not a question of analyzing the internal or external criteria that would enable the Greeks and Romans, or anyone else, to recognize whether a statement or proposition is true or not. *At issue for me was rather the attempt to consider truth-telling as a specific activity, or as a role.*[13] (Italics added.)

If, following Foucault's lead, we direct our attention away from psychological truth as content, as semantics, and focus instead on truth-seeking as an activity, we can at last begin to define truth in active rather than passive terms, that is, as a psychological *process*. If we concede that beliefs, opinions, and concepts are constructed out of the empirical experiences of everyday life and are influenced by individual motivations, both conscious and unconscious, which distort, confine, include, and exclude certain data, then we have what can be called *observational dynamics*. Observational dynamics include projection, identification, projective identification, introjection, education, propaganda, entertainment, scientific research, political spin, etc.

Two conclusions arise out of the subjective nature of observational dynamics: (1) empirical observation is a dynamic interplay of oscillating interiorized and interiorizing subjectivities that influence each other; (2) any exterior point of observation is itself an effect, *a posteriori*, of oscillating subjectivities.[14] A corollary of these conclusions is that any discourse, now or in the historical record, that relies on empirical observation, and is therefore not a product of self-reflection,[15] is *necessarily* incomplete.[16] Such discourse cannot be considered to have psychological (as opposed to political, social, religious, or economic)[17] weight *as content*, but only *as function*, that is, as propaganda, to propagate a particular opinion or belief.

The conclusion that discourse cannot have psychological value as a product of truth-seeking unless it is explicitly self-reflective is nothing new. In everyday social intercourse we hear echoes of it in statements such as, "That's just your opinion." A fair amount of what passes for political discourse relies on the implicit recognition of subjectivity, which also then becomes the basis for refuting many arguments: "Global warming is just a theory." Thus, "Evolution is just a theory," implies that Creationism and Intelligent Design hold the same status as the Theory of Evolution by virtue of the supposed subjectivity of theory—"My theory is as good as yours." As we noted earlier, scientific knowledge is not truth, but rather a set of facts that express probabilities about what the world is like or how it operates, necessarily or contingently. However, scientific discourse is not beyond the reach of subjectivity. Subjectivity is the "softening agent" that makes facts, events, knowledge, and truth plastic. Yet, even as we reflect on the problem of subjectivity and its capacity to decompose the semantics of political discourse, we must not ignore psychological syntax, the form of thought.[18]

MODERN SYNTAX, ARCHAIC SEMANTICS

Before we move on to a discussion of the psychological form of thought, we might look at some examples of the application of the semantics of an outmoded syntax to current situations. First of all, it is important to be aware that the banishment of psychological understanding from political discourse is not primarily something that politicians have foisted upon an unsuspecting electorate. Rather, it is the other way around. The electorate,[19] having abnegated its own capacity for incisive thought, has contented itself with the kind of titillation—smear campaigns, negative advertising, and expressions of righteous indignation—that mimics the endorphin rush that comes from obsessive shopping, or watching a sporting event, or looking at pornography. We need consider only a couple of examples of the difference between histrionic speechifying and genuine psychological thinking to get the idea. Here is the first example, drawn from the tragedy of the terrorist attacks of September 11, 2001.

> Like many Americans, the president had seen pictures of the devastation where nearly 5,000 people lay buried. Still, he seemed awed as he stared up at the slope of twisted steel and concrete that four days ago had been towers that dominated the Lower Manhattan skyline.
>
> Climbing atop a charred fire truck, draping his arm around a 69-year-old retired firefighter, Mr. Bush grabbed a bullhorn. "We can't hear you!" someone yelled.
>
> "I can hear you," the president bellowed back. "The rest of the world hears you, and the people who knocked these buildings down will hear all of us soon."

"U.S.A.! U.S.A.! U.S.A.!" they chanted.[20]

Those who watched this event on television may have had an immediate association to the U.S.-Soviet hockey game at the Winter Olympics at Lake Placid in 1980, and to the roar of the crowd (and the rush of endorphins) as the American team pulled off an improbable upset victory. With thousands of people lying dead under the rubble of the Twin Towers, the most "meaningful" and spontaneous—that is, unconscious—association of the collective American psyche was to a meaningless sporting event, and the crowds gathered at Ground Zero behaved as if they were in an Olympic stadium, cheering their country on. The semantics and the syntax were out of sync.

Or consider John Kerry's bungled "joke" during the 2006 Congressional campaign regarding the carnage of the Iraq War. Here is one commentator's account:

> This week … he [Kerry] botched a Bush punch line so badly, that it may qualify as the political gaffe of the year. Speaking to college students in California, Kerry said, "You know, education—if you make the most of it—you study hard, you do your homework and you make an effort to be smart, you can do well. If you don't, you get [*us*] stuck in Iraq."
>
> The remark provoked a torrent of criticism from Republicans who were quick to take it out of context and broadcast it as a slam on the intelligence of U.S. troops, rather than on Bush.[21]

Kerry's unconscious associations may well have taken him back to his days as a protester during the Vietnam War, and to the use of school deferments by millions of young men to avoid the draft. Those not lucky enough to be able to go to college were, of course, sucked into the war machine. Kerry's joke, whether poorly delivered or not, qualifies as histrionic speechifying, just as do the subsequent expressions of moral outrage and righteous indignation on the part of Kerry's detractors at his alleged denigration of the American troops in Iraq or his actual impugning of Bush's intelligence.

Now contrast these two incidents with a speech (presented here in its rather lengthy entirety) by Robert F. Kennedy on April 5, 1968 to a civic group in Cleveland the day after Martin Luther King was assassinated.

Mr. Chairman, Ladies and Gentlemen,

I speak to you under different circumstances than I had intended to just twenty-four hours ago, but this is a time of shame and a time of sorrow. It is not a day for politics. I have saved this one opportunity, my only event of today, to speak briefly to you about the mindless menace of violence in America, which again stains our land and every one of our lives. It is not the concern of any one race. The victims of the violence are Black and White, rich and poor, young and old, famous and unknown. They are, most important of all, human beings whom other human beings loved and needed. No one—no matter where he lives or what he does—can be certain whom [*sic*] next will suffer from some senseless act of bloodshed. And yet it goes on and on and on in this country of ours.

Why? What has violence ever accomplished? What has it ever created? No martyr's cause has ever been stilled by an assassin's bullet. No wrongs have ever been righted by riots and civil disorders. A sniper is only a coward, not a hero; and an uncontrolled or uncontrollable mob is only the voice of madness, not the voice of the people.

Whenever any American's life is taken by another American unnecessarily—whether it is done in the name of the law or in defiance of the law, by one man or by a gang, in cold blood or in passion, in an attack of violence or in response to violence— whenever we tear at the fabric of our lives, which another man has painfully and clumsily woven for himself and his children, whenever we do this, then the whole nation is degraded.

"Among free men," said Abraham Lincoln, "there can be no successful appeal from the ballot to the bullet; and those who take such appeal are sure to lose their case and pay the costs." Yet we seemingly tolerate a rising level of violence that ignores our common humanity and our claims to civilization alike. We calmly accept newspaper reports of civilian slaughter in far-off lands. We glorify killing on movie and television screens and we call it entertainment. We make it easier for men of all shades of sanity to acquire weapons and ammunition that they desire.

Too often we honor swagger and bluster and the wielders of force; too often we excuse those who are willing to build their own lives on the shattered dreams of other human beings. Some Americans who preach non-violence abroad fail to practice it here at home. Some accuse others of rioting and inciting riots and have, by their own conduct, invited them. Some look for scapegoats, others look for conspiracies, but this much is clear: violence breeds violence, repression breeds retaliation, and only a cleansing of our whole society can remove this sickness from our souls.

For there is another kind of violence, slower but just as deadly destructive as the shot or the bomb in the night. This is the violence of institutions, indifference, inaction, and decay. This is the violence that afflicts the poor, that poisons relations between men because their skin has different colors. This is the slow destruction of a child by hunger, and schools without books, and homes without heat in the winter. This is the breaking of a man's spirit by denying him the chance to stand as a father and as a man amongst other men. And this too afflicts us all.

For when you teach a man to hate and to fear his brother, when you teach that he is a lesser man because of his color or his beliefs or the policies that he pursues, when you teach that those who differ from you threaten your freedom or your job or your home or your family, then you also learn to confront others not as fellow citizens but as enemies, to be met not with cooperation but with conquest, to be subjugated, and to be mastered.

We learn, at the last, to look at our brothers as aliens, alien men with whom we share a city, but not a community, men bound to us in common dwelling, but not in a common effort. We learn to share only a common fear, only a common desire to retreat from each other, only a common impulse to meet disagreement with force. For all this, there are no final answers for those of us who are American citizens.

Yet we know what we must do, and that is to achieve true justice among all of our fellow citizens. The question is not what programs we should seek to enact. The question is whether we can find in our own midst and in our own hearts that leadership of humane purpose that will recognize the terrible truths of our existence.

We must admit the vanity of our false distinctions, the false distinctions among men, and learn to find our own advancement in search for the advancement of all. We must admit to ourselves that our children's future cannot be built on the misfortune of another's. We must recognize that this short life can neither be ennobled or enriched by hatred or by revenge.

Our lives on this planet are too short; the work to be done is too great to let this spirit flourish any longer in this land of ours. Of course, we cannot banish it with a program, nor with a resolution. But we can perhaps remember, if only for a time, that those who live with us are our brothers, that they share with us the same short moment of life; that they seek, as do we, nothing but the chance to live out their lives in purpose and in happiness, winning what satisfaction and fulfillment that they can.

Surely this bond of common faith, surely this bond of common goals, can begin to teach us something. Surely we can learn, at the least, to look around at those of us, of our fellow men, and surely we can begin to work a little harder to bind up the wounds among us and to become in our hearts brothers and countrymen once again.

Tennyson wrote in "Ulysses":

> That which we are, we are,—
> One equal temper of heroic hearts,
> Made weak by time and fate, but strong in will
> To strive, to seek, to find, and not to yield.

Thank you very much.[22]

I have quoted this speech in its entirety for two reasons. First, what is there in it that could possibly be edited out? As an entire thought, it is complete in itself. The logic of the message builds incrementally from one paragraph to the next, and this incremental logic would be lost in any attempt to excerpt or summarize. No "sound bite" could capture the broad scope of the thought. Second, each paragraph contains either an explicit or implicit psychological perspective: "violence breeds violence, repression breeds retaliation"; "Too often we honor swagger and bluster and the wielders of force"; "We must admit the vanity of our false distinctions ... among men"; "when you teach a man to hate and to fear his brother ... then you also learn to confront others not as fellow citizens but as enemies." Commonly understood and recognized psychological mechanisms—scapegoating, repression, projection, and projective identification, among others—are implicit in Kennedy's analysis of the situation he is lamenting, as are the emotional (and hence psychic and psychological) consequences of using those mechanisms.

Consider the powerful phrase, "The vanity of our false distinctions." It encapsulates a psychological insight, on the semantic level, that modern consciousness arrived at gradually and at great cost as it evolved, on the syntactic level, over the millennia since Aristotle and other Greek philosophers found philosophical justification for slavery. This sort of psychological thinking on the semantic level is lacking in the examples of political discourse we examined earlier from Rove, Bush, and Kerry. In its place, we find empty rhetoric and righteous exhortations (both implied and explicit) that are calculated to polarize the nation. It is precisely this kind of polarization that Kennedy is lamenting in his speech. But the speech is also a vivid illustration of the process of self-reflection at the national level, with Kennedy individually taking on for the entire nation the task that it would not collectively undertake for itself: the task of looking inward at its own soul.

Self-reflection and the syntax of psychological thought are interconnected. Self-reflection involves consideration of the meaning of what is encountered as abstract thought, and abstract thought is the lexis (or content) of our present-day syntax of thought. In an age when mechanical and quantum mechanical functions have replaced the occult substances and supernatural forces of superstition in our thinking as the immediate cause of motion and emotion, it is jarring to the ear to hear a Jerry Falwell invoke the semantics of an obsolete syntax to assert a modern, reductive, mechanical causal connection between AIDS and the wrath of God. Falwell declared: "AIDS is the wrath of a just God against homosexuals. To oppose it would be like an Israelite jumping in the Red Sea to save one of Pharaoh's charioteers. ... AIDS is not just God's punishment for homosexuals; it is God's punishment for the society that tolerates homosexuals."[23] This is the conceptual equivalent of George W. Bush, as Commander-in-Chief of the U.S. Armed Forces, sacrificing an animal to invoke the blessings of the gods before embarking on the Iraq War. Imagine the uproar that would have caused. Yet Falwell's statement barely raised a murmur among rank-and-file Americans. Few were able to recognize that Falwell's semantics were out of sync with the syntax of our times, and this is precisely because self-reflection has been abandoned, both in public and in private life.

Speaking of the human response to the shift in syntax that has taken place over the past two hundred years, Giegerich writes:

> ... [T]wo opposite stances are possible. One can *either* try to hold on to and defend the truth of the past *against* the real situation

produced by historical developments *or* own up to the new situation into which history has placed us and allow oneself to be taught by it about how to think.[24]

People like Falwell choose to adopt the first stance, often with profoundly discordant and disturbing psychological consequences for individuals as well as for groups. If the discordance is not picked up at the conscious level, it nevertheless registers at the subconscious level. The consequences for truth-seeking are obvious: the truth of the present moment cannot be reached, since the semantics are formulated within the syntactic structures of the past, structures that are known to be obsolete and are believed in purely for the sake of keeping up appearances. This is particularly true in the practice of religion, where outmoded syntactic structures have become so hardened that they are difficult to break out of. Giegerich writes:

> What is left of religion once its substance has been integrated into the logical form of consciousness is only the "conventional sign," the conventional forms without living substance: the dead snakeskin after the living snake has moved out of it into new fields. One can, however, inflate even a dead snakeskin and replace the life that it does not have of its own account with one's own breath. ... Thus fundamentalism uses the old dogmas and fills them with the subjective zeal stemming from the feeling of lack and thereby gives a secondary, rigid stability and seeming life to them. Or one can use the snakeskin like an amulet; conventional forms of religion can serve as a kind of spiritual pacifier for want of a living truth; the fossil pointing to a former real life can be used as a *token* satisfaction of one's need for a symbolic or metaphysical life; the appearance can be taken for the real thing, with the same kind of silent conspiracy that is found in the tale of the emperor's new clothes. Or, a third possibility, one can use the old forms as a mere stimulant for an attempt to work oneself up into strictly subjective, heightened emotional states that have very little to do with the experienced truths that the old forms in themselves were about, the religious origin of the stimulant sufficing to gloss over the merely subjective emotions, so that the impression is created that the religious or metaphysical needs are taken care of.[25]

Religion, however, is not the only human institution encrusted in obsolete syntactic forms. The world of politics is similarly plagued. A host of political abstractions are, like the ideas of religion, couched in the syntax of a bygone era. Nationhood, patriotism, justice, equality, freedom—these are empty words. Time has drained them of any meaning they may once have had. They are now all empty snakeskins waiting to be filled with whatever semantic content is politically expedient, with a "subjective zeal" that functions as a bulwark against psychological thinking.

It will now be much clearer why this article began with the statement, "Today it is a major challenge for anyone to carry on a civil political discussion. I would go a step further and suggest that it may be even more difficult to conduct a civil *psychological* discussion about politics." The latter assertion cuts across the entire political spectrum, from the most conservative to the most liberal. When political lines are drawn, political abstractions are treated as if they had ontological existence, whether in regard to nationalism, civil or human rights, patriotism, or any other product of the mind. If they once had ontological status under an earlier syntax, they do not any longer; they have died logically and psychologically, negated by the historical process. The syntactic structure of our times makes it untenable for us to think that ideals such as justice, liberty, and equality can have universal validity or applicability. These political relics, now merely tools in the hands of self-interest, ideology, or the lust for power, are devoid of psychological validity for they do nothing but serve the interests of political expediency in shaping public opinion. If psychological understanding is to return from exile and once again inform political discourse in our country, we must as a nation shed the snakeskin of what has already passed into logical and psychological history and engage in psychological truth-seeking within the framework of the psychological syntax of our times.

NOTES

1. Consider these statements by various political commentators: "This derangement is the signature expression of the Great Backlash, a style of conservatism that first came snarling onto the national stage in response to the partying of the late sixties"—Thomas Frank, *What's The Matter with Kansas?* (New York: Metropolitan Books, 2004), p. 5.

"In recent years, the conservative agenda has become far more radicalized. Its latest incarnation is more threatening and potentially more destabilizing to America and the world than its previous forms"— Robert Reich, *Reason: Why Liberals Will Win the Battle for America* (New York: Alfred Knopf, 2004), p. 3. "Political debate in this country is insufferable. Whether conducted in Congress, on the political talk shows, or played out at dinners and cocktails, politics is a nasty sport. At the risk of giving away the ending: It's the liberals' fault."—Ann Coulter, *Slander: Liberal Lies about the American Right* (New York: Crown Forum, 2002), p. 1.

2. *The Washington Post*, 24 June 2005.

3. *The New York Times*, 23 June 2005.

4. *Ibid.*, 24 June 2005.

5. Former Secretary of Defense Robert McNamara, in the film *The Fog of War*, declared that understanding one's enemy is an essential element in determining strategy and policy, and it might have saved countless lives if *he* had employed it as a policy during the Viet Nam War.

6. Ann Coulter, *Treason: Liberal Treachery from the Cold War to the War on Terrorism* (New York: Crown Forum, 2004), p. 1.

7. Does Coulter's reference to "Third World savages" extend to Arabs and other Muslims?

8. When Rove added in his quote "wanted to prepare indictments," he was speaking to a conservative audience that has held longstanding contempt for the *liberal* judiciary. "The Warren Supreme Court progressively recast the law to give rights to all sorts of previously excluded groups—not just blacks but also women, homosexuals, the handicapped, prisoners, the mentally ill, even pornographers. The Court found that criminal defendants were entitled to a wide range of constitutional protections: in came due process and the right to silence and a speedy trial; out went self-incrimination—and all of this at a time when the nation's crime rate was soaring. ... Momentous though it was, the *Roe v. Wade* decision on abortion in 1973 was just one in a long succession of outrages for the 'coalition of the fed-up'"—John Micklethwait and Adrian Wooldridge, *The Right Nation* (New York: Penguin Press, 2004), p. 65. Nothing in the foregoing quote or what follows differentiates between and among the categories of people described as having been *given* constitutional protections, and so one

can infer that all the decisions with regard to all listed categories of people identifying (not *giving*) the protections offered by the U.S. Constitution belong to the category of "outrages for the coalition of the fed-up."

9. Alan R. White, *Truth* (Garden City, NY: Anchor Books, 1970), p. 85.

10. *Ibid.*, p. 81.

11. Thomas Hobbes, *The English Works of Thomas Hobbes of Malmesbury*, ed. W. Molesworth, Vol. I (London: John Bohn, 1839-1845), p. 10.

12. My appreciation to Wolfgang Giegerich for pointing this out to me in a personal communication.

13. Michel Foucault, "Discourse and Truth: The Problematization of Parrhesia," Six Lectures Given by Michel Foucault at the University of California at Berkeley, Oct.-Nov. 1983, Lecture 6: Concluding Remarks, *Michel Foucault, Info.*, 2006, <http://foucault.info/documents/parrhesia/foucault.DT6.conclusion.en.html>.

14. "For Kant, the distinctions between analytic and synthetic and *a priori* and *a posteriori* judgments must be kept separate, because it is possible for some judgments to be synthetic and *a priori* at the same time. What Kant proposes is this: Surely all *a posteriori* judgments are synthetic judgments, since any judgment based solely on experience cannot be derived merely by understanding the meaning of the subject. But this does not mean that all synthetic judgments are *a posteriori* judgments, since in mathematical and geometrical judgments, the predicate is not contained in the subject (e.g., the concept 12 is not contained either in 7, 5, +, =, or even in their combination; nor does the concept "shortest distance between two points" contain the idea of a straight line). Such propositions are universal and necessary (and thus *a priori*) even though they could not have been known from experience; and they would be synthetic *a priori* judgments." Stephen H. Daniel, Texas A&M University Department of Philosophy Website, 2007, <http://philosophy.tamu.edu/~sdaniel/Notes/epi-kant.html>.

15. Self-reflection, which may be defined as discursively explicit exposure to one's own subjectivity or the awareness of self as both source and vantage point, must *not* be confused with navel-gazing. As the awareness of one's own subjectivity and those of any others as they manifest in any particular observation, self-reflection may well be the

most intense and interactive meeting of instinct, emotion, and *esprit de corps* an individual may have.

16. Cf. Foucault: "I would now like to turn to the various techniques of the parrhesiastic games which can be found in the philosophical and moral literature of the first two centuries of our era. … I think that these techniques manifest a very interesting and important shift from that truth game which—in the classical Greek conception of parrhesia— was constituted by the fact that someone was courageous enough to tell the truth to other people. For there is a shift from that kind of parrhesiastic game to another truth game which now consists in being *courageous enough to disclose the truth about oneself*" (italics added). "Discourse and Truth: The Problematization of Parrhesia," Six Lectures Given by Michel Foucault at the University of California at Berkeley, Oct.-Nov. 1983, Lecture 5: Techniques of Parrhesia, *Michel Foucault, Info.*, 2006, <http://foucault.info/documents/parrhesia/foucault. DT5.techniquesParrhesia.en.html>.

17. It is also inconceivable that something can have real, that is, psychologically real, merit as political, social, economic, or religious discourse if it, the discourse, lacks discursive exposure of its subjectivity. It may have the merit of effectively pushing a particular agenda, but the merit of that agenda cannot be known at that moment. Where logical and psychological understanding lack, history determines merit, but even then subject to the limitations of subjectivity.

18. For a thorough discussion of psychological syntax, the reader is encouraged to read Wolfgang Giegerich's *The Soul's Logical Life* (Frankfurt am Main: Peter Lang, 2001) and "The End of Meaning and the Birth of Man," *Journal of Jungian Theory and Practice* 6, no. 1 (2004): 10.

19. The electorate, of course, does not exist in reality as a monolithic force, but rather as a conglomerate of forces, which are simplistically labeled right wing, left wing, liberal, conservative, independent, libertarian, etc., as if those categories existed in reality and individuals belonged to them.

20. *The New York Times*, 15 September 2001.

21. Daniel Kurzman, "John Kerry's Botched Joke," About.com, Nov. 2, 2006, <http://politicalhumor.about.com/b/a/256889.htm>.

22. "On the Mindless Menace of Violence," *RFK: Speeches in Real Audio Format*, n.d., <http://www.angelfire.com/pa4/kennedy2/vil.html>.

23. Daniel Kurtzman, "The 10 Craziest Things Rev. Jerry Fallwell Ever Said," *About.com*, 2007, <http://politicalhumor.about.com/od/stupidquotes/a/falwellquotes.htm>.

24. Giegerich, "End of Meaning," p. 10.

25. *Ibid.*, p. 24.

A Personal Meditation on Politics and the American Soul

THOMAS SINGER

Introduction

An invitation to write about politics and the American soul should cause anyone with common sense to turn and run in the opposite direction in the same way that seeing an advertisement for the "soul of a BMW" or hearing Cadillac's newly trademarked slogan—Life. Liberty. And The Pursuit.™—induces nausea. The language of soul and politics has been so co-opted by a vast public relations machine, which instantaneously turns everything, including soul, into a marketable commodity, that there are probably only a handful of us foolish enough to tackle the subject.

The purpose of this essay is to be more impressionistic and evocative than precisely descriptive of the relationship between the American soul and politics—partly because it is so hard to give specific definitions to such essentially indefinable realities. It may be helpful to think of soul as having both a function and a content. As a function and not a specific content, we experience soul as emotional, embodied psychic movement.

Thomas Singer, M.D., is a psychiatrist and Jungian analyst practicing in San Francisco, and has written widely on the collective psyche. He is co-editor with Samuel L. Kimbles of *The Cultural Complex: Contemporary Jungian Perspectives on Psyche and Society* (Brunner-Routledge, 2004); editor of *The Vision Thing: Myth, Politics and Psyche in the World* (Routledge, 2000); and co-author with Stuart Copans, M.D., of *A Fan's Guide to Baseball Fever: The Official Medical Reference* (Elijim Publications, 1991) and *Who's the Patient Here?: Portraits of the Young Psychotherapist* (Oxford University Press, 1978).

Soul, as a function of psychic movement, can legitimately attach itself to various contents—landscape, people, events, eras, values. One can think of our individual and collective souls as being that psychic function which creates and contains the playing fields for the endless encounters between instinct and spirit. And because of the elusive nature of soul as a function or a content and the essential unknowability of whether there is even such a thing as a collective soul, our topic begs to find a hook in a specific time and place.

   Such a hook presented itself to me in 2004 when I was asked to moderate a conference on the theme of "The Soul of America" at the San Francisco Jung Institute. The topic was as overwhelming to me then as it is now. At the time, a deep divide in the American political psyche took on simplistic but potent symbolic form in the image of the Red and Blue States. It was natural for the conference's topic of "The Soul of America" to veer towards a discussion of "the political fight for the soul of America."

   As a Northern Californian for the past thirty-five years, with deep roots in both the Midwest and East coast, I chafe at the one-sidedness of most characterizations of members of one political, religious, ethnic, racial, or regional group by another. Living in a liberal region with progressive politics, I did not want to get up and proclaim that the Democrats had an inside track on the "real" soul of America or that Bush was an "idiot." Both were too easy, because those were the opinions of almost everyone in the audience, or, for that matter, of almost everyone I know. The fact is that no one group in America has an exclusive claim on either the "soul of America" or on being "idiots," even though one side will usually claim soul for itself and idiocy for its rival. (In the political rhetoric of the last few decades, the right has been most effective at staking out "the soul of America" for itself and far less stupid than most on the left have claimed).

   It is very easy to project soul into politics and politics into soul. Indeed, I believe it is the first task of an inquiry such as this to try to differentiate soul from politics. This differentiation begins with the acknowledgment that soul and politics get mixed up with each other all the time in the collective psyche and in the intermingling of myth, politics, and psyche in our cultural unconscious.[1] With the goal of differentiation in mind, the first part of this paper will address the topic of "The Soul of America" and the second part will address "Politics and The Soul of America."

PART ONE: WHAT IS THE SOUL OF AMERICA?

And if the soul
is to know itself
it must look into a soul:
the stranger and enemy, we've seen him in the mirror.[2]

I start with these lines from George Seferis's poem "Argonauts" because I believe that each of us discovers different bits and pieces of "the soul of America" as the personal journeys of our individual lives interface with the unfolding story of our nation's soul journey. When we inquire about the soul of America, I think we need to keep in mind that we are talking about a living interface between the experience of our individual souls and that of the national soul. And if looking into the depths of our personal souls often reveals mysteries, ambiguities, and contradictions, how much more complex is it to reflect on the nature of our American soul? We should begin this inquiry with the recognition that we discover the soul of America only as we discover the story of our own souls. If the Hindus speak of *Atman* and *Brahman*, perhaps we should think about an intermediary zone and speak of the individual soul and the group soul.

Let me give you a brief example that illustrates the importance of this semi-permeable membrane or interface between personal soul and collective soul. John Perry, a well-known Jungian analyst of an earlier generation, once told me the story of his meeting, as a young man, with Jung in 1936. On one of his journeys to America, Jung had visited the house of John Perry's father in Providence, Rhode Island. Perry's father served there as a Bishop in the Episcopal Church. Conversation with Jung at the Perry house touched on the Native American Indian's role in the story of America and the need for modern man to connect with the "archaic man" inside. Jung expressed his opinion that to connect with the soul of America one needed to connect with the American Indian. That night a young John Perry dreamt that *he was standing by the fireplace in the living room with his hand on the mantelpiece. A bare-chested American Indian appeared in the fireplace and threw a tomahawk directly at him. In a startled response, Perry managed to catch the tomahawk in his hands.*[3] One way to think about this dream is to say that the soul of John Perry was introduced to the soul of America in his meeting with a Native American.

Not all of us have such extraordinary meetings between our individual soul and the soul of our country, but each of us is certainly startled when some aspect of America's soul appears to us in our own psychic house. In this context of the encounter of personal soul with national soul, I want to relate a story of my own unexpected personal soul meeting with a part of our nation's soul.

In July 2004, just a few months prior to the national elections later that fall, I traveled with my family from San Francisco to Alton, Illinois. This journey helped give me an inkling of how to speak about what the phrase "soul of America" evokes in me without falling into the easy trap, at a time of presidential elections, of identifying soul with one political group or another. It is no accident that my own musings about "the American soul" began with a personal, physical journey halfway across the country, since so much of what we think of as "the soul of America" is embedded in journey—whether it be from a foreign land to America, or the journey from East to West to open the continent, or from West to East in search of our roots. The "journey" is at the heart of the "soul of America," and my journey to the Midwest in July, 2004 was no exception.

Alton sits on the bluffs of the Mississippi River, just below where the Mississippi and Missouri rivers come together (see Fig. 1). It is a proud old river town which celebrates its history of having been a safe haven for abolitionists in the pre-Civil-War era, as well as having been the site of the famous Lincoln-Douglas debates. I had traveled to Alton with my wife and children in order to bring home the ashes of my mother-in-law, Agnes, who had died in the San Francisco Bay Area earlier in the spring. Alton was the home of Agnes's ancestors, her childhood home, and the home where she had raised her own family. Such homecomings remind us that the soul connects the material and the spiritual realms just as the Mississippi River connects north and south, east and west in the heart of the country.

If you grow up in the Midwest, as I did, the Mississippi River reflects the soul of the country. The river's journey is the soul's journey as Huck Finn and Tom Sawyer taught us in our youth. The grandeur of the river and the fertile valleys surrounding it make it a real, a symbolic, and a spiritual heartland all at the same time—a flowing source of vast generosity and security. It is not an exaggeration to compare the coming together of the Missouri and Mississippi with the confluence of other great rivers of the world, such as the Tigris and Eurphrates. Proud civilizations flourish in the fertile valleys and lowlands at the confluence of great rivers, and we were returning Agnes to the generous source of her origins, where her personal soul might join the American soul in its return to the origin of all souls.

Fig. 1: A view of Alton, Illinois across the Mississippi

On July 3, 2004, having carried Agnes's ashes halfway across the country to her homeland beside the River, we traveled to the Alton Cemetery for a memorial service to honor this profoundly kind and decent woman. Agnes was widely known as "Saint Agnes" because she was like the river—vast in her giving and compassion, both to her family and friends in her personal life, and to her patients in her professional

Fig. 2: The cemetery in Alton, Illinois

life as a nurse. From the photo I took that day in the sublime cemetery (Fig. 2), you can see why I began to get fleeting recollections and intimations of Walt Whitman's *Leaves of Grass* as we placed Agnes's ashes in the grave next to her husband's. The cemetery's green canopy of trees and carpet of grass were both a soothing balm and a clear call to my soul, which felt deeply linked to the soul of my mother-in-law and, as Walt Whitman put it, the souls of "black folks ... White, Kanuck, Tuckhoe, Congressman, ..." I felt my soul resonating to the soul of the river and the soul of the town and the soul of my mother-in-law, all participating in the uniquely Midwestern incarnation of the American soul. Here is how Whitman wrote about leaves of grass, the death of old and young alike, and the meeting of individual soul and the American soul in his long poem "Song of Myself:"

> 1
> I celebrate myself, and sing myself,
> And what I assume you shall assume,
> For every atom belonging to me as good belongs to you.
>
> I loafe and invite my soul,
> I lean and loafe at my ease observing a spear of summer grass.
>
> My tongue, every atom of my blood, form'd from this soil, this
>   air,
> Born here of parents born here from parents the same, and their
>   parents the same,
> …
>
> 6
> A child said *What is the grass?* fetching it to me with full hands;
> How could I answer the child? I do not know what it is any more
>   than he.
>
> I guess it must be the flag of my disposition, out of hopeful green
>   stuff woven.
>
> Or I guess it is the handkerchief of the Lord,
> A scented gift and remembrancer designedly dropt,
> Bearing the owner's name someway in the corners, that we may
>   see and remark, and say *Whose?*
>
> Or I guess the grass is itself a child, the produced babe of the
>   vegetation.

Or I guess it is a uniform hieroglyphic,
And it means, Sprouting alike in broad zones and narrow zones,
Growing among black folks as among white,
Kanuck, Tuckahoe, Congressman, Cuff, I give them the same, I
        receive them the same.

And now it seems to me the beautiful uncut hair of graves.

Tenderly will I use you curling grass,
It may be you transpire from the breasts of young men,
It may be if I had known them I would have loved them,
It may be you are from old people, or from offspring taken soon
        out of their mothers' laps,
And here you are the mothers' laps.

This grass is very dark to be from the white heads of old mothers,
Darker than the colorless beards of old men,
Dark to come from under the faint red roofs of mouths.

O I perceive after all so many uttering tongues,
And I perceive they do not come from the roofs of mouths for
        nothing.

I wish I could translate the hints about the dead young men and
        women,
And the hints about old men and mothers, and the offspring
        taken soon out of their laps.

What do you think has become of the young and old men?
And what do you think has become of the women and children?

They are alive and well somewhere,
The smallest sprout shows there is really no death,
And if ever there was it led forward life, and does not wait at the
        end to arrest it,
And ceas'd the moment life appear'd.

All goes onward and outward, nothing collapses,
And to die is different from what any one supposed, and luckier.
...

31

I believe a leaf of grass is no less than the journey-work of the
        stars, ...[4]

In Section 21 of "Song of Myself," Whitman proclaims himself the bard of the American soul when he writes: "I am the poet of the Body and I am the poet of the Soul."[5] He is writing of the Body and the Soul of America which he likens to a blade of grass whose very existence mirrors the "journey-work of the stars" in its immortality. At Agnes's service, "a blade of grass" allowed me to participate for a moment in the immortality of her soul and the American soul.

On July 4, the day following Agnes's memorial service, my family went down to the Mississippi River to join in the holiday's festivities. We were at peace with ourselves and open to participating in the celebration of our nation's birth in the knowledge that we had truly accomplished the purpose of our ritual journey home. If you have not celebrated the Fourth of July by the banks of the Mississippi, I urge you to do so before you become a leaf of grass. Quite unexpectedly, I discovered there another forgotten part of Whitman's "Song of Myself" whispering to my soul as I wandered among the day's celebrants— adults guzzling beer and listening to rock 'n' roll music as the children danced and played and jumped up and down by the river's edge.

32

I think I could turn and live with animals, they are so placid and
    self-contain'd,
I stand and look at them long and long.

They do not sweat and whine about their condition,
They do not lie awake in the dark and weep for their sins,
They do not make me sick discussing their duty to God,
Not one is dissatisfied, not one is demented with the mania of
    owning things,
Not one kneels to another, nor to his kind that lived thousands
    of years ago,
Not one is respectable or unhappy over the whole earth.
…

52

The spotted hawk swoops by and accuses me, he complains of
    my gab and my loitering.

I too am not a bit tamed, I too am untranslatable,
I sound my barbaric yawp over the roofs of the world. ….[6] (my italics)

Fig. 3 is an image from that celebration that got me musing about the meaning of the "Barbaric Yawp." You might find yourself wondering about my choice of this image and find it repulsive, vulgar, or simply of little relevance to this journal's noble topic of Politics and the American Soul. But, on this particular Fourth of July, the day after the moving memorial service for Agnes, I was fascinated by this couple as I secretly circled around behind them in an effort to capture the image of what struck me at once as so "other" and as so "barbaric." In their unabashed celebration of their own animal force, this couple evoked some primitive connection in my psyche to Whitman's "barbaric yawp."

> I too am not a bit tamed, I too am untranslatable,
> I sound my barbaric yawp over the roofs of the world.

What is a "barbaric yawp?" Why did the quintessential poet of the American soul, Walt Whitman, link the "barbaric yawp" to the American soul? There are two parts to Whitman's phrase, a phrase that now brings up some 110,000 "hits" on a Google Internet search. "Barbaric" means "without civilizing influences, uncivilized, primitive" and a "yawp" is a "loud, harsh cry." Neither "barbaric" nor "yawp"

Fig. 3: Biker couple at the Fourth of July celebrations in Alton, Illinois

suggests a civilized approach to things. Taken together, they signify a primitive enthusiasm in the form of a non-verbal cry from the essential nature of a living being. In Whitman's imagination, the essence of the American soul is neither civilized nor verbal. The "barbaric yawp" is the fierce "voice" of a soul that is essentially unrestrained and exulting in its self-expression.

One senses in my photograph of the Fourth-of-July biker couple an animal force that does not concern itself with, or simply flouts, more conventional norms. Adding this image to the thought that George Bush's Texas swagger and his inarticulate utterances are heard by many in America as some sort of cry from our country's "body and soul," one has to accept the fact that they are as much a part of the American soul and its "barbaric yawp" as our more progressive sensibilities. Linking George Bush and this photograph to the "barbaric yawp" is intended to be both ironic and absolutely serious simultaneously. Who are we to know what or who contains the "barbaric yawp?" Who has a legitimate claim on the American soul? Again, what is the American soul?

Steven Herrmann, a Jungian with a deep scholarly interest in Whitman, wrote to me: "Whitman's "yawp" is a *conscious* cry from the Soul of America to make the barbarian in American political democracy conscious! The "barbaric yawp" is Whitman's call from the depths of the American Soul to awaken the possibility of hope in a brighter future for American democracy." Hermann goes on to write:

> The aim of Whitman's "barbaric yawp" was to sound a new heroic message of "Happiness," Hope, and "Nativity" over the roofs of the world, to sound a primal cry which must remain essentially "unsaid" because it rests at the core of the American soul and cannot be found in "any dictionary, utterance, symbol" (*Leaves,* Section # 50). The "barbaric yawp" is a metaphorical utterance for something "untranslatable," a primal cry from the depths of the American Soul for the emergence of man as a spiritual human being in whom the aims of liberty and equality have been fully realized and in whom the opposites of love and violence, friendship and war, have been unified at a higher political field of order than anything we have formerly seen in America. His "yawp" is an affect state, a spiritual cry of "Joy" and "Happiness" prior to the emergence of language.[7]

At this point, the reader may be wondering how it is possible to reconcile what might appear on the surface to be two very different aspects of the "barbaric yawp" that I have presented. How can the image of "Biker Dick" be part of the same "barbaric yawp" that sounds "a primal cry from the depths of the American Soul for the emergence of man as a spiritual being?" But, as Stephen Herrmann aptly points out, Whitman's image of man's emergence as a spiritual being

> refers to a person that can realize his earthly existence within the context of his total life pattern, including his depths of erotic passion. Whitman's barbarian is both a spiritual and a sexual being. He is not split inside, but whole and conscious of his full instinctive nature and lives it out according to the preference of his Soul.

In contemporary America, Whitman's "barbaric yawp" is as inclusive of the violence found in the television show *The Sopranos* as it is of the unitary vision of Martin Luther King's "I Have a Dream." This suggests expanding our national imagination to embrace the American soul's "barbaric yawp" as both vulgar and compassionate at the same time. It was the genius of Whitman to see in "the barbaric yawp" of the American soul the capacity for an interconnected transcendent unity.

This section on the Soul of America would not be complete without mentioning one final example of how glimpses of the American soul come through individual encounters that open up a window or interface between the individual soul and the larger, collective soul of the group. As she was gestating a novel on slavery, freedom, and the Black experience, Toni Morrison tells us in her preface to *Beloved,* she met her main character in the following way:

> I sat on the porch, rocking in a swing, looking at giant stones piled up to take the river's occasional fist. Above the stones is a path through the lawn, but interrupted by an ironwood gazebo situated under a cluster of trees and in deep shade.
>
> She walked out of the water, climbed the rocks, and leaned against the gazebo. Nice hat.
>
> So she [Beloved] was there from the beginning, and except for me, everybody (the characters) knew it—a sentence that later became "The women in the house knew it." The figure most central to the story would have to be her, the murdered, not the murderer, the one who lost everything and had no say in any of it.[8]

Like Perry's American Indian with the tomahawk, this is a soul figure that appears out of nowhere, or as Jungians might say "out of the unconscious"—personal, cultural, and collective. She emerges out of the water and presents herself to Toni Morrison, who is trying to figure how to create a fiction based on the true story of "Margaret Garner, a young mother who, having escaped slavery, was arrested for killing one of her children (and trying to kill the others) rather than let them be returned to the owner's plantation."[9]

The soul figure with the "nice hat" who greets Toni Morrision becomes the central character in her novel, *Beloved*. Beloved is the soul of a murdered innocent, which becomes a conduit for the voices of all the other black people who perished in slavery and its aftermath. These collective voices are as deep a part of the American soul as John Perry's American Indian or Walt Whitman's barbaric yawp. Here is how another character from the novel, Stamp Paid, understands the collective "roaring" soul sound that surrounds the house where Beloved has taken up residence with her mother:

> … [H]e believed the undecipherable language clamoring around the house was the mumbling of the black and angry dead. Very few had died in bed, like Baby Suggs, and none that he knew of, including Baby, had lived a livable life. Even the educated colored: the long-school people, the doctors, the teachers, the paper-writers and businessmen had a hard row to hoe. In addition to having to use their heads to get ahead, they had the weight of the whole race sitting there. You needed two heads for that. Whitepeople believed that whatever the manners, under every dark skin was a jungle. Swift unnavigable waters, swinging screaming baboons, sleeping snakes, red gums ready for their sweet white blood. In a way, he thought, they were right. The more coloredpeople spent their strength trying to convince them how gentle they were, how clever and loving, how human, the more they used themselves up to persuade whites of something Negroes believed could not be questioned, the deeper and more tangled the jungle grew inside.
>
> But it wasn't the jungle blacks brought with them to this place from the other (livable) place. It was the jungle whitefolks planted in them. And it grew. It spread. In, through and after life, it spread, until it invaded the whites who had made it. Touched them every one. Changed and altered them. Made them bloody, silly, worse than even they wanted to be, so scared were they of

the jungle they had made. The screaming baboon lived under their own white skin; the red gums were their own.

Meantime, the secret spread of this new kind of whitefolks' jungle was hidden, silent, except once in a while when you could hear its mumbling in places like 124 ....[10]

The "undecipherable language" that Morrsion describes in her novel is as much a voice of the American soul as is Whitman's primal "barbaric yawp." It is filled with the "roaring" sound of the "black and angry dead" and the "mumbling" sound of the white race's collective projection onto blacks, which is portrayed as the "whitefolks' jungle" of "swift unnaviagable waters, swinging screaming baboons, sleeping snakes, red gums ready for their sweet white blood." Beloved becomes the spokesperson for a part of our American soul that is as much with us today as when Margaret Garner murdered her baby girl rather than return her to slavery.

Like any other soul, the American soul seeks incarnation in specific place, specific time, specific event, and even specific person or groups of people. This specificity of incarnation loves location and the right person(s) at the right moment. This very specificity means that many places and times in American history can claim some piece of the American soul as their own. At the same time, the American soul should not be thought of as bound to any particular person or group, any special place on the continent, or any unique time in our nation's history. As a whole, the American soul is much broader than its particularity and specificity, reaching as far back as the American Indians' migration across the Bering Straits and as far forward as one can imagine hearing Whitman's Barbaric Yawp.

PART TWO: HOW DOES THE AMERICAN SOUL EXPRESS ITSELF IN POLITICS?

We all have complexes; it is a highly banal and uninteresting fact...It is only interesting to know what people do with their complexes; that is the practical question which matters.[11]

In the second section of this article, I want to add "politics" to the already fermenting "soul-of-America" brew that I have been stirring. The first ingredient for the political part of this American-soul concoction that comes to mind is a strangely beautiful book by Doris

Lessing, *Briefing for a Descent into Hell.*[12] The central part of the novel takes its lead from the Platonic myth that this world is only a veiled shadow of the world of ideal forms. Indeed, the main character, Charles Watkins, leads us on a science-fiction journey of his inner world, in which he discovers that each individual soul is briefed before its descent to earth and its human incarnation through birth on Earth. Earth itself is described as a "poisonous hell" for which the soul needs to be prepared. This is the "briefing" of the soul, just as birth as a human is the "descent."

For many readers of this journal, the inner world is primary, and participation in the politics of the earthly realm is in fact a "poisonous hell." Many Jungians prefer to avoid politics altogether in favor of other, "deeper" soul work. We all know something about the soul's disillusionment when it participates in the everyday politics of institutional life—be it in the Jungian community or national presidential elections. In my own personal experience, I came away from intense engagement in Senator Bill Bradley's 2000 campaign for the Democratic Party's nomination for president feeling burned by the "poisonous hell" of earthly politics. Out of that experience (which I am sure is matched by many similar experiences among this journal's readers in the political arena) I would like to share some reflections on how I am currently thinking about the relationship between politics and the American soul.

First, I don't think that the soul of America is to be located in identification with one party or the other. Neither party possesses the soul of America. Presumably, the soul of a right-wing fundamentalist is as engaged with the journey of the American soul as is the soul of a progressive liberal. Nor do I think the soul of America is located in one specific issue or another, whether it be abortion, immigration, discrimination based on race or other differences, gay marriage, the environment, the war in Iraq, or a host of other compelling issues.

Usually, a discussion of politics focuses on the rough and tumble of political struggle, 95% of which is about how to gain and exercise power. But I am going to turn the traditional discussion of politics as it relates to power a bit upside down in this meditation and focus not on Machiavelli but on some basic, recurring collective psychological themes and tensions that have coursed through our political history. These recurring themes embody deep-seated conflicts in our nation's psyche, in which neither side of the ambivalences and tensions has exclusive claim on meaning or correctness. Both sides have legitimate claim to soul.

The psychological form in which these recurring conflicts take shape over generations is what I have been exploring in the concept of "cultural complexes."[13] Each culture has its own version of how to work out basic human tensions and conflicts. The uniqueness of a culture's way of experiencing these basic human problems becomes embodied in its cultural complexes, which then play themselves out in political life. Sunnis and Shi'ites don't have the same way of dealing with their problems as Midwesterners or Southerners.

In speaking about individual complexes as revealed by the Word Association Test, Jung wrote: "Our destinies are as a rule the outcome of our psychological tendencies."[14] Another way of saying this is that our personal complexes are the hand that Fate has dealt us. How we play the hand that Fate has dealt us, or what we do with our personal complexes, determines who we become as individuals. Jung put it rather bluntly: "We all have complexes; it is a highly banal and uninteresting fact. ... It is only interesting to know what people do with their complexes; that is the practical question which matters."[15] I believe that the same is true of our cultural complexes. What we do with our cultural complexes determines not only who we become as a people, but the destiny of the American soul. A good deal of our working out (or not working out) of our cultural complexes occurs in the political arena.

Cultural complexes, underpinned by archetypal patterns, form the core of those highly charged struggles that have defined who we are as an American people throughout our national history. Such cultural complexes accrue a memory of their own, a point of view of their own, and a tendency to collect new experiences in contemporary life that validate their unchanging point of view. Cultural complexes also tend to fire off autonomously and with deep emotion when an event triggers them. We know that a cultural complex may well be on the scene when there is a highly aroused emotional reaction to current events. Emotional reactivity of the collective psyche is the calling card of a cultural complex.

For instance, our more than three-hundred-year conflict around race, as mirrored in the clamoring voices of *Beloved* in the first section of this article, is an example of an entrenched cultural complex that is always ready to detonate in the psyches of whites and blacks. The well-known radio celebrity, Don Imus, has made a successful career out of intentionally stepping on the landmines of cultural complexes in his toying with the stereotyping of many racial and ethnic groups. But no one individual or group is immune from the destruction of self and/or others that can come with detonating a cultural complex, as even Imus discovered in the national outrage that came on the heels of his racial slurs about black women basketball players from Rutgers University.

My thesis, then, is that the American soul is embedded in our various cultural complexes. Furthermore, our cultural complexes are what give political life its dynamism and its content. Both the energy and the issues of political debate spring from the autonomous, highly charged emotional material of our core cultural complexes. Political life is the natural social arena in which cultural complexes play themselves out. We forge the American soul in our struggle with our cultural complexes. In the political arena, cultural complexes seem mostly to generate heat, division, hatred; they are inflammatory and polarizing; they usually end in a stalemate without any resolution, only to recur in the next election or the next generation; sometimes they are ignored or kept unconscious for decades; occasionally they can be worked out slowly in engagement, compromise, reconciliation, and healing after generations of recurring battle. In short, they behave like complexes.

We might now reframe the question about the relationship of politics to the American soul as follows: "What are we doing with our cultural complexes in political life?" Or perhaps the question may be better phrased, "What are our cultural complexes doing with us in our political life?" In order to explore those questions, we need to ask, "What are our primary cultural complexes?" As a way of answering these questions, I would like to offer a list of themes or "relationships" around which cultural complexes have formed in the American psyche over the course of our nation's history.

As I briefly consider each of these "relationships," I will refer to "soul-making" and whether or not it appears to be happening around specific cultural complexes. I imagine soul-making as potentially occurring when there is a legitimate claim for something of deepest human value on both sides of a conflict that has come alive in the collective psyche and has been engaged in the political arena. I hope that the reader will keep in mind that the seven American cultural complexes that I outline below interweave with one another in a tangled skein and are by no means as clear or as simple as I sketch them.

1. Our Relationship to Money/Commerce/Consumer Goods

a. Core Attitude of Cultural Complex:

One of the highest values in American society has been the accumulation of personal wealth and material goods, often at the expense of or in disregard for the common good. This complex emphasizes individual achievement in the material world. On the positive side of this complex is the promised opportunity for every person to maximize his or her material well-being. The negative side of this cultural complex emphasizes our collective and individual right to eat the world, own the world, amass personal wealth, and continuously increase the "gross national product." In the name of participating in the American Dream, consumerism has become almost synonymous with the highest good.[16]

b. Specific Current Political Issue: Campaign Finance Reform

In an attempt to curb the equation of material wealth with the common good, recent attempts have been made to introduce campaign finance reform as a way of equalizing the role of money in a democratic society. These attempts have been "dead on arrival" and have been undermined by both parties. On this issue, there is no "soul-making" occurring in either major political party. There is little meaningful engagement in the political arena with the overemphasis on money and consumerism in our civic life and in our political life. We are soul-dead with regard to active, conscious engagement of this cultural complex. Our collective psyche is consumed by its consumerism. (Al-Qaeda was very conscious of this when it attacked the World Trade Center.)

2. Our Relationship to the Natural Environment

a. Core Attitude of Cultural Complex:

Historically, we have been a country of vast and seemingly unlimited natural resources. This has fostered a cultural complex based on the belief that this blessing entitles us to everything we want and that we own everything in the natural world. A growing number of people have come to understand that "stewardship" is the responsibility that goes along with the privilege of vast but dwindling natural resources.

b. Specific Current Political Issues:

There are a host of ongoing political debates related to the environment that suggest soul-making is going on with regard to this cultural complex. These include policy conflicts about global warming, clean air and water, the limitation of natural resources, and the desire to use those limited resources wisely.

3. Our Relationship to the Human Community, Including Family Life, Social Life, and the Life Cycle from Conception to Death

a. Core Attitude of Cultural Complex:

This country was built on a belief in the inalienable rights and freedoms of the individual as much as it was on utopian communalism. A core American cultural complex spins out of the unending dynamic tension between the myth of the self-sufficient individual in opposition to the welfare of the community as a whole and the reality of the community's responsibility to the individual. The good of the whole and all of its members is endlessly challenged by the rights of the individual.

b. Specific Current Political Issues:

This cultural complex is ubiquitous in our political debates and makes itself known in all sorts of issues that range from the right to bear arms and taxation to national health-care policy and how to fund pensions and Social Security. Again, national soul-making appears to be going on in the engagement of this cultural complex. The debate over the rights and responsibilities of the individual in relationship to the needs of the collective and its responsibilities to all its members engages citizens across the political spectrum.

4. Our Relationship to the Spiritual Realm

a. Core Attitude of Cultural Complex:

Our Puritan heritage launched our country both in dissent and in a tradition of strict belief in moralistic behavior. The belief that America has a special relationship to God fuels our sense of national entitlement, which is matched only by our strong tradition of religious dissent, which drives our national skepticism about privileged authority, divine or otherwise. Out of these twin foundational attitudes grew our tradition of separation of church and state. Inclusive pluralism and dogmatic fundamentalism are the vying poles of a uniquely American cultural complex that is the psychological inheritance of our religious traditions. As in many other countries, the archetypal split between good and evil in our collective psyche projects itself onto many political issues, from the clash over abortion to the debate about the war in Iraq.

b. Specific Current Political Issue: Abortion

Perhaps about as much soul-making has been going on around this issue as aound any in recent political history. Although the issue has generated murderous heat, it has also raised fundamental questions about the nature of soul and life, which, to my mind, are part of any healthy debate in society. The clash of religious fundamentalism with the rights of a woman to make choices about her own body in a society that values the separation of church and state cuts across so many of our cultural complexes that I think it forces everyone to sort out what he or she believes on an incredibly difficult series of issues. That is soul-making. It has turned many things upside down in our society. For instance, conservatives most often align themselves with the rights of the self-sufficient individual and progressives side with the needs of all in the community. But on the issue of abortion, progressives uphold the right to individual choice, while conservatives argue for a community value that applies to all.

5. Our Relationship to Race, Ethnicity, Gender—All the "Others"

a. Core Attitude of Cultural Complex:

There have been two distinct poles in the American cultural complex with regard to race, ethnicity, and gender. As much as in any other country in the world, inclusiveness in terms of race, ethnicity, and gender has been part of our national character and its proud "melting-pot" history. But ever since the nation's inception, the radioactive background behind the apparent embrace of diversity has been the premise that white, Anglo-Saxon, heterosexual men were destined to dominate the nation.

b. Specific Current Political Issues: Same-sex marriage; Immigration

The powerful unconscious hold of the cultural complex of discrimination on the basis of sex, race, ethnicity, and age has been challenged on multiple levels simultaneously in the past several decades. Indeed, the assault on the established complex has been so thorough that the new cultural complex replacing it — "political correctness" — has itself become the dominant persona of the collective, behind which lurks the shadow of stereotyping on the basis of differences. In a sense, white male dominance and the embracing of diversity can be thought of as two sides of the same coin of this cultural complex. But, most importantly for our discussion, soul-making in the collective psyche is occurring at unprecedented speed with regard to the active engagement of this complex in such potent current political issues as same-sex marriage and immigration, and in the fact that for the first time in American history, a black man, a woman, and a Mormon are running simultaneously for the presidential nomination.

6. Our Relationship to Speed, Height, Youth, Progress, Celebrity

a. Core Attitude of Cultural Complex:

As the "new land," America has always been identified with what is new—a new land with new people and new ideas, faster, higher, younger, ever progressing, ever renewing itself. The wedding of celebrity, charisma, and ingenuity are forever the hope of the American Dream and American politics. The "new land" gave substance to the belief in our nation's unique destiny, poignantly portrayed in John Gast's *American Progress* from 1872 (Fig. 4, next page). This wonderful illustration shows an archetypal anima figure who serves as a symbolic image of the American soul's identification with "Progress." "She"— the American soul as Progress—floats at the core of a national cultural complex of entitlement, exceptionalism, and the "American Dream."

b. Specific Current Political Issue: Stem Cell Research

This political debate has tremendous potential for soul-making in the collective psyche because it pits what is "god-given" against what is "new." Surely, there is soul on both sides of the debate. Our addiction to creating something new, quicker, easier, better is a source of American ingenuity and prosperity. It endlessly challenges what has existed for a long time, if not forever. For many, what has existed forever is good enough, and for some it is even God's will.

Fig. 4: John Gast's *American Progress* (1872). In John Gast's *American Progress*, a diaphanously and scantily clad woman, representing America, floats westward through the air with the "Star of Empire" on her forehead. She has left the cities of the East behind, and the wide Mississippi, and still her course is westward. In her right hand, she carries a schoolbook, a testimonial to the National Enlightenment, while in her left she trails the slender wires of the telegraph, which will bind the nation together. Fleeing her approach are Indians, buffalo, wild horses, bears, and other game, all of which disappear into the storm and waves of the Pacific Coast. They flee the wondrous vision—the star "is too much for them." [Adapted from a contemporary description of Gast's painting, written by George Crofutt, who distributed his engraving of it widely. Source: http://www.csubak.edu/~gsantos/ img0061.html.]

7. Our Relationship to the World beyond our Borders

a. Core Attitude of Cultural Complex:

The theme of the freedom of the individual vs. the individual's responsibility to the whole is writ large in the cultural complex of our relationship to the broader world beyond American borders. In this case, our nation arrogates to itself, as a nation, the same rights as the individual, whose freedom it sees as paramount. As an "individual" nation, we place our economic and security interests for the most part above our responsibility to the global community as a whole. The tension between the freedom of the individual and the individual's responsibility to the whole in this complex joins forces with another cultural complex—our sense of entitlement, which comes from our view of ourselves as exceptional and therefore as knowing what is best for the world. These two cultural complexes get acted out in peculiar ways—we wage war in other parts of the world in the name of individual freedoms just as easily as we retreat from broader engagement in the world in the name of individualistic isolationism, which renounces responsibility to the broader whole.

b. Specific Current Political Issues:

The American-led war in Iraq is a horrific contemporary example of how a cultural complex (or more than one cultural complex) can seize the collective psyche and come alive in politics. Part of the motivation for waging this war grows out of a deep-seated American belief that affirms the unique destiny of our people as guardians of democratic principles and therefore as exceptional, blessed by God with endless opportunity, perhaps even eternal youth and immortality as a nation. The conduct of the Iraq War has revealed the flaws in a cultural complex that puts the nation's rugged individualism ahead of a sense of responsibility to and participation in the global community. The experiences of the wars in Vietnam and now Iraq have begun the slow process of challenging these core beliefs which sit at the heart of those fundamental American cultural complexes in which our fierce individualism joins forces with our sense of entitlement and exceptionalism. As the deflation of bankrupt policies settles into the collective psyche, one hopes that this terrible misadventure has had its soul-making impact on the body politic.

CONCLUSION

In each of the broad areas that I have characterized as cultural complexes, a set of specific issues take center stage at any given time in the political life of our country. In the great crucible of politics, where our core cultural complexes enter the political life of the nation, the American soul gets forged and crucified—made, remade, unmade, made again—over and over. These autonomous psychological clusters of memory, affect, and repetitive historical behavior seize our collective psyche in an endless round of racial strife, economic striving, gender warfare, and unending worship of technology, progress, speed, height, information, youth, innocence, moral simplicity, heroic achievement, and insatiable consumerism, all of which have addicted the entire nation—Democrats, Republicans, independents, and the uncommitted alike. It is the "barbaric yawp" of the American soul embodied in political life.

Signs of soul life can clearly be detected in the growing conflict around our relationship to the natural environment. Such signs can also be detected in the intensifying struggles and rapidly changing collective attitudes to race, gender, and sexual identity. In these particular cultural complexes, the American soul seems to be transforming itself through highly engaged political activity. On the other hand, our country is so addicted to money, to speed, to youth, to consumerism, and to progress that our collective soul seems lost or invisible in our possession by these complexes. Our national politics with regard to these possessions seems hopelessly unengaged and unconscious. Lively debate on the current political issues generated by these underlying cultural complexes that course through our history like an underground river are essential to the continuing growth of our collective psyche and our individual souls as well.

The politics of the day that challenge our more entrenched cultural complexes are met with the same kind of fierce resistance from groups that an analyst encounters when asking a patient to take on or confront a personal complex—or that the ego faces when it encounters the unconscious resistance of an entrenched complex, which does its best to keep from being known or made conscious. Frankly, I was surprised, in taking this most approximate inventory of our cultural complexes, that I reached the conclusion that soul-making activity is taking place in so many areas of our political life. At the outset of writing this article, I would have said that there was little happening in our political life that suggested soul. Of course, many readers may disagree with my conclusions.

Many in our country would prefer that the sound of our national soul be less of a yawp and closer to the "Om" of Hinduism. "Om" evokes compassion, peace, reverence, unity. To make a bad pun, "Om" is a far cry from Whitman's primal "barbaric yawp." But the reality is that the sound of the American soul is more messy than "Om" and when the barbaric yawp sounds its discordant note in politics, it is rarely unifying or resonant of deep compassion. Rather, at its best, it vibrates with dynamism, energy, and the promise of renewal. Perhaps we should be most afraid of the time in our country when the mix of politics and soul has left us so deadened by disillusionment and distrust that we are unable even to hear the barbaric yawp.

NOTES

1. Thomas Singer, ed., *The Vision Thing: Myth, Politics and Psyche in the World* (London and New York: Routledge, 2000).
2. George Seferis, "Argonauts," in *Collected Poems: 1924-1955*, trans., ed., and intro. Edmund Keeley and Philip Sherrard (Princeton, NJ: Princeton University Press, 1967), p. 9.
3. Personal communication with John Perry.
4. Walt Whitman, "Song of Myself," in *Walt Whitman: The Complete Poems* (London: Penguin Books, 2004), pp. 63, 68-69, 93.
5. *Ibid.*, p. 83.
6. *Ibid.*, pp. 94, 124.
7. Personal communication with Steven Herrmann.
8. Toni Morrison, *Beloved* (New York: Vintage Books, 1987), p. xviii.
9. *Ibid.*, p. xvii.
10. *Ibid.*, p. 234.
11. C. G. Jung, *Analytical Psychology: Its Theory and Practice,* The Tavistock Lectures, Lecture 3 (New York: Vintage Books, 1968), p. 94.
12. Doris Lessing, *Briefing for a Descent into Hell* (London: Vintage Books, 1981).
13. See: Thomas Singer, "The Cultural Complex and Archetypal Defenses of the Collective Spirit: Baby Zeus, Elian Gonzales, Constantine's Sword, and Other Holy Wars," *The San Francisco Library Journal* 20, no. 4 (2002): 4-28; Thomas Singer, "Cultural Complexes and Archetypal Defenses of the Group Spirit," in *Terror, Violence and the Impulse to Destroy,* ed. John Beebe (Zürich: Daimon Verlag, 2003), pp. 191-209; Thomas Singer and Samuel L. Kimbles, eds., *The Cultural Complex: Contemporary Jungian Perspectives on Psyche and Society* (London and New York: Brunner-Routledge, 2004).

14. C. G. Jung, "Freud and Psychoanalysis," *The Collected Works of C. G. Jung,* Vol. 4., trans. R. F. C. Hull (Princeton, NJ: Princeton University Press, 1961), para. 309.

15. C. G. Jung, *Analytical Psychology: Its Theory and Practice*, The Tavistock Lectures, Lecture 3 (New York: Pantheon Books, 1968), p. 94.

16. Jack Beatty, *Age of Betrayal: The Triumph of Money in America, 1865-1900* (New York: Alfred Knopf, 2007).

SELECTED BIBLIOGRAPHY

Beatty, Jack. *Age of Betrayal: The Triumph of Money in America, 1865-1900.* New York, Alfred Knopf, 2007.

Gellert, M. *The Fate of America: An Inquiry into National Character,* Washington, D.C.: Brassey's Inc., 2001.

Henderson, J. "The Archetype of Culture." In *The Archetype.* Proceedings of the 2nd International Congress for Analytical Psychology. Ed. Adolf Guggenbuhl-Craig. Basel and New York: S. Karger, 1962/1964.

_____. "The Cultural Unconscious." In *Shadow and Self: Selected Papers in Analytical Psychology.* Wilmette, IL: Chiron Publications, 1990. Pp. 103-113.

Herrmann, Steven. "The Cultural Complex in Walt Whitman." *The San Francisco Jung Institute Library Journal* 23, no. 4 (2004): 34-62.

_____. "Walt Whitman and the Homoerotic Imagination." *The Jung Journal Culture and Psyche* 1, no. 2 (2007): 16-47.

Jung, C. G. *Freud and Psychoanalysis.* Princeton, NJ: Princeton University Press, 1961.

_____. *Analytical Psychology: Its Theory and Practice.* The Tavistock Lectures. New York: Pantheon Books, 1968.

Kalsched, D. *The Inner World of Trauma: Archetypal Defenses of the Personal Spirit.* London and New York: Routledge, 1996.

Kimbles, Samuel L. "The Cultural Complex and the Myth of Invisibility." In *The Vision Thing.* Ed. Thomas Singer. London: Routledge, 2000. Pp. 157-169.

Lessing, Doris. *Briefing for a Descent into Hell.* London: Vintage Books, 1981.

Morrison, Toni. *Beloved.* New York: Vintage Books, 1987.

Packer, George. *The Assassins' Gate: America in Iraq.* New York: Farrar, Strauss and Giroux, 2005.

Perry, J. "Emotions and Object Relations." *The Journal of Analytical Psychology* 15, no. 1 (1970): 1-12.

Samuels, Andrew. *The Political Psyche*. London and New York, Routledge, 1993.

Seferis, George. *Collected Poems: 1924-1955*. Trans., ed., and intro. Edmund Keeley and Philip Sherrard. Princeton, NJ: Princeton University Press, 1967.

Singer, Thomas, ed. *The Vision Thing: Myth, Politics and Psyche in the World*. London and New York: Routledge, 2000.

_____. "The Cultural Complex and Archetypal Defenses of the Collective Spirit: Baby Zeus, Elian Gonzales, Constantine's Sword, and Other Holy Wars." *The San Francisco Library Journal* 20, no. 4 (2002): 4-28.

_____. "Cultural Complexes and Archetypal Defenses of the Group Spirit." In *Terror, Violence and the Impulse to Destroy*. Ed. John Beebe. Zürich: Daimon Verlag, 2003. Pp. 191-209.

Singer, Thomas and Samuel L. Kimbles, eds. *The Culutral Complex: Contemporary Jungian Perspectives on Psyche and Society*. London and New York: Brunner-Routledge, 2004.

Psyches and Cities of Hospitality in an Era of Forced Migration:
The Shadows of Slavery and Conquest on the "Immigration" Debate

MARY WATKINS

> The borders and barriers, which enclose us within the safety of
> familiar territory, can also become prisons, and are often defended
> beyond reason or necessity.
> —Edward Said[1]

THE BORDER WORK OF DEPTH AND LIBERATION PSYCHOLOGIES

As students of depth psychologies, we learn to question what is on the other side of walls, knowing that we are apt to surround ourselves with what is comfortable and familiar. We are tutored to see through our certainties and accustomed metaphors to the ideas and commitments that forge them.[2] Depth psychologies ask us to forsake inhabiting a frozen center, cut off from relations to what and

Mary Watkins, Ph.D., is a core faculty member and the coordinator of community and ecological fieldwork and research in the M.A./Ph.D. Depth Psychology Program at Pacifica Graduate Institute. She is the author of *Waking Dreams, Invisible Guests: The Development of Imaginal Dialogues*, co-editor of *Psychology and the Promotion of Peace*, co-author of *Talking With Young Children About Adoption*, and co-author (with Helene Lorenz) of the forthcoming *Toward Psychologies of Liberation* (Palgrave Macmillan). She is a co-founder of Santa Barbara for Immigrant Justice.

who is different from us. They teach us to move to the edges where we can greet what has been repressed and marginalized by a too-narrow ego-consciousness. Attention to unbidden thoughts, images, dreams, emotions, and bodily feelings is at the core of depth psychological methods, which all seek to establish dialogue with what is customarily extruded or passively ignored.[3] This border work has been largely imagined as intrapsychic and interpersonal processes that are facilitated by the atmosphere of trust within psychotherapeutic practices and their multiple methods of welcoming psyche through free association, movement, bodywork, dreams, active imagination, and conversation that is released from the bounds of conventional discourse. The ghosts of psychic life have most often been seen as resulting from familial difficulties, traumatic and otherwise, as well as issuing from struggles with the archetypal dominants of human existence.

Euro-American depth psychologies are being bridged with psychologies of liberation that have arisen in the Southern hemisphere and also in the United States at the margins through both cultural work and community psychology.[4] These approaches understand individual psychological suffering, and human misery more generally, in the context of social, political, and economic arrangements that generate and normalize such misery. In particular, they address collective trauma, imposed by a wide range of injustices. In the small group and community approaches nourished by various psychologies of liberation, border work is done at the interface of psyche and culture. It is intrapsychic and interpersonal, occurring both within and at the borders between. It turns to history to critically understand present misconstruals.

These psychologies have been my teachers, as I stand in witness to a devastating humanitarian crisis that is misrepresented as a debate on immigration and national security.

> Perhaps the problem might be better understood as a humanitarian crisis. Can the mass migration and displacement of people from their homelands at a rate of 800,000 people a year be understood as anything else? Unknown numbers of people have died trekking through the extreme conditions of the Arizona and New Mexico deserts. Towns are being depopulated and ways of life lost in rural Mexico. Fathers feel forced to leave their families in their best attempt to provide for their kids. Everyday, boatloads

of people arrive on our shores after miserable journeys at sea in deplorable conditions. As a humanitarian crisis, the solution could involve the UN or the Organization of American States. But these bodies do not have roles in the immigration frame, so they have no place in the "immigration debate." Framing this as just an "immigration problem" prevents us from penetrating deeper into the issue.[5]

In moving more deeply into the issue, I travel paths I have learned from the intersections of depth and liberation psychologies. This humanitarian crisis of unprecedented levels of forced migration requires us to move downward through the deep intrapsychic level until we emerge into the familial, community, cultural, and collective. We must also proceed downward from the level of the global to national politics, to city government, to community and neighborhood sites of reconciliation, all the while holding tight to how psyche shows up in these regions. When there is an impasse at one level of organization, such as national politics, it can help to shift work to another level, in this case, to that of the city, town, and community. It is not that one abandons the levels above (national and global), or those below (interpersonal, familial, and intrapsychic). Rather one works to understand their interpenetration. Would we be building a wall between our neighbors and us—between Mexico and the United States—if we did not live within psychic walls? Do not these psychic divisions reinscribe social, economic, and ethnic divides? Does not border crossing in one domain work to undermine the pernicious stability of walls in interrelated domains? Can the opening and sustaining of dialogue at the borders of our experience help to create sacred sites of reconciliation where walls now stand?

WALLS BEGET WALLS

Standing on the San Diego side of the triple wall that is being constructed between the United States and Mexico, you see a vast collection of land-moving equipment; half the bright yellow Caterpillar equipment familiar to us from the toy trucks of childhood, the other half bearing drab-colored U.S. army camouflage. The presence of this partnership between a private corporation and the military is predictable, given the explosion of transnational corporations' collusion with national government policies and the armies that police them.

This border area with our southernmost neighbor is the most highly militarized border on earth between a nation and a peaceful neighbor nation. To see the wall going up is a heartache. What a legacy![6]

At the border near Tijuana, the National Guard is busy filling in deep canyons in order to stretch the wall across the uneven terrain. These actions displace tons of earth that then drain into nearby estuaries choking off their life. To accomplish this, the United States Department of Homeland Security—a misbegotten progeny of our government's misguided response to 9/11—has been given the authority to breach all environmental protections carefully crafted over decades to protect the fragile wetlands and ecology near Tijuana/San Diego.[7] The wall extends into the Pacific Ocean, as though having the God-given right to part the sea into separate national domains (see Fig. 1).

Our United States' "Berlin Wall" has affinity with other such walls. Standing on the parched earth looking south toward Tijuana across the wall, for a moment you might think you are in Israel or the Palestinian-occupied territories. The same kind of bright yellow equipment constructed the Israeli separation wall that is strangling the Palestinian settlements and refugee camps. Caterpillar is the same

Fig 1: U.S./Mexico Wall at the Pacific Ocean, Tijuana/SanDiego

company that actually created machinery to specifically demolish houses in Palestine. This demolition is a terrorizing response to whole communities where only a few are responsible for violence.[8] The day I first saw these machines, my stomach turned. You think of comparable equipment building homes and workplaces. Instead, precisely such equipment is being used to efficiently shatter houses, homes where families have enjoyed holidays and weddings, where they have cradled their children and mourned their loved ones, while under occupation.

Walls beget walls. The U.S./Mexico wall has echoes in the increased militarization of Mexico's southern border with Guatemala—a region where Central American refugees flee lives of untenable poverty and lack of hope for a better future for their families. As you drive in southern Mexico, you are stopped multiple times by police, who look inside the car to see if you look like a refugee. What is this "look?" Tired, poor, dirty, frightened, dark-skinned, indigenous? These internal checkpoints echo northward as well—in Denver and Chicago, Raleigh and Charlotte—places deep within the U.S., where we too have established unpredictable, spontaneous, and moving internal checkpoints that suddenly upset the lives of poor people on their way to work, while picking up their children at school, or sitting in an evening classroom studying English after working two shifts.

Throughout history, cities surrounded themselves with walls to prevent military seizures and occupation by foreign forces. These new walls have a different meaning. The siege that is being protected against is not military; it is not occupation by foreign rulers. It is a siege of people with unfulfilled hunger and desires, of peoples displaced by forces larger than themselves.

Recently in San Diego, I spoke with a Border Patrol spokesperson, now an employee of the Department of Homeland Security. He said that he hosts many governmental delegations from around the world that are interested in learning how to create the kind of wall we are busily constructing: the kind with thousands of ground sensors so that the carefulness of your steps do not matter; the kind with satellite surveillance so you cannot hide; the kind with infrared sensors so that your very body heat betrays you; the kind that is said to require a workforce of 28,000 border agents. Thai government officials came recently to the Border Patrol office in the San Diego sector to see what they could learn. European Union (EU) ministry representatives also came to consult on the building of walls in North Africa to stem the tide of African migration due to genocides, the AIDS epidemic, corrupt and violent governments, and starvation.[9] In an age of unprecedented forced migrations, Americans are getting quite a worldwide reputation for wall building. We have made a huge investment in our southern border: 7.3 billion dollars since 1993.[10]

How initially ironic it sounds linking such walls with freedom: an age of walls is part of an age of "free" trade. But then it begins to make sense. Walls do not impede the passing of computer parts, assembled electronics, toxic waste, or people of means and power. They do not even stop the passage of poor and desperate people. Since the beginning of the construction of the U.S./Mexico wall in 1994, which coincided with the passage of NAFTA, the North American Free Trade Agreement, the flow of migration has not stopped; migratory routes have shifted into the Arizona desert. Walls also beget subterranean tunnels, perilous alternate pathways, subjugation, and fear; walls call for expensive "experts" to guide migrants across the border, drug traffickers who are no strangers to brutality. Over 4000 people have died in the desert trying to cross into the United States in the last twelve years. They died from extremes of heat, cold, and violence. Before 1994 there were so few deaths that there were not even yearly records kept.

So if the wall does not keep out poor migrants—newly re-labeled "potential terrorists" — what does it do? American border policies aim to create a world of low wages and high profits, says Maria Jimenez,[11] a border activist in Texas. The wall and border surveillance achieve two goals. On the one hand, the poor who are immobilized in their country of origin become willing laborers in assembly plants, working for extremely low wages. On the other hand, those who do succeed in crossing, without legal residence, are then available to work at the lowest wages with the fewest benefits and rights.

Walls not only reproduce themselves between nations in an era of massive displacement of impoverished people due to genocide, civil war, and transnational capitalism's lifting of protective tariffs and environmental regulations. Such walls also snake through our communities, dividing children into poor and affluent schools, separating neighborhoods into those beset by violence and drugs and those walled off by private security. These walls reinforce daily divisions between neighbors with different skin colors, mother tongues, and economic levels. Walls in our social environments insidiously construct psychic walls, and fill psychic space with exclusionary thinking, fear of difference, and polarized divisions. In a tragic circle, such psychological wall-making begets further distance, ensuring stereotyping, and yet more divisions. Walls give some psyches a sense of superiority, entitlement, privilege, and pride, while crushing others with fear, self-doubt, angry frustration, fatalism, and pernicious feelings of inferiority.[12] If followed backwards, in America all such walls pass back into history, to the separation of families on the slave block, to children drinking at separate water fountains. They snake back to the multiple divides of reservations where the displaced and dispossessed survivors of America's mass genocide of those indigenous to the land were corralled.

The present immigration debate sadly does not even put before citizens whether or not a wall should be built on our 1,950-mile-long border. On a national, governmental level, the wall is under way and will be funded for completion. May we begin to imagine a day when our children and grandchildren gather at what used to be the site of the wall and learn how greed erupted, creating an open wound at our southern border; *una herida abierta,* where Gloria Anzaldúa says, "the Third World grates against the First and bleeds."[13] May they learn how corporate and national rights were asserted before and against human rights to shelter, food, education, and healthcare.

The question we must pose to ourselves is whether we will continue to be bystanders to America's many walls or commit ourselves to their dismantling, to moving across established divides, creating transborder relationships at all levels of our existence: psychic, interpersonal, community, intercommunity, national, international, even interspecies, and between ourselves and the natural and built environments.

Chicano playwright Cabranes-Grant says, "We are each transportable borders, enacting a separation or challenging it. The border is not a distinct geographical location."[14] Play director Joseph Velasco expands on this point, saying that "[b]orders are not crossed just when one crosses from one country into another—but rather, anytime one enters a new territory. Ethnicity, age, place, language, gender, and social borders are crossed everyday."[15] Daily, we enact the maintenance and construction of borders and walls between others and ourselves, all the while sectioning off our intrapsychic experience in corresponding ways.

Limit Situations, Limit Acts

In our lives we come up against what Alvaro Vieira Pinto and Paulo Freire call "limit-situations," situations that block our freedom, and which are often initially experienced by us as fetters and insurmountable obstacles. Refusing to accept the usual idea of "limit," Pinto says that limit-situations can be seen, not as "impassable boundaries where possibilities end, but the real boundaries where all possibilities begin": they are not "the frontier which separates being from nothingness, but the frontier which separates being from being more."[16] We can think of the border situations within ourselves, in our communities, and our nation as limit-situations. It is these that we need to dream actively about, transgressing them first in imagination and then in reality.

The U.S.-Mexico border as a limit-situation not only creates misery, but inspires transgression and creativity. Those who embrace such limit-situations engage in what Freire calls the vocation of humanization, the call to move from being objects of a culture by which we are passively used to standing in opposition to dehumanizing processes, taking on

Fig. 2: Border Dynamics—Alberto Morackis and Guadalupe Serrano. The sculpture is the property of the University of Arizona and is a permanent exhibit on their main campus in Tucson, Arizona.

the task of creating and claiming a different future. The border as a limit-situation is a potential site of making the world anew through our relationships, and through art and activism (see Fig. 2).

Aurora Levins Morales says, "Borders are generally established in order to exercise control, and when we center our attention on the historical empowerment of the oppressed, we inevitably swim rivers, lift barbed wire and violate 'no trespassing signs.'"[17] The transgression of borders requires particular kinds of selves who grasp the power to create with others, to be part of seeing through and then constructing the world anew. They are selves who search for the history of the borders they encounter, refusing to take them as necessary facts. They inquire into the history of their communities in order to know something of the present and to be able to imagine a different future. Selves-in-solidarity-with-others can imagine doorways where walls now stand.

COMMUNITIES OF HOSPITALITY

In the Old Testament, Moses is asked by God to create six cities of refuge: three in Canaan and three in Jordan. "These six cities shall be a refuge, both for the children of Israel, and for the stranger, and for the sojourner among them ..." (Numbers, 35: 15). In an address to the International Parliament of Writers, the late Jacques Derrida traced the idea of "open cities" or refuge cities, those places where migrants can seek sanctuary from the pressures of persecution, immigration, and exile. In European medieval tradition, according to Derrida, the city had a certain degree of sovereignty by which it could determine its laws of hospitality. The International Parliament of Writers, including Derrida, became interested in these laws of hospitality as migrants and asylum seekers were either turned away from borders or, once inside, treated as having inferior status due to their lack of papers or legal status.

In Europe and the United States, some cities are seeking to revive the idea of sovereignty for cities around issues of hospitality. In protest against harsh national immigration and asylum policies, they are seeking to establish themselves as cities of refuge or hospitality. In the United States, over 60 cities have adopted referenda to create more hospitable conditions in their cities for migrants. In particular, they have moved not to adopt national initiatives that would require local police to be involved in the enforcement of immigration laws, and in particular not to ask about the immigration status of those who require

police assistance, medical care, or social services (unless federally
mandated for particular programs).[18] This could be seen as a small step
toward a postnational consciousness, linked to the exercise of the
postcolonial imagination (see Fig. 3). At the same time, other cities
have moved to greater inhospitality. Under the Counterterrorism Act,
local jurisdictions can ask the Attorney General to deputize police as
immigration agents. This means that many injured and sick people
will not seek care in hospitals and clinics for fear of deportation. It means
domestic abuse and neighborhood crime will be under-reported for
fear that police will ask for papers and turn those without them over
to immigration authorities. It increases an atmosphere of intimidation,
harassment, punitiveness, and gross inhospitality.

As of this writing in the summer of 2007, national politics has ground
to a halt on immigration reform, while the national government has
augmented surveillance of immigrant communities and stepped up

Fig. 3: "Dream of Taniperla Canyon," on the Mexican side of the U.S./Mexico
Wall, Ambos Nogales, Mexico. This mural was originally painted by Zapatistas in
Chiapas, Mexico. It was destroyed by paramilitary forces. Subcomandante Marcos
called for it to be repainted throughout the world. It is a depiction of the indigenous
communities in Chiapas being able to live in peace, after 500 years of assault by
colonialism and neoliberalism.

workplace and home raids that result in deportations and a darkened atmosphere of intimidation and fear. At this political moment, we may be more effective in establishing a humane atmosphere in and through our cities and towns than struggling exclusively on the national front. Many U. S. and European cities are working to extend the sovereignty and autonomy of their cities and towns to enhance justice for immigrants, while interlinking with others nationally and transnationally who are also working to imagine a world without walls. Derrida suggests that new cities of refuge could reorient the politics of the nation: "If we look to the city, rather than to the state, it is because we have given up hope that the state might create a new image for the city."[19]

This kind of initiative—a politics of hospitality—is an exemplar of a different political strategy, one that is more laterally than vertically oriented, one that decenters centralized power. When the politics of the nation-state loses its ethical compass, it is crucial that it be countered by a combination of initiatives from civil society at both the local and the transnational levels. When a nation goes far astray in the practice of humane conduct—attacking civilian hospitals, torturing detainees, holding people without charges and without recourse to self-defense, preemptively beginning wars—then its citizens must assert and keep alive an empathic concern for our neighbors, particularly those suffering the effect of national mispolicies. Our cities could become more like autonomous zones that differentiate themselves from national agendas driven by corporate greed, thereby recovering the ethic of hospitality that we long for, and in so doing restoring our humanity. A community that aspires to such hospitality requires psychologies that study divides and creates opportunities for meeting across them.

Recent adoption of the Kyoto Protocol by several hundred U.S. mayors has shown that cities can at serious times adopt a more visionary stance than that of the national government. At the federal level, the Bush administration rejected regulation of the greenhouse gases that contribute to global warming on two counts: it had not yet been scientifically proven that humans contribute to the greenhouse effect, and further control of manufacturers' emissions would jeopardize their competitiveness on the world market.

Unfortunately, towns and cities that claim some sovereignty can also contribute to intensifying exclusionary walls within their legal limits. In the absence of national consensus regarding immigration policy, many towns and cities have passed laws that commit landlords to checking the immigration status of potential occupants, that make English the official language, that punish business owners who hire workers without documents, and that sanction police assistance in matters of immigration control, contributing to forced deportations and the splitting of families. For instance, a man in Winchester, Connecticut was pulled over for not wearing a seatbelt. When it was discovered he had no driver's license, the police called immigration officials who then began deportation proceedings.[20]

What is at stake psychologically and ethically? Derrida argues that culture itself is hospitality; that the ethical is hospitality. If this is so, we are but a shadow of our lost humanity in the face of walls between our neighbors and us. He argues that the foreigner or the stranger puts us in question, poses a question to us. The foreigner through his or her very being poses the question: What kind of neighbor are we? The stranger's presence holds a mirror to us, showing us our own face of disregard, of scorn, of fear, of interest or ignorance, of hospitality. He stresses that the essence of hospitality is its unconditional nature. It does not ask the stranger to speak our language, to visit only on our terms, to be only the wealthy. "Absolute hospitality,"[21] he says,

> requires that I open up my home and that I give not only to the foreigner (provided with a family name, with the social status of being a foreigner, etc.), but to the absolute, unknown, anonymous other, and that I *give place* to them, that I let them come, that I let them arrive, and take place in the place I offer them, without asking of them either reciprocity (entering into a pact) or even their names. The law of absolute hospitality commands a break with hospitality by right ....[22]

While political policy cannot be directly drawn from such an unconditional proposition, ought not the spirit of it be somewhere visible in the way we live our relations and craft our laws? Divided by nationality, are we not united, as Kant pointed out, by being citizens of the world?

Derrida underscores a psychological fact: we are only truly at home with ourselves when we are open to receiving the other. Is a home a home when it keeps the stranger out? The paradox he is working to unveil is that without welcoming the stranger, the host is a hostage in his own home. While the host is inside, without inviting the guest, he is on the outside of the inside. Only the invited guest can host him into the inside of his own home.

Derrida urges us:

> Let us say yes *to who or what turns up*, before any determination, before any anticipation, before any *identification* whether or not it has to do with a foreigner, an immigrant, an invited guest, or an unexpected visitor, whether or not the new arrival is the citizen of another country—a human, animal, or divine creature, a living or dead thing, male or female.[23]

Lest we drift toward an Anglo-Judeo-Protestant sense of righteousness, we must heed a caution regarding the language of hospitality. If we use it, as I am doing, we must hold tight to the shadow of this way of naming the situation, a shadow that introduces crucial and critical complexity. If one people invades and occupies another people's land, is it hospitality if the descendants of the original inhabitants are allowed to come back to visit or to live? If one people enjoys wealth and high educational and health standards partly from the profits gained from the exploitation of another people, is it hospitality when these benefits are shared? When people work very hard for small reward, while others profit grossly, when they are separated from their loved ones and their community, when they have risked their lives to provide for their families, when they suffer the loneliness of separation from their homeland, their families, and communities, should they be dependent on hospitality instead of enjoying the rights of refuge? As an idea, hospitality is a starting point for relationship. In time, its naïveté will need to be abandoned. From one vantage point on hospitality, a beneficent person gifts to another person who is less fortunate. From another vantage point, the one who could offer hospitality but does not, symbolically loses his own home. The one who might be hospitable needs the stranger in order to come home to him or herself, to live within his or her humanity and to reclaim his or her own shadow. Gloria Anzaldúa advises Anglos thus: "Admit that Mexico is your double, that she exists in the shadow of this country, that we are irrevocably tied to her. Gringo, acccept the doppelganger in your psyche. By taking back your shadow the intracultural split will heal."[24] We are in need of a different set of ways of being with one another.

"By Taking Back Your Shadow the Intracultural Split Will Heal"

Our borders could be lived as sacred places, as places for creativity and regeneration, as sites for hybridity, where we can imagine and bring into being what is most desired. Such border-work requires explorations of shadow in our local communities, its workplaces, neighborhood community centers, its houses of worship, and our town halls. What is the American shadow that falls across the U.S./Mexico border with such a violent harshness? Is it in part the shadow caused by cultural amnesia regarding slavery, genocide, and the forced displacement of Mexicans after the U.S. conquest of Mexican land?

Last month I re-visited Maclovio Rojas, a small community outside of Tijuana, founded in 1988 by a group of visionary women from Oaxaca. They imagined a better life for their families and organized an autonomous community to promote education, healthcare, and local self-governance. Their leaders are now in hiding, following periods of imprisonment by the Mexican government. Their plan for such a community is not part of the master plan for the "free" trade zone. Standing on the hill above this *colonia's* simple homes, I looked to the northeast and saw a glittering sea of metal roofs of 5000 tractor truck trailers, ready to load the products from the *maquiladores* and take them to market. On the southwest I saw a brand new ghetto under construction, rows of new housing for *maquiladora* workers. Here each family will be confined to a small room, next to hundreds of other families, each in their equally diminutive quarters. I did not see any playgrounds or *zocalos*, central town plazas for strolling and meeting.

These dwellings—springing up by the thousands—are called "pigeon houses"[25] (see Fig. 4). They are a new kind of slave quarters. Jimenez compares the Border Patrol—and the vigilantes that have grown up around it—to the slave patrols before the Civil War. She says their function is to reinforce immobility—and to bring about the conditions that, by ensuring low wages, maximize profits.[26] Human rights activists at the border understand workplace conditions as a contemporary extension of the hacienda plantation system, where workers were virtually indentured and were seen not as human beings worthy of care and compassion but as labor commodities. Jaime Cota, from CITTAC, a human and labor rights organization in Baja

California, Mexico, is assisting workers in defending their rights as human beings. In one case against a *maquiladore* manufacturer, Cota is representing workers who have suffered the amputation of fingers and hands by metal cutting machines. The machine sensors built to protect workers from being cut were intentionally turned off to force workers to move at a quicker pace out of fear of the amputation of fingers and hands. This graphic example shows how human lives are reduced to a mere labor commodity as the greed for profit replaces human regard. Mexico's history of racism bleeds into that of the United States.

We know about contemporary American slave quarters: the camps for migrant agricultural workers, the city slums that breed horizontal violence among young people, our prisons … especially our prisons. The structure of slavery has not left our bloodstream. Like a renegade gene, it keeps replicating itself, pulling in different ethnic groups to satisfy its cancerous voraciousness for profit. Africans, Irish, Italians, Chinese, Japanese, Puerto Ricans, Dominicans, Haitians, Bangladeshis, Pakistanis, Sudanese, Mexicans. The evil triplets that Martin Luther King, Jr. warned

Fig. 4: "Pigeon houses" being built around manufacturing plants near Tijuana, Mexico.

us about—racism, militarism, and capitalism—have shown up at the U.S./Mexico border, and they are busy doing their work.

It is impossible to talk with migrants without documents without being reminded of slavery and indentured servitude. Fleeing poverty, civil war, political repression and torture, or genocide, migrants describe how they work multiple menial jobs, often below minimum wage, without workplace safeguards, environmental standards, and workers' representation through unions. While contributing their labor to the common good and part of their earnings to our social security pools, they and their children will not enjoy the benefits of these pools. They are accused of exhausting local resources for health, policing, and education. In a just world the federal government would transfer these social security contributions to the municipalities where the majority of migrants live, taking the pressure off local budgets. Migrants live in the shadows of our cities, surrendering a voice for justice out of fear of being deported and unable to support their families. As DuBois said of African-Americans before them, they are "shut out from their world by a vast veil" of racism.[27]

How ironic the far Right's discourse on immigration from Mexico sounds when placed in a historical context. "Intruders," "foreigners," "parasites," "illegals," "carriers of disease." The historical amnesia is shocking. California, Nevada, Arizona, New Mexico, and Utah were the northern part of Mexico 160 years ago. Twenty-five thousand Mexicans died in an effort to retain their national lands. Upon defeat, 100,000 Mexicans became trapped within the new borders of the United States, their families separated by the forcible imposition of a new national border, many forcibly displaced from their land, others lynched and subjected to mob violence.[28] Mexicans say, "we did not cross the border, the border crossed us."

How do we engage the shadows of slavery and conquest? In this brief space I can only offer several formal and informal public community initiatives. These are suggestive of multiple available means of bringing history's legacy in the present into the conversation, so that it can be addressed and redressed.

CULTURAL AMNESIA AND THE RECOVERY OF
HISTORICAL MEMORY

In the wake of apartheid and the violence, injustice, and racism
that sustained it, a process of truth and reconciliation was created in
South Africa that has spawned similar efforts worldwide to heal the
gap between official histories and the experiences of those excluded from
these histories. In 2004, the first Truth and Reconciliation Commission
(TRC) in the United States was begun in Greensboro, North
Carolina.[29] It sought to expose and heal an intercommunity wound
that occurred in 1979, a symptom of a larger structure of racial injustice
flowing from the times of slavery in the United States. In 1979, during
a demonstration, White Klan and neo-Nazi members killed five Black
members of the Communist Workers Party, and injured 10 others.
Aware of the potential for violence at the rally, the police decided to be
absent, colluding with the violence that erupted. As many White city
officials distanced themselves from the event and never inquired into
the underlying issues, these issues continued to fester and create enmity
between White and Black communities. The TRC proceedings offered
public space for many to come forward from various sectors of the
community to give testimony regarding what happened in 1979. The
commissioners hoped that increased public acknowledgment would
lead to institutional reforms and citizen engagement and
transformation. Recommendations that arose from the TRC included
the establishment of living wages, anti-racism training, citizen review
committees to ensure police accountability, and the creation of a
community justice center.

There were representative present at the TRC proceedings from
Tulsa, New Orleans, Selma, Rosewood, and Montgomery. Attempts
at reconciliation seed other such attempts. They expose the walls that
exist in communities, inquire into their history and function, address
grievous wrongs that have been hidden, and begin a process of imagining
and embodying multiple means of reparations for the past, reparations
that create connective tissue between historically alienated
communities for the future.

The Slave Reparations Movement is a similar effort under way in
the United States.[30] The debates that have been opened through
consideration of reparations for slavery address publicly not only the

246-year history of slavery in America, but also the legacy of slavery for the continuing economic servitude of many African-Americans. Historians and economists working in this area are clear that in general while Blacks work harder than Whites, they are paid less. Despite affirmative action initiatives, the economic capital base of Whites that was built on the labor of slaves—particularly through textile manufacturing, the building of the railroads, tobacco production, and the insurance industry, where slaves were treated as material property—continues to give Whites an unfair advantage. This automatic inheritance of economic privilege by Whites happens regardless of their families' length of stay in the U.S., because it is an inheritance based on skin color. Freed slaves were never given the compensation of 40 acres and a mule promised by Sherman as part of Reconstruction. The facts that they were kept out of neighborhoods that accrued value, denied mortgages, excluded from the Homestead Act of 1862, and that economically prosperous Black areas were destroyed as in Tulsa, Oklahoma in 1921 have led to continuing equity inequality. Historian Manning Marable and others have called for a national commission whose aims would be the erasure of racialized deficits through the provision of such things as equitable healthcare and schools for Blacks, as well as more access by Blacks to managerial roles.

Many community arts projects also seek to bring extruded aspects of history into current awareness. The Confluence Project, Maya Lin's memorials along the Columbia River to mark the meetings of Lewis and Clark's group with Native American groups is one example. Another is the Ford Foundation's Animating Democracy Projects, which included museum displays of furniture and finery of the colonial period along with the telling signs of slavery—such as shackles and whipping posts—which supported such elegance.[31] Community murals and art, such as the ones presented in this article, educate new generations about histories of injustices suffered and communities' dreams of a more just future.

These movements bring into dialogue aspects of American history many would prefer not to know. For Whites, not knowing or not remembering leads to a false sense of entitlement, an unquestioning acceptance of economic privilege which distorts their image of themselves, their labors, and rights. Keeping the past at bay allows privilege to continue to accrue, balancing economic gain with soul loss.

Sites of Reconciliation

In part, the past can be metabolized and the future created differently by informal exchanges in the present between individuals from groups that have been historically divided. In most towns and cities, meetings between migrants and citizens happen only on top of economic and ethnic divides. Immigrants without documents are not free to speak of their difficult experiences on account of their fear of racism and deportation. There is a collusion of silence that keeps Whites ignorant of the challenges and heartaches borne by their fellow townspeople.

To create sites of reconciliation requires insight into the need for them and sustained effort to build bridges across separations established over a long history. The learning of each others' languages is a first step toward more personal communication. Neighborhoods, workplaces, adult education centers, and religious congregations can set up *intercambios*, where pairs of people divide the time between speaking in one mother tongue and then the other, all the while sharing the bits and pieces of daily life. Beyond language acquisition is the creation of relationships freed from the usual divisions. Knowing how unsafe migrants feel in the larger community, citizens can offer their support to community centers where migrants go for information about housing and healthcare; they can help with immigration issues; and they can assist in the learning of English.

Such intercultural meetings spawn relationships that can transcend delimited normative notions of hospitality by opening "spaces and forms of exchange that *allow* for mutual obligation, engagement, and civic participation."[32] Such spaces are also part of American history, echoing from the beginning of the settlement house movement of Jane Addams' Hull House days in Chicago.

Depth Psychology and the Border Work of Reconciliation

In contrast to ego psychology and to developmental schemas that advocate firm ego boundaries, the development of mastery and control, increasing differentiation from others, independence, and autonomy, Jungian psychology counsels us to distrust the ego and decenter ourselves to a more observant place within (the non-ego center). We are directed to approach the borders of our experience, inviting and then engaging dialogically with what has been excluded. As we can see from the example I am foregrounding in this essay, it is where borders become unduly firm and frozen, where walls are built, that projections, disassociations, historical and cultural amnesia, ignorance, and the failure of empathic imagination thrive. Rhetoric and stereotypical thinking follow; rationalizations abound. Paradoxically, walls do not quell fears, they reinscribe them, promoting increased feelings of vulnerability and paranoia.

Jungian and archetypal psychologies direct us to a different way of being in borderlands, a way that entails engaging a multiplicity of perspectives by making sure that dialogue is practiced where monologue has prevailed. Dialogue facilitates a withdrawal of projections and stereotypes as well as the development of compassion and empathic imagination. It allows us to see what we have identified with and why. To be involved in such dis-identification is to become more aware, more able to see the other's point of view. Here psychic hospitality intersects with community hospitality: both require efforts at reconciliation with what has been cast aside into unconsciousness. Through this intersection, those privileged by race, ethnicity, and class can discover ways to counter the soul loss engendered by cultural amnesia, an amnesia about the misappropriation of the labor of poor people of color and the withholding from them of recognition, witness, and hospitality.

Work in the borderlands requires stepping out of our comfort zone, into a relationship with what is unfamiliar, allowing it to challenge what we have taken for granted. The work of individuation requires that we clarify where we live within ossifying borders. These are sites of potential creativity.[33] They are places where the regeneration of community, of ecology, and of the Self are one and the same. They are not only within us; they are everywhere around us.

The psychological work of individuation can be re-framed as border work, as becoming more skillful at building hybrid spaces of connection. Such border work supplements the downward movement at stake in traditional soul work with a deepening into the depth of "between" spaces. At the borders between the familiar and the unfamiliar, self and other, connective tissue needs to grow from formal and informal efforts at dialogue.

Depth psychologically-minded people are needed at the community and intercommunity levels to participate in and help host such work. They are also needed as we attempt to understand the intrapsychic defenses that are mobilized as we try to know ourselves within a wider historical and cultural context.

The theme of this issue of the journal is "Politics and the American Soul." Sadly, the issues I have raised are not limited to America; they re-appear in all communities where the rivers and rivulets of 100 million[34] displaced people worldwide struggle to re-establish their lives in this era of unprecedented forced migration. We will need to address the psychology of unbridled greed more effectively, studying its dynamics in colonialism and their present morph in transnational capitalism. From 1994-2004, the number of international migrants doubled; 50% of these are children. Sebastião Salgado, the Brazilian photographer committed to documenting these tragic migrations, says that they are unparalleled in human history, presenting profound challenges to our most basic notions of national, cultural, and community citizenship.[35] They are also challenges to the psyche, and much depends on how we respond to them as depth psychologists.

NOTES

1. Edward Said, quoted in C. Kaplan, *Questions of Travel: Postmodern Discourses of Displacement* (Durham, NC: Duke University Press, 1996), p. 119.

2. James Hillman, *Re-Visioning Psychology* (New York: Harper & Row, 1975).

3. Mary Watkins, "Depth Psychology and the Liberation of Being," in Roger Brooke, ed., *Pathways into the Jungian World: Phenomenology and Analytical Psychology* (London: Routledge, 2000).

4. Mary Watkins, "Seeding Liberation: A Dialogue Between Depth Psychology and Liberation Psychology," in Dennis Slattery and Lionel Corbett, eds., *Depth Psychology: Meditations in the Field* (Einsiedeln, SW: Daimon Verlag, 2000); Helene Lorenz and Mary Watkins, "Silenced Knowings, Forgotten Springs: Paths to Healing in the Wake of Colonialism," *Radical Psychology: A Journal of Psychology, Politics, and Radicalism*, http://radpsy.york.ca (2000); Helene Lorenz and Mary

Watkins, "Individuation, Seeing-Through, and Liberation: Depth Psychology and Culture," *Quadrant, XXXIII*; Mary Watkins and Helene Lorenz, *Toward Psychologies of Liberation* (London/New York: Palgrave Macmillan, 2008); Lawrence Alschuler, *The Psychopolitics of Liberation: Political Consciousness from a Jungian Perspective* (London: Palgrave Macmillan, 2006); Geoffrey Nelson and Isaac Prilleltensky, *Community Psychology: In Pursuit of Liberation and Well-Being* (London: Palgrave Macmillan, 2005).

5. George Lakoff and Sam Ferguson, "The Framing of Immigration," (2006), 2-3, www.rockridgeinstitute.org/ research/ rockridge/immigration

6. Over the past six years the delegations I have been part of to the U.S./Mexico border regions of San Diego/Tijuana and Douglas/Ambos Nogales (Arizona/Mexico) have been hosted by three extraordinary organizations committed to public education about the border: the American Friends Service Committee (www.afsc.org/pacificsw/ sandiego.htm), Borderlinks (www.borderlinks.org/), and Global Exchange (www.globalexchange.org).

7. Personal communication with Mike McCoy, Tijuana National Estuarine Research Preserve.

8. Israel Committee Against House Demolition, www.icahd.org/ eng; www.catdestroyshomes.org

9. In 2002, the European Union (EU) ministerial body decided to try to stem the tide of African migration into Europe not by building a wall on their own shore, but inside North Africa. They built a 200-mile wall in Morocco to frustrate desperate migrants. Of the 45,000 migrants crossing from Africa to Europe since 2005, at least 3000 have died in the sea. C. Rajah, "Disturbing Similarities: Migration's Common Features from Africa to Mexico," *The Quarterly Newsletter of Global Exchange*, 70 (2007): 6.

10. Christian Ramirez, American Friends Service Committee, talk to human rights delegation from Global Exchange, April 30, 2006.

11. Maria Jimenez, "The Militarization of the U.S.-Mexico border, Part I: Border Communities Respond to Militarization," www.inmotion magazine.com/mj1.html (1998): 25.

12. The Southern Poverty Law Center, which monitors hate crimes, is struck by the explosion of hate groups and alarming events around "immigration" issues. For instance, during a Cinco de Mayo celebration

in 2006 in a Tucson park an armed anti-immigration extremist, Roy Warden, led demonstrators proclaiming: "Listen up, Mexican invaders. We will not permit you, the ignorant, the savage, the unwashed, to overrun us, as happened in Rome …. Land must be paid for in blood. If any invader tries to take this land from us we will wash this land and nurture our soil with oceans of their blood!" (Southern Poverty Law Center Report, 2006, 36, 2, p. 1).

13. Gloria Anzaldúa, *Borderlands/La Frontera: The New Mestiza* (San Francisco: Aunt Lute Books, 1987), p. 3.

14. Cabranes-Grant, in Joseph Velasco, Director's Notes for Bordertown and *La Barda* (The Wall), Ensemble Theater Company, March 12-13, 2004, Santa Barbara, CA.

15. Joseph Velasco, Director's Notes for Bordertown and *La Barda* (The Wall), Ensemble Theater Company, March 12-13, 2004, Santa Barbara, CA.

16. Quoted in Paulo Freire, *Pedagogy of the Oppressed* (New York: Continuum, 1989), p. 89.

17. Aurora Levins Morales, *Medicine Stories: History, Culture, and the Politics of Integrity* (Cambridge, MA: South End Press, 1998), p. 38.

18. See http://www.nilc.org/immlawpolicy/LocalLaw/tbl_local _enfrcmnt_0704.pdf

19. Jacques Derrida, *On Cosmopolitanism and Forgiveness*, trans. Mark Dooley & M. Hughes (New York: Routledge, 2001), p. 6.

20. Mishkin, "Activists Lobby for Immigrants," *Yale Daily News*, 10/04/06.

21. The "guest" worker proposals before the Senate and Congress bear no relation to hospitality, despite their name. These proposals give all power to employers regarding the coming and going of employees within strict time limits set by the federal government. Workers must accept whatever work conditions they find themselves in or else they must leave the U.S. The "guest" proposals separate families, deny migrants sufficient long-term security to enable them to develop roots in their communities, and mitigate against the dignity of being able to claim basic human rights in the workplace. A child of the *bracero* program of the 1950s, the guest worker program would more aptly be named the "exploited worker" program.

22. Jacques Derrida, *Of Hospitality: Anne Dufourmantelle Invites Jacques Derrida to Respond*, trans. Rachel Bowlby (Stanford, CA: Stanford University Press, 2000), p. 25.

23. *Ibid.*, p. 77.

24. Anzaldúa, *Borderlands/La Frontera*, p. 384.

25. Without studying the effect of "free" trade agreements on Mexican farmers, it is difficult to understand the mass migration such housing marks. The North American Free Trade Agreement (NAFTA) undermined the price of corn in Mexico. The price had been kept steady by the Mexican government as a basic welfare precaution, enabling the poorest to have food provisions. NAFTA required the Mexican government to stop their intervention in prices, while allowing the U.S. government to continue its subsidies to farmers. This resulted in a dumping of U.S. corn on the Mexican market that put thousands of small farmers out of business and contributed to the growing hunger of millions. U.S. policy through NAFTA substantially contributed to the very exodus of Mexicans many now complain about. This fact is little known or remembered when migrants are treated as illegal invaders. "Free" trade turns out to be freer for the few than for the many, disrupting local economies for the sake of unconscionable private profit by the few. Critics have argued standards for "fair" trade, to provide sufficient wages to allow people to work in their home communities.

26. Maria Jimenez, see note 11.

27. W. E. B. DuBois, *The Souls of Black Folks* (1903).

28. For some sense of the scope of racist violence, it is estimated that between 1848 and 1928 at least 597 Mexicans were lynched. William Carrigan, "The Lynching of Persons of Mexican Origin or Descent in the United States, 1848 to 1928," *Journal of Social History* (Winter 2003).

29. Pat Clark, "Greensboro Truth and Reconciliation Commission: Seeking Truth, Working for Reconciliation," One by One Conference, November 14, 2006, Riverdale, NY. See www.greensborotrc.org

30. John Eisler, "Slave Reparations: The Final Passage," CrabTree Pictures (2004).

31. Fred Wilson, "Mining the Museum," Baltimore Historical Society. See "Animating democracy: The Artistic Imagination as a Force in Civic Dialogue," 1999. http://www.artsusa.org/animatingdemocracy/pdf/full.pdf

32. Heidrun Friesen and Sandro Mezzadra, "Hospitality and Transnational Migration in Europe and the Mediterranean Middle East and North Africa," (2007): 4. http://www.iue.it/RSCAS/Research/Mediterranean/mrm2007/pdf/WS15_MRM2007.pdf

33. In the community and ecological fieldwork and research portion of the M.A./Ph.D Depth Psychology Program at Pacifica Graduate Institute, which I coordinate, we work with the idea that each of us is called to different borderlands based on our life experiences. We invite students to show up at the border(s) given to them. Through engaged fieldwork and research, students learn about the multiple viewpoints that comprise the border region, studying how it became culturally, historically, and archetypally constructed as a border, and attuning themselves to the images, dreams, metaphors, and visions maintaining and mitigating against various kinds of divisions.

34. Exhibition notes, Sebastião Salgado, "Exodus," Center for Documentary Arts, Salt Lake City, November 2005.

35. *Ibid.*

Social Suffering Through Cultural Mourning, Cultural Melancholia, and Cultural Complexes

SAMUEL L. KIMBLES

> All humanity is caught in an inescapable network of mutuality,
> tied in a single garment of destiny, whatever affects one directly,
> affects all indirectly.
> — Martin Luther King

INTRODUCTION

Is it possible, in our analytic understanding of healing, to include a wider attitude toward human suffering that encompasses the ever-present issues of poverty, social inequality, social breakdown, and violence? Can we, in our analytic work, link analysis, the helping professions, religions, political movements, and social policy into a psychological narrative that includes social suffering? Can we develop an Eros toward social suffering that would allow us to become

Samuel L. Kimbles, Ph.D., is an analyst member of the C. G. Jung Institute of San Francisco. He is on the Clinical Faculty at the Department of Family and Community Medicine of the University of California, San Francisco Medical School. He maintains a private practice in Santa Rosa and San Francisco and is an organizational consultant. He is the editor, along with Thomas Singer, of *The Cultural Complex: Contemporary Jungian Perspectives on Psyche and Society* (Brunner-Routledge, 2004).

consciously part of a moral community wherein historical injustices and present events, like homelessness and global warming, can become part of our analytic work? Some of the figures in our patients' dreams and transferences speak about their/our social context; the other becomes by definition part of the interpersonal web of our work. From the point of view of social suffering, our analytic work is constitutive of our "ontological debt" to the other.

This paper consists of four different concepts: social suffering, cultural mourning, cultural melancholia, and cultural complexes. Each of these areas could easily form the basis of an individual presentation, but in this paper I will focus on their interrelationship. Social suffering refers to suffering experienced by individuals through their membership in one or another group, on the one hand, and by being a member of the human group, on the other. Social suffering includes the monstrous injuries that social forces inflict on human beings politically, economically, and institutionally as well as the images and metaphors used to represent these injuries. It refers to the cultural appropriation of memories (i.e., slavery, genocide) for political and cultural agendas as well as the culture of denial that surrounds these memories. Focusing on social suffering is my attempt to collapse the old categories that separate the individual from the social and cultural levels of meaning and place them within a moral attitude. These old ways of separating are barriers to understanding how human suffering can be at the same time collective and individual. Social suffering, a central subject of religion and theology, is hardly taken up at the collective level by our psychological orientation, which tends to be centered on individuals.

My emphasis on social suffering is a push for our analytic community to recover and take on a wider understanding of suffering that links social and cultural factors, relationships, and meanings to individual experiences. I use the concept of cultural mourning to ask the question of what the group has done and is doing with the reality of social suffering—theirs and ours. What have we done with the injuries, the losses, the rage, shame, and guilt suffered? Cultural melancholia refers to the failure to mourn or work with social suffering at the level of the group. And finally, cultural complexes are my way of thinking about how these processes become organized by the psyche at the level of the group and the individual.

SHADES AND SHADOWS

Recently, during a silent moment in my analytic work, a patient wondered out aloud: "When a sound stops, at what point do the vibrations end in space? When does a terror experienced and shouted out end? Do the vibrations go on forever—resonating in others who get the story of what happened through some sort of intuitive feeling?" I asked him about the stimulus for this question. He had in mind a past situation that we both knew about, in which a colleague had been killed during an outdoor sporting event. The patient had for several months been preoccupied with a vague anxiety about his own dying. But this way of expressing his anxiety was new and different. For one thing, it felt like a real question that opened both of us up to a kind of reverie about the unknown. This question was distinct from the anxious questions asked by him before, which had a stale circularity to them.

My patient's questions stimulated in me a set of thoughts and fantasies about the ongoing impact of trauma, individual and collective, and its intergenerational aftermaths. I, too, in a kind of half-conscious state had been wondering how long do traumas last and spread out in time? This question was the impetus for my reflections on the topic for this paper on "Social Suffering, Cultural Melancholia, and Cultural Mourning." I realized that over the past several years as I have spoken and written about cultural complexes, I have been wondering something similar to the question my patient asked. How do group traumas get processed, mourned, and redeemed in groups and in individuals? What happens if these traumas and losses are not redeemed or processed? Do they live on in a kind of collective dissociation?

My patient had not yet been born when his parents fled Nazism in Germany before the Second World War, and he had never brought that aspect of his traumatic family history directly into his analysis, even though his family structured many of its activities around managing the parents' irrational expressions of anxiety through their participation in religious rituals. Something within his family always remained unassimilated because the trauma they experienced when fleeing the Nazis in Germany was not acknowledged as an event that had a real psychic impact on their lives. A critical aspect of this patient's family history appeared to live on, encrypted, in his own generalized anxiety symptoms, and the specific one that he shared with me concerning his anxiety about dying. Through wondering aloud, was the patient asking himself/me about some family event that he knew about on some unconsious level but dared not let himself know consciously? Or was it the phantom of his family's secret, its repression that came into the session with his curiosity?

Since Freud's paper "Mourning and Melancholia,"[1] the goal of mourning has been defined in terms of the detachment of libidinal ties from the deceased love object(s). Successful mourning means that the ego is freed up from its former attachments and is thus able to attach to new object(s) and form a new life. Losses for Freud include the loss of a person, ideal, country, liberty, identity, and, of course, the loss of a culture.

Freud states that the primary difference between the mourner and the melancholic responses to loss is that the melancholic fails to adequately mourn his loss, and so one finds in him a profoundly painful dejection, cessation of interest in the outside world, loss of the capacity to love, inhibition of all activity, and a lowering of self-regarding feelings to a degree that finds utterance in self "reproaches and self-reviling, and culminates in a delusional expectation of punishment."[2]

Utilizing the concept of the cultural complex to look at social suffering through mourning and melancholia allows us to look at how mourning, or the failure to mourn, at the collective or group level and at the group level of the individual psyche becomes linked to cultural melancholia. In using the concept of the cultural complex to look at cultural mourning and cultural melancholia, Freud's formulation becomes for me a point of departure.

But before exploring the relationship of social suffering, cultural mourning, and cultural melancholia, I must first speak about cultural complexes.

CULTURAL COMPLEXES

The concept of the cultural complex expands on Joseph Henderson's concept of the cultural unconscious[3] and extends Jung's theory of complexes, originally applied to individuals, to the life of the group. The cultural level of the psyche and the group level of the individual psyche provide structure to the cultural unconscious.

> Cultural complexes express themselves in powerful moods and
> repetitive behaviors and are basic, naturally occurring elements

> in human beings that structure the individual responses to
> biological givens such as the body, aging, and death and to
> interpersonal relations within family, tribal, and broader
> communal systems. They operate through the group's
> expectations, its definition of itself, its destiny, and sense of its
> uniqueness. We can find [group] complexes operating in and
> through the group's fears, its creation of enemies and its attitudes
> toward other groups.[4]

In short, if the personal unconscious can be understood through
personal complexes, the cultural unconscious can be understood
through cultural complexes by providing affect, image, structure, and
dynamism to individual and group life.

As is true in the phenomena of transference and
countertransference, the underlying archetype of kinship libido
energizes the field in which cultural complexes are constellated. It links
personal experiences and group expectations as mediated by ethnicity,
race, gender, and the processes of social identity by providing a sense
of historical continuity. In his essay, "The Psychology of the
Transference," Jung states:

> an endogamous relationship is an expression of the libido which
> serves to hold the family together; One could therefore define it
> as a kind of instinct which, like a sheep dog, keeps the family
> group together.[5]

Similarly, cultural complexes may be seen as workhorses that facilitate
the relationship of the individual to the group, and the group to the
individual. They work to hold together the group energies associated
with kinship libido as expressed through similar histories, identities,
and ideologies at the individual and group levels.[6]

Living, internal memories at the level of the cultural unconscious
create a cultural symbolic space in which memories and events are held,
elaborated, and come to signify the spirit of the group.

An example of the activation of a two-thousand-year-old religious
cultural complex can be seen in James Carroll's book *Constantine's
Sword*. Carroll reports the story of a religious fight at Auschwitz between
Polish Catholics and Jews over the placement and meaning of a cross
that was placed near the death bunker where a Franciscan priest,
Maximilian Kolbe, was martyred, along with quarter of a million non-

Jewish Poles and a million and a half Jews. Pope John Paul II in 1979 had celebrated Mass in an open field for his countrymen where this same cross had been mounted. The Pope prayed for and to Father Kolbe who had voluntarily taken the place of a fellow inmate in the death bunker. He also prayed for Edith Stein who died in the camp and had been declared a Catholic saint in 1998. The pope called Auschwitz the "Golgotha of the modern world" and expressed the wish that a place of prayer and penance could be built on the death site. This infuriated Jews who wanted no prayers for the Jews killed in the Shoah. As fights escalated between the two groups, Jews and Catholics, the verbal attacks spewed out with "they killed Jesus," "They crucified our God," to "leave Our Dead Alone," "Do Not Christianize Auschwitz." Within the first twelve pages of Carroll's book, we read words that are complex indicators for the reenactment of a 2000-year-old religious cultural complex. These words are: Roman Catholic Church, Cross, Auschwitz, Jew, Golgotha, Jesus, Nazis, Shoah, Holocaust, Lord's Prayer, and Ruach. Carroll says,

> In addition to signifying the problem that death puts to God, whether a Jew's God or a Christian's, the cross at Auschwitz evokes with rare immediacy everything that has separated Jew and Christian during the two-thousand-year-old conflict between the two religions.[7]

Keeping the above example in mind, I now open up and expand on the definition of cultural complexes. I have identified five basic elements of cultural complexes (of course, there could be many more): (1) they function at the group level of the individual psyche and within the group; (2) they function autonomously; (3) they organize group life; (4) they facilitate the individual's relationship to the group; and, (5) they provide a sense of belonging and identity as well as sense of historical continuity.

1. A cultural complex is a way of describing how deeply held beliefs and emotions operate in group life and within the individual psyche by mediating an individual's relationship to a specific group, nation, or culture. Cultural complexes are dynamic systems of relations that serve the basic individual need for belonging and for individual and group identity through linking personal experiences and group

expectations as these are mediated by ethnicity, race, religion, gender, and/or social identity processes. Jung's metaphor of the psyche as a spectrum can be applied: "psychic processes behave like a scale along which consciousness slides."[8] Hence, the individual and group poles of identity are different manifestations of one underlying process. At the level of this underlying process of collective and individual, a psychological attitude allows us to ask what the psyche is doing with the fact of differences and similarities both individually and culturally.[9]

In Carroll's example, the group complexes are constellated around the meaning and significance of the Shoah or Holocaust, the Christian cross, the conception of God, and Jews' and Christians' identities that define the meaning attributed to these categories. Once activated, identities are charged with affect, and individuals and groups become caught up in a kind of emotional discharging, sensory-dominated expression.

2. Cultural complexes tend to operate autonomously beneath our awareness. As expressions of field phenomena operating at the level of the cultural unconscious, their existence implies levels of meaning that bind individuals to each other and provide a sense of coherence which generates a sense of group continuity. Cultural complexes are nucleating centers that allow for a continuous movement of affect and images, leading to narratives and rituals passed from generation to generation. At the collective level, they constitute the "unthought known" of group life.[10] They are centripetal in direction, imposing constraints on the perception of differences or accentuating them, emphasizing identification with or differentiation from the group, defining enemies, and allowing for feelings of belonging or being alienated from the group.

In Carroll's example, the potential for what occurred around the placement and meaning of the cross and Auschwitz had been going on for 2000 years. Christianity claimed to be the "true Israel," and Jews were "dismissed by Christians as custodians of the false Israel." This collective contestation constitutes a boiling cauldron that can erupt at any time.

3. Energy fields created by cultural complexes constitute impersonal dynamics that function through psychic induction creating a resonance among people that produces a sense of familiarity. Negatively, they

function through collective emotional sign language, bypassing thinking and reflection, readying individuals and groups for action.

To use Bion's language, the group loses its ability to transform beta elements. These sensory-dominated, emotional, undigested expressions of the archaic and infantile psyche become activated and swallow up the participants.

4. Cultural complexes may be positively involved in the individual's sense of belonging to and identification with his or her reference group and provide a nucleating center for group life. They may also be a destructive force as they form the basis of this belonging, generate stereotypes, prejudices, and a whole psychology of otherness threat. Every group has a vocabulary of images about those who are different. Those who are different are generally pathologized or demonized, and almost never idealized.

Activated cultural complexes generate an emotional field dominated by ethnos logic. This is the blood logic that functions through participation mystique, unreflectively. This does not mean that each individual in the group internalizes and identifies with the same meaning of the trauma; rather each member of the group recognizes that something happened at the level of the group psyche that has profound implications for issues of belonging and identity.

To return to the earlier example of Carroll in his book *Constantine's Sword*, the cross becomes a kind of fetish, a sign that is a concrete expression of each group's beliefs and relationship to their specific kinship libido configuration. For the Christians, the cross is a remembrance of a sacrifice made by one of their own for Jews and Christians alike; and for the Jews, the cross becomes an annihilation of and an expression of a collusion with the perpetrators of the catastrophe. In neither case is the cross a symbol but a sign that does not mirror but encrypts; a sign that incorporates, consumes, and concretizes an identification with the dead without opening either group up to a living connection to the other world where, in Emery words, "encryption gives way to errant uncertain destination of becoming singular."[11] And, I would add, becoming connected to our ancestral tradition that opens us to a continuity with the unknown others with whom we feel a kinship.

Cultural Mourning and Cultural Melancholia

From Freud's formulation of mourning and melancholia at the individual level, I now turn to the group level and look at lost objects related to families, ancestors, homelands, places, and ideals as they are experienced and carried by the group, and losses resulting from individual traumas that come principally from being a member of one particular group or another. From the point of view of cultural complexes, losses are self-objects, and melancholia reflects lost aspects of the Self that are not mourned or acknowledged. Some losses and group traumas become part of the group and individual character structure not simply by introjections, incorporation, and identification, but through belonging to a group. I think immediately of African American experiences, Native American experiences, and, currently, losses in Israel for both Jews and Palestinians and many other groups around the world.

These losses constitute traumas that exist well beyond the immediate present and continue to be a part of how a particular group or group member responds to what Volkan has called a "chosen trauma."[12] He means by "chosen trauma" something similar to what I am referring to as a cultural complex. That is, a group's response to an event(s) that become identified with as having significance for that group's collective identity. Though individuals may not have experienced the event in question themselves, it becomes an assumed trauma through their identification with the group and the group's claim on them. I suggest that cultural complexes organized around trauma and loss will stimulate the emotional dynamics that are associated with melancholia. "The chosen trauma, or the event qua event, takes on a particular resonance for the history of the people, their most deeply felt cultural affiliations and anxieties, and collective symbols of a community."[13] When the meaning of the event has not been assimilated or worked through in relationship to the current situation, group members become conflicted between feeling burdened by (speaking negatively) and/or charged with living the dream of the group forward(speaking positively).

Continued relationship to loss and trauma at both the individual and group level is not, in and of itself, pathogenic. Relationship to traumas and related issues generated by and through group membership, in fact, may become a source of strength. It may lead to feelings of gratitude for the sacrifices made by previous generations and provide motivation for continuing the struggle to the clarify issues and values that provide a sense of group solidarity and identity. From the point of view of analysis, the individual works with the cultural complex in terms of how (s)he is making use of it or not making use of it, and/ or how a particular cultural complex is affecting their life currently.

Cultural losses and the associated symptoms of rage, shame, and anger are demands for recognition, restitution, or reparation and are an important part of the group's and the individual's healing process. Without these processes, the wound caused by the loss becomes a melancholic black hole because the group feels an unfulfilled need, at some level, both for something from the offending other(s) and for some sort of intragroup reparative effort from within. Without this work, the group is unable to move on.

The following dream illustrates the aforementioned point. I had this dream years ago, the night before my interview with the San Francisco Jung Institute to which I had applied for training.

I am sitting in a Mosque with a number of well-dressed Black Muslim men waiting for my interview. My name is called. As I get up to go into the interview, several of the Black Muslim men bar the door to stop me. They say they will not allow me to leave until I demonstrate to them that I remember the secret handshake. This gesture will demonstrate that I will not forget them.

At the time, the Black Muslims were the carriers of the most conservative aspect of race consciousness in the Afro-American community. They emphasized hard work and racial pride as ways to deal with the legacy of slavery and discrimination. In a way, the Black Muslims expressed an attitude that allowed blacks to deal with the ongoing cultural projective identifications that were internalized as negative self-esteem and self-destructiveness in the black community. I took the dream as a reminder that the issue of race and identity must be remembered and worked with as I entered this next phase of my life. My work on cultural complexes may be seen as a continued amplification of that dream.

I believe the dilemma as expressed in my dream is a common cultural complex dilemma for many minority group members.

Particularly, in the experience of many immigrants to America, a bind is created when homeland, family, language, identity, property, etc. are left behind and assimilation is not forthcoming.

In a paper entitled "A Dialogue on Racial Melancholia," Eng and Han, both Asian Americans, one a social worker and the other an assistant professor of English, state the following about the relationship to Asian experience with immigration and assimilation:

> It might be said to deny him or her the capacity to invest in new objects. The inability to invest in new objects is part of Freud's definition of melancholia. If the losses suffered by first-generation immigrants are not resolved and mourned in the process of assimilation—if libido is not replenished by the investment in new objects, new communities, and new ideals, then the melancholia that ensues from this condition can be transferred to the second generation. At the same time, however, can the hope of assimilation and mastery of the American dream also be transferred? If so, mourning and melancholia are reenacted and lived out by the children in their own attempts to assimilate and to negotiate the American dream.[14]

Looking at issues around loss, mourning, and melancholia as a movement toward the internal transformation of identity that allows for a sense of continuity at both the individual and the group level is to move beyond the pathogenic bias. I believe the group makes claims on us to continue the work of transforming; that the dead make claims on the living through the process of dealing with the past. These claims and demands are part of the process of moving from cultural melancholia to cultural mourning. Not through relinquishing the experiences of the past and present that relate to identity and belonging, but through claiming, internalizing, and redeeming. As Jung said,

> it frequently happens that when a person with whom one was intimate dies, either one is oneself drawn into death, so to speak, or else the burden has the opposite effect of a task that has to be fulfilled in real life. One could say figuratively that a bit of life has passed over from the dead to the living and compels him towards its realization.[15]

This would require that we bring a symbolic attitude to our awareness of cultural complexes and social suffering. This attitude makes all the difference between encapsulation, encryption, and the capacity to utilize our losses to dream life forward.

CONCLUSIONS

Cultural mourning and melancholia are different attitudes that identify the individual and group relationship to social suffering. An Eros attitude towards social suffering is one that links analysis, the helping professions, religions, political movements, and social policy in a way that may lead to the creation of a cultural anima—or, to use Andrew Samuels' term, "a moral imagination." By this he means "the means by which we consider complex social and political issues."[16] We become self consciously part of a moral community wherein historical injustices and present events, like homelessness and global warming, become enfolded into our therapeutic concerns. Social narratives as expressed in racial, ethnic-specific memories of suffering become consecrated. Our relationship to the other becomes part of the interpersonal web of our work. "Melancholia considered as pathological grief may be read as a mourner's (group's) response to loss that is not socially acceptable or socially understood and it is therefore hard to tolerate or explain."[17]

Cultural mourning and cultural melancholia call our attention to the cultural complexes that bring together the individual and the cultural within the larger ongoing relational and historical context in which we all live. Turning cultural melancholia into cultural mourning involves developing a kind of cultural anima, a new cultural attitude, a "moral imagination" that has a working contact with social feeling that can assist us in transforming events into experiences that can be thought about, consciously experienced, reflected, and acted upon.

> If social regard for the meaning of the loss is inadequate or withheld, we must consider the possibility that mourning itself may manifest a depressive loss of individual self-regard. This loss may be more accurately interpreted as a social rather than a self construction.[18]

Mogenson states a mythic attitude on a vertical dimension:

> History's genetic aspect has roots in the object representations, which our forebears introjected during their lives, roots that

> implicate us in a profound manner through the complexes. Yet our ancestral sense of soul does not come from our literal genealogy, but from a mythical genealogy projected upon the literal, through which we are linked by our forebears to our first ancestor, Adam's parent, God.[19]

Mogenson is describing archetypal/ historical connections that point to a transcendent dimension, to object representation and continuity that live beyond the personal. I am reminded of a statement by Winnicott in which he says, "In some specific setting of which the patient is unaware, hate is more powerful than love," and in melancholia, "the illness is an attempt to do the impossible. The patient absurdly claims responsibility for general disaster, but in so doing avoids reaching his or her personal destructiveness."[20] In other words, we must find our personal potential for destructiveness at the level of our participation in and identification with the group. Otherwise, our use of the group's aggression can cover over our personal relationship to aggression and hate in our everyday life.[21] For instance, we can feel outraged at the genocidal madness expressed in ethnic cleansing and in racial and cultural hatred. However, the ongoing ways that we participate in the unjustified suffering of others, the collusions involved in privileges that exclude and/or exploit others and resources which is corrosive to human connectedness, require another kind of imagination that can hold our relationship to the impact of the "narcissism of minor differences," our potential for destructiveness, and our relationship to our group's shadow.

I will close with an acknowledgement of Martin Luther King's attempt through his ministry to express an attitude that had a cultural Eros as the basis of his message. Thematically he held three components together: The beloved community, the metaphor of the dream, and the Promised Land. These became metaphors that embodied an attitude beyond tribalism and toward opening up a community beyond individualism. In a way, the empowerment suggested by this vision constitutes his way of addressing cultural melancholia. King said, "I think not in terms of external factors, I think the greatest victory was what this period did to the psyche of the black man."

NOTES

1. Sigmund Freud, "Mourning and Melancholia" (The Institute of Psycho-Analysis and the Hogarth Press, 1959), American ed., pp. 152-170.

"The testing of reality, having shown that the loved object no longer exists, requires forthwith that all the libido shall be withdrawn from its attachments to this object. Against this demand a struggle of course arises; it may be universally observed that man never willingly abandons a libido-position, not even when a substitute is already beckoning to him. This struggle can be so intense that a turning away from reality ensues, the object being clung to through the medium of a hallucinatory wish psychosis. The normal outcome is that deference for reality gains the day. Nevertheless its behest cannot be at once obeyed. The task is now carried through bit by bit, under great expense of time and cathectic energy, while all the time the existence of the lost object is continued in the mind. Each single one of the memories and hopes which bound the libido to the object is brought up and hyper-cathected, and the detachment of the libido from it accomplished. Why this process of carrying out the behest of reality bit by bit, which is in the nature of a compromise, should be so extraordinarily painful is not at all easy to explain in terms of mental economics. It is worth nothing that this pain seems natural to us. The fact is, however, that when the work of mourning is completed the ego becomes free and uninhibited again." (p. 154)

And later, "the object-choice had been effected on a narcissistic basis, so that when obstacles arise in the way of the object-cathexis it can regress into narcissism. The narcissistic identification becomes a substitute for the erotic cathexis." (pp. 159-160)

2. *Ibid.,* p. 244.

3. Joseph Henderson, *The Cultural Unconscious in Shadow and Self* (Wilmette, IL: Chiron, 1990).

4. Samuel Kimbles, "The Cultural Complex and The Myth of Invisibility," in *The Vision Thing,* ed. Thomas Singer (Routledge, 2000), p. 159.

5. C. G. Jung, *Collected Works*, tr. R. F. C. Hull (Princeton: Princeton University Press, 1953), vol. 16, para. 431 (all future references to Jung's *Collected Works*, abbreviated to *CW*, will be by volume and paragraph number).

6. Samuel Kimbles, "Cultural Complexes and the Transmission of Group Traumas in Everyday Life," *Psychological Perspectives,* 2006, vol. 49(1): 96-110.

7. James Carroll, *Constantine's Sword* (New York: Houghton, 2001), p. 58.

8. C. G. Jung, *CW* 8 § 408.

9. Samuel Kimbles, "The Cultural Complex and The Myth of Invisibility;" Thomas Singer and Samuel L. Kimbles, *The Cultural Complex: Contemporary Jungian Perspectives on Psyche and Society* (Routledge, 2004).

10. Christopher Bollas, *Forces of Destiny* (London: Free Association Books, 1989), pp. 213-214.

11. E. Emery, "Into the Labyrinth: Threads, Specters, and Dreams in the Work of James Grostein." Presented at the Div. 39, Annual Spring Meeting, April 26, 2001.

12. V. D. Volkan, G. Ast, and W. F. Greer, *The Third Reich in the Unconscious* (New York: Brunner-Routledge, 2002).

13. R. Khanna, *Dark Continents: Psychoanalysis and Colonization* (Durham, NC: Duke University Press, 2003), p. 14.

14. D. L. Eng and S. Han, "A Dialogue on Racial Melancholia," *Psychoanalytic Dialogues,* 10 (4): 667-700, 2000, p. 670.

15. C. G. Jung, *Letters, Volume One: 1906-1950* (Princeton: Princeton University Press, 1973), p. 347.

16. Andrew Samuels, "Original Morality in a Depressed Culture," *The Archetype of Shadow in a Split World*, ed. Mary Ann Mattoon (Einseldn, SW: Daimon, 1986), p. 73.

17. E. Sanchez-Pardo, *Cultures of the Death Drive* (Durham, NC: Duke University Press, 2003), p. 215.

18. M. Fowlkes, "The Morality of Loss: The social construction of mourning and melancholia," *Contemporary Psychoanalysis,* 27 (3): 529-551 at p. 550.

19. Greg Mogenson, "Mourning and Metapsychology: An Archetypal View," *Spring,* 1995, p. 65.

20. D. W. Winnicott, *The Sense of Guilt, The Maturational Processes and the Facilitating Environment* (Madison: International Universities Press, 1987), p. 21.

21. Andrew Samuels, "Original Morality in a Depressed Culture."

America's Selective Remembering and Collective Forgetting of Martin Luther King, Jr.

JENNIFER LEIGH SELIG

> What an individual, a culture, a people, or even a species chooses
> to remember and forget, where it makes the cut between what
> will be allowed in and what will remain outside, defines that entity
> even more than one's fingerprints or biological heritage. Our
> identities are bound up with what we—as a people and a
> culture—choose to forget as well as what we select to remember.
> — Dennis Patrick Slattery[1]

As early as 1957 and at the tender age of 28, Martin Luther King, Jr. formed the Southern Christian Leadership Conference (SCLC), was elected its president, and declared in no uncertain language his personal and professional mission in its motto—*to save the soul of America*. Such language befitted King in his role as a powerful preacher, but as I argued elsewhere,[2] he was also one of the country's most effective depth psychologists and cultural therapists, and as such, he was just as likely to use psychological language to discuss the ailing

Jennifer Leigh Selig, Ph.D., is Chair of the Depth Psychology Program at Pacifica Graduate Institute. She considers Martin Luther King, Jr. one of the greatest depth psychologists of the 20th century, and has researched and written extensively on King from a multitude of angles.

soul of the country. Thus, he looked deep into the psyche of America and declared his diagnosis—schizophrenia, psychosis, and neurosis.

King's sermons, speeches, and books are rife with this psychological language. In a typical example, he wrote, "America has been something of a schizophrenic personality, tragically divided against herself. On the one hand we have proudly professed the great principles of democracy, but on the other hand we have sadly practiced the very opposite of those principles."[3] King just as often referred to America as neurotic, telling his staff, "we live in a sick, neurotic nation" and that the campaign he would never live to see complete, the Poor People's campaign, was based on "the hope that we can move this sick nation away from at least a level of its sickness."[4] He even went so far as to express fear that America would move from being neurotic to psychotic, writing,

> but it is not too late to return home. If America would come to herself and return to her true home, "one nation, indivisible, with liberty and justice of all," she would give the democratic creed a new authentic ring, enkindle the imagination of mankind and fire the souls of men. If she fails, she will be victimized with the ultimate social psychosis that can only lead to national suicide.[5]

This highlights one of King's greatest contributions to depth psychology: he took terms originally associated with the individual psyche and applied them to the nation at large, bringing them to the forefront of American consciousness.

King offered the country not only diagnosis, but cure. His treatment of the country paralleled Karen Horney's treatment of the neurotic: he helped his client—the country—to see the gap between her ideal self and her real self.[6] He used marches and protests and demonstrations to bring America's shadow to the surface where she could no longer deny its existence, and then, rather than leaving her wallowing in guilt and shame, he offered her specific redemptive measures she could take toward healing and wholeness. These measures in turn would ultimately lead toward the manifestation of what King called *the beloved community*, his term for an individuated culture. For a while, America subjected herself to the treatment he extolled, and demonstrated back to King some willingness to work on her issues, particularly around race. Some of King's greatest victories were won during the early to middle years of the movement, including the passage of the Civil Rights Act of 1964, and the Voting Rights Act of 1965.

I believe it is *this* King that *this* country selects to remember, the King that led a successful Civil Rights Movement that abolished most overt forms of racism and segregation. We remember the King Victorious, the man raising his arm high and declaring his dream for his country. We remember the King of "We Shall Overcome Some Day," a day most Americans today would consider largely realized. What we don't remember is the King that was overcome himself by depression and despair, the King who spoke of his own shattered dreams, the King who died days before he was to preach a sermon called "Why American May Go to Hell." No King and country victorious here, but *this* King we collectively choose not to remember.

As Dennis Patrick Slattery says in the epilogue to this essay, "Our identities are bound up with what we—as a people and a culture—choose to forget as well as what we select to remember." That we have selected as a country to remember King is clear. He is one of only two Americans who has a Federal holiday in his name, guaranteeing a *time* set aside to remember him.[7] He is one of only five Americans in history, all others Presidents, to warrant a memorial on the Mall at our nation's capital, guaranteeing a *place* set aside to remember him.[8] However, in this essay, my interest is to bring to light the King we have chosen to forget in order to illuminate something of the shadow of America and point to the way back toward "a more perfect union."

THE EVIL TRIPLETS

After achieving his initial victories in the Civil Rights Movement, King came to understand that they were not enough, in and of themselves, to bring about the kind of cultural transformation he sought. He realized that America's neurosis extended beyond the dysfunction of racism, and thus he needed to extend himself beyond racism to facilitate her healing. He stated,

> I now had to give a great deal of attention to the three problems which I considered as the largest of those that confront mankind: racial injustice around the world, poverty, and war. Though each appeared to be separate and isolated, all were interwoven into a single garment of man's destiny.[9]

The garment analogy is an appropriate one—the more he unraveled the threads of racism in this country, the more he came to see how those threads were interwoven with other threads, and as he began to tug on those, he came to see that the whole garment was flawed and needed to be re-made. He began to see that

> the black revolution is much more than a struggle for the rights of Negroes. It is forcing America to face all its interrelated flaws—racism, poverty, militarism and materialism. It is exposing evils that are rooted deeply in the whole structure of our society. It reveals systemic rather than superficial flaws and suggests that radical reconstruction of society itself is the real issue to be faced.[10]

He narrowed the interrelated flaws down to three, which he termed the three evils, or "the giant triplets of racism, extreme materialism, and militarism."[11]

The Evil of Materialism

King's initial sensitivity to the second of the evil triplets, "extreme materialism," came early in life during his youth in Atlanta. He was born on the verge of the Great Depression, and he recalled "how I questioned my parents about the numerous people standing in bread lines when I was about five years of age. I can see the effects of this early childhood experience on my present anti-capitalistic feelings."[12] Of his youth, he writes,

> I had also learned that the inseparable twin of racial injustice was economic injustice. Although I came from a home of economic security and relative comfort, I could never get out of my mind the economic insecurity of many of my playmates and the tragic poverty of those living around me. During my late teens I worked two summers (against my father's wishes—he never wanted my brother and me to work around white people because of the oppressive conditions) in a plant that hired both Negroes and whites. Here I saw economic injustice firsthand, and realized that the poor white was exploited just as much as the Negro. Through these early experiences I grew up deeply conscious of the varieties of injustice in our society.[13]

His concern about economic injustice continued as he entered his twenties. His wife Coretta wrote that King "knew that the basic problem in our society had to do with economic injustice... the contrast of wealth between the haves and the have-nots."[14] She recalled discussions they had during the early months of their courtship, when King was only twenty-three years old, regarding his concern for the masses. "He talked about the unequal distribution of wealth, and he said, 'It's so unfair that a small percentage of the population could control all of the wealth.' He felt that there could be a more equitable distribution of wealth."[15] He told her that though his "old man" was a capitalist, "I don't believe in capitalism as it is practiced in the United States."[16]

King was not a communist, either, though the accusation was wielded against him later during the Civil Rights Movement. As a preacher, he was not afraid to critique communism from the pulpit. In fact, he gave a sermon titled "How Should a Christian View Communism" where he clearly states that communism is antithetical to Christianity and advises Christians to "pray for the Communist constantly, but never...tolerate the philosophy of Communism."[17] Yet, in that same sermon he criticizes Christianity for being "content to mouth pious irrelevancies and sanctimonious trivialities" while failing to be truly concerned about the economic and social conditions that strangle people's souls.[18] He says, "Surely it is unchristian and unethical for some to wallow in the soft beds of luxury while others sink in the quicksands of poverty."[19]

He increasingly came to see that capitalism was not a system that fostered the noblest expression of our humanity. He stated,

> The profit motive, when it is the sole basis of an economic system, encourages a cut-throat competition and selfish ambition that inspires men to be more concerned about making a living than making a life. It can make men so I-centered that they no longer are Thou-centered.[20]

In his sermon "Paul's Letter to American Christians," he spoke his feelings through the voice of the apostle Paul, professing "I still contend that money can be the root of all evil. It can cause one to live a life of gross materialism."[21] He believed that America had become a "nation suffocating with material corruption,"[22] and although there had been social reforms in the twentieth century to address poverty, "True compassion is more than flinging a coin to a beggar. It comes to see that an edifice which produces beggars needs restructuring."[23] The edifice could be restructured in two ways: by a return to humanistic and spiritual values whereby capitalism would be used for the highest good of all people, with the profit motive replaced by the people motive, and/or by embracing a new economic system such as democratic socialism.

He was exposed to democratic socialism in December of 1964 when he traveled to Norway to receive the Nobel Peace Prize. Days later he visited Stockholm for a reception for all the prize winners. Speaking to the SCLC staff in 1966 about the trip, he reminisced,

> I am always amazed when I go there [Sweden], they don't have any poverty. No unemployment, nobody needing health services who can't get them. They don't have any slums. The question comes to us, why?... Something is wrong with capitalism....There must be a better distribution of wealth, and maybe America must move toward a Democratic Socialism....[24]

He admonished his country,

> to work within the framework of democracy to bring about a better distribution of wealth. You can use your powerful economic resources to wipe poverty from the face of the earth. God never intended for one group of people to live in superfluous inordinate wealth, while others live in abject deadening poverty. God intends for all of his children to have the basic necessities of life, and he has left in this universe "enough and to spare" for that purpose. So I call upon you to bridge the gulf between abject poverty and superfluous wealth.[25]

THE EVIL OF MILITARISM

King declared militarism the third of the evil triplets, and sought its elimination from the national psyche. King deplored violence; his loyalty to the philosophy of nonviolence makes that clear. Yet while most Americans are familiar with his insistence on nonviolence during the domestic Civil Rights Movement, fewer are aware that he extended nonviolence into a critique of militarism itself, taking a radical, anti-war stance during the last few years of his life and vociferously critiquing American foreign policy.

The first year in which King spoke publicly about the Vietnam War was 1965, telling a group at Howard University, "The war in Vietnam is accomplishing nothing,"[26] and later calling for an end to the war. In July of that year, after making his strongest statements yet, reporters questioned him about his interest in a subject not tied to civil rights. He replied, "I'm much more than a civil rights leader," and "I feel that it is necessary for me to continue to speak on it."[27]

He spoke out against the war rather timorously by his own accounts until 1967. Early that year, King went away to Jamaica to work on a book. While in the airport, he bought a handful of magazines, and flipping through one, he came across an illustrated story called "The Children of Vietnam." His close advisor and friend, Bernard Lee, never forgot King's reaction to seeing the photos.

> When he came to *Ramparts* magazine he stopped. He froze as he looked at the pictures from Vietnam. He saw a picture of a Vietnamese mother holding her dead baby, a baby killed by our military. Then Martin just pushed the plate of food away from him. I looked up and said, "Doesn't it taste any good?," and he answered, "Nothing will ever taste any good for me until I do everything I can to end that war."[28]

Lee stated "That's when the decision was made. Martin had known about the war before then, of course, and had spoken out against it. But it was then that he decided to commit himself to oppose it."[29]

In Jamaica, with plenty of time to think, reflect, and meditate, Vietnam weighed heavily on his mind. He stated, "I came to the conclusion that I could no longer remain silent about an issue that was destroying the soul of our nation."[30] When he returned in February, he gave his strongest speech yet, saying that the war was causing America's "declining moral status in the world," and was evidence of America's "deadly western arrogance," "a new form of colonialism," and "an ominous expression of our lack of sympathy for the oppressed."[31] He returned to reminding America of the gap between her idealized and her authentic self, telling her, "before it is too late, we must narrow the gaping chasm between our proclamations of peace and our lowly deeds which precipitate and perpetuate war."[32]

In April of 1967, one year before his assassination, he delivered his famous speech, "A Time To Break Silence." He began by noting all the questions he was receiving as to why he was speaking out against the war, given his obvious fame as a civil rights leader. He pointed out that winning the Nobel Peace Prize in 1964 charged him with the mission of bringing peace to all, not just to blacks and whites in America but to communists and capitalists and all God's warring children worldwide.

He reiterated his advocacy for a revolution of values, a recapturing of the revolutionary spirit that would send Americans out "into a sometimes hostile world declaring eternal hostility to poverty, racism, and militarism."[33] If the revolution of values was genuine, it would mean that "our loyalties must become ecumenical rather then sectional. Every nation must now develop an overriding loyalty to mankind as a whole in order to preserve the best in their individual societies."[34] He ended the speech with a call for America to begin to "rededicate ourselves to the long and bitter—but beautiful—struggle for a new world."[35]

SHATTERED DREAMS

Publicly, King continued to speak his hope that America could hear and would answer the call, but privately he struggled with depression and despair over his own shattered dreams for the country. King biographer David Garrow chronicles King's bouts of depression during many moments in his life, but especially in his final days, referring to him as dispirited, despondent, and melancholy.[36] To begin with, he questioned the efficacy of the Civil Rights Movement. Harry Belafonte, a loyal supporter of the movement and of King, wrote,

> I remember the last time we were together, at my home, shortly before he was murdered. He seemed quite agitated and preoccupied, and I asked him what the problem was. "I've come upon something that disturbs me deeply," he said. "We have fought hard and long for integration, as I believe we should have, and I know that we will be victorious. But what bothers me is that I've come to believe that we're integrating into a burning house."[37]

King came to realize that his victories over segregation meant very little unless economic conditions changed. He wondered, what good was it if blacks won the right to eat a hamburger at a lunch counter with whites when they couldn't afford the burger? What good was it if blacks could vote when they had nothing substantive to vote for? SCLC put out a policy statement in January of 1968 that reflected King's concern. "The right to vote or to eat in any restaurant, while important....does not actually affect conditions for living."[38]

Near the end of his life, King spoke to a longtime family friend, confessing with despair,

> I have found out that all I have been doing in trying to correct this system in America has been in vain. I am trying to get at the roots of it to see what ought to be done.... The whole thing will have to be done away with.[39]

The deeper King came to realize the magnitude of the problems, the deeper he sank into despair. Publicly, he projected his feelings onto "the movement," saying "The movement for social change has entered a time of temptation to despair, because it is clear now how deep and how systematic are the evils it confronts."[40]

KING'S DREAM TODAY

There is a curious plaque outside the Lorraine Motel where King was assassinated. It reads, in part, "They said one to another, Behold, here cometh the dreamer. Let us slay him, and we shall see what will become of his dreams." So let us ask, how have we progressed against the evil triplets which King felt kept his dream from being fulfilled?

Without a doubt, much progress has been made on racism, both during King's life and continuing after his death. Though institutional and individual racism still exist in both covert and overt forms, the country has come a long way in closing the neurotic gap between our ideals and their realization. For example, Barack Obama is being taken seriously in his run for President and, in fact, is often compared to King, though the oft-raised question by political pundits of whether he is *black enough* is disturbing enough to make us question how deep our dialogue on race really goes in this country. Still, the man can have a hamburger at a lunch counter in Birmingham when he campaigns there, and if he rode a bus he could sit in the front no matter how many white people were on it, and that is progress.

But are we any less materialistic now than we were in 1968 when King was killed? King called for the elimination of world poverty and poverty in our own country; he called for the creation of full employment or a guaranteed income for all citizens—none of these dreams have come true. He called for the closing of the income gap, but the gap has widened even more since his death, and in fact is now the widest it has been since 1929.[41] "The income gap between the rich and the rest of the U.S. population has become so wide, and is growing so fast, that it might eventually threaten the stability of democratic capitalism itself." These are not words spoken by King in 1968, but by Alan Greenspan in 2005.[42]

Similarly, has equal progress been made since the 1960's on King's third evil of militarism? Has King's dream of nonviolent conflict resolution on a national and international level come true? King once critiqued the militarism of the United States, asking:

> Why has our nation placed itself in the position of being God's military agent on earth, and intervened recklessly in Vietnam and the Dominican Republic? Why have we substituted the arrogant undertaking of policing the whole world for the high task of putting our own house in order?[43]

But since his death, the examples of militaristic intervention have only grown: Grenada, Panama, the Persian Gulf, Afghanistan, Iraq, the list goes on. King admonished us,

> We must find an alternative to war and bloodshed. Anyone who feels, and there are still a lot of people who feel that way, that war can solve the social problems facing mankind is sleeping through a great revolution. President Kennedy said on one occasion, "Mankind must put an end to war or war will put an end to mankind." The world must hear this. I pray to God that America will hear this before it is too late, because today we're fighting a war.[44]

In how many of the nearly forty years since King's death, can we find America still fighting one war or another?

As a nation we are *more* materialistic, *more* militaristic, not less. We have elevated King, the slayed dreamer, but shattered much of his dream, and the only way we can live with ourselves is to focus on remembering the dream come true. The most iconographic image we have of King is that hot summer day in 1963, his hand raised above the integrated crowd, declaring to all the world his dream of racial harmony. His "I Have a Dream" speech consistently appears as one of the top ten most influential speeches of the 20th century.

Every year on January 15th, the same old video clip, the same old sound-bite. On that same day of the year, and in the following month known as Black History month, students all over America are taught the same story of Martin Luther King, Jr. They can repeat the myth to you verbatim. Blacks versus whites, locked in a power struggle for freedom, a struggle that was largely won, and won largely by Martin Luther King, Jr., a man with a dream.

Indulge me in an example. My nine-year-old niece Hayley called me one day and told me she was doing a report on Martin Luther King, Jr. I asked her what she had learned about him in school. This is her completely unedited response.

> He wanted to have the right to have freedom from the white people, because the white people have always bossed the black people around, and he felt that that was wrong. And so he told the other black people that they are strong. They need to have the right to become free. And, it worked! And so that made them all happy, and so that made life easier. And that's how it is now.

In her response, I believe, lies part of the reason why we have selected to remember only one-third of King's message. I believe we do this because it serves as a self-congratulatory story. It makes us feel good to think of King this way, as a man who helped us come to our senses about the most overt forms of racism and discrimination. It is our defensive story, allowing us to keep our neurosis in place by patting our ideal selves on the collective back. We remember just the part of King's message that we can bear to remember. And no more.

THE PSYCHO-POLITICS OF SELECTIVE REMEMBERING AND COLLECTIVE FORGETTING

It was Ronald Reagan who institutionalized this collective back-patting by signing the holiday honoring King into law in 1983. He said of King, "He made it possible for our Nation to move closer to the ideals set forth in our Declaration of Independence."[45] The feel-good part is that yes, our nation moved with King and moved far and moved quickly, and though almost everyone will follow this up by saying but we still have a way to go—the teachers asking students for examples of times they've been discriminated against and the journalists showing how statistically blacks still aren't equal in all ways yet—for the most part, at least for white America, we feel done. "And, it worked! And so that made them all happy, and so that made life easier. And that's how it is now."

I used to think there was something almost sinister about the fact that it was the very far-right leaning conservative President who literally placed his seal of approval on this very far-left leaning, radically liberal man. Now, I just find it sadly ironic that it was President Reagan, a subsequent sufferer of Alzheimer's, who institutionalized this collective forgetting, this selective remembering, who led us by his example to see that the only way we can bear to remember King is, in truth, to forget him.

But Reagan was a man who, if he understood nothing else, understood the power of image. He did not want to sign the Martin Luther King, Jr. holiday into law, but felt pressured into it. When one Republican governor wrote to him expressing concerns over elevating a radical to such stature, Reagan wrote back, "I have the reservations you have, but here the perception of too many people is based on an image, not reality. Indeed, to them the perception is reality."[46] So, the conservative politicians got to work on the perception of King, and to hear them tell it now, King was one of them. One of Reagan's biographers, Peggy Noonan, wrote this of Reagan:

> He did not believe in racial preferences, did not believe in quotas or what has come to be institutionalized as affirmative action and thought it necessary that no one be given special treatment on account to his race or religion. In this he felt he was consistent with the thinking not only of his parents and the good liberals of the 1940's and 1950's, but also of Martin Luther King, Jr., himself: We must be judged not by the color of our skin but by the content of our character.[47]

The last line is the conservatives' favorite line of King's—George W. Bush relied heavily on it in 2003 when he declared King's birthday a Federal holiday.

Look no further for evidence of America's neurotic defensiveness. In no way are Ronald Reagan and George W. Bush leaders whose actions are consistent with the thinking of King—nor was George H.W. Bush, who added another conservative seal of approval onto King by signing a Martin Luther King Holiday Proclamation in 1989. To use King's language, these three politicians have grossly sinned in their allegiance to the evil triplets; they are presidents who have fallen into the worship of the golden calf of materialism, of the silver bullet of militarism, and who have certainly not supported in any way King's platform for the remediation of racism. King was *for* racial preferences, was *for* affirmative action, was *for* quotas, and even more radically, was *for* reparations for slavery.

These were not views King kept hidden from the public. In his 1964 book *Why We Can't Wait*, he wrote,

> No amount of gold could provide an adequate compensation for the exploitation and humiliation of the Negro in America down through the centuries...Yet a price can be placed on unpaid wages. The payment should be in the form of a massive program by the government of special, compensatory measures which could be regarded as a settlement in accordance with the accepted practice of common law.[48]

In his 1968 book *Where Do We Go From Here?*, he stated that "a society that has done something special against the Negro for hundreds of years must now do something special for him, to equip him to compete on a just and equal basis." To do this he expressed support for quotas. He wrote, "If a city has a 30% Negro population, then it is logical to assume that Negroes should have at least 30% of the jobs in any particular company, and jobs in all categories rather than only in menial areas."[49] Yet many people continue to invoke that one poetic comment of King's, made in 1963—about judging black children by the content of their character not their skin color—to argue against the imposition of quotas and affirmative action, measures King himself clearly supported.

A man named Charles Adams once asked,

> Could it be that Mr. Reagan understood that the easiest way to get rid of Martin Luther King, Jr. is to worship him?
> To honor him with a holiday that he never would have wanted. To celebrate his birth and his death, without committing ourselves to his vision and his love. It is easier to praise a dead hero than to recognize and follow a loving prophet. The best way to dismiss any challenge is to exalt and adore the empirical source through which the challenge has come.[50]

I would add to *exalt* and *adore* the words to *fix* and *freeze* the source. In my view, King has come to be primarily associated with three archetypal roles—that of the warrior-hero, the peaceful dreamer, and the martyr-savior. At the start of the Montgomery Bus Boycott in 1955, King was seen as an archetypal warrior-hero, fighting the dynamic and dramatic battle against racism through the weapon of non-violent resistance. Later, in 1963 during the March on Washington, I would argue that King became fixed in the public eye and adored in another archetypal role as well, that of the peaceful dreamer. Then, still later in 1968 when he was assassinated, King's image became frozen and exalted by the public as an archetypal martyr-savior. What he did between 1963 and 1968 is mostly forgotten. Frankly, it is not politically expedient or psychologically safe for an ever-more militaristic, ever-more materialistic America to remember.

This selective remembering, repackaging, and retelling of the story, though I have portrayed it politically quite cynically, can be viewed in another light as a rather predictable psychological process. From very early in his career, King was already both man and myth, and with his assassination he ascended in the American psyche as a mythical figure, virtually guaranteeing that much of the actual man would be forgotten. Lionel Corbett writes,

> Mythic characters personify intrapsychic processes, but there are
> many characters and plots in any story on which attention can
> be focused, and only certain of them pertain to the individual
> self....This helps to explain why different observers select
> different themes on which to focus; we are drawn to aspects of
> the story that resonate personally.[51]

I would add to that argument that we are drawn to aspects of the story that resonate *safely*, that provide us with just the right amount of challenge our psyches can hold. In the case of the still-neurotic, still-addicted, and still-violent American psyche, it is obvious that she can hold very little of the challenge that King the man provided, so she selected certain aspects and themes of his story to mythologize, certain places where she can safely worship the King.

INTERLUDE: A TRIP TO THE BOOKSTORE

I know I am painting a simplistic and rather dark picture here. Of course there are people who remember King's strong critique of militarism during those later years, and there are also people, though many fewer I suspect, who remember his even stronger critique of materialism. But I paint the picture this way because I fear that the people who remember the triple challenge King's message and wish to express it could lose the battle to those who remember King's message and choose to forget or suppress it. Those of us who lived through and remember the time will die, and for those who do not remember it, it will live for them through history books and the stories their teachers tell them.

My niece did not know that King was against war, and therefore did not know that the reason why George W. Bush was booed while memorializing King was because Bush was *for* war and was, in fact, raging war as he praised the King of peace. My niece did not know that King was against the rich getting richer while the poor got poorer, and therefore did not know that another reason why Bush was booed while memorializing King was because Bush had done everything in his political power to make sure that economic gap increased.

So to counteract this story she had been told, to make sure she had the full report for her report, I rushed down to my local bookstores to buy her some reference books. Of the six children's and young adult books on King available in the biography section of my local Barnes and Noble (none were available at Borders that day, though the biographies of pop stars Hilary Duff and Lindsay Lohan were in stock), *only one of them* made mention of both King's concern with militarism and materialism.[52] The other five *made no reference to Vietnam at all* or to his anti-militaristic stance. (Though some noted he won the Nobel Peace Prize, they connected this with his peaceful protests regarding race). Three of those five *made no mention of his concern about materialism at all* and of the two that did, they made cursory mention of his support for garbage workers striking for better wages, but only to contextualize why he was in Memphis at the time of his death, and not to illustrate his vehement position on materialism itself.

If Slattery is correct and "our identities are bound up with what we—as a people and a culture—choose to forget as well as what we select to remember," I would assert that those five books on King define America more than they define King, that they are more about America's identity, her idealized identity, than they are about the identity of the King she idealizes.

Toward a New Collective Remembering

So, is there a solution, or is America simply a helpless and hopeless case? No, let's not give up on our client just yet. Depth psychology suggests a solution, and it's a simple one. We can change what part of the myth we focus on. We can fix the archetypes we have fixed onto King, and thus begin to fix ourselves. If we could collectively remember another side of King, we could resurrect more of the man and redeem more of his message.

While space does not allow me to fully explore what all of those "archetypal fixes" might be, I do want to offer one: the role of the gadfly. The literal gadfly is the annoying fly that circles around cows and pesters them. The archetypal gadfly is a social critic, the one whose task is to open up dialogue; the intention of that dialogue is to stimulate awareness followed by action undertaken with the goal of improving societal conditions. An early gadfly was Socrates, who said of himself, "I am that gadfly which God has attached to the State, and all day long and in all places am always fastening upon you, arousing and persuading and reproaching you."[53]

I am suggesting that we need to hear King's voice buzzing in our collective ear, arousing us and persuading us and reproaching us for all we have not done yet. Perhaps the peaceful dreamer could give way to the provocative gadfly if we would forget for a while King's "I Have a Dream" speech and remember his gadfly sermon mentioned earlier, "Why America May Go to Hell." In doing this, we could shift from remembering King by patting ourselves on the back to really honoring him by waking up and getting to work on the monumental task of manifesting King's vision of heaven on earth—the beloved community.

Here we are not creating a mythological role where none exists, for it is clear that King saw himself as this sort of gadfly. He wrote, "If something doesn't happen soon, I'm convinced that the curtain of doom is coming down on the U.S." Continuing, he said,

> America, I don't plan to let you rest until that day comes into being when all God's children will be respected, and every man will respect the dignity and worth of human personality. America, I don't plan to allow you to rest until from every city hall in this country, justice will roll down like waters and righteousness like a mighty stream.
> America, I don't plan to let you rest until you live it out that "all men are created equal and endowed by their creator with certain unalienable rights."[54]

But rest we do when we mythologize King as a warrior-hero who won the battle, a peaceful dreamer whose dream came true, a martyr-savior who gave his life and saved us. Rest we do when we are taught, like my niece, "And, it worked! And so that made them all happy, and so that made life easier. And that's how it is now."

Socrates said of himself,

> You will not easily find another like me, and therefore I would advise you to spare me. I dare say that you may feel out of temper (like the person who is suddenly awakened from sleep), and you think that you might easily strike me dead as Anytus advises, and then you sleep on for the remainder of your lives, unless God in his care of you sent you another gadfly.[55]

King can be seen as that gadfly sent by God to America, but America did not spare him and struck him dead too, then went back to sleep. Now we even have a holiday in King's name upon which to catch up on our sleep, and a new batch of drugs—these ones legal—to make our apathy more comfortable and our lethargy less depressing.

King is asleep now too. He lies in a tomb which reads "Free at last, free at last. Thank God almighty, I'm free at last." King is free at last, but it is we who are still enslaved, still shackled to our worship of weapons and our idolization of money. The true axis of evil we have yet to fight is not those countries declared to be evil by George W. Bush, but those concepts, "the three triplets," declared by Martin Luther King, Jr.—racism, militarism, and materialism. These are the real evils that terrorize Americans every day—these are the real evils Americans use to terrorize the world every day. I know I suffer from a case of homeland insecurity, and I know I am not alone. I have a dream—that one day someone will rise up, call 911, and declare the so-called United States a disaster area.

But wait. We had a King who already did that. Rabbi Abraham Heschel, introducing King to an audience in Memphis right before his death said "The whole future of America will depend upon the impact and influence of Dr. King."[56] This is not mere hyperbole. King, like Jesus, like Gandhi, like the other warriors and dreamers and martrys and gadflys before him, gave us enough wisdom to live by for centuries. Recall G. K. Chesterson's line, "The problem with Christianity is not that it has been tried and found wanting, but that it has been found difficult, and left untried."[57] The same can be said of King, that his message has been found politically dangerous to the status quo and psychologically dangerous to the American soul, and therefore has been left, for the most part, untried.

But in order for us to try it, we have to remember it.

"OUT OF THE MOUNTAIN OF DESPAIR, A STONE OF HOPE"

In 2008, the Martin Luther King, Jr. Memorial will open on four acres at the National Mall in Washington, D.C. The centerpiece of the memorial will be a 30-feet-tall rough stone called "The Stone of Hope" in tribute to one of King's oft-repeated statements, "With this faith, we will be able to hew out of the mountain of despair, a stone of hope."[58] On the side of the stone facing the Jefferson Memorial, King's likeness will be carved. Standing at the Lincoln Memorial where King delivered the "I Have a Dream" speech, the stone will be visible.

From perusing the pages of the Memorial website, it appears that soon a much richer story of King will be told there for future generations to read than those now available in our local chain bookstores. When explaining why now the time is right to build the Memorial, the site states,

> Dr. King once reminded the nation of "the fierce urgency of now" while warning against "the tranquilizing drug of gradualism." The time is now a historical perspective. Many young people have heard of Dr. King, but are unaware of the significance of his contributions to America and the world.[59]

From looking at the site design plans, there are references to the struggle against racism, of course, but there are also references to peace and economic justice. In fact, the vision of the Memorial is described as such:

> The Memorial will evoke the memory and spiritual presence of Dr. King. It will honor not only a great man, but the values that empowered his leadership, including courage and truth, unconditional love and forgiveness, justice and equality, reconciliation and peace.

It is an appropriate turn, to look not just at the man and the myth and the movement, but at the message that encircles them all. In the end, everything came down to values for King, a revolution of values. He wrote,

> For its very survival's sake, America must re-examine old presuppositions and release itself from many things that for centuries have been held sacred. For the evils of racism, poverty and militarism to die, a new set of values must be born.[60]

For every new generation that is born, this Monument will serve, literally, as a touchstone for those values.

Though I have taken on the role of a gadfly myself during much of this essay and resonate with King's despair over the future of this country, I do have hope as well, and it is this Memorial in part which gives me that hope. Against the movement of the American psyche to forget King, there seems to be a countermovement always to remember him and the radical integrity of his message, a countermovement even in the political realm where his message is most dangerous. In Slattery's words, "where [a country] makes the cut between what will be allowed in and what will remain outside, defines that entity even more than one's fingerprints or biological heritage." The American psyche is not definitively defined: the cut is not carved in stone.

NOTES

1. Dennis Patrick Slattery, "Remembering the Terezin Ghetto," *The Progressive Christian* 181, vol. 8 (May, 2006): 14.

2. An expanded analysis of King's work with America's neurosis, as well as other themes in this essay can be found in my dissertation entitled *Cultural Therapy: Martin Luther King, Jr.'s Work with the Soul of America* (2004).

3. Martin Luther King, Jr.,"The American Dream," in *A Knock at Midnight: Inspiration from the Great Sermons of Reverend Martin Luther King, Jr.* (New York: Warner Books, 1998), p. 87.

4. King, quoted in David Garrow, *Bearing the Cross: Martin Luther King, Jr. and the Southern Christian Leadership Conference* (New York: William Morrow and Company, 1986), p. 584.

5. Martin Luther King, Jr., *Where Do We Go From Here: Chaos or Community?* (New York: Bantam Books, 1967), p. 99.

6. Karen Horney, *The Neurotic Personality of Our Time* (New York: W. W. Norton & Company, 1937) and *Neurosis and Human Growth: The Struggle Toward Self-Realization* (New York: W. W. Norton & Company, 1950).

7. George Washington is the only other American honored with a Federal holiday. Abraham Lincoln's birthday is a legal holiday in some states, but not a Federal holiday, though some states have joined his birthday and Washington's into one called President's Day, which coincides with the Federal holiday for Washington. There is only one other Federal holiday that honors an individual: Columbus Day.

8. Those Presidents are Theodore Roosevelt, Thomas Jefferson, George Washington, and Abraham Lincoln.

9. King, in *The Autobiography of Martin Luther King, Jr.*, ed. Clayborne Carson (New York: Warner Books, 1998), p. 262.

10. Martin Luther King, Jr., "A Testament of Hope," in *A Testament of Hope: The Essential Writings and Speeches of Martin Luther King, Jr.*, ed. James M. Washington (San Francisco: HarperCollins, 1969), p. 315.

11. King, *Autobiography,* p. 340.

12. Martin Luther King, Jr., "An Autobiography of Religious Development," in *The Papers of Martin Luther King, Jr.: Vol. 1. Called to Serve, January 1929-June 1951*, ed. Clayborne Carson (Berkeley: University of California Press, 1950), p. 359.

13. King, *Autobiography*, p. 9.

14. Coretta Scott King, "Thoughts and Reflections," in *We Shall Overcome: Martin Luther King, Jr. and the Black Freedom Struggle*, ed. Peter J. Albert and Ronald Hoffman (New York: Pantheon Books, 1990), p. 253.

15. King, quoted in *Bearing the Cross*, p. 46.

16. *Ibid.*

17. Martin Luther King, Jr., "How Should a Christian View Communism?," in *Strength to Love* (Philadelphia: Fortress Press, 1963), p. 100.

18. *Ibid.*, p. 102.

19. *Ibid.*, p. 103.

20. *Ibid.*

21. King, "Paul's Letter to American Christians," in *A Knock at Midnight*, p. 28.

22. King, quoted in *Bearing the Cross*, p. 429.

23. Martin Luther King, Jr., "A Time to Break Silence," in *A Testament of Hope*, p. 241.

24. King, quoted in Robert M. Franklin, "An Ethic of Hope: The Moral Thought of Martin Luther King, Jr.," *Union Seminary Quarterly Review* XL, no. 4 (1986): 46.

25. King, "Paul's Letter to American Christians," pp. 28-29.

26. King, quoted in *Bearing the Cross*, p. 394.

27. *Ibid.*, p. 430.

28. Lee, quoted in *Bearing the Cross*, p. 543.

29. *Ibid.*

30. King, quoted in *Bearing the Cross*, p. 543.

31. *Ibid.*, p. 545.

32. King, *Where Do We Go From Here*, p. 213.

33. King, "A Time to Break Silence," p. 242.

34. *Ibid.*

35. *Ibid.*, p. 243.

36. David Garrow, *Bearing the Cross: Martin Luther King, Jr. and the Southern Christian Leadership Conference* (New York: William Morrow and Company, 1986), p. 598.

37. Harry Belafonte, "Is America a Burning House: We Need a Voice of Moral Courage to Offer a Vision for the Twenty-first Century," *Essence* 27, November 1996, p. 218.

38. King, quoted in *Bearing the Cross,* p. 591.

39. *Ibid.,* p. 580.

40. *Ibid.,* p. 581.

41. Bill Moyers, http://www.racematters.org/josephhough.htm

42. Peter Grier, "Rich-poor Gap Gaining Attention," *Christian Science Monitor,* June 14, 2005, http://www.csmonitor.com/2005/0614/p01s03-usec.html

43. King, quoted in James H. Cone, "Martin Luther King, Jr., and the Third World," in *We Shall Overcome,* p. 207.

44. King, "Remaining Awake During a Great Revolution," in *A Knock at Midnight,* p. 219.

45. Ronald Reagan, "Message to the Congress of Racial Equality on the Observance of Martin Luther King, Jr. Day," http://www.reagan.utexas.edu/archives/speeches/1986/11686b.htm

46. Marcus Epstein, "Myths of Martin Luther King," http://www.lewrockwell.com/orig/epstein9.html

47. Peggy Noonan, *When Character Was King: The Story of Ronald Reagan* (New York: Viking Books, 2001), p. 234.

48. Martin Luther King, Jr., *Why We Can't Wait* (New York: Signet Classic, 1963), p. 127.

49. King, *Where Do We Go From Here,* p. 170.

50. Adams, quoted in Michael E. Dyson, *I May Not Get There With You: The True Martin Luther King, Jr.* (New York: The Free Press, 2000), p. 283.

51. Lionel Corbett, *The Religious Function of the Psyche* (London: Routledge, 1996), p. 89.

52. The one that mentioned all of the triplets was *Martin Luther King, Jr.: A Photographic Story* of a Life (2004) by Amy Pastan. The others reviewed that day were *Heroes of America: Martin Luther King, Jr.* (1996) by Herb Boyd, *My Brother Martin* (2003) by Christine King Farris, *I Have a Dream: The Story of Martin Luther King* (1986) by Margaret Davidson, *Martin Luther King, Jr.* (2003) by Mary Winget, and *Martin Luther King, Jr: Young Man With a Dream* by Dharathula H. Millender (1983).

53. Socrates, *The Apology,* http://socrates.clarke.edu/aplg0106.htm

54. King, quoted in Vincent Harding, *Martin Luther King: The Inconvenient Hero* (Maryknoll, New York: Orbis Books, 1996), p. ix.

55. Socrates, *The Apology.*

56. Heschel, quoted in *Martin Luther King: The Inconvenient Hero*, p. ix.

57. G. K. Chesterton, "What's Wrong with the World?" (Dodd, Mead and Company, 1910. Reprinted, San Francisco: Ignatius Press, 1994), p. 37.

58. King, "Remaining Awake," p. 224.

59. http://www.mlkmemorial.org/

60. King, *Where Do We Go From Here: Chaos or Community?*, p. 157.

FUNDAMENTALISM IN THE USA: WORD WORSHIP VERSUS THING WORSHIP

ANN CASEMENT

...it has even been said that the highest praise of God consists in the denial of him by the atheist who finds creation so perfect that it can dispense with a creator.

— Marcel Proust[1]

INTRODUCTION

I have been invited as a non-American to contribute to this special issue of *Spring* on "Politics and the American Soul" and have selected the topic of fundamentalism out of the possible titles I was sent by the Editor. A few words about myself would seem to be a starting point for this article, and, in order to do this, I will follow the French structural anthropologist, Pierre Bourdieu's approach set forth in what he calls *participant objectivation*. He expounded upon this at the Huxley Memorial Lecture at University College London in 2000 which is where I last saw him shortly before his death from cancer in January 2002. In

Ann Casement is a Senior Member of The British Association of Psychotherapists and a New York State Licensed Psychoanalyst. She served on the International Association for Analytical Psychology (IAAP) Executive Committee from 2001-2007. Her most recent edited books are *The Idea of the Numinous: Contemporary Jungian and Psychoanalytic Perspectives* (Routledge, 2006), with David Tacey; and *Who Owns Jung?* (Karnac, 2007).

brief, *participant objectivation* lays stress on the point of view of the objectivizer and the set of cognitive structures that underlie her objectivation. My point of view may be seen to derive from being a middle-aged, middle class British Indian woman, classical/contemporary Jungian, licensed psychoanalyst, and social anthropologist. In the context of the theme I have chosen, it also seems appropriate to add that I am a Catholic. Under its appearance of banality, *participant objectivation* is about the overturning that consists in taking a point of view on one's own point of view, and, thereby, on the whole set of points of view in relation to which it defines itself as such.

As to my point of view on fundamentalism, I would say that though I have been a frequent visitor to the United States (US) since the late 1960s, most often to the Eastern Seaboard but also to the South, including the Deep South, the Mid-West, and the West, I have had little firsthand experience of US fundamentalism. Nevertheless, it has intrigued me for a long time while at the same remaining latent in my psyche until now. I have used as background material for this piece recent articles on the religious right in the US (about such figures as James Dobson, Jerry Falwell, Pat Robertson, and Ted Haggard) that have appeared in the pages of *The Economist*,[2] to which I am a long-time contributor. Other sources include the 19th-century French politician and thinker, Alexis de Tocqueville,[3] one of the best foreign observers of the US scene, and the French philosopher and journalist, Bernard-Henri Lévy's *American Vertigo*,[4] an homage to de Tocqueville. I have also looked at Richard Dawkins' recent bestseller in the United Kingdom (UK) *The God Delusion* whose pages are full of references to US fundamentalism.[5]

I want to state at the outset, though, that my brief is different to *The Economist*, Dawkins, Lévy et al. as I have been asked to bring a depth psychological perspective to bear on the topic. To address this, I have looked at what relates to fundamentalism in the literature from clinicians and scholars in the Jungian, Freudian, Kleinian, and neo-Kleinian movements, to garner insight into fundamentalism as a psychological phenomenon. In particular, I am indebted to my friend and colleague the Jungian psychoanalyst, George Hogenson, who is the most knowledgeable person I know about fundamentalism and its connections to neo-conservatism in the US.

ORIGINS

In order to start writing anything intelligible about fundamentalism, I went in quest of further information about its origins from sources that include data I discovered online; in the three volumes on *Modern American Religion* by Martin E. Marty,[6] an historian and religious writer; and in the *Encyclopedia Britannica*. From these, I discovered that the roots of fundamentalism appear to lie in 19th-century Protestant evangelical churches which comprised a mixed group of theologically conservative communions that stressed the full, and often *verbal*, inspiration of the Bible and its complete authority over faith and practice. The message that was imparted to the faithful by these communions was that a happy eternal life is won only as the gift of God's grace through a radical conversion and commitment to Christ as Savior. This either gave rise to or found an echo in a messianic complex in the American psyche which Freud classes as "something analogous to a delusion..."[7]

The starting point of fundamentalism dates from the American millenarian movement in the 1830s and 1840s when expectations were aroused of the second coming of Christ. From this it was claimed there would ensue a thousand years of peace (the millennium), which attracted thousands of supporters. The movement failed when the expected advent did not occur. It is worth noting that though fundamentalism is stereotyped as a Southern phenomenon, the millenarian movement and its sequel in the 1870s were located in the East and Northeast of the US. Suffice to say there was a corresponding movement taking place in the South which will be discussed further in this paper. Millenarianism arose in the US when confidence in its destiny began to wane among some Protestant leaders due to labor unrest, social discontent, and the rising tide of Roman Catholic immigrants. These phenomena combined with interpretation of the Scriptures as predicting apostasy in Christendom and degeneracy in society which only the return of Christ could remedy.

The term "fundamentalist" was coined in the 1920s to designate those doing battle in the name of such fundamental credos as the inerrant inspiration of the Bible, the virgin birth, Atonement, Resurrection, and the miracle-working power of Christ. As Marty states: "...all Fundamentalists were inerrantist."[8] At the same time there appeared a 12-volume collection of essays written in the period 1910-1915 entitled *The Fundamentals,* the contents of which were heavily reinforced at the Niagara Bible Conference of 1878 and the Presbyterian General Assembly of 1910.

The neo-Kleinian psychoanalyst, Ron Britton, has borrowed the term fundamentalism in order to apply it to particular phenomena in the analysis of some narcissistic disorders in a clinical setting. He uses the term "word worship" where it applies to idealization of the analyst's words and "thing worship" where the analyst's physical identity is idolized. In the case of "word worship" the analyst's "words were adopted and idealised..."[9] In relation to "thing worship," he states:

> My identity...extended beyond the boundaries of my physical body to include the couch, the carpet, the walls, probably most of all the blanket...This became in her mind a shared skin providing absolute congruity. [10]

He concludes that both these defensive organizations are meant to prevent the recognized co-existence of more than one psychic reality. He goes on to say about "word worship" and "thing worship" that "the two modes existed as alternatives and were in opposition to each other."[11] In relation to "word worship" an explanatory experience in analysis is sought along with a corresponding avoidance of emotional dependence: "texts become the word of God."[12] Following Britton's hypothesis, "word worship" may be applied to fundamentalism in the USA where their tracts

> based their authority on the infallibility of the Bible because it was said every word in it was the Word of God. The movement had two particular hated targets, Roman Catholicism and modernism. The former was regarded as infatuated with religious idols and the latter with materialism; both were seen as evil opponents of the one God and his Word.[13]

In this vein, Roman Catholicism, depicted as idolatry, as well as materialism would be anathematized as "thing worship." Jung also alludes to the "power-word" in writing about the US as follows: "There is no country on earth where the 'power-word,' the magic formula, the slogan or advertisement is more effective than in America."[14] And Marty states: "A relentless logic lay behind the development of fundamentalism, which was chiefly doctrinal."[15]

AMERICAN EXCEPTIONALISM

This section provides a résumé of the views of the recently departed Seymour Martin Lipset, the Harvard sociologist and political scientist, himself a second generation Russian Jewish immigrant, who wrote extensively on the topic of what he called "American exceptionalism." He posed what seems to me to be the fundamental question about fundamentalism which is to ask why the US has sky-high levels of religiosity. Lipset traced this back to the revolution of 1776 which not only got rid of feudalism but also shattered what he termed the confessional state, which imposed by law what the hierarchy considered to be right. The void left by this led to the creation of a free market in religion.

Even before the revolution, the "First (there were three more) Great Awakening" proclaimed by the Puritan pastor, Jonathan Edwards, in colonial days saw significance for millennialism in the discovery and settlement of the New World. He foretold the establishment of Christ's kingdom sometime near the end of the 20th-century in the New Jerusalem. Before this, John Winthrop, in his famous 1630 sermon *A Model of Christian Charity* to the Massachusetts Bay Colony Puritans, told them they would found "a city upon a hill," a term he borrowed from the Sermon on the Mount. This had a powerful effect on the New England Puritans in implanting the idea that their community was ordained by God just as it had been earlier covenanted between God and the Children of Israel. This rhetoric found an echo in speeches by John F. Kennedy and in Ronald Reagan's 1989 "Farewell Address" when he spoke of the United States as a city on a hill. The rights protected by the Constitution in 1776 of "life, liberty, and the pursuit of happiness" were seen to be created by God and given to humankind. This principle echoes throughout American history in, for instance, George Washington's "First Inaugural Address;" Martin Luther King's "Letter from a Birmingham Jail;" and the recent call to war by President George W. Bush.

The "Second Great Awakening" preceded the Civil War of the 1860s, the key to that being the Abolitionist movement. The fundamentalism associated with the Southern states of the US emerged out of the Civil War which resulted in the institutionalizing of racial segregation. Segregationists in the South pointed to the story of Noah to justify the lower status of blacks and even slavery as the children of Ham. This is depicted in the Book of Genesis which presents Noah as the first to plant a vineyard. His drunkenness and the disrespect it provoked in his son, Ham (or Canaan), resulted in Noah's curse on Ham and his descendants. The ethnic and social division that resulted in the separation of the Israelites (from the line of Shem) from the pre-Israelite population (Canaan) meant that they would live in subjection to the Hebrews. The splitting evident here is an example of classical Kleinian theory where denigrated parts of the self are split off and projected into another. "This links to a particular form of identification which establishes the prototype of an aggressive object-relation. I suggest for these processes the term 'projective identification.'"[16]

There is a strong link from classical Kleinian theory to the concept of *shadow,* consisting of inferior or rejected parts of the self in Jungian theory, as follows: "…when the *shadow* is activated, usually through projection, it is charged with affect and takes on an autonomous life of its own beyond the ego's control."[17] However, Jung also buys into the inferiority of what he terms "the Negro" and the psychological influence that exerts on the way white Americans express themselves in "the peculiar walk with loose joints, or the swinging of the hips so frequently observed in Americans, also comes from the Negro…The expression of religious feeling, the revival meetings, the Holy Roller and other abnormalities…"[18]

Both classical Kleinian and Jungian theory on splitting and shadow projection can be applied to the segregationist view of keeping whites separated from blacks in the South. This became reified in the "separate but equal" policy that was prevalent from the 1890s until the historical ruling of the Supreme Court in 1954 that brought about the most significant social transformation since the Civil War.

The case of *Brown v. Board of Education of Topeka,* 347 U.S. 483 (1954), was heard by the 14th Chief Justice of the US, when he spoke for a unanimous court in declaring unconstitutional the separation of public school children by race. In doing so, he rejected the "separate but equal" doctrine that had prevailed since 1896 and declared that separate educational facilities were inherently unequal. This ruling also removed tax exemptions from schools and religious colleges that discriminated against black students. The formation of the Moral Majority and related right-wing fundamentalist groups resulted from this decision, underlining the fact that racism was the initial stimulus for the emergence of the religious right, not the obsession with abortion and homosexuality which came later. A recent survey on the American South in *The Economist* states:

> So as the South has become less racist, it has lost none of its religiosity. Nearly half of southerners believe the Bible is the literal word of God—twice the proportion in the north-east or the West. Such beliefs have political consequences. Southerners vote for politicians they judge devout. Their faith lends passion to national debates about abortion, homosexuality and bioethics. It affects foreign policy, too: some 56% of southerners think God gave Israel to the Jews.[19]

ANGLO-SAXON WORLD VIEW

To return to Lipset, he claimed that US moralism explained both what he saw as its reforming zeal and its suffocating self-righteousness that led to American exceptionalism, and it is the latter which is flourishing once again under the neo-conservatives. This can be cited as a major reason why there are growing differences with Europe about issues ranging from military intervention to capitalism. On the other hand, the special relationship between the US and the United Kingdom (UK) has led to what is called the Anglo-Saxon worldview which underwrites globalization. Martin Marty uses source material from another French visitor to the US, André Siegfried, an economist, political scientist, historian, and journalist, of whom Marty says as follows: "He was not a genius, as his predecessor Alexis de Tocqueville a century earlier had been, but he had an instinct for discerning and elaborating the central plot of American spiritual life."[20] As Siegried states: "the Americans as a whole pride themselves on their original stock, which was Anglo-Saxon and inherently Protestant."[21] The old American majority promoted "unity of spirit by insisting impatiently that their centre of gravity still lies in the Anglo-Saxon and Puritan stock."[22] In his most quoted line, Siegried stated: "Protestantism is the only national religion, and to ignore that fact is to view the country from a false angle."[23] Analytically, this would be seen as the need to establish a core identity without which there exist anxieties of annihilation and disintegration.

With regard to Anglo-Saxonism, my viewpoint may be depicted as both that of an outsider as a non-American but also that of an insider as a putative participant in the Anglo-Saxon philosophy of life. The term suggests consensus both in the US and the UK, but the underlying reality is that there exists a split in both countries—politically in the US between what may be seen as the Republican and Democratic standpoints, and in the UK between strong supporters of Atlanticism and those who are vehemently anti-American. It is important to posit the existence of this split in both the American and the British psyches, but beyond the scope of this article to attempt to find answers to complex geopolitical questions.

Furthermore, there are significant differences between the US and the UK, one being the role religion plays in both societies. In the US, for instance, religion and politics blend in a potent mix such as the messianic democracy that is part of the crusading zeal of the neo-conservative philosophy of life. It is this kind of democracy that has been tried in Iraq as a result of what Al Gore refers to as President Bush's faith-based policies. As Marty puts it: "If the Christian ideal was worthy to be followed in America, it was worthy to be presented in every land."[24]

In the UK, on the other hand, religion and politics tend to be kept separate, though it used to be said that the Church of England was the Conservative party at prayer. The Labour party, on the other hand, has its roots partly in the Methodist church which explains its reforming zeal over social issues. Although George Bush is a neo-conservative Republican, he found an ally in the former Labour Prime Minister, Tony Blair, as they both share deeply held religious convictions evidenced by Blair, somewhat unusually for a British Prime Minister, basing many of his actions on a belief in the righteousness of them. A recent book *The Hubris Syndrome* by David Owen, a former British Foreign Secretary, examines the messianic unshakable belief that underlay both Bush and Blair's conduct of the war in Iraq and the nemesis that has followed.[25]

To summarize this section, it is generally true to say that the UK as a whole is uncomfortable with a religio-political mix. It has been said that the British hold nothing sacred apart from cricket, and they were largely bemused by a Prime Minister who not only holds strong beliefs but who is also converting to Catholicism. American readers may be interested to know that the British monarch may not marry a Catholic and, as Defender of the Faith, would be dethroned if he or she did. US politics, as has already been attested to in this article, is inherently at ease with this mix. Freud's famed dislike of the US was probably, in part, an extension of this as was his contrasting fondness for England. Jung, on the other hand, felt warmly towards the US, which may be ascribed to his positive view of the religious issue. It is well known that Freud pathologized religion as an illusion, even a delusion, going so far as to say that its psychological characteristics were "sanctity, rigidity and intolerance, the same prohibition of thought for its own defence."[26] His analysis of religious belief was based on his hypothesis that its roots lay in repeating childhood fears of the power of the parents linked to the need for their protection. His conclusion was that the very premises of science, and, hence, of psychoanalysis, are incompatible with those of religion. My own view of the latter, which owes much to my friend and colleague, the philosopher and anthropologist, Ernest Gellner, is that psychoanalysis lets religion in through the back door in having a prophet, dogma, eschatology, and congregation. It even has its own heretics.

THE SCOPES MONKEY TRIAL OF 1925

By the end of World War I, the rise in immigration led to the increasing spread of Roman Catholicism in the US, which, in turn, led to growing concerns amongst some Fundamentalist Protestant leaders. As the Catholic Church "competed for the soul of America"[27] it captioned its mission as *"adaptation and conquest."*[28] "It was the latter concept that frightened non-Catholic Americans."[29] These fears were fuelled by what they saw as mounting social degeneracy which Fundamentalist Protestants linked to the growth of science and materialism. The teaching of evolution was a particular source of displeasure that, combined with anxiety over the spread of biblical criticism, led to legislation in March 1925 in Tennessee declaring unlawful the teaching of any doctrine denying divine creation of humans as taught in the Bible. This came to a head in the so-called Scopes Monkey Trial of 1925, a brief account of which follows.

John T. Scopes, a science teacher in the small town of Dayton, Tennessee, offered to serve as the defendant against the charge of having taught evolution. Two of the foremost public figures of the decade, William Jennings Bryan, a conservative Presbyterian Fundamentalist, and Clarence Darrow, a defense counsel in notable criminal trials, served respectively as counsel for the prosecution and the defense. Scopes was found guilty of teaching evolution and fined $100, though on appeal the state supreme court upheld the constitutionality of the law, but acquitted Scopes on the grounds that the fine had been excessive. The law was eventually repealed in 1967.

Richard Dawkins and Bernard-Henri Lévy both make mention of the trial in their recent books, and Freud alludes to it in *The Future of an Illusion,* written shortly after the event, as "the 'monkey trial' at Dayton." In his critique of religion, Freud states that the evidential value of religious documents has been whittled away as "natural science has shown up the errors in them, and…the fatal resemblance between the religious ideas which we revere and the mental products of primitive peoples and times."[30]

Lévy's reference to the monkey trial depicts it as "the battle between faith and science—and the latter was often ordered to give in to the former."[31] As Lévy goes on to say:

> Today…the strategy has been refined. It has even been reversed. Instead of opposing science…contrasting a soulless science with the eternal human soul and natural theology, the creationist camp has had the clever idea of fitting itself into the adversary's mould…and starting to speak in the name of science.[32]

"Intelligent design" is one outcome of the new strategy which developed a teleology of the history of species with the support of the Nobel Prize winner and spiritualist John Eccles. One object of a series of International Conferences for the Unity of Science has been the undermining of the theoretical foundations of Darwinism. "Scientific creationism" is a pretence at accepting Darwinism by elevating "to the rank of 'science' what is patently superstition and pretence…"[33]
. A quote from Jung is apt here:

> …these harmless creatures form a mass, and there emerges a raging monster; and each individual is only one tiny cell in the monster's body…Having a dark suspicion of these grim possibilities, man turns a blind eye to the shadow-side of human nature.[34]

Richard Dawkins also alludes to the "Monkey trial" in Dayton, Tennessee, where Bryan College is named after William Jennings Bryan, who was the prosecutor at the trial. "Think critically and biblically" is the motto displayed on the Bryan website. Dawkins states:

> I am hostile to fundamentalist religion because it actively debauches the scientific enterprise...It subverts science and saps the intellect.[35]

Jung has several references in the *Collected Works* to what he calls "This magic word, which always ends in 'ism.'"[36] He suggests this is particularly at work in those who have the least access to their interior selves "and have strayed the furthest from their instinctual roots into the truly chaotic world of *collective consciousness.*"[37] The result of becoming absorbed by the opinions and tendencies of the latter is "the mass man, the ever-ready victim of some wretched 'ism.'"[38] He warns that possession "by a supraordinate idea"[39] can manifest as materialism, intellectualism, atheism, and he would, no doubt, have added fundamentalism if he were alive today. However, Jung also viewed religiosity as innate in humans which was not only negative, as he expresses in the following quote: "Confrontation with an archetype or instinct is an *ethical* problem of the first magnitude...a spiritual goal toward which the whole nature of man strives."[40] And he adds: "The archetype behind a religious idea has, like every instinct, its specific energy, which it does not lose even if the conscious mind ignores it."[41]

In this last statement, Jung is unwittingly echoing de Tocqueville in *Democracy in America,* which he wrote after spending nine months in the U.S. from 1831-32 studying its penal system, politics, and religion. He states:

> The soul has wants which must be satisfied, and whatever pains are taken to divert it from itself, it soon grows weary, restless, and disquieted amid the enjoyment of sense...I should be surprised if mysticism did not soon make some advance among a people solely engaged in promoting their worldly welfare...But they feel imprisoned within bounds, which they will apparently never be allowed to pass. As soon as they have passed these bounds, their minds do not know where to fix themselves and they often rush unrestrained beyond the range of common sense.[42]

In this study of America, de Tocqueville pre-empts Jung's theory of *enantiodromia* borrowed from Heraclitus, which means running counter to and which proposes that everything that exists turns into its opposite. "I use the term enantiodromia for the emergence of the unconscious opposite in the course of time."[43]

De Tocqueville and Jung are remarkably similar in their attitude to religion where, for instance, the former states "these lofty instincts are not the offspring of his capricious will; their steadfast foundation is fixed in human nature..."[44] De Tocqueville thought that because Americans held to Christian values in seeing all citizens as equals they could not tolerate a tyrant. Christian values also imposed a restraint upon government in a form which would harmonize earth with heaven. But he displays remarkable prescience in what he says about the extreme form religion can take in the U.S. as follows:

> Here and there in the midst of American society you meet with men full of fanatical and almost wild spiritualism, which hardly exists in Europe. From time to time strange sects arise which endeavour to strike out extraordinary paths to eternal happiness. Religious insanity is very common in the United States.[45]

Richard Dawkins takes up de Tocqueveille's theme of "religious insanity" in the United States with several quotes from representatives of what he calls the "American Taliban." The following are some examples: "We should invade their countries, kill their leaders and convert them to Christianity." "Don't use the word 'gay' unless it's an acronym for 'Got Aids Yet?'" "We don't have to protect the environment, the Second Coming is at hand."[46] *The God Delusion* is a critique of all religion, not just fundamentalism, as exemplified in the following extract from it: "Our Western politicians avoid mention the R word (religion) and instead characterize their battle as a war against 'terror,' as though terror were a kind of spirit or force, with a will and mind of its own."[47] The psychoanalyst, Harold Bloom's words may be of interest to Dawkins here:

> One of the uses of religious criticism is that it is the appropriate instrument for dissecting, understanding, and perhaps someday destroying Fundamentalism, which is the shadow side of what is most spiritual and valuable in the American Religion.[48]

Jung's complex theory can shed light both on representatives of the "American Taliban" and also on Dawkins himself, who appears to be in the grip of an anti-religious complex. Complexes function as "splinter psyches"[49] which, when one of them is activated, function with a degree of autonomy that is outside conscious control "and therefore behaves like an animated foreign body in the sphere of consciousness."[50] Jung was influenced by the French psychopathologist, Pierre Janet, in his thinking on "the extreme *dissociability* of consciousness."[51] A complex can assimilate ego-consciousness step by step and lead "to a neurotic dissociation of the personality."[52]

The case of Ted Haggard, one of the religious right's brightest stars, close friend of James Dobson, the leader of the religious right and ally of President of Bush, and president of the thirty million strong National Association of Evangelicals, is an example of a man caught in a complex. Haggard, a leading campaigner against same-sex marriage, was denounced in November 2006 by a male escort accusing him of paying for sex on a regular basis and using methamphetamines. Haggard first denied the accusations but eventually stated: "There's a part of my life that is so repulsive and dark that I have been warring against it for all my adult life."[53] Jung warns of the dangers of repressing the shadow and says no one has a more dangerous enemy than his own unknown self:

> ...somewhere we have a sinister and frightful brother, our own flesh-and-blood counterpart, who holds and maliciously hoards everything that we would so willingly hide under the table.[54]

Neo-Conservativism

A brief account follows of neo-conservativism, most of the material for which has been culled from the pages of *The Economist,* from various online websites dedicated to the neo-conservatives, and, most interestingly, from exchanges with George Hogenson. In recent years, the fundamentalist movement in the US found its soul mate in the neo-conservatives who currently hold power in the US with the President, George W. Bush, at their head. This has led to a political marriage of convenience between these two groups with major repercussions for US foreign policy and the geopolitical scene.

The neo-conservatives, or neo-cons as they are widely known, started off as a small, East Coast group of sophisticated intellectuals, initially largely Jewish, who were in no position to get elected or to influence elections. They began early on to align with the old guard conservative movement in the Republican Party, headed by East Coast intellectual Catholics like William Buckley, but still had limited access to real electoral power. When Richard Nixon ran for President in 1968, however, a sea-change came over the Republican Party as he engaged what was called the "Southern strategy" to lure the populist vote in the South that had traditionally been Democratic due to the Civil War and Lincoln's being a Republican, despite the racial divide between Northern and Southern Democrats. Nixon was also trying to hold off the racial politics of George Wallace. This was the opening for the white Southerners to move to the Republican Party which Carter may have moved further along. The result of the Nixon years was that the populist white evangelicals in the South got a foothold in the electoral process, becoming the Republican base that now dominates the primary process for the Republican Party.

 With the election of Ronald Reagan, the neo-cons came into positions of power when Richard Perle and others worked their way into the upper levels of the foreign policy and defense bureaucracies. The marriage of convenience between the neo-cons and the fundamentalists started from the premise that their mutual interest in Israel would be the fulcrum on which it would rest. Thus, the neo-cons were the intellectual insurgents who could not get elected, while the fundamentalists were political insurgents whose intellectual standing was suspect at best, if not downright crazy. It was only with George W. Bush that the fundamentalist social and religious agenda and the neo-conservative foreign policy and political agenda came to be fully aligned with one another in the American political system.

The neo-cons themselves trace their intellectual descent back to the 1930s and the German-born political philosopher, Leo Strauss (1899-1973). He was a protégé of the existentialist philosopher, Martin Heidegger, and the Nazi jurist, Carl Schmitt. The latter personally arranged for the Jewish Strauss to leave Germany on a Rockefeller Foundation fellowship in 1932 to study in London and Paris, from where he took up teaching posts in the US ending up at the University of Chicago. It is an irony of the current marriage of convenience between the religious right and the neo-cons that Strauss himself was opposed to the invocation of religious revelation in the pursuit of political ends, a phenomenon that has become an essential characteristic of US right-wing politics.

To summarize some of Strauss's main thinking, it is important to stress the influence on him of Heidegger, who politicized Nietzsche (both existential thinkers) in rephrasing Nietzsche's saying that one had to fabricate a myth. Heidegger believed Nietzsche's tragic nihilism was itself a "myth" and emphasized that nihilism properly understood contained the possibility of humankind's salvation. Strauss, on the other hand, was more sympathetic to Nietzsche's idea of tragedy, and he also advanced the idea that philosophers wrote esoterically to avoid persecution by the state or religious authority in claiming that esoteric text forced the reader to their own thinking by inviting a dialogue with the reader.

Most famously, Strauss claimed that Plato's *Republic* should never be used as a proposal for a real regime. Central to Strauss's model is his idiosyncratic reading of Plato that the enlightened man is under constant threat from his intellectual inferiors and must resort to dissimulation and ellipsis in pursuit of the great ends which only the initiated can comprehend. This philosophy is, in essence, a valorization of the ancients (Socratic thinkers and their heirs) versus the moderns (Machiavelli on). Strauss and his followers, Harvey Mansfield at Harvard and Alan Bloom at the University of Chicago, Irving Kristol, Norman Podhoretz, and Gertrude Himmelfarb, made up the first generation of neo-cons whose worldview also incorporated Trotskiesque characteristics such as the concept of rolling revolution. This became in essence the blueprint for the Middle East plan whose brief was to pursue a policy of benevolent global hegemony by the US as set out by the second-generation of neo-cons that included Dick Cheney, Donald Rumsfeld, Douglas Feith, and Richard Perle, some of whom were also connected to hardliners in the Likud party in Israel. Dawkins, amongst other sources, writes about this as follows:

> I could have cited those American 'rapture' Christians whose powerful influence on American Middle Eastern policy is governed by their biblical belief that Israel has a God-given right to all the lands of Palestine…and actually yearn for nuclear war

because they interpret it as the 'Armageddon' which...will hasten
the Second Coming.[55]

The recently departed fundamentalist minister, Jerry Falwell, was
a central figure in the link-up between neo-conservatism and
fundamentalism. In an article on his career immediately after his death
in May 2007, the Lexington column in *The Economist* described him
as having "a genius for religious entrepreneurialism."[56] Ever since the
Scopes Monkey Trial in 1925, the religious right had shunned the
national political scene. Two things changed this: the first was the
leftward drift of the Supreme Court in the 1960s and 1970s, which
infuriated fundamentalists by pronouncing on school prayer,
pornography and, above all, abortion. The second was the Carter
administration which raised the religious right from obscurity by
calling upon its members to participate in politics. Carter was himself
a born-again Southern Baptist but as a result of their disaffection with
his administration, the religious right defected *en masse* from the
Democratic Party, the ancestral home of white southerners, to the
Republican Party.

Once he had discovered conservative politics, Falwell embraced it
with religious fervor stating: "If you would like to know where I am
politically I am to the right of wherever you are. I thought Goldwater
was too liberal."[57] In the process, Falwell helped create the Moral
Majority which he defined as pro-life, pro-family, pro-morality, and
pro-American. His views became increasingly cranky leading to his
laying the blame for the terrorist attacks of 11th September on lesbianism
and homosexuality which had persuaded God to remove his protective
mantle from the US. His followers were also given to extreme
pronouncements such as blaming Ariel Sharon's stroke on God's
punishment for giving away Israeli land.

To stay with the religious metaphor, it may be interesting to express
the resulting coniunctio between fundamentalism and neo-
conservatism in the same vein as one that seemed to its followers to be
conceived in heaven but to its critics is viewed more as a marriage made
in hell. The Luciferian energy that propelled its coming into being has
been transformed along the way into a satanic bond. To quote Jung:
"This bond is often of such intensity that we could almost speak of a
'combination.' When two chemical substances combine, both are

altered."⁵⁸ The immersion in this coniunctio is akin to what Jung speaks of as the night sea journey which is a "kind of *descensus ad inferos*—a descent into Hades and a journey to the land of ghosts somewhere beyond this world, beyond consciousness, hence an immersion in the unconscious."⁵⁹

The Luciferian light that blazes for a while from this combination can only too easily gutter out, which appears to be happening as both the fundamentalists, as various leaders from the religious right, and the neo-conservatives are discredited with even the President's reputation becoming increasingly tarnished. Even a leading neo-con theorist, Francis Fukuyama, has served up a powerful indictment of the Bush administration's war in Iraq in his book *America at the Crossroads*. He critiques the neo-con doctrine of "benevolent hegemony" in pointing out "it is not sufficient that Americans believe in their own good intentions; non-Americans must be convinced of them as well."⁶⁰ By adopting a belief system that conforms to the wishes of the super-ego, the arbiter of morality, the neo-cons have satisfied impulsive destructiveness and gained God's approval at the same time. Destructive action based on an ideological belief of which the super-ego approves is bound to be gratifying and free of guilt. The resulting degeneration can lead to regeneration for as Jung says: "No new life can arise...without the death of the old."⁶¹ What that new life may be is impossible to envisage as the alchemical process is still in progress.

CONCLUSION

The Luciferian energy that has fuelled the upsurge of a fundamentalist and neo-conservative takeover of large groups in the US may be seen as an epidemic that has much in common with Dionysian experiences. These often lead to a relapse into a pagan form of religion where the joyful intensification of moods akin to heroic and godlike heights is inevitably followed by "an equally deep plunge into the abyss."⁶² This was only too evident in the aftermath of the invasion of Iraq where early military victory has been followed by chaos. Jung's view of American "exceptionalism" is that it is based on "an extremely high conscious level of culture and an unconscious primitivity. This tension forms a psychic potential which endows the American with an indomitable spirit of enterprise and an enviable enthusiasm which we in Europe do not know."[63] This helps to throw light on the disparaging remarks made about "Old Europe" by a leading figure amongst the neo-conservatives.

This Luciferian energy also gives rise to a messianic savior complex such as has been described in this article in relation to some of the leaders of the religious right. Jung has interesting things to say about this as follows: "If the ego is dissolved in identification with the self, it gives rise to a sort of nebulous superman...Such a personage, however saviourlike or baleful his demeanour, lacks the *scintilla,* the soul spark..."[64] He goes on to say that the ego lives in space and time and must adapt itself to their laws if it is to exist at all. If, on the other hand, it becomes identified with the self, it becomes stifled and can no longer work to integrate the unconscious in which the work of realization can take place: "The separation of the empirical ego from the 'eternal' and universal man is therefore of vital importance, particularly today, when mass-degeneration of the personality is making such threatening strides."[65]

The neo-Kleinian, Wilfred Bion, as a result of his work with groups talked of the basic assumptions that may be detected in the group as a whole. One of these is the pairing basic assumption which suffuses the group with a mysterious kind of hope, often with behavioral pairing between two members, or a member and the leader, as if all share the belief that some great new idea, or individual, will emerge from the intercourse of the pair.[66] This messianic belief underlies the marriage of convenience between fundamentalism and neo-conservatism in the US. Jung was aware of this phenomenon when he wrote that the mass psyche inevitably becomes the focus of fascination, drawing everyone under its spell. "That is why masses are always breeding-grounds of psychic epidemics..."[67]

To return to Britton's writing on fundamentalism touched on earlier in this article wherein he highlights the basic fear that underwrites this phenomenon is that of *malignant misunderstanding* which is "an experience of being so *misunderstood* in such a fundamental and powerful way that one's experience of oneself would be eliminated and with it the possibility of establishing meaning annihilated."[68] This is akin to Bion's concept of *nameless dread* that arises from failure of understanding in infancy and leads to part-object relating which results in the conviction that the whole of knowledge is contained within one belief system. This is the reason why fundamentalism cannot tolerate any knowledge that is not in agreement with the text on which the fundamentalist belief system rests and should be abolished. Word worship will tolerate no rival.

As Jung says of the Self, it is both ego and non-ego and is "the uniting symbol which epitomizes the total union of opposites...As such and in accordance with its paradoxical nature, it can only be expressed by means of symbols."[69] In neo-Kleinian language, regressive object relating results in symbols becoming symbolic-equations. Perhaps the ultimate explanation of fundamentalism as a psychological phenomenon rests on the lack of a capacity for symbolization and a transcendent function amongst its adherents with a resulting reification of "the Word" which remains absolute and incontestable and gratifies the infantile ego with wish-fulfilling feelings of omnipotence.

NOTES

1. Marcel Proust, "The Geurmantes Way, Vol. III," in *In Search of Lost Time* (London: Chatto & Windus Ltd. 1992), p. 479.

2. Lexington, "Inner Demons," *The Economist,* 11th November 2006; Lexington, "God without the godfather," *The Economist,* 19th May 2007.

3. Alexis de Tocqueville, *Democracy in America* (Indianapolis/ Cambridge: Hackett Publishing, 2000).

4. Bernard-Henri Lévy, *American Vertigo: On the Road from Newport to Guantámo* (London: Gibson Square, 2006).

5. Richard Dawkins, *The God Delusion* (London: Transworld Publishers, 2006).

6. Martin E. Marty, *Modern American Religion: The Irony of It All: 1893-1919, Vol. 1* (Chicago and London: The University of Chicago Press, 1986); *Modern American Religion: The Noise of Conflict: 1919-1941, Vol. 2* (Chicago and London: The University of Chicago Press, 1991); *Modern American Religion: Under God, Indivisible: 1941-1960, Vol. 3* (Chicago and London: The University of Chicago Press, 1996).

7. Sigmund Freud, *The Future of an Illusion* (London: W. W. Norton & Company Ltd., 1927/1989), p. 39.

8. Marty, *Modern American Religion: The Irony of It All: 1893-1919, Vol. 1,* p. 237.

9. Ronald Britton, "Fundamentalism: Ideological Genocide and Suicidal Idealism." Paper given at the Institute of Psychoanalysis in April 2007, p. 3.

10. *Ibid.*, p. 3.

11. *Ibid.*, p. 7.

12. *Ibid.* p. 7.

13. *Ibid.*, p. 2.

14. C. G. Jung, *Collected Works*, tr. R. F. C. Hull (Princeton: Princeton University Press, 1953), vol. 10, para. 102 (all future references to Jung's *Collected Works*, abbreviated to *CW*, will be by volume and paragraph number).

15. Marty, *Modern American Religion: The Irony of It All: 1893-1919*, *Vol. 1*, p. 237.

16. Melanie Klein, "Notes on Some Schizoid Mechanisms," in *Envy and Gratitude and Other Works 1946-1963* (London: The Hogarth Press Ltd., 1975), p. 8.

17. Ann Casement, "The Shadow," in *The Handbook of Jungian Psychology: Theory, Practice and Applications*, ed. Renos Papadopoulos (London: Routledge, 2006), p. 94.

18. Jung, *CW* 10 § 95.

19. "A Special Report on the American South," *The Economist,* 3rd March 2007, p. 6.

20. Marty, *Modern American Religion: The Noise of Conflict: 1919-1941, Vol. 2*, p. 63.

21. *Ibid.*, p. 63.

22. *Ibid.*, p. 64.

23. *Ibid.*, p. 65.

24. Marty, *Modern American Religion: The Irony of It All: 1893-1919*, *Vol. 1*, p. 312.

25. David Owen, *The Hubris Syndrome: Bush, Blair and the Intoxication of Power* (London: Methuen Publishing Ltd., 2007).

26. Freud, *The Future of an Illusion*, p. 66.

27. Marty, *Modern American Religion: Under God, Indivisible: 1941-1960, Vol. 3*, p. 421.

28. *Ibid.* (Original italics)

29. *Ibid.*

30. Freud, *The Future of an Illusion*, p. 49.

31. Lévy, *American Vertigo*, p. 124.

32. *Ibid.*, pp. 124-125.

33. *Ibid.*, p. 126.

34. Jung, "The Other Point of View: The Will To Power," in *Two Essays on Analytical Psychology* (Princeton: Bollingen Foundation 1953), § 35.

35. Dawkins, *The God Delusion*, p. 284.

36. Jung, *CW* 8 § 405.

37. *Ibid.* (Original italics).

38. Jung, *CW* 8 § 425.

39. Jung, *CW* 9 § 125.

40. Jung, *CW* 8 § 410, § 415.

41. Jung, *CW* 9 § 129.

42. Alexis de Tocqueville, *Democracy in America* (Indianapolis/Cambridge: Hackett Publishing, 2000).

43. Jung *CW* 6 § 709.

44. de Tocqueville, *Democracy in America.*

45. *Ibid.*

46. Dawkins, *The God Delusion*, p. 288.

47. *Ibid*, p. 304.

48. Harold Bloom, *The American Religion: The Emergence of the Post-Christian Nation* (New York: Simon & Schuster, 1992), p. 39.

49. Jung, *CW* 8 § 204.

50. Jung, *CW* 8 § 201.

51. Jung, *CW* 8 § 202.

52. Jung, *CW* 8 § 207.

53. Lexington: "Inner Demons," *The Economist,* 11th November 2006, p. 62.

54. Jung, "The Other Point of View: The Will To Power," § 51.

55. Dawkins, *The God Delusion*, p. 302.

56. *Economist* 2007, p. 52.

57. *Ibid.*

58. Jung, *CW* 16 § 358.

59. Jung, *CW* 16 § 455.

60. Francis Fukuyama, *America at the Crossroads: Democracy, Power and the Neoconservative Legacy* (New Haven, CT: Yale University Press, 2007).

61. Jung, *CW* 16 § 467.

62. Jung, "The Other Point of View: The Will To Power," § 41.

63. Jung, *CW* 10 § 103.

64. Jung, *CW* 8 § 430.

65. Jung, *CW* 16 § 502.

66. Wilfred Bion, *Experiences in Groups* (London: Tavistock, 1961).

67. Jung, *CW* 9 § 228.

68. Ronald Britton, "Fundamentalism: Ideological Genocide and Suicidal Idealism," p. 4.

69. Jung, *CW* 16 § 474.

WHO MADE YOU GOD?
POLITICS AND THE GOD-IMAGE

DRUSCILLA FRENCH

The architects of the Constitution of the United States of America were a patriarchal assemblage, fifty-five affluent white men whose vision was not flawless, but nonetheless inspired. They planned a new republic, prohibiting governmental practices they had come to abhor. In these United States there would be no rulers by reasons of ancestry or divine right. The chief executive and his stand-in would be elected for a term of four years, at which point the citizens could re-elect, or toss them out in favor of other free, white males, provided they were native born and had lived thirty-five years or more. Affairs of state would be conducted separately from those of any religious institutions. There would be no established religion, no mandatory support—financial or otherwise—of any doctrine, and "no religious test shall ever be required as a qualification to any office or public trust under the United States."[1]

Druscilla French, Ph.D., sits on the Board of the Institute for Conflict Analysis and Resolution at George Mason University, where she endowed the French/Cumbie Chair in Conflict Studies. She has lived in the Washington, D.C. area for thirty years and has been politically active through five administrations. Currently, she is engaged in returning Senator Clinton to the White House, this time as the occupant of the Oval Office. She is a founder and the president of the Foundation for Mythological Studies (mythology.org).

These constitutional clauses have been interpreted to mean that no legal measures may be taken to prevent political participation by any citizen for reasons of religious beliefs. In practical application, this has rarely been the case. It has been, and continues to be, hazardous for an American candidate to be something other than a monotheist in the Judeo-Christian tradition. There have been times when it was inadvisable to be either a Jew *or* a Catholic Christian. In today's world, there is no right to privacy of religion for candidates; indeed, there is very little privacy of any kind. The collective seems to have decided that the public has the right to know everything about anyone who steps forward to stand for office as a public servant.

Nevertheless, freedom of or from religion is theoretically the law of the land. Would that it were so in the realm of the psyche. Political choices are influenced by religious beliefs or by an unconscious archetypal god-image. That god-image exists in all of us, even those who maintain that the gods are either dead or imaginary. The god-image can be the psychological basis for both religious beliefs and political affiliations.

There are those who blame not only our domestic malfunctions on religious delusions, but also see global conflict as collisions of the great monotheisms, and are convinced that "religion poisons everything."[2] Christopher Hitchens writes, "Violent, irrational, intolerant, allied to racism and tribalism and bigotry, invested in ignorance and hostile to free inquiry, contemptuous of women and coercive toward children: organized religion ought to have a great deal on its conscience."[3] Equally disenchanted is Richard Dawkins, author of *The God Delusion*. "The God of the Old Testament is arguably the most unpleasant character in all fiction: jealous and proud of it; a petty, unjust, unforgiving control-freak; a vindictive, blood thirsty ethnic cleanser; a misogynistic, homophobic, racist, infanticidal, genocidal, filicidal, pestilential, megalomaniacal, sadomasochistic, capriciously malevolent bull."[4] History supports these accusations. The religious impulse has cast some long, dark shadows.

Religion can be a catalyst for large-scale conflict, or can provide an ethical basis for resolution. Former Secretary of State Madeleine Albright writes, "When participants in a conflict claim to be people of faith, a negotiator who has the credentials and the credibility to do so might wish to call their bluff. If the combatants argue the morality of their cause, how is that morality reflected in their actions? Are they allowing their religion to guide them or using it as a debating point to advance their interests? Has their faith instilled in them a sense of responsibility toward others or a sense of entitlement causing them to disregard the rights and views of everyone else?"[5]

Perhaps with greater diplomacy than his secretary of state, former President Bill Clinton is less willing to "call their bluff." With his mercurial charm and ability to understand multiple points of view, he feels that religious faith contributes to diplomatic endeavors. "'If you're dealing with people who profess faith,' he said, 'they should agree that God created everyone. This takes them from the specific to the universal. Once they acknowledge their common humanity, it becomes harder to kill each other; then compromise becomes easier because they've admitted that they are dealing with people like themselves.'"[6] This approach has sometimes proven expedient, but does not address the proliferation of violence in the name of religion.

Joseph Campbell published *The Hero With a Thousand Faces* in 1949, four years after the bombings of Hiroshima and Nagasaki. Americans desperately wanted to believe that the horrible sacrifices of two global wars had opened up possibilities for peaceful co-existence in the modern world. In this book, Campbell is searching for commonality, a thread of human nature that might connect us at the level of soul. "[T]here's one mythology in the world. It has been inflected in various cultures in terms of their historical and social circumstances and needs and particular local ethic systems, but it's one mythology."[7] That one mythology, the hero's journey, he called the *monomyth,* and he demonstrated how this myth appears in diverse cultures and religions. Other scholars argue that he failed to consider consequential cultural differences. Feminist scholars have identified an unconscious sexism in his focus on the hero, with females featured only in supporting roles.

Like Clinton's hopeful diplomacy, Campbell's optimism has proven to be unwarranted. The monomythology of humanity (the commonality of the human condition) has yet to unite us in a search for the common good. In these years following World War II, we have seen an escalation of religious discord. Scholars of conflict analysis know that wars resolve nothing. Rather, they lay the groundwork for the next dispute. Surrender may bring about the cessation of gunfire, but not hostilities.

The optimism contained in Campbell's observation is part of the reason that he has generated such a following. He elucidates the idea of a universal human experience, a shared archetypal reality that he felt would provide a basis for cross-cultural understanding. Recognizing the validity of the criticisms of his theory, there is nonetheless value in looking at the story that we all have in common—the tale of the human condition. Somewhere, back in time, we all meet in our ancestry. Every life, no matter the length, has a beginning, a middle, and an end. We are fellow travelers on an odyssey that begins with birth and moves inevitably toward death. We are all the product of one sperm and one egg.

Freud's sense that religion acted like a cultural neurosis was based upon his analysis of the projections of parental figures on god-images.[8] As infants, we have very little information, but our need to survive compels us to pay attention. When tummies are empty, we let out a howl. Magically a big breast appears to alleviate discomfort. Our first divinity is a food supply. Usually maternal, she is the source of safety and sustenance. There resides a lingering memory of the time when support on demand was available unconditionally and we would like to have this deity with us forever. According to Freud, another deity appears, the powerful paternal figure, omnipotent and omniscient. (For many children, this Freudian fantasy of the attentive mother and father isn't a reality. Nevertheless, someone has to sustain life and teach self-protection, or child's life will be extinguished.) These two archetypal energies become locked in the psyche, inextricably linked to a sense of survival. We are left with a longing for a reunion with these divinities. When this longing remains unconscious, we fall into the neurosis of the god-delusion, an exaggerated amplification of an imaginal reality, a nostalgic sense of a time when all was right in the world and there was nothing to fear.

This internal image of a me-centered universe imprinted upon the psyche as the wholly divine is the source of what scholars have called the *numinous*. It resonates with these earliest memories of unnamed, loving, all-powerful figures who created us in their own image—same but different. Why wouldn't we spend the rest of our lives trying to find that sense of total acceptance, invulnerability, immortality, and steadfast devotion? Why wouldn't we believe, with all our being, in its reality? We can't remember this blissful state except at some deep, pre-conscious level, but the risk is that we shall spend our lives desperately longing for what never was and never will be. We commit ourselves to a futile search for an infantile fantasy, a misunderstanding of the covenant between parent and newborn. The parent/child relationship was never meant to go on forever, but we keep insisting that it *might*, if we could only find the right god, the right person, the right boss, the right president for our country.

Wars without end, children gunning down children, sex trafficking, rapes, murder, and mayhem—the more these impossible desires are thwarted, the greater the outrage. Some are convinced that they have been deprived of their inalienable rights, and are victims of a conspiracy to defraud them of their rightful place at the top of creation's hierarchy. Some believe that their very existence is threatened. Some commit terrorist acts in the name of their god. The god-image can morph into an image that is as distorted and dangerous as that described by Dawkins in his depiction of the God of the Old Testament. The *God-Delusion* is an ill-informed archetypal energy that has led mankind not only into some of its finest hours, but also its darkest deeds.

From Jung's perspective, the god-image is more accurately replaced by the concept of *Self*. In *Aion*, Jung tells us repeatedly that *God* is a form of self-knowing. Jung's god *is* an image, a *god-image* which contains our longing for union with something outside ourselves, bigger than the personal ego. It is not really a literal god or goddess that we seek, but rather a life-giving link to Other, More, Greater. We are seeking redemption from our insignificance and dread of mortality. Vera von der Heydt points out that

> Jung called the centre of totality the Self; this central archetype is the dynamic nucleus from which consciousness and its centre the ego evolves, and it is the source of all creativity. It is the place where the image of God is born, the dimension from where religious symbolism, feelings, thoughts and longings arise and filter through into consciousness. Jung had discovered that this area is a psychological reality and not only a metaphysical assumption.[9]

Jung deconstructs the myth of Jesus and regards him as a symbol of Self. The Christ symbol, often portrayed as an emaciated human being—stripped of everything including life, hanging tortuously from a cross, sucked completely dry—is an archetypal image that resonates with most of humanity. We all have experiences that feel like crucifixions. For Jung, the image of Christ symbolized the human condition. This was true for Campbell as well, for the story of the life of Jesus includes all the elements of a perfectly structured monomyth. Jung, like Campbell, insists that archetypal experiences are basically the same for all human beings.

The concept of Self refers to an energy that can carry us beyond the idea of Me and Other, into a state of union with all that is, a completion of wholeness (Campbell's term is *bliss*). Jung writes,

> Unity and totality stand at the highest point on the scale of objective values because their symbols can no longer be distinguished from the *imago Dei*. Hence all statements about the God-image apply also to the empirical symbols of totality.[10]

Often misunderstood, the Jungian term *Self* can be problematic, implying a narcissistic relationship with an inflated image. The association with selfishness is not at all what Jung intends. The image that Narcissus perceives in the pool is diametrically opposed to Self. The narcissistic image is intended to isolate from Other, to dissolve any ties to an outside world, to deny the conditions of existence, and to remain absorbed in one's own fantasized self-image. Rooted in fear, narcissism is a state of isolation, not self-love so much as self-absorption and exclusion of all that is threatening.

Jung's understanding of the process of maturation, which he called *individuation*, involves retracting the projections that give rise to religious beliefs and becoming aware of the unconscious dynamic at the root of our god-delusion. William James, in his chapter "The Divided Self," uses a different word. He calls it the "unification" of the divided self. His position on the god complex was ahead of his time. In 1903, he was wrote,

> [T]o find religion is only one out of many ways of reaching unity; and the process of remedying inner incompleteness and reducing inner discord is a general psychological process, which may take place with any sort of mental material, and need not necessarily assume the religious form.[11]

American iconology includes many symbols of totality, the "more perfect union" to which we aspire. Our motto, *E Pluribus Unum*, speaks to this longing for belonging. In our songs and oaths, we pledge allegiance to the image of our country, using language appropriate to sacred vows. In 1940, Don Raye wrote these lyrics, "This is my country! Land of my birth! /This is my country! Grandest on earth! /I pledge thee my allegiance, America, the bold/For this is my country to have and to hold."[12] Not unlike other countries, we have rituals of *worship* to express and sanctify our relationship with our Father/Mother land. This dynamic leads us to project upon our president an image of the Almighty. This chauvinistic inflation leads us to imagine ourselves as the rightful heir to a position of leadership, rulers of a global hierarchy. It is the god-image that is projected when we speak of our president as the "Leader of the Western World," "The Great White Father," "The Father of our Country," or even "The Decider." The founding fathers clearly warned us against just such inflation.

We remain in pathological denial of the terrible acts committed in the name of gods as long as we are stuck in a longing for an omnipotent figure that can redeem our fearfulness, as long as we persist in believing that there is Something that loves us deeply, that wants us to thrive and become the best we can be. We want a god that finds us worthy of an endless bounty of love and nurturing—abundant milk or crude oil. We want an omnipotent, omniscient source, concerned with our welfare. Even though we may suspect that this god is only a character in an infantile, imaginal drama, a construct created by each of us at a time when we knew almost nothing and relied on intuition for survival, we often don't want to give it up.

Jung's concept of Self has the advantage of placing our knowledge of existence in the context of a greater whole—not only reaching wholeness in and of ourselves, but cognition of the connection to something greater. The challenge is to notice whether the religious impulse is leading us toward maturation or pathology. Separation *is* an illusion. Our longing for connection is a kind of psychological blindness, for we all participate in the continuum of life on an interdependent planet. Once we achieve a greater consciousness we make the disappointing discovery that tantrums no longer get the desired result. June Cleaver is gone forever and John Wayne was just a movie star. When the god-image is "all about me," or all about us as Americans, we have started down the narcissistic path. Patriotism becomes sociopathy.

Becoming conscious brings this terrible burden of responsibility. We can no longer pretend to be fooled, not to know. My country is not my parent and my president is not my god. It is time to assess our candidates by criteria that have nothing to do with the god-image. A president is a head of state, not a deity. The office conveys significant power but not omnipotence (another gift of our constitution.) As I write, two candidates—one black, one female—are entering the 2008 race for the presidency. There are those who say that one or the other cannot win for a similar reason the defeat of John F. Kennedy was inevitable. "The country is not ready for a Catholic/racially-mixed/woman president." I would say this is precisely what we are ready for—the deconstruction of a patriotic mythology gone seriously awry.

NOTES

1. *U. S. Constitution of the United States*, art. VI, sec. 3.

2. Christopher Hitchens, *God is Not Great: How Religion Poisons Everything* (New York: Twelve, 2007).

3. *Ibid.*, p. 56.

4. Richard Dawkins, *The God Delusion* (New York: Houghton Mifflin, 2006), p. 31.

5. Madeleine Albright with Bill Woodward, *The Mighty and the Almighty: Reflections on America, God, and World Affairs* (New York: Harper Perennial, 2007), p. 75.

6. *Ibid.*, p. 78.

7. Joseph Campbell, *The Hero's Journey: Joseph Campbell on His Life and Work,* ed. Phil Cousineau and Stuart Brown (San Francisco: Harper, 1990), p. 127.

8. Sigmund Freud, *The Future of an Illusion*, ed. James Strachey, trans. W. D. Robson-Scott (New York: Anchor, 1964).

9. Vera von der Heydt, "Jung and Religion," in *Jung and the Monotheisms: Judaism, Christianity and Islam,* ed. Joel Ryce-Menuhin (London: Routledge, 1994), pp. 12-13.

10. C. G. Jung, *Psyche and Symbol: A Selection from the Writings of C.G. Jung*, ed. Violet S. deLaszlo (Garden City: Doubleday, 1958), pp. 30-31.

11. William James, "The Divided Self and the Process of Its Unification," *The Varieties of Religious Experience: A Study in Human Nature*, (New York: Modern Library), p. 172.

12. Don Raye and Al Jacobs "This is my Country," 1940. *Wikipedia* http://en.wikipedia.org/wiki/This_Is_My_Country_%28song%29 (accessed June 12, 2007).

THE MEMORY OF THE HERO AND THE EMERGENCE OF THE POST-HEROIC ATTITUDE

JOHN BEEBE

PROLOGUE: THE HERO MYTH AGAIN

The hero myth is always with us, but our fantasies about it change as we and our cultures develop. My present perspective has emerged in a United States that has grown increasingly ambivalent about the hero. When I was in my late twenties and had my first exposure to Jungian lectures, analysts were already warning that it was very hard to get beyond the hero. Through most of my middle years, it was repeatedly brought home to American men that we were living in post-patriarchal times and that it was important to disidentify from the hero archetype. At the same time, however, there was a countermovement. During the 1980s, Ronald Reagan, Joseph Campbell, and Robert Bly all asked us, in their very different ways, to

John Beebe, M.D., is a psychiatrist and Jungian analyst in San Francisco who lectures and writes frequently about issues of integrity and character in persons and nations. His essay "*The Wizard of Oz*: a vision of development in the American political psyche" can be found in *The Vision Thing*, edited by Thomas Singer.

Editor's Note: The first version of this paper was read at the 16th Congress of the International Association for Analytical Psychology held in Barcelona, Spain, August 29-September 3, 2004, on the theme, "Edges of Experience: Memory and Emergence." It has been revised for this issue of *Spring*.

resurrect the hero, and when George W. Bush was elected president, hero psychology turned out to be very much alive. What had happened to the postmodern discourses that had come to seem so secure and that had taught us to stay with the project of deconstructing the hero?

By the time of the long count of the 2000 election, I was an established Jungian lecturer myself, trying to help others see through, and disidentify with, the hero myth. As the early months of the Bush presidency revealed that we were far from out of the pattern, I began to feel anachronistic giving lectures that showed how Jungian psychology might look if individuation were conceived as a story that leads beyond the hero, and I realized I needed to give the topic a fresher look if I was to make any more difference than my own teachers had. Between 2001 and 2004, I took time to re-examine some of the classic hero texts, expecting to expose in them in some more fundamental way the psychological limitations that I thought it was my generation's duty finally to get everyone to see.

Early in my research, I was surprised to discover that in most of the hero stories I looked at, the postheroic attitude was already present. Not infrequently, the hero's story comes in two parts—the first illustrating the rise of the hero, but the second showing a deconstruction of the values so carefully advanced in the first. This two-part structure can be observed, for instance, in David Lean's 1962 film *Lawrence of Arabia*, in which the two, rather different phases of T. E. Lawrence's career in World War I Arabia are divided by an intermission. The first part shows the effeminate, feckless Lawrence angling his way up the ladder to leadership in the struggles for Arab independence and finally surrendering to the ecstasy of battle. The second part reveals his capture and re-emasculating rape by a Turkish general, which awakens Lawrence to his masochistic proclivities and leads him almost to savor the disintegration of his own authority in the denouement that follows.

Fritz Lang's 1924 silent film *Die Niebelungen* follows the same structure, with the first part, *Siegfried*, showing the rise of a hero with a will to save the world and the second part, *Kreimhild's Revenge*, which begins after the death of Siegfried, revealing the other side of the archetype in the treacherous revenge of Siegfried's widow Kreimhild, whose incendiary destructiveness annihilates the world beyond any hope of heroic redemption.

These movie depictions of the hero myth led me to a paradoxical insight that I have begun to check against literary texts as well, that disillusionment with heroic fantasy is embedded in the structure of the myth itself. I decided to seek out a literary text in which this structure is an explicit part of the artist's handling of the theme.

It was not hard to land upon what now seems to me the obvious choice. The Program Committee for the then upcoming 2004 Congress of the International Association for Analytical Psychology (at which I had vowed to present something about the hero) issued its Call for Proposals. At that time, a poll of 100 noted writers from fifty-four countries had just named *Don Quixote* the best book in history. Here surely was an ironic approach to the hero myth, and I hadn't read it! That the Congress would be held in Spain, on the eve of the hundredth anniversary of the book's publication, made the opportunity seem propitious. Only now, three years later, do I see that I was desperately seeking a homeopathic elixir, in this book about madness in late Renaissance Spain, for the madness infecting my own country.

For by now it is commonplace to realize that our national motive-hunting for the war in Iraq has been as futile as one of Iago's paranoid soliloquies: the war itself was a psychotic reaction, fuelled like all psychoses by a delusion (weapons of mass destruction) and a displacement (the assumption that Saddam Hussein was somehow responsible for the events of September 11). Certainly the years after Bush announced on May 1, 2003 that our "mission" had been "accomplished" in Iraq have been like a psychotic depression, punctuated by the strangest cinema I have seen in my lifetime, by which I mean the most fragmentary and incomplete, like the dreams that follow but never quite encapsulate a psychosis. The film that most heralded our era turned out to be *Memento*,[1] since without memory our collective hero-mind has had to ask how we got to this place when we can't even recall the most recent nastiness. And still the heroic imagery comes up. Reviewing two movies released this spring that had no problem advancing the theme without irony, David Denby wrote, "Made in a time of frustration, when Americans are fighting a war that they can neither win nor abandon, *300* and *Shooter* feel like the products of a culture going slowly and painfully mad."[2]

So my intuition was sound in turning to fiction, and no doubt right to settle on *Don Quixote*. Didn't fiction, as we know it now, start with this first modern (and postmodern) novel? Moreover, *Don Quixote* was in two parts. Perhaps it would follow the same rising and falling pattern as *Lawrence of Arabia* and *Die Niebelungen*. As I labored to get through the nine-hundred-forty-page Edith Grossman translation,[3] celebrations of the book were occurring all over the world, and they cheered me on, the way Don Quixote himself had experienced being celebrated in the second part of the novel, which appeared in 1615.

That my ambition to read the novel was heroic was obvious, but I could ride it through as a final gallop of midlife grandiosity. The execution of my project to cover the literature about it well enough to write something interesting was shadowed, however, by the kind of postheroic irony that Cervantes appreciated. As the time got away from me, as it usually does for a working analyst, I discovered that if I was to have a paper to include in the advance proceedings of the Congress, I was going to have to start to write about the massive novel even before my reading of it was complete.

Fortunately, my intuition about its two parts proved reliable. *Don Quixote Part One* recalls a man's mad attempt to claim an already archaic heroic identity. *Don Quixote Part Two* deals with the emergence in the same man of a truly post-heroic attitude, with astonishing anticipations of present day notions of individuation.[4] I chose to imitate this two-part structure to organize my own remarks, dividing them, according to the themes of the Congress, memory and emergence, into meditations on the *memory* of the hero as we rediscover the archetype in *Don Quixote Part One* and reflections on the *emergence* of the postheroic attitude, as the archetype proceeds to qualify and finally limit itself in *Don Quixote Part Two*. It has not escaped me that I presented the first version of this paper the August before our last presidential election, as Bush's Democratic challenger John Kerry was struggling to get the country to look at its national psychosis and only succeeded in getting his own heroism deconstructed. It is good to have a chance to revisit this paper now, as a second chance to expose the psychology that I think is continuing to harass our American culture.

THE MEMORY OF THE HERO

Analytical psychology itself got its start in the two parts of Jung's *Wandlungen und Symbole der Libido*. Part I introduced the hero's journey through the night sea of the unconscious, and Part II complicated this vision by postulating that heroic consciousness itself would have to be sacrificed for the development of the mind to proceed. To make sense of this contradiction, depth psychologists, following Jung himself, have assumed that the hero is the archetypal image of the strong ego formed in the first half of life, which rises, like the sun, to prominence only to set, or be set aside, in the second half of life. This has, however, been a hard prescription to follow.

Don Quixote is a text with much to tell us about the ego's continuing wish, well beyond middle life, to wrap itself in the mantle of the hero. In Cervantes' depiction of the "peculiar madness" of this fiftyish *hidalgo*, I was able to identify three problematic aspects of heroic consciousness when it persists into the second half of life. The first problematic aspect, easily recognized in the Don, is *an inordinate modeling of the ego's identity upon fictions*. Quixote, belonging to the first century of ordinary citizens who could read and therefore model their consciousnesses on what they found in books, is ever citing fictional precedents for the kind of life he would like to live. His favorites were the chivalric romances. In an unconscious parody of the way some of his contemporaries were reading *Imitation of Christ*, Don Quixote makes a book called *Amadis of Gaul* the model for his own life.

The biggest fiction that Don Quixote espouses is that the world is arranged to occasion the display of chivalry—that life is organized to offer opportunities for a hero to intervene. I have seen just this assumption operating in the minds of men throughout the second half of life who become agitated by all they feel called upon to do. Surely there is a flavor of paranoia in the presumption that the world is always setting tests for the ego to master.

A second aspect of the elderly bachelor Don Quixote's madness involves his naive display of desire for the heroic life. The Jungian analyst Ruth El Saffar, also a leading Cervantes scholar, called this, in a book that she co-edited, "quixotic desire,"[5] which I take to refer to an assertion of romantic will that is a bit ridiculous to everyone who sees it. On the basis of Cervantes' own explanation of what motivated his character's "fervent desire" to the life of a knight-errant, an *andante caballero*, Miguel de Unamuno wrote that Don Quixote "was driven mad by reading books of chivalry, and he fell into the folly of wanting to appear in their pages..."[6] But that interpretation of the quixotic obsession ignores something else Cervantes tells us in the first chapter of the novel:

> The poor man imagined himself already wearing the crown, won
> by the valor of his arm, of the empire of Trebizond at the very
> least; and so it was that with these exceedingly agreeable thoughts,
> and carried away by the extraordinary pleasure he took in them, he
> hastened to put into effect what he so fervently desired. (21-22)

Fame, in other words, the mad *hidalgo* already assumes he has, and
will only get more of in the course of living the chivalric life that he
has been called, by reading about it, to follow. *This is the desire to enact
what one believes—deludedly—one is already famous for.* I once attended
a Catholic funeral, where one of the speakers, a woman I shall call Mary
Finnerty, told us, "Let it never be said that Mary Finnerty ever left
someone unvisited in the hospital." (She was particularly praising of
the deceased, for having shown more gratitude than anyone else for
the visits she had paid.)[7]

A third aspect of Don Quixote's madness can be described as
monomania. Mania derives from the Greek mῆνιν, given (in the
accusative case, mῆνιν) as the first word in the *Iliad*, where it refers to
the wrath of Achilles. The ego's capacity for psychotic ire when in heroic
mode is carried forward by the English word "mad," which puns on
the rage that clouds reason exactly when it feels itself to be right,
superior, in need of asserting its own position. Although Don Quixote
is sometimes violent to the point of being unconsciously cruel,[8] his
basic pathology is grounded neither in anger, sadism, nor what
psychoanalysts nowadays call narcissistic rage. Rather, it stems from
what Jungian type psychology might formulate as the insistence on
using one function of consciousness, in his case intuition, exclusively,
resisting any compensation or advice from the other functions. (We
saw this monomania in our own country in the widely held belief,
impatient of the pleas of inspectors to give them time to verify the
suspicion, that Iraq was a storehouse for "weapons of mass destruction.")
This is a problem that inevitably compromises reality-testing. When
he is displaying his madness, Don Quixote insists on using his intuition
to the exclusion of thinking, feeling, and sensation. An example might
be the way he handles the process of arming himself, in the opening
chapter of the novel:

> And the first thing he did was to attempt to clean some armor that had belonged to his great-grandfathers and, stained with rust and covered with mildew, had spent many long years stored and forgotten in a corner. He did the best he could to clean and repair it, but he saw that it had a great defect, which was that instead of a full [knight's] . . . helmet with an attached neckguard, there was only a simple headpiece; but he compensated for this with his industry, and out of pasteboard he fashioned a kind of half-helmet that, when attached to the headpiece, took on the appearance of a full . . . [one]. It is true that in order to test if it was strong and could withstand a blow, he took out his sword and struck it twice, and with the first blow he undid in a moment what it had taken him a week to create; he could not help being disappointed at the ease with which he had hacked it to pieces, and to protect against that danger, he made another one, placing strips of iron on the inside so that he was satisfied with its strength, and not wanting to put it to the test again, he designated and accepted it as an extremely fine . . . [knight's helmet] (22).

Perhaps it is because Don Quixote is unable to use a balance of psychological functions in testing reality that he suffers from an agitated depression of exactly the kind that I have seen in men possessed by the *senex* archetype[9] in psychiatric practice where one recognizes easily enough the Knight of the Sorrowful Face. As Terry Castle has noted in a recent report on her reading of the new Grossman translation,[10] "for much of the fiction" Quixote "comes off as a senile man-child: fey, withered, dissociated, lost in his archaic, estranging dreams."

She helps us to see that Quixote is in fact not archetypally a hero at all. Archetypally, the character we encounter personifies the senex. According to Hillman's classic delineation,

> *Senex* is the Latin word for 'old man.' We find it still contained within our words *senescence, senile* and *senator.* . . . As natural, cultural and psychic processes mature, gain order, consolidate and wither, we witness the specific formative effects of the senex. . . . Longings for superior knowledge, imperturbability, magnanimity express senex feelings as does intolerance for that which crosses one's systems and habits. . . . The temperament of the senex is cold, which can also be expressed as distance.[11]

One critic,[12] in line with Castle's notion of Don Quixote as a "senile man-child," has described the *hidalgo* as a *"puer senex,"* the kind of man

Hillman and also von Franz have taught us to recognize, one who is identified with the archetype of the *puer aeternus* in youth and then, lacking a relation to the anima, slips in age into an identification with the archetype of the senex. He becomes an occasionally wise, often pontificating, and finally foolish old man, like Don Quixote. From this perspective, one has to view Don Quixote's reaching out to embrace the hero archetype less as a particular natural affinity for this archetype, and more as a last ditch attempt to hold onto the idealism of the puer aeternus in order to avoid petrifaction—the cynical despair of the old man who has failed to prosper at life. Don Quixote's monomaniacal embrace of the hero is thus not just a simple inflation of the ego's superior function by a narcissistic (or perhaps we should say egoistic) character.

In an individual taken over by the senex, the superior function can be hard to spot. All one sees is the senex that has preempted the ego. Looking at the psychological lifeworld of *Don Quixote* taken as a whole, the novel's actual heroic standpoint is quite hard to identify in the midst of all Don Quixote's arrogating. If there is an authentic hero within the novel, and I think there is, it is Miguel Cervantes himself (who coyly hides behind his pseudonymous Arab narrator, Cide Hamete Benengeli—Sir Ahmed Eggplant, as Terry Castle translates this name— to conceal the degree to which Cervantes dominates the story with his extraordinary narrative gifts). We have little secure information about Cervantes' personality, but we do know that, though ill, he fought bravely in the decisive battle of Lepanto against the Ottoman Turks, he was captured by Barbary pirates and held for ransom by a Muslim viceroy in a prison in Algiers for five years, during which time he led several escape attempts that failed, and even though he refused to tell on his co-conspirators, insisting on taking sole responsibility for the plans to escape, he so impressed the Viceroy that he avoided being put to death. It is also recorded that, after two years in prison, when his family had finally managed to raise the money to ransom him, their firstborn son, he had the funds applied to free his younger brother Rodrigo who had been captured with him, even though that meant further years of imprisonment for himself. According to the priest who eventually did ransom him—in chains on a ship that he was just about to have to row with other slaves out of the harbor of Algiers, presumably never to be heard from again—the future author of Don Quixote "showed a very special grace in everything."[13] I read him as an introverted feeling type, with auxiliary extraverted intuition—introverted feeling, the author's private unerring sense of value, and extraverted intuition, his endless capacity to entertain us with the possibilities of his material. His character Don Quixote attempts to adopt the introverted feeling style of the knights-errant in the books he has read, but he does so in a senescently introverted intuitive way. I would say that the character's introverted intuition is a creative personification of the shadow side of Cervantes' enabling auxiliary extraverted intuition.[14] In my explorations of typology, I have found that the shadow of a man's auxiliary function, meaning that function used with the opposite attitude with respect to extraversion or introversion, is associated with the archetype of the senex.[15] This archetype can take center stage in later life by appropriating the natural superior function, normally associated with the archetype of the hero, to its own agenda.

In this way, the senex tries to commandeer the hero archetype in a clumsy, driven, and finally self-defeating way, not unlike what we have seen in our own government with such figures as Donald Rumsfeld. Within Cervantes' novel a heroic introverted feeling type's reputation for natural gentlemanliness and service to honor is what Quixote's intuition aspires to as a religious ideal, one that he can only comically attempt to realize in his own person. According to the logic of Cervantes' irony, his very attempts to embody this ideal actually serve to reify it, so that the reader of Part One finds himself rooting against common sense for the possibility that the character will actually stumble his way into the tao of chivalry.

Some would say that the Don, for all his inattention to the constructions of everyday reality, is sublimely present to his goal. The great literary historian of Zen sensibility, R. H. Blyth, was so impressed by Don Quixote's unquestioning embrace of knight-errantry in Part One that he wrote, "the man who in the history of the world exemplifies all that is best in Zen . . . is Don Quixote de la Mancha, Knight Errant."[16] Blyth refers to the *hidalgo's* instinctive way of embodying the heroic ideal, however fumbling: "he lived twenty four hours every day, following his instincts (his ideals,) as wholeheartedly, as truly, as naturally, as the blooming of flowers in spring, as the falling of leaves in autumn."[17]

However, the instinctive idealization of the hero is not maintained in *Don Quixote* by the title character alone. The other half of the archetypal pair that supports the habit of living by fictions, the desire to enact fame, and the monomania of staying within a single typological perspective is Sancho Panza. One of the great achievements of the novel is that this man of another social class, educational background (Sancho cannot read), body type, and psychological type is able to team up with Don Quixote to form a pairing that is really an organic unity. We cannot imagine them apart. As G. N. Orsini has observed, "it may be said that Sancho is not an extrinsic addition to Don Quixote, but that the Don belongs to Sancho just as much as vice versa: the great comic situation would not be what it is if one of the two were omitted."[18]

They define polar ends of the irrational, perceptive dimension of consciousness.[19] Sancho Panza uses the extraverted sensation function to construe reality as insistently as Don Quixote relies on introverted intuition. This contrast produces the comic misunderstandings in scenes like the one in which, despite Sancho's concrete warnings that what he is seeing is nothing but windmills, Don Quixote proceeds to charge at what he claims, not entirely unjustifiably, are long-armed giants come to rob and dominate the countryside.

Because Sancho and his Don each hold the inverse attitude and function from the other, their dominant function-attitudes fall on the same "axis" of consciousness—in their case, an irrational axis, which enables them on many occasions in the course of the novel to function together in a *folie à deux*. On the rational, planning side of personality, one thinks of the combination of introverted feeling and extraverted thinking that got us into the Iraq war, the two functions on this axis feeling themselves so complete that information and wisdom which could have been gleaned from the other six functions of consciousness, extraverted sensation, introverted sensation, extraverted intuition, introverted intuition, introverted thinking, and extraverted feeling, were thrust aside.

We can use this insight into their complementary typologies to illuminate the way a shadow pair of functions of consciousness can conspire to produce an anachronistic heroic expectation in someone in the second half of life. From an archetypal standpoint that recognizes that every type of function-attitude that seeks to assert its consciousness is also expressed by an archaic image, Sancho Panza is trickster to Don

Quixote's senex. We often think of senex and puer as opposites, but the trickster is actually the more natural sparring partner for the senex. (In the contemporary American political drama, Democrats and Republicans take turns playing trickster and senex. It seems hardly to matter which party is in power and which is recoiling in protest: the dynamic is not disturbed, and the notion that government should rise to greatness by playing a heroic role is not seriously challenged.)

It should be pointed out that in *Don Quixote Part One*, Sancho Panza is largely a passive trickster. In Part One, the major scene involving him occurs when others toss him into the air in a blanket, a target of humiliating sport at an inn. Although Sancho engages in a few conscious deceptions, he is largely unable to put anyone else in a double bind, as he will do in Part Two, when he comes into his own. In Part One, Don Quixote is oblivious to Sancho's irony. Sancho's trickster nature shows, however, in the way his speech is "stuffed with words,"[20] an endless string of proverbs that are so adroitly fractured as to cancel themselves out within a single sentence. Such "self-erasing"[21] and overstuffed prose is a hallmark of the trickster.[22]

In this first part, it is the senex, Don Quixote, who, though mad, has the greater agency in guiding the action to keep the idea of the hero alive. Sancho Panza mostly defers to him. Senex and trickster collude in creating the illusion of a heroic future, when there is no actual reason to believe this is more than a vanished ideal. I believe this was Cervantes' symbolic perception of the situation in his nation's cultural unconscious at the time he published *Don Quixote*, and it suggests a way of understanding the psychodynamics of both individuals and cultures when powers they have deployed with confidence are waning. Without much direct reference to contemporary history, the author conveys the feeling of the unconscious situation of a Spain entering the 17th century, still shaken by England's defeat of the Spanish Armada, which had signalled the first clear limit to the future influence of the Spanish empire. By 1605, Spain had become, not unlike the United States today, a famous, influential, and proud country whose "greatest generation" was already past, even though it was not psychologically ready to give up the illusion of its transcendent power.

Under such circumstances, an individual or country that is losing its heroic position may start to keep its pride and its sense of ongoing agency afloat by a combination of fictions, desire to live up to its reputation, and monomania. In an older man, or a patriarchal country past its prime, the energy for these dynamics is fueled by the joint agency of the archetypes of the senex and trickster. As knight, Don Quixote personifies a senex-deployed introverted intuition that has a religious urgency about restoring lost honor and integrity to Spain. Sancho Panza represents a tricksterish extraverted sensation that sees a realistic opportunity to gain something by playing along with this senex grandiosity (Don Quixote has promised Sancho the governorship of an island when his fame is suitably rewarded). This is a picture of what any psychological entity—whether individual or culture—can look like when the powers that were so important in its ascendancy have declined, when heroic mastery no longer seems to be a realistic possibility, and when there is not the will to accept a diminution of status. In such a case, out of the shadow, a manic drive to reinstate the lost heroic possibility ensues.

In Don Quixote's story, the continued distance of the self-proclaimed hero from the anima suggests that this kind of effort at regeneration of heroic authority is not deeply restorative. Although Don Quixote has pledged his fealty to his Lady, Dulcinea, who is actually a young peasant woman in the neighboring village of El Toboso, he hardly knows this woman. Sancho is supposed to go back to El Toboso to take a message to her, but he only pretends to do so. Meanwhile, in the various interpolated stories, a series of anima figures appears, so that the reader is led to feel, with each new woman, perhaps at last the true soul mate has arrived. But Don Quixote is often sleeping while these stories are being told.

Don Quixote's most exact feminine counterpart is neither to be found in Dulcinea nor among the various female figures in the interpolated stories that are able to make connections to their beloveds, but in the very first of the unknown women he encounters, Marcela, a rather Artemis-like woman who wants never to have to do with any man.[23] Her chief pursuer, Grisostomo, has died of a broken heart, echoing the isolation of Don Quixote's own ego from the anima. It is that state of affairs that obtains throughout Part One of the novel: the hero is remembered, but in a way that renders him impotent to unite the psyche and lead from a place of integrity. And with no connection to the anima, there is none to the inferior function,[24] just as our current

American administration can admit no weakness or error, no inferiority in itself.[25]

THE EMERGENCE OF THE POST-HEROIC ATTITUDE

Part One of *Don Quixote* repeatedly teases us with the possibility that against all odds the mad *hidalgo* will succeed in his quest to gain recognition as a champion, like the over-the-hill fighter in Sylvester Stallone's film, *Rocky*. Part Two, which Cervantes published fully ten years after Part One, seems to carry that possibility forward, for it begins with the fame of its eponymous hero established—on the basis of so many people having read Part One! Cervantes already recognizes that his character is destined to have a fame even greater than Amadís of Gaul. Certainly Don Quixote is no less worthy of the honor, being equally fictional. Such a contextualization of the character suffering from a literary madness within his own publishing history is dazzling—postmodern before its time—and inevitably foregrounds the author. It returns us to the way Cervantes has consciously invited us to scrutinize his narrative, starting with the actual identity of the person narrating the greater part of Don Quixote's history. It is possible, as some have suggested, that Cervantes claims that that person is really Cide Hamete Benengeli to avoid prosecution. The Inquisition might easily have taken offense at the way the Priest and the Barber are shown burning Don Quixote's books, for instance. Cervantes' attempt to put a screen between himself and the reader may also be an effort at modesty in a narrator who is otherwise a show-off. The effect of this distancing, however, is to problematize the exact point of view the author is taking toward his character, thus inviting the reader to question whether *Don Quixote* itself is a straightforward heroic narrative, or something else again. If not even the identity of the narrator is clear, we are less willing to take the character's self-identification with the archetype of the hero for granted, and we're moved to look twice at heroic narrative itself.

This narrative ambiguity, a rich source of pleasure as one reads the novel,[26] has the paradoxical effect of making the characters on the page brim with significance: they are our footholds in reality as we climb the daunting literary edifice of this long novel. Yet they, too, seem to have changed when we get to Part Two. As R. H. Blyth observed, "the Don Quixote of the First Part is the quintessence of all the chivalry of the Romances, all the knighthood of the Middle Ages, together with spiritual and noble qualities derived from Cervantes himself" and "[h] is madness is partly his idealism (of which we sane people have so little)" and "partly an overstrung imagination at the service of this same idealism," but the "Don Quixote of Part Two is a kind of travelling lecturer, whose senility is taken advantage of in the most odious way by a couple of impudent, sophisticated creatures, the Duke and Duchess…"[27]

It is not only his characters' personalities that Cervantes permits himself to tamper with. He is extremely free, throughout both parts of the novel, with the names of characters. He plays fast and loose with words that ought not to change, parodying himself in this regard by the fractured proverbs and neologisms he puts so amusingly into the mouth of the illiterate Sancho Panza. In the very first line of the novel, Cervantes tells us that he does not "care to remember" the exact name of Don Quixote's village, telling us only that it is "Somewhere in La Mancha." We also learn that Don Quixote is an assumed name, adopted by a man whose real last name was either Quixada, Quexada, or Quexana: at the end of the novel, when Don Quixote has regained his sanity and can tell us himself who he is, he will tell us he is "Alonso Quixano."

The seminal Cervantes critic Leo Spitzer has described these narrative feints as creating a "linguistic perspectivism:"

> Cervantes' perspectivism, linguistic and otherwise, would allow
> him qua artist to stand above, and sometimes aloof from, the
> misconceptions of his characters.[28]

There is something demonic about the way the thinking process of naming is used, consistently undermining the conceptions of the reader. Clarity and integrity of naming, which in this introverted feeling universe should be carried by an extraverted thinking anima, is missing. In the shifting field of words, the reader's confidence in any predictable outcome is shaken. Hope for a coherent resolution becomes a quixotic desire.

In *Don Quixote Part One*, we yearn along with the central character for a feminine figure that can restore order and purpose. While Don Quixote is pining for the doubtful Dulcinea, Cervantes unveils to us a series of fascinating women to gratify the reader's wish to "see" the anima that can bring a happy ending. In Part Two, however, our hope of such an outcome is consistently disappointed. Early in Part Two, Sancho tries to convince Don Quixote that Dulcinea herself is at hand, when in fact he has pointed to a coarse peasant girl. Don Quixote decides that she is really the enchanted Dulcinea, but that does not stop the girl from using her own agency to leap onto her donkey and hightail it out of the narrative in an enormous hurry, never to return again (except in the Don's fantasy). Don Quixote's most important relational integrity in this story occurs with Sancho, with whom he sustains an affectionately adversarial dialogue, even as he is being tested by the multitude of characters that try to trick, embarrass, and defeat him in a concerted campaign to get him to relinquish his madness and know his true place in the world.

The second part of the novel moves toward getting the senex to give up its hold on the hero; the trickster no longer works in tandem with the senex to support heroic fantasy. Sancho Panza undergoes a remarkable individuation, using his trickster energy in an increasingly conscious way, learning to overturn the traps the world would like to set for him as the companion of Don Quixote. In this Second Part of the novel, the world order is symbolized by two extraordinarily sophisticated characters, the Duke and the Duchess, who personify a darker and more purposive aspect of the Self. They devise situations that are designed to break the fictions, crush the desire, and subvert the monomania that Sancho and Don Quixote are prone to enact together. Cruelly, they give every appearance of honoring the fame Don Quixote and Sancho have earned by being the subjects of a popular book, making the Don, in effect, a knight of their court (which undercuts his desire to continue as a knight-errant, off on quests). They even set up Sancho with a governorship, in which he displays an uncanny capacity, Solomon-like, to put others in double binds to resolve the tricky disputes they bring to him. But Sancho elects, eventually, to step down from this office, withdrawing all interest from the heroic role. In this way, he takes his cue from the Duke and Duchess to engineer the humbling of his own ambition.

The valorization of the hero that pervaded Part One of the novel is deconstructed in Part Two through three deliberate narrative strategies. One, famously, is *irony*, particularly the irony that the two protagonists' fame is founded on their absurdity.

A second hero-deconstructing strategy is *repeated frustration of desire*, a fate shared in common by all the characters. As Governor, Sancho is kept from eating the delicious meals that are cooked for him by the intrusion of a government doctor who has taken it upon himself to supervise Sancho's diet. Even the Duke and Duchess, in the midst of their many elaborate efforts to humiliate Don Quixote, are repeatedly stymied by Don Quixote's courteous chivalry. On more than one occasion, he actually succeeds in heroically rescuing someone in their retinue. But most often, it is Quixote himself who is frustrated, particularly in his efforts to reach Dulcinea.[29]

Irony and frustration are not, in themselves, enough to deconstruct the hero. Cervantes' third strategy toward this end, deployed by him in a sublime way, is his *irreverence*, which he can get away with because, somewhere behind it all, his own feeling for what is appropriate reigns supreme. Cervantes can defeat the fictions of his characters; he doesn't need to revere his creations to give them life. Exposing the artifices by which they live, he leaves it to the reader to decide their value.

There is a fourth strategy, however, that seems to emanate from Don Quixote and Sancho Panza themselves, who invent the modern novel along with Cervantes by coming to *self-knowledge*.[30] As their own haplessness dawns on them, they see the realistic limits of a life lived to perpetuate the hero myth.

But we will also have to notice that there is a cost to the deconstruction that dominates the second part of Cervantes' novel. Under the pressure of the debunking, the archetypal underpinnings of Don Quixote's ethical universe begin to fragment and lose their mystery. In a famous scene, the knight-errant begins attacking the puppets in a puppet show, to rescue some of the puppet characters from others who are persecuting them. In another scene, he comes upon some religious statues that are covered in white cloth—St. George, St. Martin, St. James the Moor-slayer (the patron saint of Spain), and St. Paul: seeing the figures of these men whom he regarded as spiritual knights who had "conquered heaven," he begins to wonder what, if anything, he has achieved. It's as if finally getting in touch with true archetypes of the hero at a religious level shames his intuition from the project of trying to make himself the archetype. But with his disillusionment with his own possibilities for sacred achievement, we enter a secular, and not very imaginative, universe. The very next scene has him trampled by bulls, and from that point on the old knight is repeatedly defeated.

This is not, for a culture or an individual, an entirely happy outcome to the loss of confidence in the hero. One might have hoped for a move from the trickster to the anima and a corresponding shift of emphasis from ego to Self. But despite Don Quixote's belief that Dulcinea has been enchanted and can be disenchanted if only Sancho will flog himself 3300 times (a prescription delivered by the Duke's majordomo dressed up as Merlin), Dulcinea never appears again in the novel, not even as the original peasant girl she had been. There is a woman interested in Don Quixote, one of the Duchess's servants, who is so obnoxious we agree with him that he would be better off without this particular woman. Without any viable access to the feminine, however, his capacity to sustain with any semblance of integrity his heroic identification disappears.

At the end, Don Quixote can only submit, once again, to someone's trick. His friend, Sansón Carrasco, dressed as the Knight of the White Moon, catches up with him in Barcelona. Sansón, who has read *Don Quixote Part One,* knows that Don Quixote's commitment to knight-errantry demands of him that he submit to any condition imposed on him by any other knight who defeats him. Challenging Don Quixote to a duel, he defeats him and makes him promise to return home and eschew the practice of chivalry for a period of one year. Tricked through his own text, Don Quixote can no longer continue as a knight.

Sansón's costume as Knight of the White Moon suggests that Don Quixote is submitting to lunar masculinity,[31] a style that subverts the solar heroic aspirations that appear, for instance, in Picasso's famous lithograph of Don Quixote on his horse beside Sancho Panza on his mule, where, in the foreground of the drawing, the sun is prominent.

The lunacy of *Don Quixote Part Two* is what finally moves the old man into the post-heroic attitude, which means, among other things, the narrowing of the horizon of possibilities. The narrator himself steps forward in the final chapter to make this clear, saying:

> Since human affairs, particularly the lives of men, are not
> eternal and are always in a state of decline from their beginnings
> until they reach their final end, and since the life of Don Quixote

> had no privilege from heaven to stop its natural course, it reached
> its end and conclusion when he least expected it...

At the end of the novel, Don Quixote—the fictitious persona—simply
ceases to exist. The old man who remains to carry his life to its
conclusion, now definitively naming himself as Alonso Quixano, refuses
the efforts of his old friends to trick him into believing that Dulcinea
will be disenchanted soon and that his heroic adventures can resume.
As the dying Quixano puts it to Sancho, "there are no birds in
yesterday's nests."

In the prologue to his posthumously published book, *Persiles*,
completed on his deathbed just a year after *Don Quixote Part Two* was
published, Cervantes penned a farewell to life that in stressing the limits
of what any writer can say to his contemporaries perhaps conveys the
degree to which he personally had got beyond the hero:

> A time will come, perhaps, when I shall knot this broken thread
> and say what should be said but which I cannot say here. Good-
> by, thanks; good-by, compliments; good-by, merry friends. I am
> dying, and my wish is that I may see you all soon again, happy
> in the life to come.[32]

Reading Cervantes from an American perspective nearly four centuries
later, a participant observer in the cultural madness of our own late-
stage heroism is grateful to find such a reliable guide.

NOTES

1. Directed by Christopher Nolan (2000), from his screenplay
based on "Memento Mori," a short story by Jonathan Nolan.

2. David Denby, "Men Gone Wild," *The New Yorker*, April 2, 2007.

3. Miguel de Cervantes, *Don Quixote*, trans. Edith Grossman (New
York: HarperCollins, 2003). Page citations refer to this edition.

4. Howard Mancing, in *The Chivalric World of Don Quijote: Style,
Structure and Narrative Technique,* locates a noticeable decline of
enthusiasm for the chivalric ideal on the part of the protagonist as early
as the last half of Part One, but the clear defeat for the reader of the
Don's heroic possibilities does not come until Part Two.

5. Ruth Anthony El Saffar and Diana de Armas Wilson (eds.), *Quixotic Desire: Psychoanalytic Perspectives on Cervantes* (Ithaca, New York: Cornell University Press, 1993).

6. Miguel de Unamuno, "Glosses on *Don Quixote*," in *Our Lord Don Quixote* (Princeton: Princeton University Press, 1976), p. 356.

7. This is an imagination that is funneled, therefore, into imitation: as the French critic Marthe Robert has observed, "The most radical quixotic act, then, is never the accomplishment of some personal ambition, but on the contrary, the imitation of an ideal fixed by tradition, indeed by literary convention, and consequently stripped of all originality." Marthe Robert, *The Old and the New: From Don Quixote to Kafka*, trans. Carol Cosman (Berkeley: University of California Press, 1977), p. 12.

8. "Unprovoked, except by chivalric paranoia, Don Quixote beats up a carrier ("with such good will," "so effectually mauled") and shatters the skull of his innocent companion. Interfering in a squabble, he then causes a blameless young rustic to be flogged "so severely, that he had like to have died on the pot." Martin Amis, "Broken Lance," a review of a reissue of the Smollett translation, in *The War Against Cliché: Essays and Reviews 1971-2000* (New York: Vintage, 2002), pp. 427-432.

9. James Hillman, "Senex and Puer," in *Puer Papers* (Dallas: Spring Publications, 1979); "On Senex Consciousness," *Spring* (1970), pp. 146-165; "The 'Negative' Senex and a Renaissance Solution," *Spring* (1979), pp. 77-109.

10. Terry Castle, "High Plains Drifter," in *Atlantic Monthly,* January/February, 2004. http://www.theatlantic.com/doc/200401/castle

11. James Hillman, *A Blue Fire*, Thomas Moore (ed.) (New York: Harper and Row, 1989), p. 208.

12. Eduardo Urbina, "Son Quijote, *puer-senex*: un tópico y su transformación paródica en el *Quijote*," *Journal of Hispanic Philology*, 12 (1987-88), pp. 127-38. See also the discussion of the *puer senilis* or *puer senex* in Ernest Robert Curtius, *European Literature and the Latin Middle Ages,* Princeton: Princeton University Press, 1953, pp. 98-101, in the section of his chapter on Topics entitled "Boy and Old Man." Curtius tells us that "This is a topos which grew out of the psychological situation of late Antiquity," adding that "[a]ll early and high periods of a culture extol the young man and at the same time honor age. But only late periods develop a human ideal in which the polarity youth-

age works towards a balance" (p. 98). That imaginal balance does not come forward in Don Quijote's case until very late in the novel, when he begins to consider taking up the pastoral life with Sancho, thus replacing the chivalric ideal with another literary trope, described by Steven Marx in "*Fortunate Senex:* The Pastoral of Old Age," *Studies in English Literature*, Spring 1985, online http://cla.calpoly.edu/~smarx/Publications/YouthAge/Chap2.html

13. Terry Castle, *op. cit.*

14. The "shadow" of a particular function will have the opposite attitude with respect to extraversion or introversion.

15. See John Beebe, "Understanding Consciousness through the Theory of Psychological Types," in Joseph Cambray and Linda Carter (eds.), *Analytical Psychology: Contemporary Perspectives in Jungian Analysis* (Hove and New York: Brunner-Routledge, 2004), pp. 83-115.

16. R. H. Blyth, *Zen in English Literature and Oriental Classics* (Tokyo: Hokuseido Press, 1942), p. 201.

17. *Ibid.*, p. 211.

18. G.N.G. Orsini, "Organicism," in Phillip P. Wiener (ed.) *Dictionary of the History of Ideas*, Volume 3 (New York: Scribner's, 1973), p. 422.

19. Michael Ryle has demonstrated this elegantly in his paper "Don Quixote: A Fictional Representation of the Perception Dichotomy," presented at the Fifteenth International Convention of the Association of Psychological Type, Toronto, Canada, July 23, 2004.

20. Warwick Wadlington, *The Confidence Game in American Literature* (Princeton: Princeton University Press, 1975), p. 246, quoted in Beebe, "The Trickster in the Arts," p. 43 [see n. 22].

21. R.W.B. Lewis, "Afterword" to the Signet edition of *The Confidence Man* (New York: New American Library, 1964), p. 272, quoted in Beebe, *op. cit.* p. 43 [see n. 22].

22. John Beebe, "The Trickster in the Arts," in *The San Francisco Jung Institute Library Journal*, 2/2, 1981, pp. 21-54.

23. Ruth Anthony El Saffar, "In Marcela's Case," in *Quixotic Desire*, pp. 157-178.

24. The idea that the anima "carries the inferior function" in a man is discussed in my essay, "Understanding consciousness through the theory of psychological types," *op. cit.*, p. 102.

25. The idea that the inferior function of our typology is associated with integrity is developed in my 1992 book *Integrity in Depth*, College Station, TX: Texas A & M University Press, pp. 106-7.

26. Anthony Close, in *Miguel de Cervantes, Don Quixote*, Cambridge: Cambridge University Press, 1990, pp. 109-25, argues that some of the ambiguity a present-day reader finds in the character of the *hidalgo*, who in his own time might have seemed more like a straightforward burlesque, is a consequence of the way the literary tradition Cervantes' novel set in motion has increasingly emphasized the romantic, as opposed to the simply ironic, aspects of the would-be heroic character.

27. R. H. Blyth, *Zen in English Literature and Oriental Classics*, p. 198.

28. Leo Spitzer, *Linguistics and Literary History: Essays in Stylistics* (Princeton: Princeton University Press, 1948), p. 50.

29. Frustration might even be described as the archetypal field that emanates from the novel itself. Certainly, this property has eluded many filmmakers who have attempted to make a movie of it, even as it has defeated the attempts of master critics to put its special qualities into words. Mike Todd was planning a film version of *Don Quixote* to follow his great success, *Around the World in Eighty Days*, when he suddenly died; Terry Gilliam, has recorded his own unsuccessful attempt to film the novel in the documentary, *Lost in La Mancha*, which was released in 2003; and—most famous, and frustrated, of all, Orson Welles ended up only with pieces of the Quixote film that he tried to make over a period of twenty years. Jess Franco's reconstruction of Welles' *Don Quixote* conveys that Welles managed to visualize Don Quixote nearly perfectly through his actor Francisco Reguera, but was deeply uncertain how to make his story meaningful for our time.

30. Anthony Close, *Don Quijote*, p. 108, calls this "a long painful process of *self*-enlightenment."

31. "Lunar masculinity" is a concept introduced by the psychologist Howard Teich. See John Beebe, *Integrity in Depth, op. cit.*, pp. 93-95; 97, 98; 104. The South African novelist André Brink, looking at the issue from the standpoint of the fate of the anima, takes a different view that "The decisive event in this process, and also the culmination of the Dulcinea theme in the novel, is one of the sublime moments in Western literature. It is the last encounter with the Bachelor Samson Carrasco, masquerading as the Knight of the White Moon: defeated in the

skirmish, Don Quixote is bound by the terms of their pact to acknowledge that his adversary's mistress is superior to Dulcinea del Toboso: 'Then, battered and stunned, without lifting his vizor Don Quixote proclaimed in a low and feeble voice, as if he were speaking from inside a tomb: 'Dulcinea del Toboso is the most beautiful woman in the world, and I am the most unfortunate knight on earth; nor is it just that my weakness should discredit that truth. Drive your lance home, knight, and rid me of life, since you have robbed me of honors.' [*Don Quixote*, J. M. Cohen (trans.) (London: Penguin Classics, 1950), p. 890] Eighteen years before Galileo, this is Don Quixote's *Eppur si muove* ["And yet it moves," the phrase Galileo was said to have muttered to himself, after agreeing with the Inquisition to repudiate the Copernican doctrine that the earth is not stationary, but revolves around the sun.] It is also a profoundly liberating experience: by announcing Dulcinea's status as the most beautiful mistress in the world, irrespective of whether he abjures her or not, he grants her an autonomous existence, releasing her from all dependence on *his* faith and *his* imagination. But by the same token he can now no longer be dependent on *her*—and if he relinquishes the lady who has provided the ultimate justification for all his exploits, there is, quite literally, no sense in continuing to live. And so, irrespective of what the Bachelor or the code of chivalry requires of him, Don Quixote hereby condemns *himself* to death. Which indeed follows soon afterward." André Brink, *The Novel: Language and Narrative from Cervantes to Calvino* (New York: New York University Press, 1998), pp. 43-44.

32. Miguel de Cervantes, "Foot in the Stirrup: Cervantes Farewell to Life," from *The Troubles of Persiles and Sigismunda,* in *The Portable Cervantes,* Samuel Putnam (ed.) (New York: Viking Press, 1958), p. 802.

I would like to acknowledge the scholarly assistance of Charles Stewart with this paper, and the helpful feedback of David Abel, Millicent Dillon, Adam Frey, Carol Lucero, and Mary Webster. — John Beebe

THE FRENCH AND THE REVOLUTION SYNDROME

VIVIANE THIBAUDIER

(Translated by Anita Conrade)

Aux armes, citoyens, Take up arms, citizens,
Formez vos bataillons, In battle formation,
Marchons, marchons! March on, march on!
Qu'un sang impur abreuve May our fields be watered
nos sillons. with impure blood.

—*La Marseillaise*

The two main differences between American and French history are that Americans never had royalty and that their revolution was against the British rather than against other Americans.

As a child learning French history in elementary school, I recall being appalled by the behavior of my forebears. We French people, the proud heirs of the Enlightenment, had thought it necessary to chop off the head of our king (and so many others, on the same occasion), in the belief that this physical act of savagery would institute democracy.

Viviane Thibaudier is the former president of the Société Française de Psychologie Analytique (SFPA), the French analytical society, and was the director of the Paris Jung Institute for 14 years. She is also the liaison between the developing analytic training group in China and the International Association for Analytical Psychology. She has published numerous articles in different journals as well as co-published with 4 other French analysts a Jungian dictionary. She lives and practices near Paris.

Later, I learned that most of the countries in northern Europe had seen no need for such behavior. The constitutional monarchies they set up in the early 19th century—certainly the most elaborate forms of democratic government—were, for the most part,[1] able to include the monarch, tempering his power by balancing it with that of a legislative assembly. I wondered why every attempt to do something similar in France ended in failure, and even in a ritual bloodbath.[2]

In 1858, Alexis de Tocqueville wrote to his friend Kergolay:

> There is...something peculiar in this *disease* of the French Revolution, which I can feel without being able to describe it properly, or analyze its causes. It is a new and unknown species of *virus*. The world has seen other violent revolutions, but the unbridled, violent, drastic, bold, and *almost mad,* yet powerful and effective, character of the French revolutionaries is unprecedented .... Where does this new *rage* come from? Who produced it? Who made it so effective? Who perpetuates it? ... Aside from all that can be explained about the French Revolution, there is *something unexplained* in its spirit and its deeds. I sense the whereabouts of the unknown object, but no matter how I try, I cannot lift *the veil that covers it.*[3]

Tocqueville died some months later without solving the riddle. Since his time, historians, philosophers, sociologists, economists, politicians, psychoanalysts, and many others have tackled it. The French Revolution has been the subject of countless speculations, and yet no one has truly succeeded in lifting the veil. Though I make no claim to encounter more success than those who preceded me, I shall nevertheless try to shed some light on the question, and dare to make my own interpretation of this "unexplained" thing that so intrigued Tocqueville. To this very day, *"something"* seems to haunt the French soul: since 1789, "revolutions" have caused upheaval, at every level of French society. Several have been of a purely social and political order, setting the nation aflame, but others have been more private and discreet in nature—involving corporate disputes, perhaps, or arising from within a community, group, agency, or institution.[4] In France, revolution is practically a conditioned, Pavlovian response to any conflict which emerges. This is what I call *the revolution syndrome.*

What is it about this Revolution which has such a strong impact on people's minds? Why does it still exert so much fascination on the

French? Indeed, like the Phoenix, it is continually being reborn from its ashes. It rears its head with the same ferocity whenever something new seeks to emerge—a reform, a different structure, or any sort of change—whenever new ideas are in conflict with the old.

What in the world were we trying to accomplish, by chopping off all those heads? What were we attempting to drown in these successive bloodbaths, what were we seeking to destroy in the massive and hateful destruction of human life, of souls, and of artistic and architectural treasures in these reigns of terror which seized the French again and again over two centuries? These killing frenzies were most frequent from 1789 to the Commune of 1871, but there were also the terrifying purges of the "National Revolution" instituted in 1942 under the Vichy regime,[5] "purification measures" following the Second World War, and the police brutality of the dark years of the Algerian War between 1956 and 1962. Lest we forget, there was also the "revolution" of 1968 with its barricades, and, in the autumn of 2005, the riots in the suburbs.[6] Amid widespread looting and destruction, these most recent incidents led to the burning of several thousand automobiles (perhaps, in an era when people identify so heavily with their vehicles, the cars themselves are appropriate victims?) and hundreds of injuries and arrests.

It is not so much the "revolutionary phenomenon" in itself which puzzles me and for which I would like to find a meaning here, but rather its ritualized repetition over the centuries—even if only on a small scale, via the recurring strikes and other street protests which invariably demand the "head"[7] of such and such a cabinet minister or other political or corporate villain. (Being in charge = charged.)

HISTORIC UNCONSCIOUS

From its beginnings, French history has been imbued with a three-part tradition which forged the French mentality. First and foremost, that of an absolute monarch by divine right. Next, to legitimate this right, a powerful Catholic church and clergy, convinced of the claim to be the universal religion. In the name of this conviction, heretics were persecuted and interminable wars of religion fought throughout nearly all of the 16th century. Lastly, starting in the early 5th century, salic law prohibited women from inheriting land and, towards the 14th century, definitively excluded them from the royal succession.[8] Women could neither rule nor transmit the right to rule. Thus, France is the only country in Europe where a queen has never reigned. However, when the king was too young to govern, several women acted as regents: Blanche de Castille,[9] Catherine de Médicis,[10] and Anne of Austria,[11] for example.

On the one hand, this millennial tradition engendered an absolutist conception of power, based on no authority other than that of God. To oppose the king was the same as opposing God Himself, with whom the king was identified. Indeed, the king was seen as the omnipotent and sanctified Father of his subjects. The most extreme example of absolute rule was that of Louis XIV, known as the Sun King, who had the splendid Château de Versailles built to reflect his grandeur.

On the other hand, recognition of the sovereign's divine right was a source of equally absolute power for the Church itself. In the name of an intransigent Catholicism which claimed to be the universal religion, France engaged in crusades against heretics[12] and wars of religion both inside and outside its borders. On August 24, 1572, the day of the tragic Saint Barthélémy Massacre, some 3,000 French Protestants[13] were slaughtered in the streets of Paris in a single night. Within the week that followed, there were 30,000 victims throughout the kingdom.[14] The bloodthirsty violence was such that, two centuries later, it might have aroused the envy of the revolutionaries. Salic law was actually chiefly related to the power of the clergy in royal circles[15] and the desire of the Church superiors to manage the affairs of State according to the ideal of the Church or even the Papacy, i.e., between men.

These various aspects of French history are the threads woven into a fabric of the unconscious which has fashioned the French mentality since its origins. This is what I call the historic unconscious.

Another expression of the French unconscious is our national anthem, composed in 1792 during the Revolution. A national anthem is a strong symbol of belonging, with quasi-sacred signification: an emotionally charged collective identity, conveying the unconscious ideals and desires of an entire people, passed down from generation to generation.

Out of curiosity, I read the words and listened to the music of about twenty national anthems: those of most of the European countries and the world's great powers. Although many of the melodies were inspired by marches, and thus sound military, on the whole their lyrics tend to be rather "romantic." They praise the beauty and sweetness of the land, the sunrise, the mountains, the flowers, nature in general; they speak of their pride in their flag, the benefits of freedom, hope, and love; they invite the nation to unity. Some praise God or call upon Him to protect their noble queen. That of Belgium declares the national motto to be "the immortal words, The King, the Law, and Freedom." France is the only nation (except China, perhaps) to have such a violent anthem, encouraging its citizens to take up arms and prepare to shed the blood, which, moreover, is described as "impure," of a virtually designated enemy. "*La Marseillaise*" (a stanza of which was quoted at the beginning of this article) is a war chant, composed to stoke the ardor of soldiers on the march to battle a threatening foreigner, a fierce enemy.[16]

SEMANTIC SPACE

To summarize the foregoing, we are dealing with a set of attributes constituting a millennial semantic memory. These can be conceptualized as a semantic space composed of the ideas, emotions, and attitudes which are paradigms of the French mentality. We could also describe this phenomenon as a sort of group unconscious shared by all the French people, deeply rooted in history.

As we have seen, this semantic space is structured by a foundation which is characterized by:

- An absolutist conception of power.

- The importance of the image of the divinized and all-powerful Father, which, as a corollary, necessarily implies the servility and immaturity of His sons.

- A universal faith which justifies the brutal and definitive elimination of all difference or dissension.

- The exclusion of women from the right to rule.

- Crusades and "religious" wars by virtue of the Dogma, which cannot tolerate any challenges or competition.

- The designation of an enemy who must be destroyed, whose defeat quenches a thirst and makes the victors feel united and strong.

The motto "*Liberté, égalité, fraternité*"[17] and the chorus of "*La Marseillaise*," engraved in the minds of all French people, urging them to shed the blood of the foreigner, form the foundation of French democratic thought produced by the Revolution. However, these two axioms give rise to a paradoxical whole which is, generally speaking, characteristic of the "French way of thinking." This, in turn, leads to a specifically French way of functioning. The subtext of this way of thinking can be read as containing hints of the myth of the scapegoat, which must be sacrificed (its blood[18] must flow) to guarantee the unity and harmony of the people (liberty, equality, fraternity). This theme is also reflected in the statement uttered by Robespierre, the most bloodthirsty of the Revolutionary leaders, to justify the death sentence meted out to Louis XVI: "The king must die *that the Republic may live*." Robespierre's paranoid assertion mirrors the traditional proclamation made when the king died: "The King is dead. Long live the King!" It expresses the continuity of the monarchy and the sovereignty beyond the death of the individual king. However, distorted by Robespierre, the idea is no longer that, despite the death of the king, the monarchy and all that it implicitly contains continues. On the contrary, the death of the king is defined as the prerequisite to the birth of the "public thing" (*res publica*). It's one *or* the other, and this decision necessarily involves a radical amputation: the decapitation of the king.[19]

IN THE NAME OF THE FATHER

Commenting on the Bible, René Girard reminds us that any serious decision made by a culture has a sacrificial nature. In ancient times, the Latin word *decidere* meant "to cut the throat" of the victim.[20] Pursuing "the accomplishment of a long thought-out and carefully studied plan,"[21] Robespierre, in making his declaration, shows the degree to which both his words and deeds were penetrated and possessed by the mythical and mystical figure of the executioner and the sacrificial victim. Under this spell, he acted and convinced the people of Paris to take action. Today, in France, it is still widely believed that in slaying the king, the revolutionaries were expressing the desire to "kill a symbol." This belief implies that the act was intended to have a symbolic effect. However, the revolutionary deed, in mistaking the container for the thing contained, was, to my mind, more like an act of de-symbolization similar to a psychotic explosion. It prevented the French people from becoming aware of and elaborating what was truly seeking expression at this important turning point in their history. Hence the need to return to it again and again, like something which has never been resolved. Actually, the act of beheading the king destroyed the possibility of ever symbolizing its real contents. In other words, the decapitation played the role of an "acting-out," short-circuiting the psychic elaboration of the grief and suffering caused by the abrupt transformation of the image of the king which had always been cherished by the people. By trying to run away,[22] Louis XVI suddenly revealed his utter lack of divinity. He came back down to the world of men, irreversibly, a concept which the Enlightenment had prepared people to accept. As is always the case with ritual sacrifice, his execution was a means of discharging a primal form of violence arising chiefly from the feelings of fear and frustration aroused by news of the king's betrayal. More specifically still, these feelings were caused by the collapse of the coalescence between image and reality. The execution put an end to the elaboration of the complex contents hitherto associated in people's minds with the image of the king: a sacred and absolute power, an all-powerful, divinized father. The time was probably ripe for the French people to collectively mourn the loss of this primitive image of the king, like individuals reaching adulthood, and replace it with a more human and fallible one. However, it would seem that neither the king, by running away, nor the people, in chopping off his head, were able to interpret the signs of the times. When something which embodies so much power mingled with holiness is destroyed, it is a matter of magical thought (on which all rituals are based) to believe that the extraordinary energy the image contained will die with he who embodied it. The numinosity dwelling in such representations remains. At best, it withdraws into the unconscious momentarily, to reappear at the first opportunity and take on new life. At worst, it becomes as devastating to the society as the psychotic explosion is to the individual, as was the case following the slaying of the king.

French history is chockful of men who have stepped into the king's place, donning the mantle of divine and holy omnipotence embodied for centuries by the king, and left vacant by his abrupt disappearance. Robespierre was the first. In his meteoric rise, freighted with paranoia, he ordered the execution of the king and then unleashed the Terror, sending thousands of people to the guillotine. But Robespierre was followed by many others: Napoleon, who crowned and consecrated himself emperor;[23] Louis XVIII; Louis-Philippe, and, in more recent times, Marshal Pétain,[24] whose nickname was "The Father of the Country;" General de Gaulle, France's "Savior;" the Machiavellian prince François Mitterrand, who ruled for fourteen years... One could also cite the extremely sectarian Jean-Paul Sartre, who dictated the thinking of an entire generation or, as paradoxical as it might seem, the French Communist Party which, for several decades, fascinated French intellectuals and shaped their way of thinking.

For all of these reasons, the sanctified image of the ideal and all-powerful Father, inherited from centuries of history, is still a highly influential element in French life, especially in the realm of political power. The deeds of the new president elected in May 2007 are hardly likely to reverse this tendency: quite the contrary. In perfect harmony with what the French people unconsciously expect, from the outset the President assumed the position of the absolute monarch. Most of the members of his cabinet are young and inexperienced, which enables him to maintain absolute control over them and make their decisions for them. However, in an entirely different realm, one might also cite Lacan, the all-powerful father of his "subjects," whose attitude turned them into children. His theory of the "name-of-the-father," a pure product of the semantic space described above, could gain credibility only in a country like France.

This is why the sons and daughters of France, fascinated by the unconscious image of the ideal Father, are completely subjugated by authority and hierarchical principles which, in France, are the favored organizational scheme, in both the public and private sector, the governmental and the corporate.[25] At the same time, these sons and daughters are also inclined to sudden and violent rebellion, in an attempt to escape the grip of this key-imago to the way French society functions. In these brutal upheavals, they have sought, as individuals do in adolescence, to free themselves by committing glorious acts of opposition. Generation after generation, and century after century, this has yielded revolutions great and small; however, ultimately, this process only perpetuates the power of the imago, without ever transforming it and reducing its impact.

UNIVERSAL VALUES

The principles of freedom of religion and the separation of Church and State, although they have elicited fierce conflict, occasionally resulting in massacre, and had numerous ups and downs over the decades,[26] are certainly among the greatest achievements of the French Revolution. However, as we have seen, for centuries the king's divine right to rule was based on an omnipotent Church, the only authority able to grant such a power. In exchange, this Church always sought to impose its supremacy over the State. Thus, just as the image of the divinized Father transcended the death of the king, retaining considerable influence over the French way of thinking, the dogmatic spirit of Catholicism which is historically closely associated with this image also endures, although it now holds sway in more secularized forms. Because the Catholic Church intended to be the universal religion, it refused to either acknowledge the right of any other faith to exist or allow anyone to worship God differently (ostracism of Jews, persecutions and massacres of Cathars and Protestants). Of course, in our times, Jews, Protestants, Muslims, Buddhists, and many other believers are entitled to practice their religions in France.[27] Nevertheless, it is important to note that, to replace the Christianity he had ousted, Robespierre intended immediately to found the religion of the Supreme Being. Apparently, he too was aware that the lack of a religion would leave a vacuum to be filled. For, as we have seen for the king, the Church was merely the "container" for far more complex contents associated with spiritual beliefs; apparently, it is quite difficult to deprive human beings of their religious feelings, regardless of their nature.

The French tradition of secularism dates back to the Revolution of 1789. Yet the Church had accustomed the French to a need for dogma, for absolute Truth. This leads to the next question: where did this need go? For millennia, people believed in a universal Word containing the Truth, a Word which was impossible to challenge, which excluded all others, in which they had total faith. With that gone, what could guide their lives and give them meaning?

In a country where the dominant function is thought, it is not surprising that it was in the realm of ideas that the religious contents theoretically destroyed by the Revolution sought and found refuge. Naturally, the physical acts of burning churches, destroying crucifixes, and guillotining bishops did not suffice to rid France of Catholicism forever. This was another illusion. Orthodoxy has survived in French intellectual life, highly authoritarian and hierarchical, operating in the same way as an all-powerful and dogmatic church. It has its own rituals, its gods and martyrs, religious wars, witch hunts, anathemas, excommunications, commandments, taboos, etc. Countless original and complex thinkers were figuratively guillotined in public by the Robespierres and Saint-Justs of the French intellectual world, because they were "guilty" of refusing to obey the "revolutionary catechism."[28] To name only a few: Albert Camus, Arthur Koestler,[29] Gaston Bachelard, François Furet, René Girard, Raymond Aron, Paul Ricoeur, Hannah Arendt, etc. Of course, C. G. Jung also falls into this category; it is still heretical to utter his name in any French university. They were all ostracized by those who believed, and still believe, they are guardians of the Truth. Likewise, French politics are burdened with dogma: according to the traditional left/right dichotomous structure, one must be on one side *or* the other. Systematically and unthinkingly, any initiative taken by the enemy must be destroyed.

In the last presidential campaign, Ségolène Royal's attempts to edge towards the center without losing her party's support were sharply criticized by the more prominent members of the Socialist Party (all men who had served as cabinet ministers). Likewise, when Bernard Kouchner (from the left) accepted the invitation of the new president (from the right) to serve as the government's Foreign Minister, he was immediately expelled (excommunicated) from the Socialist Party. As usual, it's one *or* the other. The absolutely impermeable nature of the split rules out any possibility of a middle path, a third way. The slightest attempt to introduce this concept is immediately vilified as "treason," one of the prized rhetorical flourishes of the French intelligentsia.

These dogmatic beliefs and arbitrary ideas, among the primary characteristics of French thought, make any real debate difficult in the realm of politics, science, or philosophy. Instead of yielding an exchange or confrontation of different viewpoints, which might be mutually beneficial to both sides, the practice of debate consists of proving at any price that the other, the adversary, the enemy, is wrong. He must be pulverized; his "blood must flow"... The spirit of the Revolution has perverted the *disputatio* common in medieval universities.[30]

Identity and Otherness

Officially, salic law was abolished in France following the fall of the monarchy. Nevertheless, for the reasons noted above, it still has a profound influence on French attitudes. For example, French women were not granted the right to vote until 1946 (whereas Turkey instituted women's suffrage in the early 1930s). To open a bank account without written permission from their husbands, French women had to wait until 1970!

In the career world, women are still clearly underrepresented in executive positions. Subject to the "glass ceiling," for the same job responsibilities, they are paid 20% to 33% less than their male colleagues. Likewise, despite the constitutional amendment of June 2000 instituting male-female parity in civil service positions, they are still a minority in the upper echelons of government administration. Currently, with barely 20% of our MPs being women, France ranks 59th worldwide (between Estonia and Equatorial Guinea!).

In *The Bacchae,* by Euripides, Dionysus returns to Thebes as an effeminate stranger after a long exile. He has come from India, singing and dancing the whole way, with a following of exotic women, the Maenads. King Pentheus, who is incredulous, has Dionysus and his disturbing female acolytes imprisoned. But Dionysus escapes and, to avenge the insult, sets the palace on fire and bewitches the women of Thebes (including Agave, mother of Pentheus), driving them into a frenzy of madness. He leads them out of the city to indulge in worshipping him in the most excessive ways. Though Pentheus has banned the cult, he is curious about it. Dionysus tricks him into visiting Mount Cithaeron where the scene is in full swing by promising him that, dressed as a woman and concealed, he will be able to spy on the women communing intimately with nature. But the Maenads, blinded by a spell cast by Dionysus, see Pentheus as a wild animal. Agave, not realizing it is her own son, tears the creature to pieces, and triumphantly returns bearing his head on the end of her thyrsus.

Like King Creon in Sophocles, Pentheus represents the rigid order of the State. He is the vessel for rational, masculine values who rejects the diversity Dionysus is attempting to introduce to the City. Jean Pierre Vernant[31] says that Pentheus simultaneously represents rationality shunning faith, warrior-like violence, and withdrawal into the confines of a single identity.

I do not know whether Tocqueville was aware of this play by Euripides, and if he was, whether it might have begun to answer some of the questions he had. In any case, if we linger upon it for a moment, it can teach us a great deal about human attitudes, and how people may interact with each other in certain circumstances.

This blind and irrepressible force, this uncontainable drive, this bloodthirsty instinct which eagerly rips apart its prey, this intoxicating ecstasy of destruction, this exultation in parading the victim's head on a spike, like a trophy... all these are visions we can glean from revolutionary iconography, visions which perplexed Tocqueville, as a great democratic thinker.[32]

What teachings, what understanding of the human soul can we distill from the myth of Dionysus, which might enable us to decipher the processes at work in the behavior of men of yesteryear and today?

The "madness" of the women is set in motion by Dionysus in response to the rigidity of Pentheus, his scorn for diversity, for the foreigner, the Other; his uncompromising stand in favor of exclusively rational and virile positions. However, despite his unilateral rejection, as an arrogant and repressive male, of what is foreign, Pentheus is secretly curious about and envious of it. This contradiction seems to be the element that provoked a reversal to the opposite extreme, which culminated in an irreparable, bestial massacre. Jung calls this dynamic enantiodromia: the sudden emergence of an unconscious counterposition: "This characteristic phenomenon (which) practically always occurs when an extreme, one-sided tendency dominates conscious life."[33]

There is no doubt that the French "masculine"[34] is closely akin to Pentheus, sharing his fear of weakness and the irrational, his tendency to shun the Other, and his scorn for and exclusion of women, who must remain in an inferior, subservient position, rather than seek a voice in men's affairs. The mediocrity of the masculine image projected by Louis XVI, who was a weak character with little interest in politics and who was manipulated by his wife, a foreigner,[35] must have done much to arouse the rage, despair, and "mad" extremism of the revolutionaries.

In this respect, the 2007 presidential campaign was a turning point in French history. For the first time, a woman was able to achieve recognition as a credible candidate for the presidency of the country. Despite the overt hostility of the men (and women) in her own party and that of her opponents, despite the criticism, sarcastic remarks, macho jeering, and even vulgar insults she had to confront, she still succeeded in winning over a large portion of the French public, garnering 47% of the vote by direct universal suffrage. Even though the male candidate was finally elected, the fact that she passed the electoral test with such success nevertheless tends to denote a significant shift in attitudes which can only enrich French culture.

MYTHS AND HISTORY

A certain interpretation of historic events suggests the hypothesis that three great myths have intersected to form the foundation of the French semantic space since the Revolution. First, the myth of the Phoenix, reflecting the continual repetition and reawakening of similar events over the course of time. Second, that of the scapegoat, the belief that the sacrifice of a victim whose "blood" must be shed in order to rid the society of a threat and provide catharsis for its primitive violence. Lastly, that of Dionysus, which expresses the rejection of diversity, reacting to it with an explosion of blind wrath and indiscriminate murderous folly.

As Tocqueville so perceptively noted, this subterranean archetypal current muddies the clarity of political discourse and contradicts rational explanations. At certain times in history, it has exerted so much pressure that it has forced the community to act out the myth, in all its ancient savagery.[36] However, the language of the myth conveys a message in an archaic language, and the message must be heard and elaborated. Otherwise, the forces it is expressing, and driven to act out, cannot be assimilated as conscious and rational motivations. I have tried to show how, since the Revolution of 1789, mythical processes, the heritage of centuries of history, have continually flared up at the very center of the large and small events occurring in the life of French society, although they have never been understood as such, or heard for what they really were. The 2005 riots in the suburbs ("*la crise des banlieues*"), for example, were a striking resurgence of the Dionysus myth. The alien, the outsider, the foreigner, was demanding that his diversity be accepted by the City and granted a place. The cold, intransigent refusal this demand elicited from the ruling party triggered the explosion of destructive drives and the irrational fury which ensued. This means that withdrawal into one's own identity and the warrior's rational position are an irresistible appeal to irrationality and blind destructiveness. In other words, the arrogant posture of the all-powerful Father cannot fail to arouse his opposite, the destructive Great Mother.

To reply to the various questions raised in this essay, the thing that haunts the French soul seems to me to be a meaning that has escaped it since the Revolution, compelling the French people incessantly to repeat events structured along similar lines. As I have shown, though the Revolution of 1789 called for major social changes, a less radical change would perhaps have been more suitable than the definitive "chopping-off" and the strange and paradoxical belief that democracy could be instituted through the zealous use of the guillotine and wanton destruction. As we have seen, this radicalism has been a theme ever since, even though, in France, persons judged guilty of "treason" and "enemies" perceived as a threat to orthodoxy are no longer beheaded in the same way! Nevertheless, through the rejection of diversity and thus of the Other, associated with a shadow which must in no case be allowed to tarnish the spirit of Enlightenment so dear to the French, ideological splits of every sort stubbornly persist in preventing any dialogue between opposites, both harming French intellectual life and endangering social stability.

It is still too early to judge whether the current openness to bipartisan decision-making displayed by the new president is merely a political maneuver or the sign of a true change of attitude. Yet, regardless of their political views, the two candidates for the 2007 presidential election will each in his or her own way have made an historical impression by forcing the French people to take a second look at their eternal divisions.

Were the French able to succeed in finding the lost meaning I have described above, they might become aware that the persistent tendency to erect the image of an ideal and all-powerful Father is, in reality, an appeal to the Mother in her most destructive and mortiferous form. Consequently, this bars access to the most fertile forms of the feminine, which is literally crushed and confined to its most archaic aspect.

Like Jung, I know that life is sense and nonsense, and that is the essence I hope to have expressed in these few reflections, truly subjective, about the history of my country, France. And I hope as anxiously and fervently as Jung did that sense will win out over nonsense, and the French will soon find a remedy for their long "illness:" the syndrome which hinders their advancement as a society and prevents them from embarking on modern life.

NOTES

1. Except England, which instituted constitutional monarchy in the 17th century.

2. 1789, 1830, 1848, 1871, etc.

3. *Correspondance Tocqueville-Kergolay*, letter dated May 16, 1858, as quoted by François Furet in *Penser la Révolution Française* (Paris, Gallimard, 1978), [trans. from French to English by Elborg Forster and published as *Interpreting the French Revolution* (Cambridge University Press, 1981.]

4. Including societies of psychoanalysts, of course.

5. Systematic trial and dismissal of all government workers refusing to take an oath of loyalty to Pétain, hunt for Jews, etc.

6. In France, the Northern and Eastern suburbs around the biggest cities are a form of ghetto.

7. Echoes the Revolution and the guillotine, but now means "resignation."

8. See, on this subject, Éliane Viennot, *La France, les femmes et le pouvoir* (Paris: Perrin, 2007).

9. Louis IX was 11 years old when he was crowned King of France upon his father's death in 1226.

10. Charles IX was only 10 when he acceded to the throne in 1560.

11. Louis XIV was five years old when he became king upon his father's death in 1643.

12. Within French borders, against the Cathars; abroad, against the Arabs.

13. They were guests invited to the wedding of the Protestant prince Henri de Navarre (later Henri IV) to Marguerite de Valois, sister of King Henri III, better known by the nickname Reine Margot.

14. In other words, a proportion of the total population comparable to the number of Jewish victims sacrificed by Vichy France during the last World War.

15. For example, the enormous political influence wielded by Cardinals Richelieu and Mazarin during the reigns of Louis XIII and Louis XIV.

16. Austria, in this case.

17. Coined by Robespierre.

18. On this theme, refer to the fascinating book by Richard D. E. Burton, *Blood in the city, violence and revelation in Paris, 1789-1945* (Ithaca and London: Cornell University Press, 2001).

19. Carried out on July 21, 1793.

20. René Girard, *Le bouc émissaire* (Paris: Grasset, 1982); *The Scapegoat*, Canadian Broadcasting Corporation (CBC Audio), September 2001.

21. Gérard Walter, *Maximilien Robespierre* (Paris: Gallimard, Coll. NRF biographies, 1989).

22. On June 21, 1791, the King and Queen fled under cover of night, but were caught and arrested at Varennes.

23. And dictated into the Napoleonic Code, which is the foundation of modern French law, that "the man is an all-powerful *pater familias.*"

24. The premier adulated by the French people from June 1940 to August 1944, who collaborated with the Germans by signing a peace treaty with them in June 1940.

25. The British and American employees of French corporations are always surprised by the lack of horizontal communication and the way it is impossible to express one's views directly, without going through the proper hierarchical channels.

26. From 1789 until the law on the separation of Church and State passed in 1905.

27. Excepting those which are classified as "cults."

28. An expression coined by F. Furet.

29. Cf. Jean Louis Faure and Pierre Pachet, *Bêtise de l'intelligence*, (Paris: Editions Joca seria, 2006).

30. The *disputatio* was a formalized debate between the participants: an *opponens* would present the objections to the initial thesis. Next, the *respondens* offered arguments to counter the objections of the *opponens,* leading to a true debate of ideas. Once all of his points had been discussed, the master of the *disputatio* handed down a final verdict as a reasoned solution, called a *determinatio.*

31. Jean-Pierre Vernant, *L'univers, les dieux, les hommes* (Paris: Seuil, 1999, [translated from the French by Linda Asher and published as *The Universe, the Gods and Mortals: Ancient Greek Myths* (New York: Harper Collins Publishers, 2001)].

32. Whose parents, "guilty" of belonging to the aristocracy, narrowly escaped the guillotine.

33. C. G. Jung, *Types psychologiques* (Genève: Georg, 1977), p. 425, *Collected Works*, vol. 6 § 709 (London: Routledge).

34. I intentionally do not use the word "men."

35. Marie Antoinette was an Austrian princess.

36. The decapitation of Louis XVI, of the Queen, the Commune, the Dreyfus affair, the Vichy Regime, etc.

BIBLIOGRAPHY

Beurtheret, Yves. *Frères réformés, si vous saviez... Ephémérides des guerres de religions.* AMDG Éditions, 2006.

Brunet, Eric. *Être de droite, un tabou français.* Paris, Albin Michel, 2006.

Burton, Richard D. E. *Blood in the city, violence and revelation in Paris, 1789-1945.* Ithaca and London, Cornell University Press, 2001.

Camus, Albert. *L'homme révolté.* Paris, NRF, 1951.

Caute, David. *The demonstration, a play.* London, André Deutsch, 1970.

Debray, Régis. *Aveuglantes Lumières.* Paris, Gallimard, 2006.

Erman, Michel. *Les mots qui ont fait élire Nicolas Sarkozy,* in Le Monde du 23 mai 2007 and Medium n° 12, 2007.

Faure, Jean Louis & Pierre Pachet. *Bêtise de l'intelligence.* Paris, Editions Joca seria, 2006.

Furet, François. *Penser la Révolution française.* Paris, Gallimard, 1978; *Interpreting the French Revolution,* translated from the French by Elborg Forster. Cambridge University Press, 1981.

Fraisse, Geneviève. *Muse de la raison, démocratie et exclusion des femmes en France.* Paris, Aliena, 1989. *Reason's Muse: Sexual Difference and the Birth of Democracy.* University of Chicago Press, 1994.

Fraisse, Genevieve. *Les femmes et leur histoire,* Paris, Gallimard, 1998. *A History of Women in the West: Emerging Feminism from Revolution to World War,* Belknap Press, Reprint 1995.

Girard, René. *Le bouc émissaire*. Paris, Grasset, 1982. *The Scapegoat*, Canadian Broadcasting Corporation (CBC Audio), September 2001.

Glucksmann, André. *Le discours de la haine*. Paris, Plon, 2004.

Jung, C. G. *Collected Works*. London, Routledge.

Jung, C. G. *Memories, Dreams, Reflexions*. New York, Vintage Books, 1989.

Pagès, Max *Le phénomène révolutionnaire, une régression créatrice*. Paris, Desclée de Brouwer, 1998.

Raynaud, Philippe. *L'extrême gauche plurielle*, Paris, Autrement, 2006.

Vernant, Jean-Pierre. *L'univers, les dieux, les hommes*. Paris, Seuil, 1999. *The Universe, the Gods and Mortals*, translated from the French by Linda Asher. New York, Harper Collins Publishers, Inc.Viennot, Éliane, *La France, les femmes et le pouvoir*, Paris, Perrin, 2007.

Voltaire. *Traité sur la tolérance*. Paris, Gallimard, 1975.

Voltaire. *Letters on the English or Lettres Philosophiques*. Whitefish, Kessinger Publishing, 2004.

Walter, Gérard. *Maximilien Robespierre*. Paris, Gallimard, Coll. NRF biographies, 1989.

LETTER FROM SWITZERLAND

MURRAY STEIN

Some years ago while attending a conference at Oxford, I had the good fortune to meet a retired British economist with a distinguished reputation from the Thatcher years who told me that he had discovered the solution to the world's political and economic problems. I couldn't help asking him to say more. He continued: "It's simple. All the countries of the world should become like Switzerland." It was that plain to him! Every country in the world should shrink its size to around 5 or 6 million inhabitants, reduce its tax rates to the levels enjoyed in most of the Swiss cantons, educate its people to the nearly one hundred percent literacy rate of the Swiss, instill the values of hard work, cleanliness, and sobriety, and so forth.

Murray Stein, Ph.D., is a graduate of the C. G. Jung Institute in Zurich and is a training analyst at the International School of Analytical Psychology in Zurich. He is a founding member of the Inter-Regional Society for Jungian Analysts (USA) and the Chicago Society of Jungian Analysts, and was President of the International Association for Analytical Psychology from 2001 to 2004. He has written several books, including *The Principle of Individuation: Toward the Development of Consciousness* (Chiron, 2006); *Transformation: Emergence of the Self*, Carolyn and Ernest Fay Lecture Series (Texas A & M University Press, new ed., 2005); *Jung's Map of the Soul: An Introduction* (Open Court, 1998); *Jung's Treatment of Christianity: The Psychotherapy of a Religious Tradition* (Chiron, 1985); and *In MidLife: A Jungian Perspective* (Spring Publications, 1983). He is also the editor of *Jungian Analysis* and of the Chiron Clinical Series.

I am not sure if he also included that they should promote the typical Swiss values of psychological introversion and political neutrality, but probably he did.

Having lived in Switzerland now for four years, I agree with him. If the rest of the world would only be more like this country, it would be a finer planet. There would be a lot less war and a lot more prosperity and contentment. (I cannot speak for creativity, which seems to thrive on a certain amount of chaos and polarization.) But alas, there can be only one Switzerland. It is so very specific.

Sometimes the Swiss are criticized for being conservative and behind the times. At the present moment in Switzerland's history, however, a woman, Micheline Calmy-Rey, holds the title of President. Calmy-Rey is a member of the Social Democratic Party (SP), which of the four major political parties in Switzerland is the furthest to the left and in recent years has lost much of its political influence, while the right-wing Swiss People's Party has exploded in numbers and importance. The President comes from the Canton of Geneva in the French-speaking part of the country, less powerful than the German Cantons to the north, though tremendously elegant and international. In addition to this position, she holds the title of Foreign Minister, and in that regard has been criticized for showing too little neutrality with respect to the conflict between Israel and the Palestinians. While Switzerland lagged behind other Western nations, especially the United States, in granting voting rights to women (by referendum only in 1972), it is not at all a laggard in advancing women to high office. The Swiss (along with the English and the Germans) have beaten the U.S. to the goal of putting a woman into the highest political office in the land. Still, women are not doing so well in the executive suites of the Swiss businesses.

In Switzerland, it should be said, the Presidency is a far cry from the dominant political presence it is in the United States. The position rotates annually among the seven members of the "Bundesrat," the Federal Councilors, so no-one gets terribly identified with the role. The Bundesrat as a body holds executive authority in the country, and the President speaks for that body, not in advance or beyond it. The seven Federal Councilors constitute an Executive Committee of the Parliament, and the positions in this important body are filled by a vote of the Members of Parliament every six years.

A rather special feature of the Bundesrat's functioning is that it operates by consensus. Switzerland therefore always has a coalition government. The major parties must all agree on policies carried out by the Federal government. The result is the well known glacially slow movement in Swiss political affairs. It is sometimes wrongfully said that everything happens ten years later in Switzerland than anywhere else. This is because consensus is not achieved easily or quickly, especially in times such as these when there is severe polarization around issues like immigration, asylum seekers, participation in the European Community, the role of the military, and agricultural subsidies. On most important issues that affect the lives of the majority of the people, there are deep fissures among the political parties. The President of the country must represent the consensual standpoint of the seven Councilors, and only after that does she also represent the country as a whole on certain official occasions.

The four major parties of the Swiss electorate cover a range in the political spectrum from fairly moderate left (the Social Democratic Party) to pretty far right (the Swiss People's Party), with two parties (the Christian Democratic People's Party and the Free Democratic Party) standing in the middle and altering the balance of power now a bit in favor of the left, now of the right. In addition, there are eleven smaller parties that extend the spectrum to both left and right and do have some voice in political affairs but cannot muster enough votes to make a difference in the Federal Parliament. From time to time these threaten the majors and produce a political dust up in the press.

This country is a construction that took some six centuries to come together. It consists of twenty-three Cantons, or states, each of which has its own distinctive character, history, and set of local governments and communities. Some Cantons were members of the Swiss Confederation since its beginning in the 14th Century; others joined as late as the 19th Century. The inhabitants of these Cantons speak four languages (German, French, Italian, and a dialect of old Latin called Romanish), and all of them are represented in the Federal Parliament in Bern. Creating Federal law is a translation nightmare. The twenty-three Cantons, like the fifty U.S. states, retain a good deal of autonomy and local authority. Each is able to pass laws, to set and raise taxes, and to run schools. When a particular issue affects the country as a whole, the Swiss hold a national referendum. Every citizen has a vote on the big issues. The individual counts. It was such a referendum that gave women the vote in 1972 and another that narrowly kept Switzerland out of the European Community in the 1990's. All things considered, the Federal government is less powerful and oppressive in Switzerland than it is in the United States: As the president is a weaker figure, so the Federal government has less authority over the lives of the citizens. The greatest share of tax money is collected by the Cantons, not by the Federal government.

Four parties, four languages—Jung was impressed by this number as a symbol of wholeness, and for him Switzerland symbolized a political solution to the problems of difference and diversity that was able to hold polarizations in tension instead of seeking to eliminate them in favor of uniformity. So much that is typically and specifically Swiss can also be said about Jung. For the Swiss as for Jung, the individual retains the highest value. At the same time, group pressure toward conformity within the small Swiss communities (the Gemeinde, the basic atomic units of the Swiss political system) can be extreme.

While the Swiss tend naturally and instinctively to look inward, reality forces them also to look cautiously outward at the larger world. Switzerland lies exactly in the heart of Middle Europe. If I've heard it once, I've heard it a hundred times: Switzerland is a tiny country surrounded by giants. There is Germany to the north, Italy to the south, France to the west, and Austria to the east. To survive through the many centuries of bitter military conflict among these adjoining monsters, the Swiss have clung doggedly to a position that they refer to as neutrality. They have had to be careful not to step on the tail of a nearby sleeping tiger. This is the reason for their policy of neutrality. If they had taken sides with France and the Allies in WWI, for instance, they would have become the enemy and therefore the target of the aggressive armies of Germany and Austria. In WWII, they were terrified of an attack from Germany and its allies, which surrounded Switzerland, and so they carefully maintained a neutral position throughout the war years. This neutrality is not seen as a particularly ethical or moral position or as the privilege of elite, but rather as a rational defense of the small against the threat of invasion by the large. Over the centuries, the attitude of neutrality has seeped into the very bones of the Swiss. Non-committal, even-handed, seeing both sides of an argument, refusing to engage in treaties and staying clear of foreign partnerships, the result has been that Switzerland remained outside the United Nations until only very recently, declined the invitation to join the European Union, and continues to hold itself apart from foreign entanglements. At the same time, it is famous for the global reach of its businesses and as being the home of many international agencies. Switzerland is by no means free of paradox and contradiction.

I asked my neighbor in Zurich—a retired Swiss international businessman who lived abroad for many years, including more than a decade in the United States, a country he continues to admire and to visit with pleasure—why Switzerland declined joining the European Union. "It would mean another level of rules and regulations," he said, "and the Swiss have enough of these. They don't want to be told further what to do and not to do—by Brussels!" There may be other important reasons for staying at arms length from the European collective, but it is true that many Swiss feel their lives are already overregulated. They cherish their independence and freedom, and they do not relish having foreign politicians regulating their lives from beyond their close borders.

The Swiss do not see themselves as better than others; they just want to go on living quietly and securely in their mountain retreat. They are individual, and not oriented by group pressure. They tend to think for themselves. Small and local are seen as better and safer than large and collective. They are suspicious of the big and the powerful. They have no interest in setting up colonies, and imperialism is not in their history. On the contrary, they prefer to stay at home and mind their own business. Paradoxically, however, their businesses reach far afield into the global scene. The country thrives economically today because of its big internationals. They have two of the world's largest banks housed in Zurich, some of the world's largest pharmaceutical companies in Basel, and other important international manufacturing and engineering firms (like the Georg Fischer Company in Schaffhausen). The Swiss have a mentality that is at once profoundly provincial and amazingly global—a *complexio oppositorum*.

Swiss neutrality and particularity, it goes without saying, is not without its shadow features. To compensate for their insularity, the Swiss have famously made themselves hospitable to asylum seekers from around the world. But the steady influx of culturally diverse peoples has also created problems and pushed the electorate to the right in recent times. A furious debate has taken place in the past year between the liberals who favor leniency and greater numbers of political refugees and the right-wing Swiss People's Party that wants to place tighter restrictions and rules on entry. The country is quite evenly divided between the two camps. Unfamiliar bouts of violence and unrest in some secondary schools and increased crime rates have fueled anxiety. Recently a proposal to build a large mosque in Bern heightened tensions and led to discussions in the press and on TV about religious tolerance. Switzerland is discovering it is not so different from its neighbors after all. They share the same identical problems, though perhaps on a smaller scale, with Western European friends and neighbors like France, Germany, the Netherlands, and the United Kingdom.

If anything it seems today, therefore, that instead of other countries becoming more like Switzerland, in fact Switzerland is becoming like the other countries, for better or worse. My Oxford acquaintance must find this disheartening.

JUNGIANA

Embodied Imagination: A Conversation with Robert Bosnak

BARBARA PLATEK

Introduction

Robert Bosnak is a Jungian analyst in Sydney, Australia. Born and raised in the Netherlands, he earned a law degree from Leiden University before receiving his Diploma from the C. G. Jung Institute in Zurich. He maintained an analytic practice for twenty-six years in Boston, where he also served as a training analyst at the Boston Jung Institute. He is the past president of the Association for the Study of Dreams, and was a visiting professor of clinical psychology in Kyoto, Japan. In the late seventies, he pioneered a method of working with dreams that he calls "embodied imagination," and he currently holds dream practicums throughout the world as well as in cyberspace. He is the author of four books about dreamwork: *Embodiment: Creative Imagination in Art, Medicine, and Travel* (Routledge, 2007); *A Little Course in Dreams* (Shambhala, new ed., 1998); *Dreaming with an AIDS*

Barbara Platek, M.A., LMHC, is a Jungian-oriented psychotherapist and author in Ithaca, New York. A graduate of Pacifica Graduate Institute, she has completed four years of training with the Ontario Association of Jungian Analysts.

Patient (Diane Pub Co., 1997); and *Tracks in the Wilderness of Dreaming* (Delta, 1997).

I interviewd Bosnak in October 2006, at a home overlooking the East shore of Seneca Lake, about twenty miles from Ithaca, New York. Bosnak had just returned from Australia via time spent in Amsterdam, and was preparing for a dream practicum that same evening. The afternoon was perfectly crisp and beautiful, and we had a distant view of the lake. We sat together, a woodstove nearby and two large dogs at our feet, and I was reminded again of his willingness to challenge preconceived notions of dreaming, including his own, and his seemingly endless desire to explore the landscape of the dreaming mind.

THE INTERVIEW

Platek: You have worked with dreams professionally for more than thirty years. You travel all over the world running dream groups, you teach dream work, you write books on dreaming: why is it important for people to pay attention to their dreams?

Bosnak: Well, first let me say that I am not sure whether it is important for people to pay attention to their dreams. In some cultures they believe that we only dream when we are sick, for example. So I don't know whether it is objectively important that people pay attention to their dreams. I can say, however, that I first became interested in my dreams while in analysis, and that they proved very useful. I think that once we pay attention to dreams, they are absolutely fascinating. And once we bring attention to our dreams, they have a tendency to become helpful in the healing process, in the creative process, and in our relationships.

Platek: I think it would be fair to say that our culture has lost touch with the dreaming process. Most people today place far more emphasis on external events than on exploring their internal landscapes. In fact, I recently heard an article on National Public Radio suggesting the fact that widespread use of antidepressants and sleep medications may be causing people to remember fewer dreams.

Bosnak: My reading of the research suggests that antidepressants like Prozac may increase dream recall. So there doesn't have to be a conflict between psychopharmacology and dreaming. But we have been at a cultural low point in terms of interest in dreams. Interest peaked in the 60's and 70's, and then we hit a lull. At this point, though, we may be experiencing a resurgence. Wherever I have traveled, I have experienced a new interest in dreaming on a global level. In fact, I have just returned from Amsterdam where they celebrated Freud's 150th birthday with a big event at the National Theater called The Night of The Dream. This event was sold out two months in advance. Dreaming and other forms of imagination are becoming interesting to people again.

Platek: The ancient Greeks had a particular understanding of how dreams healed. People would sleep inside a special temple dedicated to the god Asclepios in order to have a dream that might cure them of their illness—whether mental or physical. They believed that the god would appear in their dream and cure them directly. What do you think happens when we dream?

Bosnak: People in every culture of the world—while dreaming—are convinced that they are awake and surrounded by a real world. So the only thing we can say for sure is that, while dreaming, we are in a quasi-physical environment where events take place and where the environment feels utterly real. We can touch a table, smell flowers—all our senses are engaged in the dream. Of course we know that the dream is not an actual physical environment because as soon as we awaken, the physicality evaporates. That's why I call it a quasi-physical environment. While we are dreaming, we are someplace. We can know this simply by observing the phenomenon. Anything else we say about dreams is really just conjecture.

Platek: You mean we can't really know anything else about dreams directly?

Bosnak: Everything we have to say about dreaming is entirely shaped by the culture we are in. The only thing we know for sure is that, while dreaming we are somewhere, something happens to us, and we are in an environment that we believe to be real at the time. So here in our Western individualist culture, we believe that dreams are about us. But this belief says nothing about dreams, it only says that we are individualists.

Platek: You certainly have traveled to many cultures to explore dreaming and dream work. In the book *Tracks in the Wilderness of Dreaming*, you describe sitting with an Aboriginal spirit doctor to discuss your respective work with dreams. How did being in that culture influence your sense of the dreaming process?

Bosnak: Well, I was only able to do that because I was completely and utterly naive! I did not know very much about Aboriginal culture. I know a bit more now, but then it was as if I'd landed on another other planet. But that's where I learned with enormous shock that the notion that our dreams are about us is entirely culturally based. For example, a woman told me that a dream was created by the Mountain in order that a dance could be created and the Mountain could experience that dance. That is a very different way of looking at dreams. Even so, it is a cultural perspective.

Platek: I am thinking about your original training at the Jung Institute in Zurich. You tell a story about attending a class in which everyone was asked to interpret a dream, even though the dreamer was not present. That approach felt disembodied to you—in fact you call your own style of working with dreams "embodied imagination." You clearly feel that it is important to bring body into work with dreams.

Bosnak: A dream is not an intellectual occurrence. When we dream, our whole body is involved. In fact, neuroscience has disproved the notion that cognition is central to dreaming. Neuroscientists fight about many things, but the one thing they all agree upon is that affects and emotions shape dreams. Affects and emotions are physical. And we know from neuroscience that the affective system runs throughout the entire body, that it is not just centered in the brain. So, if our dreams are shaped by affects, then it stands to reason that our work with dreams needs to be affect-focused. And when we work with affects, we are of course working with the body.

Platek: Perhaps you could describe something of how this process of embodied imagination works—how you actually work with a dream.

Bosnak: The first thing we do is move back into a state of consciousness that is more like the dream consciousness. So, for example, at the Jung Institute, we stayed in our usual waking consciousness to look at dreams. I like to have people move in to a state just between waking and sleeping, what the sleep laboratories call the hypnagogic state. This is a kind of liminal state where we hover just above the sleep state without actually falling asleep. From within that state of consciousness, we re-enter the dream as an actual environment. Here's the interesting thing. When we re-enter the dream from the hypnagogic state we can trigger what we call a flashback experience. The notion of a flashback memory comes out of trauma work. Flashback memory works differently than ordinary memory. With ordinary memory we remember the narrative. So, for example, you might remember entering through the door, greeting me, sitting down with your recording device, beginning our conversation, and so on. You recall a narrative in a linear sequence. In a flashback memory, however, the whole environment is present—smells, sensations—even things we were not consciously aware of the first time around. It all comes back in its entire form.

Platek: And you are attempting to create a flashback experience in the dream work?

Bosnak: Exactly. My feeling is that the best memory with which to work with dreams is flashback memory. So we essentially create an artificial flashback. We are trying to sense what is happening to us in the dream environment. When you work on dreams using narrative memory—like at the Jung Institute—you are using a completely different mode of the brain. If you were to do brain imagery, you would see that a different part of the brain is activated in each case. We are trying to physically feel the dream and its experiences.

Platek: This is a very different notion of dream work than that of the analyst mining the dream for important insights and life-changing "aha" moments.

Bosnak: Trying to understand conceptually what is going on is a fool's errand with dreams. The important thing about being in the hypnagogic state and using the flashback is that we can slow things down. In this slowing-down process, the details of the dream really begin to become apparent. The more we slow down the experience of the dream, the more it can begin to enter the body. And this includes the experience of the dreaming ego—the "I" character in the dream— as well as that of the other characters. I see self as a habit of consciousness. We can move out of this self by identifying with the other characters in the dream using a kind of interior miming—like an actor might do. So we feel these states in the body, locate where they are felt most intensely, and then we "etch" them into the body, so to speak—we implant them in the body so that when they are activated the whole experience comes back. At the end of the work we have many states that can be triggered simultaneously. Many of them are completely incompatible emotional states. But this has always been the grail of psychoanalysis: to hold incompatible states without splitting them off. When we can hold all these states at the same time—even those arising from other characters and perspectives in the dream—it changes our way of being in the world.

Platek: I have had the opportunity to participate in your dream groups. My sense is that emotional healing occurs not only for the dreamer—as he or she moves more deeply into the dream environment—but for those participating as well. It seems that the dream itself has a kind of atmosphere that others can experience.

Bosnak: We are moving around in a world. That is the definition of dream that I am using. When we use flashback, the others also participate in the flashback environment. This is a privileged participation in someone's most intimate life. Through this we experience our own most intimate experience, and we begin to realize that, even though intimacy feels personal, it can also be collective. So we are in a collective state of intimacy with an environment that feels important to the dreamer and actually becomes important for everyone there. Even people who don't remember their dreams sometimes come to these groups. They find it valuable to touch the experience, to become part of the dreaming. It is a very different world from the waking one.

Platek: You have developed a special form of dream work, one that you call "somatic" dream work, which you have developed in your work with people with AIDS, cancer, and other serious illnesses. How does this way of working with dreams promote healing?

Bosnak: We don't quite know what somatic dream work does. We only began to do some scientific research on it a few years ago. We do know from patient testimonials, though, that this type of working with dreams and the body does something that the patient appreciates. Of course, that doesn't mean there are measurable scientific effects. It just means that the patient likes the outcome of the work. This type of working with dreams is based upon what I call classical medicine. You mentioned the Asclepian model earlier—where the sick person would go to the temple to have a dream to cure him or her of illness. In classical antiquity, Asclepian medicine went hand in hand with Hippocratic medicine.

Platek: Hippocratic medicine is what we think of as conventional medicine.

Bosnak: Yes. Our doctors still take the Hippocratic oath. Hippocratic medicine works on the body as object. That is its force as well as its lack. Asclepian medicine, on the other hand, works with dreams and imagination. At the beginning of Western medicine, dreams were thought to be important to the healing process. Imagination was important. Classical medicine had these two forms of medicine, the Asclepian and Hippocratic, intertwined. That is what I am interested in. These two streams of Western medicine that were initially intertwined and then split—I would like to see them brought together again. So, for example, when a person is sick, they go for Hippocratic treatment. Hippocratic medicine has accomplished extraordinary things. I have enormous respect for this form of treatment; without it, I would be dead. But again, this method sees the body as object. We have no sense of agency here. We are being worked upon.

Platek: Like bringing our car in for repair.

Bosnak: Yes. But this creates a passive state of being worked upon in the patient. What the imagination side does is create a sense of receptivity in us, in the body. We can be active in our own treatment. My notion is that when we create receptivity in the person, then the overall treatment can be more effective. This is the classical combination—both the body treatment side and the imaginal receptive side. I work on the receptive end, not the treatment end. So, if a person has cancer, for example, we can have them incubate dreams about cancer.

Platek: I believe that the term "incubate" comes from the process of sleeping in the Asclepian temple and awaiting a dream.

Bosnak: That's right. Dream incubation is a method of intentional dreaming. It is a way of seeding dreams. In ancient times, if we went to the dream temple and brought our illness, we assumed that the illness would seed our dreams and that the god of healing would come. So, with the cancer, we also attempt to seed dreams. We call upon the body to imagine. We say to the body: "please give me your imaginings about what is going on with you." We offer the body an imagined experience of the poison in the illness and then ask it to start imagining. Then we work with those imaginings, those dreams. When we are able to enter into the imagination of the body, it can be more open to the treatment it is receiving. Someone with cancer told me recently that when they go for their chemotherapy, they imagine their treatment as a kind of healing poison. This is a similar idea. The people I work with in this way tell me that it makes the quality of their life better. I think it goes beyond simply improving quality of life to actually improving the treatment itself. Of course, we still have to prove this. It is incumbent upon us to show scientifically that what we are doing is useful.

Platek: Do you think this work actually affects biochemistry?

Bosnak: I do. I think that neuroscience has more or less proved that this kind of work affects neurochemistry. That no longer needs to be proven. But what are we going to do with this? That is my great interest. What does the treatment center of the future look like? We are trying to start such a place in Santa Barbara, California. Our intention is to create a center where Hippocratic and Asclepian medicine can happen side by side. I believe that in this kind of environment the treatment will work better than just doing the standard medical treatment on its own. And we will be scientifically evaluating to see whether these methods on the receptive end really help.

Platek: After the events of 9/11, you and others set up a Nightmare Hotline in New York City. You have mentioned that you received many dreams of terrorists and planes falling out of the sky, even by those who were not directly impacted by the events that day. It sounds like you were working with the way that this trauma impacted our collective psyche.

Bosnak: That was my sense, as well. But the interesting thing is that the trauma came out in personal images. A traumatic event like 9/11 triggers personal memories that are similar to the current event. In other words, trauma triggers previous trauma. This is because we are always responding from within an associative network. That was Freud's brilliance to tell us that we are always in an associative network. For example, when the plane flew into that apartment building on the West Side of Manhattan recently, a lot of people were likely dreaming of 9/11—that is the associative process happening. So then we might get a person calling up the Response Line with a nightmare about 9/11 that was actually triggered by this more recent event and even, perhaps, compounded with the time they fell out of a tree when they were five years old, and so forth. All of these trauma responses are in a kind of interactive pattern. We had to change the name, by the way. It is now called the Nightmare Response Line. That's because we don't actually provide treatment. Instead, people are just debriefed of their nightmares, which is already a very useful thing. This is especially true for children. Children have a lot of nightmares. It is helpful for them to know that they can call and talk to someone for ten or fifteen minutes about their nightmare and receive an empathic response. Empathic responses are intensely useful for nightmare sufferers. We are obviously a society in a nightmare, and that nightmare is being manipulated all the time by the politicians. So it is important to debrief people of their nightmares. Nightmares have become one of the central political issues of our time. The nightmare is called terrorism.

Platek: You have written that terror is at the heart of psychoanalysis: that psychotherapists work with the soul in agony. How can dreams help us with experiences of terror and the anxiety and depression they leave in their wake?

Bosnak: The way that I look at the psyche is as a multiplicity of selves with a tendency to dissociate. This tendency is actually a helpful process. If we were to experience trauma directly, for instance, it would be horrendous. The dissociation protects us from having to feel the trauma fully. There are selves that have experienced this trauma, but they are left out of our awareness. This work with nightmares and trauma allows those disconnected selves to reattach to our habitual network of consciousness. At the end of the work, we have a larger energetic system than before. Before doing the work, there was a smaller system characterized by fear and terror. Actually, the fear and terror are about the possibility of the terror happening in the future.

Platek: Fear that the trauma that has already occurred will take place in the future.

Bosnak: Yes. The work diminishes the fear of the trauma happening in the future because it allows reattachment of the experience of having had it in the past. It allows us to experience the trauma that happened without dissociating. This lessens the fear for the future, because we have more fully experienced the actual event. I think that one of the ways in which the Bush administration is able to manipulate fear of terrorism is because much of what happened on 9/11 was dissociated. So people fear it for the future instead of reattaching to what happened. As long as we have not fully experienced what happened, we are very suggestible, and this can be used for political profit.

Platek: I have heard you suggest that dreams are the purest form of creativity that we can experience, that they are our closest connection to the creative force in the universe.

Bosnak: In dreams we experience pure imagination. During waking life, we also experience the imagination, but there is a physical world present. In the dream state everything is comprised of imagination. I think there is enormous advantage in dealing with this pure imagination. By allowing it to inform us, we can touch the creative process in a real way. In the dreaming process, we are exposed to the unconventional, the unexpected. Most of us fall into a routine. If there is anything that can break us out of routine, it is dreaming.

Platek: So you are saying that work with dreams can move us out of our habitual standpoint?

Bosnak: Yes. I like to imagine that we have access to a large number of actors or characters. Typically, one or two of these takes center stage and jealously guard their leading roles like divas. The rest of the cast winds up being part of the chorus. What this means, of course, is that a whole lot of our potential is not being used.

Platek: Perhaps an example would be useful. Let's say that a person's leading actor is "ambition."

Bosnak: Okay. So, the ambitious self sees only through the eyes of ambition. It does not recognize the importance of anything other than that perspective, such as being with one's children, walking through a field, and so on. Naturally, there are other selves, other actors, that would like to do these things, but they have been pushed to the background. But it is possible to work with the dreams so that the person can have an experience of these other actors. For example, a dream might allow the ambitious diva to see itself through the eyes of another character, a small child, say. It is not that the person should suddenly abandon the ambitious character and become a small child. The point is not to flip into another self. But the small child should also be allowed to enter the drama, to take its place on the stage.

Platek: The various facets of our psyche can begin to influence each other through work with dreams.

Bosnak: Right. And if we can have more actors involved in the act, we can have a greater show.

Platek: You speak about dreams as providing tracks into the wilderness of who we are. This seems especially important as we are constantly bombarded by messages about who we should be. In other words, if we trace our dreams over time, we might get some sense of the direction that our lives are trying to go—dreams can help us stay connected to what really matters to us.

Bosnak: I have this fantasy that dreaming is connected to our sense of direction. We are constantly trying to figure out where we are, where we are headed. I am a traveler and I find myself in strange places all the time. So this is my fantasy. I think that when we work on dreams, when we expand our sense of our many selves, we are honing our sense of direction. I don't think that dreaming provides a conceptual sense of where we need to go, but it can make us more sensitive to direction. I have observed this through my work. I have seen that when people work with dreams, when they enlarge their sense of the many characters influencing their lives, when they work with imagination, they create a more differentiated sense of direction. I think this is so important in the world because, as you say, we are constantly being bombarded and if we don't have a sense of direction, we get lost or become completely conventional. We need a good sense of direction, and I think that can be trained by working with dreams to include as many elements or selves as possible.

Platek: Have you seen this in your own life?

Bosnak: Oh, absolutely. I just made a huge move from the United States to Australia, and I could not have done that if I hadn't worked on my sense of direction for many years by allowing many images to participate in the decision process.

Platek: In the end, dreams seem to be truly mysterious. In your book, *Dreaming with an AIDS Patient,* you initially hope that your work with Christopher, your client, will make him well. Instead, he dies during the course of your work together. How would you explain healing—the way that dreams bring healing—in the context of what happened there?

Bosnak: Christopher died differently than he would have if we hadn't done the work together. One of the things that is said about the god Asclepios is that he cheated death, and he was punished for that. We cannot cheat death. Death will always happen. But death does not mean that the treatment has failed. If we had not done the work, Christopher would have died a death that he perceived as meaningless and as punishment for his homosexuality and his fast lifestyle. He would have died in a prison of punishment. Instead, his death occurred within a context of a spiritual experience that allowed him to feel received into the arms of another world. That experience helped quiet down his death experience—not that he didn't struggle, he absolutely did not want to die. And if he had had AIDS fifteen years later, he would not have died, he would be living with a chronic illness. But, in the end, he died with a sense of being received by another world, a world that was kind to him. That is hugely different from dying as a form of punishment.

Platek: It is also highlights a difference between the Asclepian and Hippocratic methods of healing. From the Hippocratic perspective, death is seen as a failure of treatment.

Bosnak: Yes, that's true. Naturally, when we are ill we want to live as long as possible. That is, unless we are in unbearable pain that can't be relieved. But for the Asclepian strand of medicine, there are other life elements that are just as important as the length of existence. Dreams allow us to experience these other elements. That is why we need both. We need to weave both these aspects of healing back into our method of treatment. That is the classical medicine of the future.

FILM REVIEWS

LA VIE EN ROSE. Marion Cotillard, Gerard Depardieu, Sylvie Testud, Pascal Greggory, Emmanuelle Seigner, Pauline Burlet, Jean-Pierre Martins. Written by Oliver Dahan and Isabelle Sobelman. Directed by Oliver Dahan.

REVIEWED BY DELDON ANNE MCNEELY

I was having coffee with some friends and mentioned that a film about the life of Edith Piaf was playing and I wanted to see it. Said one, "Don't go see that! My wife saw it and it was horribly depressing...she really regretted seeing it!" I couldn't imagine what could be more depressing than watching television news on any given day in America, so I entered into *La Vie en Rose*—a French film that cannot be technically called a biography, but better an impressionist expression of the source of Piaf's soulful voice. For those who want all the facts of her life, there are many biographies of Piaf available. This film does not attempt to be complete, only psychologically accurate.

La Vie en Rose introduces us to Edith Giovanna Garrison as a child and takes us through significant phases in her life until her death at

Deldon Anne McNeely, Ph.D., ABPP, is a Jungian analyst practicing in Virginia Beach. She is the author of several books and published articles, and is a training analyst with the Inter-Regional Society of Jungian Analysts and the New Orleans Jungian Seminar.

age 47. Director Oliver Dahan's intention is to portray "what drives the artist." He has said in interviews that he sees Piaf as someone who placed no barrier between her life and her art—a fitting vision for this emotionally and cinematically dark, disorderly mess. The plot jumps around, flashbacking on flashbacks, pulling us from one catastrophic scene to another in a different time and place. There's no rest for the wicked—or the wounded. There is squalor. There are drugs. Abandonment abounds. Over and over we endure being literally wrenched from the arms of the one being who has shown some iota of caring or loyalty—wrenched by the police, by would-be saviors, by sickness, and by death.

We begin to feel something akin to sad relief when we realize the end is near; but just before breathing its last labored breath, the blasted movie jumps back to a scene of Edith and a child. It seems she had a daughter which we hadn't heard of before now. Just when we thought we might get out of here, more life and another soul-wrenching experience of abandonment and death. Now can we die, please?

Sacré merde. Like Edith, this movie is a spectacular, holy broken glass of champagne. I loved it. Loved her, loved the authentic scenery and costuming, loved the lighting and the play of chiaroscuro, the effect of her bright red lips and bright red blood in the immense darkness, loved the acting, loved every character: the doomed parents, the psychotic prostitute, the exquisitely alluring and charismatic lover, the compassionate friends and hapless entourage, but most of all, the intrepid Edith, her defiance of death, her devotion to Saint Teresa, and her irresistible voice—that spirit messenger from the other world beyond the world.

If we need to be reminded of the psychological fallout from parental neglect, of the ambivalence of the abused child, we have it all. We feel her contempt for the groveling mother, her idealization of the male mentors and lover, her seeking comfort in oblivion, her mocking of authority, and most palpably, beneath it all, her fear. Time and again she is forced to push through devastating fear because life will not let her go. Fear of sickness, of blindness, of nauseating stage-fright, of not having access to the blessed drug, but always, of loneliness, the unquenchable and lifelong loneliness of the orphan.

Although Edith had parents, she was a virtual orphan. In this fluid schema we viewers must piece together for ourselves the chronological facts of her paradoxical life, which are presented in a brilliant array of disconnected images that may be deathbed memories, or just a montage of the director's choosing. She was born in 1915 in a destitute section of Paris known as Belleville, but the movie enters her childhood at about the age of four, as she watches her mother singing on the street for coins. Through the artistry of cinematographer Tetsuo Nagata the muted scenery, costumes, and makeup envelop us viewers in the moth-eaten, rough and cruddy fabric of penury. We see that Mother is young and ravaged by illness, alcoholism, or drug addiction, and unable to care for little Edith (Manon Chevallier) who is scabby, sick, and filthy.

Father comes home from military service and rescues Edith, moving her from a life of deprivation to one of depravity, by taking her to his mother's brothel in Normandy, while he disappears again. One dynamic that runs through Edith's life, as it does through all Dionysian conditions, is the play of simultaneous pleasure and pain. Grandmother is a cold and barely adequate maternal figure, and the brothel exposes Edith to appalling scenes of abusive treatment of the women by their disgusting customers. These scenes are not shoved in our faces, but are brought to our awareness through brief, barely exposed images which convey more horror by their delicacy of coverage than outright blatantly sexual scenes could do. But the child enjoys the attention of the prostitutes who introduce the joys of the flesh by bathing and feeding her, taking her for walks, and cheerily showing her how to play. Color becomes a welcomed feature in some of these scenes.

Titane (Emmanuelle Seigner) is a troubled young prostitute who falls into an enchanted state immediately upon seeing Edith for the first time, and projects her wishes for divine comfort on their relationship. When Edith goes blind as a result of an eye disease, Titane takes her to the shrine of Ste. Therese of Lisieux and teaches her to pray. This is a significant scene, as Dahan continually makes the film, like Edith and her life, a study of contrasts. Edith, the angel-child, on her knees with eyes toward heaven, lives on in the fierce, foul-mouthed hellion that Edith becomes at times in her adulthood. Titane, so sincere in her goodness, is subject to demonically crazy episodes. Edith recovers her sight, and the two wounded orphans cling to each other until they are dragged apart by Edith's father, now needing her to join his circus lifestyle.

The scenes now include adolescent Edith (Pauline Burlet) and her contortionist father as they struggle to survive in the tension of pre-World War II France. We see her debut as a singer when a street crowd demands something of her as well as of her father and he pushes her forward to perform. She manages her terror by remembering *La Marseillaise*, and reveals a voice that is at once sweet and thrilling, with just a soupcon of the grit that will mark the mature voice. (One of the aspects of Piaf's life that the film omits is her reputation for having an important role in the French resistance. Her war efforts included entertaining and posing for pictures with French POWs and participating in making fake passports for escapees.)

Marion Cotillard takes up the role of Piaf at about age eighteen with amazing skill at lip-synching, maneuvering the mood swings and physical changes through thirty years of drama, and offering to us the woman in all her contradictions. Edith's lifelong companion through the underworld is friend Momone (Sylvie Testud), and the two of them as young women seem destined for lives of women of the street. But that archetypal orphan captures the imagination of an entrepreneur, Louis Leplee, played majestically by Gerard Depardieu. He divines the vulnerable little bird behind the feisty, in-your-face street singer, christens her *La Mome Piaf* (a colloquialism for little sparrow), and employs her in his disreputable nightclub. Street-sparrow, *paraclete*— the passionate cry of that orphan, destined, at least for a while, to survive her fear, reaches us in the soul's deep. When Leplee is murdered, Edith is suspect because of her underworld associations, and she withdraws into the street scene again for a time, but then contacts Raymond Asso who becomes her Pygmalion. She is said to have given him credit for making her a human being.

The movie is vague about Piaf's men, two marriages, and numerous lovers. We are left unsure about whether her daughter, Marcelle, is a figment of Piaf's drug-induced fantasy or an actual child and left wondering if it is more than coincidence that hers is also the name of Piaf's great love, the middle-weight world champion boxer, Marcel Cerdan (Jean-Pierre Martins). Other sources indicate the child came first, early and briefly in Edith's life.

Seen through a psychoanalytic lens, the passionate affair between Edith and Marcel is a classic example of therapeutic transference that cannot be worked through. Originally Edith treats Marcel with casual disdain, imposing self-absorbed demands which would have driven less confident men to grab their crotches and run for their lives. She is, after all, not just another exhausting narcissistic personality, but an international celebrity. (Marlene Dietrich called her voice "the soul of Paris;" she was on intimate terms with Yves Montand, Jean Cocteau, Charles Aznavour, and so on). Marcel sees through the tough-girl show and deflects insulting psychic blows with the empathic aplomb of a martial artist or a seasoned analyst. Edith melts and adores him.

As hot as Marcel is as lover, he is cool and realistic in his openly double life as a happily married pig-farmer in a desperate love affair. When he is on his way to be with her, Edith begs him to take a plane, so eager is she to be with him. That is a fatal flight. Edith can accept the reality that he will never be completely hers, but not his ironically tragic death. The scene of her creating their reunion in fantasy, and then being forced to see the hard truth, is one of the most powerful of the entire movie, and probably one of the most taxing from an actor's view: For those who accept the Dionysian way, Cotillard in her all-stops-barred style is a maenad, magnificent and convincing. After this abandonment to trump all abandonments, Edith retreats from reality for some time. (Biographers report that she continued to try to reach him beyond the grave, and spent much of her fortune on occultists.)

It is not clear how much her morphine habit requiring multiple injections per day is a result of physical pain—she suffered car crashes and other illnesses, became frail and bent with arthritis—and how much is a balm for psychic anguish. In any case she does not endure her dependency or her carrot-juice cocktails gracefully, and her death scene is creatively filmed in close-up and flashbacks to illustrate her ambivalent journey. Exhausting as it was, I wanted her life to go on longer; forty-seven years was not enough, but her longevity would have been for my selfish need, not hers.

Perhaps the fact that there is no Hollywood ending is what makes some viewers less than appreciative of this work, but then Piaf never expected American audiences to understand her. Anticipating failure at her first engagement in the United States, she said, "I don't get them and they don't get me." That turned out to be not quite true. Americans and much of the rest of the world took her in. Why? Would any other singer with such a vibrant vibrato and unique musical phrasing have ignited such idolatry? Was it dumb luck that brought her into the limelight with the rich and famous? Perhaps it was the gestalt, the petite frame around the astoundingly large and gravelly sound that fascinates us, as the strange energies of hummingbirds do. Perhaps we envy the contrast of delicacy and brutishness, of heights and depths of soul, and find there a comforting paradox that confirms our faith in a sustaining force beyond our human egos.

Edith Piaf wrote many of her own lyrics, including "La Vie en Rose." Some bio-pics concentrate on the events in the subject's life at the expense of giving us the art that made their subjects notable. Not so this. The voice and music of Piaf soars throughout, engulfing us in a blanket of pleasure that keeps us one degree of survival beyond the pain. Unlike my friend, I did not regret seeing *La Vie en Rose*; in fact, I intend to see it again. *Non, je ne regrette rien.*

BOOK REVIEWS

GINETTE PARIS. *Wisdom of the Psyche; Depth Psychology after Neuroscience*. London and New York: Routledge, 2007.

REVIEWED BY MAUREEN MURDOCK

*W*isdom of the Psyche: Depth Psychology after Neuroscience is a fascinating book with many layers of meaning. It can be read as a memoir of a brilliant scholar, experiencing a life-threatening injury to her brain, who sustained such brokenness of the heart and body that all the theories about the suffering of the soul suddenly appear in a different light, as well as a beautifully written dialogue between philosophy and depth psychology. Paris asks the questions: What is truly alive and what is outdated in the field of depth psychology? What ideas are fresh and which ones have the potential to harm us even more?

Maureen Murdock is a depth psychotherapist in private practice in San Francisco and was Core Faculty in the MA Counseling Psychology Program at Pacifica Graduate Institute. She is the author of the best-selling book, *The Heroine's Journey*, as well as the newly revised *Fathers' Daughters: Breaking the Ties that Bind*; *Unreliable Truth: On Memoir and Memory*; *Spinning Inward: Using Guided Imagery with Children*; and *The Heroine's Journey Workbook*. Her books have been translated into over a dozen languages.

Paris uses her extensive background in philosophy, mythology, and the humanities as well as her expertise as a clinician to explore the realms of depth psychology and how it evokes in us a desire to think deeply about the life of the psyche. The richness of her ideas, as well as the elegance of her style, make this book an essential reference for every student of depth psychology, particularly for psychotherapists and those beginning clinical practice.

Paris redefines the goal of psychotherapy by giving the reader a taste of the awe-inspiring mysteries of life and how the present models of psychotherapy (medical, financial, and redemptive) work against this ability to find a deeper meaning in life. I was especially appreciative of her differentiation of the concept of redemption with that of individuation. She asks the reader to look at how the myth of redemption, which derives from a monotheistic mythology, informs the goals of the therapeutic process. The client starts therapy "in pursuit of consciousness, but covertly the process can conceal a quest for redemption" in which he believes he will ultimately get rid of his internal monsters, change his behavior, and evolve into an enlightened being with flawless psychological health. (p. 54) Paris' atheistic understanding of Jung's approach offers a much needed alternative to faith. "Instead of prayer, active imagination; instead of redemption, individuation; instead of belief, the archetypal images of gods and goddesses." (p. 95)

Paris uses potent examples from her clinical practice to demonstrate how to help the patient examine both the facts and affect of his personal story or myth. As the patient recalls a particular life situation, he becomes more conscious of how he has interpreted it, created a particular version of the story, and shaped the plot with a certain archetypal inflection. Naming the oppressive myth allows the beginning of its dismantling, forcing it into the open for examination and scrutiny. Paris reminds us that a myth working in the background becomes invisible; one thinks it is a personal choice, but it is not. The goal of depth psychotherapy is to become aware of the reigning myth and discover how it shapes the patient by expanding or contracting his being.

Her approach is both theoretical and practical: She listens carefully to the images and symbols in her patient's tale and emphasizes why it is crucial to remain centered on the imagination of the patient. She cautions against instances in which the therapist exerts too much influence, interpreting the images, with the result that the patient ends up with a story that reflects the therapist's imagination or theoretical orientation. She writes, "The goal of depth psychology is to evoke: to bring to mind a memory or feeling, to provoke a particular reaction or feeling, to make beings appear who are normally invisible."(p. 80)

I particularly valued her deconstruction of the prevailing maternal and paternal myths in our culture. Paris writes that the individual mother is still the focus of blame in therapy, diverting attention away from the collective maternal responsibility of our cultural, political, and educational institutions. She calls for a revisioning of the maternal myth—a revolution in values, manners, education, aesthetic sensitivity, city planning, and welfare programs. She examines how the mother archetype has been used to keep women powerless in the role of mother and to keep certain adults infantile. She writes, "We come into the world with our mother, but we die alone. Between these two events, the infantile illusion of safety must thin out until the child is strong enough to bear the responsibility of his or her decisions." (p. 115) What defines an adult psyche is not independence from a need for compassion and protection but a basic orientation toward achieving responsibility. She quotes Sartre: "To be free, one must be responsible for oneself." (p. 100)

This is where the paternal principle comes in. Her description of the Father archetype is a much needed act of re-balancing the archetype of Mother with that of the Father. She gives value to the will to win, self-discipline, a fascination for strategy and tactics, a willingness to face conflict, a love of victory, a desire for power, and a capacity to take risks.

One of Paris's greatest contributions in *Wisdom of the Psyche* is to warn against bringing too much Great Mother nurturance into therapy. When a patient expresses a need or a wound, it is tempting to take on the maternal role and give the support that seems to be lacking. She cautions the beginning therapist, in particular, to avoid psychological coddling and encourages her instead to bring in the paternal principle to help the patient develop responsibility. Pouring too much maternal love into the therapeutic container deludes the patient into expecting such positive attention in every subsequent relationship. "Too much sweet attention and support breeds an intense neediness that is at the core of egotism." (p. 152)

Wisdom of the Psyche has the power to encourage one to participate in "*amor fati,*" the love of one's fate, to endure the absurd, to cope with the insufferable, to lose one's innocence, and to embrace the totality of one's story as it unfolds, as Paris herself did in re-envisioning her own "knock on the head."

A brilliant look at how the field of depth psychology is enlarging our consciousness.

BOOK REVIEWS

LAWRENCE N. ALSCHULER. *Psychopolitics of Liberation: Political Consciousness from a Jungian Perspective.* New York: Palgrave Macmillan, 2006.

REVIEWED BY SYLVESTER WOJTKOWSKI

It is a pleasure to read a Jungian book that offers a comprehensive, profound, and original view with the clarity and structure of a good textbook. This work offers a deeply informative and informed take both on the application of Jungian thought to the study of political consciousness and the precise articulation of Jungian concepts regarding individuation in general. I second Andrew Samuels praise for Alschuler for accomplishing "what had been thought to be virtually impossible:" elucidating the political dimension of psyche through ideas of analytical psychology without compromising clinical understanding.

In brief, Lawrence Alschuler undertakes a timely project to construct a Jungian model of the development of political consciousness of the oppressed, and succeeds. In the process he manages to traverse a vast psycho-socio-political territory without compromising any field, and

Sylvester Wojtkowski, Ph.D., is a Jungian analyst in private practice in New York City. He is a founding member of the Jungian Psychoanalytic Association (JPA) and a graduate of the C. G. Jung Institute of New York. He received his doctorate in Clinical Psychology from the New School. He is a board member of the C. G. Jung Foundation for Analytical Psychology.

to provide practical insights for psychotherapists, sociologists, political scientists, and lay readers. He calls his study the psychopolitics of liberation. It encompasses both a theory of the transformation of oppressed consciousness and a practice of developing programs to raise consciousness of the politically oppressed, to assist with healing of psychic wounds of subjugation, and to organize actions challenging oppression (p. 4).

He brings ideas of Albert Memmi, Paulo Freire, and C. G. Jung together to provide structure for his model. Memmi, a Tunisian-Jewish sociologist, provided an immediately influential analysis of social dynamics of the imperialistic project in *The Colonizer and the Colonized* published in 1957. His ideas were instrumental both in predicting African movements toward sovereignty and providing ideas for the liberation of political consciousness of the colonized. Freire, a Brazilian social educator, developed programs to assist the poor, disadvantaged, and subjugated with expansion of political consciousness. (See his 1969 book *Pedagogy of the Oppressed*.) Followers of Freire have helped to organize social liberation movements throughout Brazil and the Third World.

It is inspiring to hear Alschuler read Jung politically, so the familiar metaphors of the ego-unconscious relationship sound fresh and inspire different reflections. Whether it is ego versus the unconscious locked in a "power struggle"(Jung's *Collected Works* 9i § 522-533), or the original unity of the psyche as a "tyranny of the unconscious," or dominance of the ego as a "tyrannical one-party system," or a relativized ego as a negotiator with the unconscious on the basis of "equal rights" in format resembling "parliamentary democracy" (in Jung's foreword to Erich Neumann's *Depth Psychology and a New Ethic*), they all indicate how psyche and politics are intertwined. In our habitual prejudice inherited from Jung over "group consciousness," we tend to read these metaphors as reflective of internal conflicts. But what is resonating here is also the Aristotelian *"politikon zoon,"* psyche as a reflection of the polis, and the tortured history of twentieth century. From this perspective, Alschuler critically appraises Jung's ideas on politics. He sees Jung's political thinking as overemphasizing psychological, individual causes of political phenomena, and undervaluing the social reality of politics, leading to pathologizing mass movements, and thus representative of the "naïve" stage of political consciousness based upon Freire's scale of *conscientization.*

Freire analyzes the development of political consciousness, or *conscientization*, by studying the way individuals name political problems, reflect on them, and act to resolve them. The initial stage, he calls "magical." In it, the oppressed feel "powerless before an awful reality and an awe-inspiring powerful irresistible force that changes and maintains things according to its will." (Alschuler, p. 18) The individual exhibiting the second stage—that of naïve consciousness— is characterized by the perception of political issues in terms of problem individuals, others' evil intentions or one's own failures, and seeks to either remove unjust rulers or change himself according to the oppressor's view. In the third stage, called critical consciousness, a person is capable of understanding oppression as a result of normal workings of unjust and oppressive sociopolitical systems, moves toward his own self-actualization, and works on the transformation of the system.

The innovative contribution of Alschuler to this schema lies in his relating it to the Jungian stages of individuation: magical consciousness corresponds to the emergence of the ego from collective identification with the self; naïve consciousness to ego-alienation; and critical consciousness to the relativization of the ego. In the process, Alschuler provides most useful definitions of many Jungian concepts, all described with unsurpassed precision. I would highly recommend the parts of the book dealing with the description and exact articulation of Jung's concepts to Jungian training candidates, to guide them through what often seems like a wild, intuitive forest of Jungian definitions. We, as Jungians, have become unconscious (that is collectively so) of our own jargon, which has long stopped revealing psyche in its native, often-dangerous imaginal complexity and instead has hypnotized us into magical participation in Jung's ideas. It is as if we have abdicated our responsibility to constantly wrestle with them and their application to contemporary life. So it is really refreshing to encounter such conceptual accuracy.

As I've read through Alschuler's enlightening exposition of Freire's depiction of the *consciousness of the oppressed*, it was not hard to hear it as a portrayal of *oppressed consciousness*, the consciousness haunted by shadows of "inner dictators" and bipolar complexes of paternalism and dependence. These descriptions provide useful illustrations for clinical phenomena as well. At the same time, it is reassuring that theoreticians from various fields have formulated similar views of human consciousness facing larger social-political forces or dealing with "purely" psychological issues. Of course, it is conceivable that Memmi and Freire, both younger than Jung by two generations, have benefited from Jung's insights into the dynamics of the psyche. Alschuler's analysis traces many commonalities among the views of these theoreticians and Jung's.

In their social critiques, Memme and Freire are much more aware of symbolic implications of their concepts than some psychoanalysts are: "Freire understands a human relationship to be possible between two persons, both of whom are 'subjects' and neither is an 'object.'" For Freire, *object* is synonymous with *thing*, essentially inanimate, serving as an instrument for the satisfaction of another's needs. A subject-object relationship is dehumanizing by this very definition. One wonders how much the terminology of object relation theory, by insisting on its nomenclature originating in Freud's discussion of "objects of drives," contributed to the obsession about "relationships" in our culture that throws a dark and oppressive shadow. Psychological discourse in general could benefit further from the notion of "horizontal violence" in oppressed societies (misdirected violence, leading to victimization of one's children or spouse, rather than resisting the oppressive system) that could add a missing dimension to the "dysfunctional family" concept, by considering that our consumer capitalism has contributed to the psychological violence within our families. Alschuler's detailed analysis of the psyche of the oppressed deepens not just our knowledge of horrible abuses far out in the developing world but also enriches our understanding of complex and "complexed" dynamics of any oppressed psyches.

The book is at its best regarding comparisons between narcissistic and colonial personalities. Alschuler is not afraid of bold claims: "I consider the collective healing of narcissistic disturbances during the process of decolonization to be a variation of therapies found in the analytic encounter." Through his psychopolitical analysis, Alschuler erodes a century-old wall between the socio-political understanding of the human condition and the psychoanalytic one, the wall that has been erected by a young, insecure science that desperately needed to differentiate itself from other emerging disciplines, like sociology and anthropology, and protect its own "psychic territory" from their incursions. Fathers of psychoanalysis narcissistically privileged the psychological explanation of political conditions (See Freud's *Civilization and Its Discontents* and Jung's *Undiscovered Self*, for instance) and even exerted substantial influence over significant parts of the social sciences (particularly the Freudian school). However, the influence of socio-political thought on depth psychology has been limited, only emerging in the last quarter of the century. Thus, for the most part, psychoanalytic thinking has escaped the influence of social constructivism, and persisted in developing its theories through notions rooted in the 19th century, with little or no awareness of the socio-linguistic impact of culture on psyche. Thus it has been with a singular satisfaction that I have read *The Psychopolitics of Liberation*. The direct comparison of psycho-socio-dynamics of colonial oppression with psychodynamics of narcissistic oppression is illuminating and enriching for the understanding of both.

In the 20th century we had parallel "liberation" movements: in the colonizing-Western world, psychological liberation through therapy would expand steadily (even if social liberation has been often delayed through totalitarian regimes); and, in the colonized-Southern world, movements for political sovereignty through civic disobedience and armed struggle would progressively succeed, although they would leave a host of unresolved of social-psychological problems.

I recall a grandiose fantasy from my early analytic training regarding healing narcissistic personalities. Given that the dynamics of the disorder were so similar from case to case, varying only in intensity, it seemed terribly inefficient to treat narcissistic disorders individually. Christopher Lash's analysis of narcissism as a cultural disorder in his classic book *Culture of Narcissism* moved the notion of narcissism beyond psychopathology towards the pathology of culture. My analogy for that process was a wheat field infected with ergot fungi. Ergot itself has hallucinogenic properties, and has often been used in initiations, like in the mysteries of Eleusis. And incidentally, it led to the development of LSD, a rather narcissistic drug. It would be futile to try to eradicate the fungi by individually treating each blade of grain, while some chemical spray could work over the whole population. It would be nice, I mused at that time, if we were able to develop an equivalent of such a spray, say an alchemical one, that would penetrate our narcissistic culture at large and retard the growth of narcissistic complexes. The vehicle that I thought could deliver this alchemical spray was education. So, I welcome Alschuler's pedagogic approach to psychosocial liberation as providing such a vehicle.

BOOK REVIEWS

ANN CONRAD LAMMERS, ADRIAN CUNNINGHAM, MURRAY STEIN (eds.), *The Jung-White Letters,* London & New York: Routledge, Philemon Series, 2007.

REVIEWED BY JOHN DOURLEY

Returning to the dialogue between C. G. Jung and the theologian Victor White is like meeting once again an old and familiar friend. I published on the Jung-White dialogues and the closely associated Jung-Buber dialogues in 1991, 1994, 1995, and 2007.[1] But this time the friend is a much more revealing and intimate friend, thanks to the work of Ann Conrad Lammers, Adrian Cunningham, and Murray Stein. Theirs is a finely edited presentation of all the extant letters of Jung and White to each other as well as a number of revealing letters written to and by others about the relationship between them. Lammer's footnoting is exhaustive and informative. She excels in translating the many references in other languages—German, Latin, and Greek—and in occasionally contextualizing the content of the letters themselves.

John Dourley is a Jungian analyst (1980, C. G. Jung Institute, Zurich), and professor emeritus of the Religion Department, Carleton University, Ottawa, Canada. He is also a Roman Catholic priest with the Oblates of Mary Immaculate. He has written frequently on the religious implications of Jungian psychology.

Adrian Cunnigham's short but knowing biography of Victor White is also a piece of surpassing scholarship. It is of considerable interest to learn, for instance, that White's thesis for his licentiate in theology was on Aquinas' Platonism. (p. 311) Aquinas is renown for his synthesis of Christian thought with Aristotle. That White was early on interested in Aquinas' Platonism contributes significantly to our understanding of his later attraction to Jung and to the distinctively Platonic elements in archetypal theory. Cunningham's scholarship is particularly in evidence in his detective work unraveling the mystery of White's being denied the regency, the headship of theological studies, at Blackfriars, the Dominican faculty of theology, at Oxford University in 1954. Few would have known that White's rejection was peripherally related to the post-war suppression of the worker-priest movement. Cunningham ultimately traces White's unacceptability for this position to the Vatican and its Holy Office. Cunningham's work here speaks volumes of the repressive Catholic atmosphere in which White did his courageous, pioneer work as a bridge builder between the then conflictual worlds of religion and depth psychology. Cunningham also broadens one's appreciation of White through his recounting of White's critique of a spiritually moribund and authoritarian Catholicism much earlier than his engagement with Jung. This is not to deny that White's difficulties persisted well after the height of his encounters with Jung. In this context, Cunnigham cites a revealing statement by White as late as 1958. In it, White confesses that he can no longer live in the medieval, romantic and "phoney" Catholicism of Chesterton and Belloc initially so attractive to him, but as yet he had no alternative vision. (p. 330) The wasteland apparently continued well after the period of the discussion with Jung.

And so with the publication of the White letters, the old familiar friend takes on a fuller face, deepened by the emotion, passion, and agony of both correspondents, but especially of Victor White. For if truth be told—and this in no way diminishes the immense contribution this work makes to a scholarly appreciation of their dialogue—most of what this new publication adds to our understanding already can be gleaned to some extent from the one-sided approach heretofore afforded by the long-since-published two volumes of Jung's letters. But with the publication of this work, which contains *all* of Victor White's letters to Jung as well some previously unpublished letters by Jung, the drama is greatly deepened and our appreciation of the conflict with it. It is as if the play has to be put on one more time with a greatly expanded script, though the outcome remains tragically the same.

This new play impresses with some personal details that add greatly to the human dimension but probably not much to the substance of the Jung-White interchange. One such insight is the stress that both men underwent throughout the exchange and the toll this stress took on their bodies. Jung was seventy when his dialogue with White began in 1945. White was forty-three. Throughout the fifteen-year correspondence till White's death in May, 1960, it is interesting to note how many times Jung reports various forms of illness in his letters to White, some of which Jung relates to struggling with the writing of some of his major works like the *Mysterium Coniunctionis*. (p. 185) White on his part also confesses to a raft of what would have to be called psychosomatic effects over the issues which surfaced in their relationship. (p. 217) The illnesses themselves seem to evidence the intensity of the interchange and the profound importance for both participants of the substantial issues in it.

The personal dynamic of the relationship between the two men also becomes more transparent with the addition of the White letters contained in this new publication. Initially, and to some extent throughout, White looked up to Jung as a great but familiar mentor, one to whom he could repeatedly confess not only his admiration but his love. At the same time, neither his admiration nor his love for Jung prevented White from a heated, if not aggressive defense, of his Catholic Thomistic/Aristotelian theology. Occasionally both of these sides of White appear in a single letter to Jung where White's profession of love for Jung is accompanied by near personal attacks on him and some of his followers. (p. 268, p. 273) Jung's attitude to White is characterized initially by a long sought and now welcomed appreciation by someone with a theological background who could take his psychology seriously, who shared his conviction that psychological and religious experience had much in common, if not a point of identity, and whom, Jung confesses in a letter after White's death, he thought at one point might have carried his psychology into the future. (p. 300) One gets the impression of a forbearing, long-suffering paternal embrace of White by Jung which in the end endured even the impossibility of intellectual reconciliation.

The warm human dimension of the relationship between the two is again in evidence in the many invitations that Jung extended to White to stay with him in Bollingen, his very private and somewhat primitive, rural residence to whom only the chosen were invited. From the first summer of their engagement in 1946, White visited Jung there every summer till 1953. The almost joyous enthusiasm of their mutual discovery in their earlier meetings began slowly to cede, first to a mysterious sense of alienation. In December of 1948, Jung writes of a door that had been shut, "softly but tightly," while White had been traveling that year in the U.S. A year later on New Year's eve 1949, Jung opened the discussion on evil which proved to be the major barrier between them. It soon evolved into the debate on the Catholic understanding of evil as a privation of the good. As the discussion proceeded, Jung came to insist that all opposites discernible in creation must be present in the origin of creation. This meant that God could no longer be imagined as the *Summum Bonum*, the greatest good in whom there was no darkness. The positing of good and evil in God as creator struck at White's Catholic faith itself and at his Thomism, both of which lacked the theological imagination to assimilate such a notion. White's essentialism, derived through Aquinas from Augustine, presupposes a point where good and being coincide. Evil is then understood as removal from such a point. Moderns like Tillich can use such essentialism to argue that creation and fall are simply two sides of the same process. Moving out from the divine retains a relation to the essential good even in the current existential remove from it. The first moment of this dialectic can then affirm that creation is good; the second moment that it is fallen. Both moments describe the same movement.

Against this imagination, Jung's perceptions are closer to those of Jacob Boehme (1575-1624), the most cited mystic in Jung's work. Boehme was the mystic whose visionary experience placed all opposites in an unconscious divinity seeking its own self-consciousness in a humanity called upon to unite in time what the divine could neither perceive nor resolve in eternity. The work, reviewed in this publication, contains a hand-drawn sketch (p. 122) of what Jung called a "Moses quaternity," which I had not seen in this form elsewhere. Jung presents it at some length in *Aion*,[2] but it is not diagrammed in the way it is here. This sketch describes a movement from the formlessness of an initial chaos in which the opposites would be united as undifferentiated to a final formlessness in which they would have been differentiated and united beyond opposition. The basic movement is from the formless to the formless. In this sense one might be allowed to say that being and good unite in a culminating formlessness beyond and uniting all opposites. However, this affirmation would identify a divinely based evil as an element at least latent in the primal formlessness and integrated with its opposite in the fullness of an eschatological formlessness. It would involve evil in the beginning and in a final but formless synthesis. It would hardly meet White's need for that moment in which good and being would coincide in such a manner that removal from that point of coincidence would constitute the basis of perceptible evil. In a second line of criticism, Jung was also of the opinion that the denial of evil as an *ousia*, essence, in the divine as the precondition for its reality in the human could well lead to a denial of shadow in the individual and to destructive outbursts of epidemic proportion in the collective in the form of the archetypally induced unconsciousness enlivening all "isms."

Further difficulties were to emerge between Jung and White over the relation of the purely spiritual or symbolic understanding of religious discourse to historical facticity. The doctrine of the Assumption was infallibly declared Catholic dogma on November 25, 1950. White, the theologian, had written on the declaration using distinctions Jung himself had drawn between the universal and particular appearance of the archetypal in historical consciousness. Jung's point was that the particular appearance of an archetypal concretion was always a variant of the universality of the underlying archetype. With Jung, archetypal expression was always symbolic or spiritual and never to be understood as literally historical. White tried to use this distinction no doubt to bring to the fore the symbolic meaning of the Assumption but at the same time to reconcile it with a literal historical fact, the assumption of the body of Mary into heaven two thousand years ago. Jung's describes White's historical literalism as a "parapsychological stunt," (p. 158) which wholly obscures the spiritual and only meaning of the dogma, namely, the introduction of "the feminine principle," effectively a Goddess, into the Christian Godhead itself. Read in this manner, the declaration becomes for Jung, "the most important religious development since 400 years." (p. 159) He meant since the Reformation.

The deepening impasse seems to have reached a critical turning point in White's stay with Jung in Bollingen from the 17th to the 27th of July, 1952. White signaled in a letter, written eight days before his arrival, that he wanted put on the agenda ten precise points on the issue of evil as privation before any progress beyond that issue was possible. (p. 200-204) The letters in the wake of the visit remain cordial, but the widening gulf between the men had hardly narrowed with their meeting. Rather, it became increasingly apparent that the impact of the discussion on White was taking an immense toll. A crucial letter of November, 1953 reveals that White had apparently begun to assimilate not only Jung's idea of evil as endemic to divinity as creator, but had also been deeply shaken by Jung's critique of the Christ figure as a truncated image of the self. (p. 216, p. 217) His dilemma as a Dominican, a theologian, and simply as a believing Catholic was this: Faith in Christ must be "unconditional," and this was no longer a possibility if Christ is not an adequate symbol of the self, but rather, "very inadequate, one-sided, unintegrated, and harmful." (p. 216) Even though he was a priest who had helped many of his troubled clientele out of the Church, he could not go on as priest because his faith was no longer that of his flock. "Their God simply isn't mine any more; my very clerical clothes have become a lie." (p. 216) At a more practical level, he confessed he did not know how he would earn a living in a world for which his clerical and theological training had ill equipped him. And so he wavered between leaving in the interests of honesty and staying for reasons at that time hard to define.

Jung's answer on November 24, 1953 contains many of the themes that became foundational in his late writings. (pp. 218-223) The conflict between Christ and Satan would be overcome in an age of the Spirit in which, by implication, both would embrace. Before this age eventuated, White must suffer the opposition between absolute good and evil. Such agony was the meaning of the pain in his life. Holding the tension was White's greatest contribution to the religious future. The psycho/ spiritual meaning of incarnation was the ongoing historical realization of the fullness of the unconscious in consciousness. The Christian epoch was not yet complete and the battle between absolute good and evil must continue. And yet its continuance is in the interests of a future myth which would indeed invalidate the Christian myth. The invalidation would take the form of a richness of opposites reconciled and would be worked by the same Paraclete who had created the Christian Aeon. The Christian period was not to be surpassed by its premature dismissal but rather through the revelatory compensation that would complete it even as it superseded it.

In the following March of 1954, White's anguish continued. In a letter dated March 4, he concedes, after many readings of Jung's letter of the preceding November, that Jung was "in the main right." (p. 228) Such capitulation only increased his problem. As a theologian he simply could not see how "this view could be squared with Catholic Doctrine: what I am supposed and under oath to teach, and for teaching which I am provided with my bread and butter." He continued to struggle with the idea that Christ could have a shadow and projected it, much as the current Church projected its own shadow in its obsession with sex and communism. At the same time, the Church was possessed of "treasures" which White could never relinquish. The question "Can I stay where I am?" continued to be a torturous moral issue. (p. 230)

Jung's response to White on April 10th again develops themes at the core of his later writings. First, he tried to assuage White's problems with a Christ possessed of a shadow and a dubious omniscience by encouraging White to take his Christology as mythology rather than literal dogma or a modern biography. Then he turned to the main point: what are the features of the supplanting myth upon which the unconscious is currently working. Jung identified its substance but not its details in the imagery of the cross. The significance of the symbol of the cross lies in its intimation that Christ, conscious humanity, must die symbolically through union with nature or the unconscious, the cross as natural wood, in working the unity of conscious and unconscious in history. Religiously speaking, the psyche directs history to that point where "man will be essentially God and God man." (p. 237) Jung fully acknowledges the ecclesial obsessions to which White refers in his previous letters, "pharisaeism, law consciousness, power driven, sex obsession and the wrong kind of formalism." Yet, in this letter, Jung encourages White to stay in the Church. Those of White's vision must stay behind to help in the maturation of those in dependency on the Church as a questionable "support." White's intelligent and sensitive introversion changes the doctrine itself as he integrates it personally and has an invisible, unspoken, though real, impact on those in his surroundings. He should keep up his fight. "The man allowing the institution to swallow himself, is not a good servant." (p. 239) Nor should he be overly worried about his doubts. "Doubt and insecurity are indispensable components of a complete life." (p. 240) As for the institutional pathology in which he lives, Jung suggests that White, "take the Church as your ailing employer and your colleagues as the unconscious inmates of a hospital." (p. 241) The letter seemed to have worked. In White's reply on May 15th, 1954, he tells Jung that he has decided to stay. The letters thus prove that Jung was responsible for White's staying in the Dominicans and the priesthood not only at that time but till White's death.

In 1954, after he was refused the regency, as the head of studies at Blackfriars in Oxford, the Order sent White to the U.S. There he had considerable time in his lectures and travels to diagnose the state of American Catholicism of that period. In a letter in January, 1955, he writes to Jung that he is glad that Jung's *Answer to Job* had yet to appear in English to an American public. "It would queer my pitch rather badly among these mostly very naive, but very well meaning Catholics." (p. 254) Later that month, Jung responded that indeed it would and apologized in advance for the discomfort its publication would inflict on White.

When *Answer to Job* was published, White's pain first took the form of a devastating review he wrote of it in *Blackfriars*, March, 1955. This review is reprinted in this work as Appendix 6 in its full original text, including the personal attacks on Jung in enlarged script which White later was to edit out in certain revisions. In writing to Jung from the Queen Mary on his return trip to England after the publication of this review, White concedes that Jung might find it unforgivable. This does not stop him from going on to wonder what Jung could gain from such an "outburst." (p. 259) He also makes a dubious claim that Jung earlier had promised he would not publish *Answer to Job* when he originally gave it to White in manuscript form.

Here Lammers' excellent editing is so helpful. She points out that in October, 1951 and again in April, 1952, White expressed only his "...eagerness and gratitude for its publication." (fn. 24, p. 259). In fact, there exists no evidence anywhere that Jung had ever stated that he did not intend to publish the essay. White saw only harm coming from its publication undermining his own efforts to "...make analytical psychology acceptable to & respected by, the Catholics & other Christians who need it so badly." The line is simply a restatement of White's ongoing dilemma. Jung's "outburst" expressed a psychology that White admitted his Catholic and Christian constituency badly needed to recover a life-giving spirituality, but its recovery was beyond the boundaries of Catholic and Christian orthodoxy.

White's dilemma still exists. Can a Christian spirituality recover currently the life that historical Christianity has lost in its self-emasculating expulsion of the gnostics, the alchemists, the seekers of the grail and the more radical mystics and still be Christian? More succinctly, if its contemporary health lies in the appropriation of its heresy, can it heal itself and still be itself?

Jung's responses in his letter of April 2, 1955 to White's own outburst were measured. He simply states that he felt he had to publish *Answer to Job* to alert the world to the unspecified collective unconsciousness drifting toward "...an impending world catastrophe." (p. 261) He probably meant the Cold War. He encourages White to continue in his personal suffering as the form that God's suffering took in White's life. But then he turns from his former unqualified encouragement that White remain in his religious order and priesthood. In a statement that takes on added weight in the context of a psychology that arose in large part out of and against the prolongation of puerile dependency into adulthood, Jung affirms that he is freer in his life than White who must limit his independence, if not of mind then at least of expression, as the "...hard rule for everybody fed by an institution for services rendered." (p. 264) Put more concisely, "If you take their money you hew their line, at least in public."

Incredibly, at the end of this letter, Jung still extends an invitation to White to visit him in Zurich when White would lecture at the Institute that summer, though at Kusnacht not Bollingen. Again in preparation for this meeting, as he did for their water-shed meeting of 1952, White drew up an agenda, this time of five points around *Answer to Job*. (pp. 267-270) But when he arrived in Zurich, he found that Jung was caring for Emma, now recovering from an operation from the cancer that would take her life in November of that year. The discussion never took place. White did meet Jung but at a convalescent home in Mammern.

In his first letter after the meeting, White refers to his own "...ruthless tactlessness..." which ruined the chance for a dialogue and probably whatever remained of the possibility of a truly dialogical relationship between them from that date forward. They did meet once more in 1958, but little came out of the meeting. In a letter prior to it, White confesses that he was unhappy about their last meeting nearly two years before at Mammern, takes responsibility for the estrangement between them, and defensively assures Jung that he will never write anything under pressure from his ecclesial superiors (p. 276).

In April, 1959, White had a motorcycle accident and suffered serious injuries to the head. In March, 1960, he writes to Jung that he had undergone an operation for intestinal cancer. He died from a sudden thrombosis on May 22, 1960. The final months were filled with the poignancy and drama characteristic of the whole relationship. A certain rapport had been reestablished between them by a Prioress of a contemplative convent with whom White had been associated. But even at this late date and with White suffering from cancer, Jung wrote a final letter to him responding to a critical review of his *Answer to Job* or of his *Collected Works*, volume 11 and urging White to go beyond a personal to an archetypal perspective to avoid the final negativities of Freudian psychoanalysis. (p. 285) The differences were never resolved. Jung was to apologize for this letter and to assure White of his friendship and loyalty. (p. 285, p. 305) His personal age and health were all that kept him from White in his final situation. White's last words to Jung were, "May I add that I pray with my heart for your well-being, whatever that may be in the eyes of God." (p. 292)

In some sense it ended there. In another sense the debate transcended the individuals and engaged an archetypal opposition whose resolution still challenges humanity with survival issues. That is why this book is so important. Jung himself, after White's death, best describes what was at stake in their dialogue in a letter to the above-mentioned prioress. He writes, "I have now seen quite a number of people die in the time of a great transition, reaching as it were the end of their pilgrimage in the sight of the Gates, where the way bifurcates to the land of Hereafter and to the future of mankind and its spiritual adventure." (p. 306) Jung surely implies in these words that White's death meant that he and his theology would have had continued difficulty in joining humanity's future spiritual adventure.

Murray Stein writes in his foreword that Jung's discussion with White was formative to Jung's late writings. The dispute is mentioned textually in *Aion*.[3] Stein notes that Jung's *Answer to Job* was, in fact, his answer to White, one which "...flew directly in the face of the received doctrine that had anchored White's life and career." (p. x) In these remarks, Stein shows his usual analytic acuity and, in so doing, extends the Jung-White interchange into the present.

For, if the "...future of mankind and its spiritual adventure" are to be anchored in the profound themes of Jung's *Answer to Job,* is there any real hope of such an adventure being realized especially in the specific contribution that the world's religions might make to it? How many of them can grasp the point that humanity's relationship to God is wholly contained in the relationship of consciousness to the archetypal unconscious and that humanity's historical vocation is to resolve in historical consciousness the divine self-contradiction that divinity could neither perceive nor heal in eternity and this at the insistence of divinity itself? Can incarnation be reconceived as the progressive concretion in finite consciousness of its unconscious source? Can religion, and especially the monotheisms, endorse Jung's understanding of the "relativity of God" as a process in which divinity and humanity as polar opposites in an eternal organism, the psyche, confer a mutual redemption on each other as the former becomes conscious in the latter?[4] Can especially the monotheistic mind locate an endemic archetypal evil in God and work to the embrace of Christ (or their preferred good God and historical representatives) with Satan in history, or must they remain, in Jung's words, "...victims of the Summum Bonum...", the God without shadow?[5] Are human archetypally bonded collectivities up to the "symbolic death" which the late Jung thought could alone avoid "a universal genocide?"[6] In other words, can they lose their specific faiths in time to save their common humanity? Or is what we now see not more likely, namely, religious and political communities bonded by archetypal and collective unconsciousness in faith, patriotism, and other ideological commitments continuing to kill each other for their always noble causes? These are the ground questions and issues that the Jung/White dialogue surfaced, issues that humanity's current and future "spiritual adventure" must address and solve if it is to survive the drive of God to become incarnate in humanity.

Nor have current forces outside of psychology failed to pick up on these issues. Samuel P. Huntington has identified religion as the bonding force of civilizations and so at the basis of the clash of civilizations.[7] He rightly sees current and future wars as religious wars, though he lacks the resources of an archetypal analysis toward resolution of such enmity in a more conscious collective inhesion in the deeper psyche itself as the creator of the religions, their Gods, and their cultures beyond and behind their differences. Daniel Dennet[8] and Richard Dawkins,[9] among others, currently sponsor a militant atheism from an evolutionary perspective which makes of all forms of supernatural theism such as White's a far too easy target of ridicule. From a Jungian perspective, one feels that there are more choices than those between White's supernaturalism and a sterile, somewhat grating, rationalist atheism with its narrow appeal to evolution and natural selection. Shades of the nineteenth century conflict! There is the option of an immediate dialogue with the source of external divinity and its numinous power in the depths of the human being. Somewhat along the lines of Huntington, Sam Harris documents the appalling desolation that faith in the trinity of one and only Gods now works in and beyond America.[10] One is reminded of Tillich's wry suggestion that the major cause of atheism is theism. "The protest of atheism against such a highest person [God] is correct."[11] Again, the question is whether there is an option between a religiously and unconsciously based aggressiveness so easily inspired by tribal faith in a supernatural power, on one hand, and a supposedly redemptive atheism, on the other. Jung could be a major provider of such an option, but it would mean a recovery of the liberating power of human interiority, and this is unlikely if the Gods remain in heaven and humanity is reduced to reason. Perhaps it is time to bid adieu to our old friend, the Jung/White dialogue, and get on with humanity's present and future spiritual adventure, redeeming God in human consciousness without destroying humanity in the process.

NOTES

1. John Dourley, "The Jung-Buber-White exchanges: exercises in futility," *Studies in Religion* (1991), 20, 3, 299-309; "In the Shadow of the Monotheisms: Jung's Conversation with Buber and White," *Jung and the Monotheisms, Judaism, Christianity and Islam*, ed. Joel-Ryce Menuhin (London and New York: Routledge, 1994), ch. 10, pp. 125-145; *Jung and the Religious Alternative: The Rerooting* (Lewiston: Edwin Mellen, 1995), ch. III, "The Uprooting: God as Summum Bonum," pp. 71-134; "The Jung-White dialogue and why it couldn't work and won't go away," *Journal of Analytic Psychology* (2007), 52, 3, pp. 275-295.

2. C. G. Jung, *Collected Works*, tr. R. F. C. Hull (Princeton: Princeton University Press, 1953), vol. 9ii, pages 226-242 (Jung's *Collected Works*, abbreviated hereafter as *CW* and references are to page numbers not paragraph numbers).

3. Jung, *CW* 9ii, p. 61, fn. 74.

4. Jung, *CW* 6, pp. 241-258.

5. Jung, *CW* 18, p. 725.

6. Jung, *CW* 18, p. 735.

7. S. P. Huntington, *The Clash of Civilizations and the Remaking of World Order* (New York: Simon and Shuster, 1996).

8. D. Dennet, *Breaking the Spell: Religion as a Natural Phenomenon* (New York: Penguin, 2006).

9. R. Dawkins, *The God Delusion* (Boston: Houghton Mifflin, 2006).

10. S. Harris, *Letter to a Christian Nation* (New York: Alfred A. Knopf, 2006).

11. P. Tillich, *Systematic Theology, Volume I* (Chicago: Chicago University Press, 1951).

BOOK REVIEWS

MURRAY STEIN. *The Principle of Individuation: Toward the Development of Human Consciousness.* Chiron Publications, 2006.

REVIEWED BY SUSAN ROWLAND

Important books clarify the mind, portray problems in the context of possible solutions, and leave the reader energized and more fully alive. Murray Stein's *The Principle of Individuation* is an important book. In particular it shows how the terrors and joys of living in the modern world are always part of our individuation as individuals, as members of families and groups, and as growing communities. It is individuation we need to develop if we are to be *conscious* of who we are as humans on a frail planet. And the great blessing of this book is that it is a lucid welcome to a beginner in depth psychology as well as being, for the more experienced reader, the wise culmination of deep analytic practice. Some writers whose clinical work is the healing of the soul know instinctively how to reach out to the reader. Few succeed so well as Murray Stein in presenting reading itself as an individuation initiation into knowledge.

Susan Rowland, Ph.D., is Reader in English and Jungian Studies at the University of Greenwich, UK, and author of *Jung as a Writer* (Routledge, 2005). She was Chair of the International Association for Jungian Studies, 2003-2006.

The Principle of Individuation is structured rather like several of Jung's *Collected Works* by starting from the dual movement in the psyche, a separation from the other (initially m-other) and a corresponding desire for joining or union with the other. After a marvellously clear discussion of the core ideas, Stein takes the complexity of individuation through ancient and historic cultural forms of Greek myth and fairy tales. Then the book begins to address the complex problems of living in modern culture. A chapter is devoted to the tricky notion of psychological space for individuation. This topos is then lived out by the book, and so for the reader, as the possibility of healing the large wounds of Christianity is explored.

What are the challenges of attempting to individuate a tradition? Are we individuating a religion by embracing it, or is some more conscious cultural intervention required? These are vital questions to which Stein offers cogent and stimulating perspectives. The final section of the book on politics and international relations is a daring and persuasive argument about how our global culture may learn to survive. Here Murray Stein joins the political conversation held among analytical psychologists such as Andrew Samuels and Michael Vannoy Adams. By taking the essential concept of individuation, and *making* it so essential in this book, *The Principle of Individuation* enacts its own *coniunctio* with political theory.

Murray Stein uses the notion of the "journey" to orient *The Principle of Individuation*, and contrasts it with an earlier metaphor of a "map" of Jung's model of the mind. To me, the especial success of the book is the way that Jung's prospective movement of the psyche, the energy of individuation, moves the reader to contemplate large spheres of history, religious narrative, symbols, stages of life, politics, and numinosity. Stein examines the term "numinous" in some detail, showing deftly the ways in which Jung does and does not treat it as a religious idea. This scholarly approach to Jungian ideas is essential if they are to be understood and find new homes fertilizing arid intellectual forms of knowledge. So *The Principle of Individuation* does what only a work of wisdom can, combine scrupulous scholarship with the arts of making complicated ideas engaging. It is scholarship devoted to life.

The sections using fairy tales and the adventurous private lives of the Greek gods are placed in a relationship with case histories. This is a very effective way of seeing the typical and archetypal in the unique story of the individual. Arresting for me was the *treatment* of Hephaistos, born afflicted because of his mother, Hera's rage at her husband, Zeus. Initially Hephaistos inherits that rage when he is rejected as a child. Fortunately, he is loved and raised by sea nymphs, Thetis and Eurynome. Yet his first marriage is a disaster. His wife, Aphrodite is spectacularly unfaithful with war god, Ares. Hephaistos is forced to fall back on the only part of his-self that he has allowed to be creative, his work with metals in the forge. Eventually, he builds a life from his creativity, is appreciated by the gods, and gains a loving wife. Thetis comes to Hephaistos for a special shield for her son, Achilles, who is going off to Troy. Hephaistos produces a work of wonder—its destination only shows how much cultural individuation needs to be promoted!

Using myth and fairy tale, Murray Stein illuminates individuation, just as he shows the whole idea of individuation enriching modern life. The book grants the axes of time and space to the modern person, by showing how we are and are not creatures of myth, and how we are and are not shaped by potent cultural and political institutions. Individuation is an essential tool for survival in our perilous new century. *The Principle of Individuation* is the best place to find out about it.

BOOK REVIEWS

ROBERT BOSNAK. *Embodiment: Creative Imagination in Medicine, Art and Travel.* London and New York: Routledge, 2007.

REVIEWED BY GINETTE PARIS

My reaction was visceral. I read this book late into the night, curled snugly in my bed. When Morpheus overwhelmed me, I reluctantly laid it on the bedside table, turned out the light, and entered the land of my dreams, where I was powerfully visited. Upon waking, I used Robert Bosnak's approach to see what *embodied imagination* had to say about my life through my dreaming.

I am walking in a garden that I have visited a couple of times in my life. I am particularly delighted by the red color of some unidentified flowers. It's unclear exactly what was the shape of these oneiric flowers, but upon awakening, I remember vividly their particular hue of red.

Ginette Paris, Ph.D., is on the Core Faculty at Pacifica Graduate Institute in Santa Barbara. Her most recent book is *Wisdom of the Psyche: Depth Psychology after Neuroscience* (Routledge, 2007). Her other works include *Pagan Meditations: The Worlds of Aphrodite, Artemis, and Hestia* (Spring Publications, 1991); *Pagan Grace: Dionysus, Hermes, and Goddess Memory in Daily Life* (Spring Publications, 1990); and *The Psychology of Abortion* (Spring Publications, 2nd ed., 2007).

Applying Bosnak's simple, but profound method, I discovered that this particular red belongs to the peonies that are abundant in this garden. This deep red, like no other, carries a precious essence, a quality that belongs not to me, but really belongs to peonies. This red carries a sensation of calm and beauty. Red peonies, and the beauty of that garden, are in a sense *alien* because the garden is not mine and I am not a peony. Bosnak moves away from the usual "peony-in-me" kind of interpretation and into a typically archetypal approach which is suggesting a look at that red as a quality of the sensate world to which you can relate.

I am convinced. This method works!

Bosnak's approach to dream interpretation differs from most other interpretive methods in its emphasis upon opening the realm of the senses. He places the sensory experience of the dream image at the center of the exploration. Because much of our feeling life is lived in the senses, it is worthwhile to examine the sensual memories expressed in dream images.

Working with a patient's dream of a bull, Bosnak writes: "If we see the bull as *really* belonging to Berthe's person, as a kind of sub-personality, we lose the truly alien nature in which the bull presents himself while dreaming. Phenomenally speaking, we lose a central aspect (its alien-ness) of the bull as an autonomous presence. The central tenor in this book is that embodied imagination is a true meeting with alien substantive intelligences which can possess our subjective bodies and influence our physical body."

The "embodied image," the quality that is part of the otherness of red peonies, tells me exactly what atmosphere I need to create in my life this week. In other words, I feel I know how to fetch for my psyche that little touch of peony red! Esoteric though it may be, but I surely understand what the dream is suggesting. I get it *sensually*.

It is difficult to describe sensory experiences. Who can describe the exact pleasure of licking a vanilla ice cream cone, in the company of a loved one, on a pleasant Sunday walk, on a perfect summer day? How much of my inner reality can I communicate by writing that my psyche needs a touch of peony red? What does my patient mean when he says that the smell of the house in his dream carries the misery of his childhood? We are confronted with the poverty of language when it comes to depicting sensory elements, and that difficulty explains why the sensual memory of dream images is often left unexamined. That great longing for expression is what Bosnak is attending to. He teaches us how to work with the ineffable.

This is an important, powerful book, written by a great master of dream analysis. His approach is most original, yet immediately useful.

BOOK REVIEWS

DENNIS PATRICK SLATTERY. *A Limbo of Shards: Essays on Memory, Myth and Metaphor.* Lincoln, NE: iUniverse, 2007.

REVIEWED BY ROGER C. BARNES

Early in this wonderful collection of 29 essays, Dennis Patrick Slattery comments that the narrative of William Faulkner's *Absalom, Absalom!* raises a primary question: "By what means do we give validity to experience, either to what we live out in the world of experience and/or to what and how we re-collect those moments?"(p. 5). In many respects, this question is the organizing question for the entire set of these essays, for the center of Slattery's interest is experience and imagination, memory and myth, knowing and being. Slattery, who teaches at Pacifica Graduate Institute and is a first-rate Jungian scholar, takes the reader on an exciting ride through memory, myth, and metaphor, but *A Limbo of Shards* contains some insights that even a non-Jungian should find stimulating.

Slattery's essays span the years 1984 to 2006, and while he originally had them organized chronologically, prompting by a friend got him to reshuffle them under the "distinct terrains" (p. xxii) of memory, myth, and metaphor. It turned out to be a most effective decision as

Roger C. Barnes, Ph.D., is a professor of sociology at the University of the Incarnate Word in San Antonio, Texas. He is a Phi Beta Kappa graduate from the University of Kansas, where be also obtained his doctoral degree in sociology.

the themes of memory, myth, and metaphor are adeptly drawn and conveyed.

Memory, which Slattery describes as the "act of imaginally remembering the future" (p. 136), is both personal and collective. It is connected to a "large vessel of belonging" (p. 144) and is obviously connected to what and how we remember. This is no small matter, as Slattery makes clear in a moving essay about the Terezin Ghetto and concentration camp north of Prague. As Slattery's tour group walked in silence through the camp, it was clear that everyone had to "yield" to "the act of remembering." (p. 141) But it turned out that this was not quite the case for everyone. Slattery and his wife met a Jewish woman whose 18-year-old daughter would not come to the camp because she didn't want to get depressed. Slattery then writes a solid account of what denial, of not remembering, of subverting memory, means for a person and for a culture.

Myths, Slattery notes, "have comprised and contain the body of beliefs and values that gave a people a sense of identity, a history and a destiny." (p. 244) In a 2004 essay, "Addicted to the Myth of Development," Slattery tells about a planned housing project not far from where he lives that will only contribute more to the "clogged arteries" of his city "already overstrained with traffic, bacteria and people." (p. 243) The myth operating in the corporate world of real estate developers is obvious: land is useful only when developed. This myth is "whirring out of control" (p. 245), threatening to remove natural places of reprieve, sanctuary, and solitude. Myths, those cosmic visions of the world, as Joseph Campbell reminded us, can work to emancipate and liberate, but they also can, as in the developers' myth, constrain and coerce us.

Metaphor, the third "terrain" in these essays, is fleshed out in 9 essays that range from a dandy description of Dostoevsky's "The Peasant Marey" to a spirited account of hospitals and hermitages. Slattery borrows from Colin Turbayne's definition that "metaphors represent the facts of one sort in an idiom appropriate to another." (p. 309) They are "a form of sort-crossings; we observe one thing in terms of another." (p. 309) This can become rather tricky, however, as memory, metaphor, and imagination come colliding together, making the very act of remembering quite complicated. Slattery shows the reader how Dostoevsky's "literal remembrance re-orders, re-forms experience, finally in language." (p. 318) In other words, "the literal assumes and exposes properties of metaphor." (p. 318)

Slattery raises an engaging question when he asks whether "memory re-order(s) events by way of metaphor, or does metaphor remember in a particular way to bring a unity, a sense of a formed experience, to what is recalled." (p. 315) This a superb question for which our author offers the view that "to say that memory is metaphorical is to implicate the memorial quality of metaphor." (p. 318) What comes from this view? Actually, quite a lot. Ask yourself the following questions: What do you remember? How do you remember it? Can you answer those questions without linking memory and metaphor? Our consciousness and language is fixed in metaphor, as is our memory.

Dennis Patrick Slattery has grounded these essays around three intellectually sensible principles—memory, myth, and metaphor. For this reviewer, who is neither a depth psychologist nor a Jungian scholar, but rather, a sociologist, I found myself pulled to some other themes that while not as forceful as memory, myth, and metaphor, are present nonetheless and give the collection a powerful voice.

If I had been the friend suggesting to Slattery how to organize these essays, I might have responded that the "terrains" I saw were literature, politics, and family. For example, some of the deepest analyses we are presented deal with literature. Slattery's scholarly expertise in literature leads him in search of Homer, Dante, Faulkner, Melville, Dostoevsky, Shakespeare, and Sophocles, among others. He devotes more attention to Dostoevsky than the rest, but taken as a whole, the essays provide thoughtful criticism and insight into some of the world's greatest literature. Any serious student of literature will want to read through these essays closely.

Lest anyone imagine that Slattery lives only in the world of great literature and the ideas of C. J. Jung and Joseph Campbell, they should go through those essays that directly tackle politics and decision-making. Here, in a collection of essays about war (Vietnam and Iraq), protests (anti-war and civil rights), and power (presidential and terrroristic), Slattery demonstrates a savvy political instinct.

Let me go to a passage that opens his 2005 essay "Vietnam's Open Wound, Ritual, and a Failed Imagination:"

> What is it about the energy the war in Vietnam still carries so forcefully in our collective memories decades after its completion?

Perhaps *completion* is the wrong word to use as I listen to the
ferocious toxicity surrounding war wounds, war records, good
service, bad service, reporting for duty, and then witness the
pathologies continually spinning off the current war in Iraq, so
close in design and disease to our earlier battles in Southeast Asia.
Is it because we have never, as a nation, collectively grieved in
some formalistic ritualistic way, for the dead and for families of
the dead? (p. 114)

One of my favorite essays is Slattery's 2004 "The Politics of
Apocalypse" where he argues that "in our collective recoil from
terrorism"(p. 241) we are transforming ourselves into the very thing we
hunt. Slattery comments, "The apocalyptic rhetoric of terrorism is
not only upon us: it is U.S." (p. 242) There is some good, hardheaded
political thinking in these essays, revealing that memory, myth, and
metaphor exist in the lived reality of our social and political pathways
and institutions. There is no flight from reality in them. Quite to the
contrary, Slattery gives us a tough message about the folly of not
remembering the past and the failure of imagination to design a better
future.

Lastly, I saw issues of family in this collection. The fine essay
"Housing the Eye of Memory" takes us to Cleveland where Slattery
and his younger brother Bill find themselves wandering through their
grandparents' vacant house. The sounds and smells of childhood come
back as the memory of old wall clocks and magic windows return.
And there is the essay about eros and psyche that opens with a story:
Slattery had stopped at a small diner in rural Washington state and
noticed that his waitress had a tongue post that she clicked against her
teeth. Asking her why she had a piece of steel in her mouth, she
unraveled a story that at the age of 22, married with a child, she felt
stuck, with her life well on the way to being over. The tongue post,
however, gave her a feeling of being alive, of having some experience of
meaning. Slattery comments: "A parcel of Eros had been returned to
her through the wound in the tongue." (p. 193) Wonderful!

I suggest these additional themes of literature, politics, and family
only to illustrate that memory, myth, and metaphor wander into these
realms of life and have some powerful messages for us. Much of *A
Limbo of Shards* is personal. Perhaps that is why I like it. Dennis Patrick
Slattery has asked us to hear his narrative, share his memories, visit his

imagination, and see his myths. It's a good experience, and after all, isn't that where we can find meaning?

BOOK REVIEWS

LAURA SHAMAS. *"We Three:" The Mythology of Shakespeare's Weird Sisters*. New York: Peter Lang, 2007.

REVIEWED BY SUSAN ROWLAND

The very form of theatre preserves ancient shamanic roots. We speak easily of dramatic *ritual* without consciously recalling the modern play's archaic origins in incantations, spells, and invocations to the gods. An actor is a vehicle for a dramatic spirit. Embodying the words of an Other, she gives breath to an alternative reality. And if some characters and plays seem to be haunted by a primitive world of ghosts and rites, none in the English tradition is more afflicted than Shakespeare's *Macbeth* with its eerie and malevolent three witches.

To unlock the mysteries of these dramatic enigmas, we now have the excellently researched, *"We Three:" The Mythology of Shakespeare's Weird Sisters* by Laura Shamas. Essentially, Shamas traces the archetypal pathways of these three characters from myth to folktale to demonization of "wise" women as witches. Shakespeare's play itself, she shows, contains the route

Susan Rowland, Ph.D., is Reader in English and Jungian Studies at the University of Greenwich, UK, and author of *Jung as a Writer* (Routledge, 2005). She was Chair of the International Association for Jungian Studies, 2003-2006.

of literary metamorphosis from goddess to witch. By serving Hecate, we have reference to Anglo-Saxon fates or "wyrd sisters," conspiring with a Greco-Roman triple-headed deity. This creative weaving of the mythological heritage is unique to Shakespeare. It suggests that the politics of *Macbeth* is more mysterious than other scholars have perceived. For while the play came into being at the behest of King James 1 as a political instrument to magnify his legitimacy on the English throne and indict the perpetrators of the Gunpowder Plot with the evil of witchcraft (by using the term "equivocation"), its art is more daring. *Macbeth's* mythological innovations brought the triple goddess onto the dramatic stage.

A highly persuasive second chapter explores the triangulations of *Macbeth* and of feminine archetypes in literature. In a daring argument, Shamas excavates the maternal resonance of the witches and reveals them to be allied to Lady Macbeth. At a time of a determined cultural movement to wrest the healing arts from untutored women, the witches' cauldron forms an horrific image of the maternal archetype in action. The cauldron is the womb of future events. It signifies that the witches are Shakespeare's own creation of a cosmology of female Trinitarian archetypes. They will finally clash with a Christian patriarchal Trinity late in the play. And what is most frightening and equivocal about them is that it is impossible to tell who wins in the downfall of Macbeth. Shakespeare refuses to give the wierd sisters definite origins, motives, aims, and destinations. They remain hysterically powerful and equivocal agents of the drama.

Another very valuable aspect of this book is in the amplification of the theme of the three weird sisters into other myths, fairytales, and later literature. The trio of feminine beings appears to frequent the underworld and to be bound up with fate and prophecy. Meanwhile, witches can be found as far back as Homer in Circe and Medea. Clues as to the ritual element of Shakespeare's figures come from recognizing the connection between the spinning of the spinster, to production, reproduction, and seduction. Witches dance in a ring to mark out the path of their spinning of fate, as they do in *Macbeth*, marking a sacred or demonic space on stage. Hence the witches invite projection of the dark side of the great mother, and indeed could be called a cultural shadow image.

Today, witchcraft in culture is still a means of representation of the illicit. Still it constellates in three sisters, as the television show, *Charmed*, indicates. Laura Shamas is to be congratulated for giving to Shakespeare's most dramatically powerful creatures of darkness their proper place as guardians of the 'weyward path' to the Other. While the book would be even better with more consideration of the effect of this analysis on the dramatic form of Shakespeare's tragedy, "*We Three*" is now an indispensable resource for that most spell-binding of plays.

The Foundation for Mythological Studies (FMS)
www.mythology.org ◆ www.mythplace.org

"Dionysian consciousness requires a Thiasos, a community, and this community is not only exterior, in other people, but it is a communal flow with the 'other' souls and their Gods, a consciousness that is always infiltrated with its complexes, flowing together with them."
-- James Hillman

The Foundation for Mythological Studies (FMS) was created in 1997 with the purpose of educating and enriching communities, both local and global. FMS seeks to widen perspectives by cultivating intellectual ideas and exploring the depth of human experience. We seek a better understanding of who we are as a species and how we may live on this planet in a conscious, sustainable manner.

Join us at Myth Place, our virtual international community. Blog with creative and interesting people, form discussion groups, keep up with the latest books, research, and track global events.

FMS Events for 2008

January 12, 2008
WRITER'S SERIES - check website for details.

February 1-3
HYPNOSIS AND ARCHETYPAL PSYCHOLOGY:
Archetypes Showing Up Under Hypnosis
A Weekend Seminar with John Tamiazzo, PhD., and Ginette Paris, PhD.

April 4-6
FMS 2nd Annual Conference: Nature and Human Nature:
The Mythology of Violence
Speakers: Lionel Corbett, Chris Downing, Thomas Moore
Co-Sponsors: Spring: A Journal of Archetype and Culture, Pacifica Graduate Institute

May 9 -10
MOTHER'S DAY - A Special Weekend at La Casa de Maria

June 7-8
ANIMAL EMOTIONS: Why They Matter and The Healing Professions, Marc Bekoff, PhD.

June 28
WRITER'S SERIES - Myth and Memoir with Maureen Murdock

July 26-27
WRITER'S SERIES - A Weekend of Myth and Mystery: Susan Rowland and other mystery authors.

August 16-17
MYTH & MEANING - James Hollis

Sept. 6
A DAY With DIONYSOS: FMS Annual Fundraiser

For more information please go to www.mythology.org

THE JUNGIAN SOCIETY FOR SCHOLARLY STUDIES VIIᵀᴴ ANNUAL CONFERENCE

Making the Darkness Conscious

A Jungian Exploration of Psyche, Soma, and the Natural World in an Age of Crisis

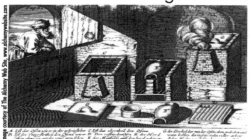

August 7-10, 2008
Champlain College, Burlington, Vermont

Call For Papers

Filling the conscious mind with ideal conceptions is a characteristic feature of Western theosophy, but not the confrontation with the shadow and the world of darkness. One does not become enlightened by imagining figures of light, but by making the darkness conscious.
— C. G. Jung (1954)

The Jungian Society for Scholarly Studies was founded in 2002 by a group of academics seeking opportunities for scholarly discourse on analytical psychology, focusing on the research and theories of C. G. Jung and those who have come after him. TJSSS organizes a yearly interdisciplinary academic conference through which members can present scholarly papers, organize roundtable discussions, and provide interactive workshops.

Continuing with the theme of transformation from Conference VI, TJSSS Conference 2008 will provide academics from across the disciplines, practitioners of analytical psychology, and others interested in the work of C. G. Jung and the post-Jungians an opportunity to explore the impact of the unexamined shadow in the world today. The conference theme is inclusive and serves as an umbrella for issues related, but not limited to, our human condition, the relationship between individual and collective, and our human embeddedness in the natural world.

Proposals in the form of abstracts of 500 words or less are invited for papers, workshops and/or panel presentations related to the conference theme. We welcome submissions from students of Jungian Studies.

Proposals should be submitted by November 30th 2007 to:
Dr. Marie-Madeleine Stey, TJSSS Conference Coordinator,
Capital University, Dept. of Modern Languages,
1 College and Main, Columbus, OH 43209-2394,
mstey@capital.edu

All submissions must include your C.V., full name and full contact information of mailing address, email address, and telephone numbers (if in the U.S. & Canada). Conference information will be posted in the near future at: www.theJungiansociety.org/

THE JOURNAL OF ANALYTICAL PSYCHOLOGY
VIIIth INTERNATIONAL CONFERENCE
Tradition and Creativity:
Reframing Analysis in a Changing World
Thursday 15th May to Sunday 18th May 2008
Hotel San Rocco, Orta San Giulio, Italy

'It is not possible to be original except on the basis of tradition'
(D.W. Winnicott)

This residential conference offers an opportunity to consider the ways in which analytical psychology can make a creative response to the social, cultural and scientific developments of the early 21st century while maintaining its roots in the accumulated knowledge and experience of the analytic tradition.

Speakers will include **Sue Austin, Stefano Carta, Massimo Giannoni, Christopher Hauke, Jean Knox, and Vittorio Linguardi.** *The opening address will be given, in Italian, by Umberto Galimberti. (It will be available in English prior to the address.)*

Address for a registration form and further information:
Journal of Analytical Psychology Conference
1 Daleham Gardens, London NW3 5BY
Tel 44+ (0) 20 7794 3640; Fax 44+ (0) 20 7431 1495.
Email: journal.jap@btconnect.com

2008 Programs

Founded 1989 by Michael Conforti, Ph.D., Director

ASSISI INSTITUTE

Dreams, Eternal Wisdom and the Objective Psyche: Expressions of the Transcendent

May 15 – 18
Brattleboro, Vermont

with:

MICHAEL CONFORTI, PH.D.
Jungian analyst, author

MARION WOODMAN, PH.D.
Jungian analyst, author

and others...

July 8 – 15
Assisi, Italy

with:

MICHAEL CONFORTI, PH.D.
Jungian analyst, author

JEAN HOUSTON
Researcher, author

DENNIS PATRICK SLATTERY
Author, Faculty, Pacifica Graduate Institute

and others...

For additional information or to register, please contact the Assisi Institute office:
Tel: **(802) 254-6220**   E-mail: **assisi@together.net**   **www.assisiconferences.com**

Our programs are open to clinicians, consultants, and laypersons. Continuing Education Units are available.

New from Assisi Institute Press

Threshold Experiences: The Archetype of Beginnings

BY MICHAEL CONFORTI

Author of *Field, Form & Fate: Patterns in Mind, Nature and Psyche*

Threshold experiences draw us into the reality of *a priori* archetypal fields, and learning to creatively interact with them can allow us rich access to sources of eternal wisdom. Drawing from the fields of Jungian psychology, biology, quantum physics, and the new sciences, this important book provides a unique lens for viewing the central archetypal dynamics operating within an individual life.

$22.95, paper   184 pages   ISBN 978-0-944187-99-9

To order, contact the Assisi Institute Press — Tel: **(802) 254-6220**
E-mail: **assisi@together.net**
Website: **www.assisiconferences.com**

ASSISI INSTITUTE PRESS

NEW FROM SPRING JOURNAL BOOKS

EVOCATIONS OF ABSENCE
Multidisciplinary Perspectives on Void States

Edited by Paul W. Ashton

ISBN 978-1-882670-75-8 • Price: $22.95 (US) • 214 pp.

If absence is the most compelling form of presence, then emptiness is pregnant with fullness, and the Void is not a place of darkness, but of potentially healing light. That is the unifying theme and under-lying message of this wide-ranging collection of essays, brought together in this volume. The essays are drawn from fields as diverse as music, art, poetry, religion, neurobiology, dance/movement therapy, and philosophy, and many are written against the backdrop of Jungian psychotherapy. While each of the contributors brings his or her own unique perspective—and, in some cases, per-sonal experience—to bear on the painful experience of the void state, they unanimously strike a note of unqualified optimism that we can, if we embrace that pain, return from the abyss transformed.

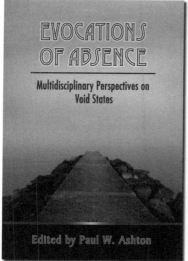

EVOCATIONS OF ABSENCE

Multidisciplinary Perspectives on Void States

Edited by Paul W. Ashton

This book fills an important gap in the literature of depth psych-ology. The presence of absence has long been the province of the mystical traditions and psychoanalysts, but we now have a collection of fascinating essays from other disciplines, including the Jungian tradition, on an important subject. The authors provide a glimpse into the problem of the opposites of empti-ness and fullness.
—**Lionel Corbett**, author of *Psyche and the Sacred*

Our lives today are crammed with consumerism, instant com-munication, immediate gratification—open, empty spaces are foreign to us. This timely book examines our daily existence from that other side, urging us to think about and find meaning in nothingness. It offers abstract and intellectual debates inter-woven with descriptions of personal experiences of a state of being too large to comprehend. This rich and nuanced gather-ing of material will speak to a wide readership.
—**Astrid Berg**, Vice-President, International Association for Analytical Psychology

I wholeheartedly recommend this splendid multidisciplinary collection of essays on the primordial image-experience of Absence. Paul Ashton and his co-authors invite the reader to enter into and explore the Void, its expressions and transform-ations, guided by the ample spirit of the imagination itself. A significant and fascinating book!
—**Joan Chodorow**, Editor, *Jung on Active Imagination*

CONTRIBUTORS
Stephen Watson; Stephen Bloch; John Dourley; Helen Anderson; Anne Graaff; Peter Hodson, Tina Strom-sted; Paul Ashton; Peter Collins

ABOUT THE AUTHOR:
Paul W. Ashton is a psychiatrist and Jungian analyst living in Cape Town, South Africa. He has lectured widely and written on mythology, art, and psychology, and has a special interest in the Void. His latest book is entitled *From the Brink: Experiences of the Void from a Depth Psycho-logical Perspective* (2007). His articles and book reviews have appeared in the Jungian journal *Mantis* and *The San Francisco Jung Library Journal*.

To order, please visit our online store at
www.springjournalandbooks.com

The friends of James Hillman
invite you to join them in a celebration honoring
the lifetime achievement of

JAMES HILLMAN
June 19-22, 2008
Venue:
The Sheraton Hotel, Station Square
Pittsburgh, PA
Registration fee: $140
The weekend's activities will include dialogues, discussions,
entertainment, trips, and a banquet in honor of James Hillman.

For registration forms and more information, contact:
Stanton Marlan
5400 Hobart St.
Pittsburgh, PA 15217, USA
e-mail: SMarlan@aol.com

The event will correspond with the release of a book entitled
Archetypal Psychologies: Reflections in Honor of James Hillman
edited by Stanton Marlan
and published by Spring Journal Books.
Many of the contributors to the book will be present at the event.